Children of Afghanistan

Book Thirty-Six
Louann Atkins Temple Women & Culture Series
Books about women and families, and their changing role in society

Children of Afghanistan

The Path to Peace

EDITED BY JENNIFER HEATH AND ASHRAF ZAHEDI

University of Texas Press ◆ *Austin*

The Louann Atkins Temple Women & Culture Series is supported by Allison, Doug, Taylor, and Andy Bacon; Margaret, Lawrence, Will, John, and Annie Temple; Larry Temple; the Temple-Inland Foundation; and the National Endowment for the Humanities.

Library of Congress Cataloging-in-Publication Data
Children of Afghanistan : the path to peace / edited by
Jennifer Heath and Ashraf Zahedi.
    pages   cm. — (Louann Atkins Temple women & culture series ; book 36)
    Includes bibliographical references and index.
    ISBN 978-0-292-75931-2 (cloth : alk. paper)
1. Children—Afghanistan—Social conditions.   2. Child welfare—Afghanistan.
3. Afghanistan—Social conditions.   I. Heath, Jennifer.   II. Zahedi, Ashraf, 1947-
    HQ792.A3C45   2014
    305.2309581—dc23
                                                                    2014013885
doi:10.7560/759312

To Mary MacMakin
—JH

To Ashok Mehta
and to the memory of Soheyla Rafieezadeh
—AZ

In memory of Hamida Barmaki and Paula Lerner.
Most of all, this book is dedicated to the children of Afghanistan.
May your futures be bright with promise in peace and justice.

Contents

Acknowledgments

We want first to thank our contributors—writers and photographers—for their marvelous work. They have kindly and generously shared their knowledge with us so that readers might develop a clearer picture of the situation and possible solutions. We are honored by their participation.

We wish also to thank, for information, inspiration, help, support, and enthusiastic assistance of all kinds over the long and short hauls: Haleh Afshar; Bernard Amadei; Nahid Aziz; Valerie Behiery; Jim Burr; Lynne Chapman; Jack Collom; Sandra Cook; Hafizullah Emadi; Pierre Fallavier; Erika Friedl; Shahla Haeri; Mary Elaine Hegland; Kayhan Irani; Ghada Kanafani; Karen Leggett; Marsha McColl; Mary Jo Meyers; Margaret Mills; Senzil Nawid; Soraya, Sabrina, and Suleiman Omar; Kathleen Rafiq; Kavita Ramdas; Margaret Rogers; Naomi Schneider; Avideh Shashaani; Patricia Silberman; Mary LaMotte Silverstein; Rickie Solinger; Elizabeth Stites; Mathew Varghese; Zaher Wahab; Sima Wali; Andrew Wille; and our friends and family. We are all, as Bishop Desmond Tutu says, prisoners of hope.

In peace and gratitude,
Jennifer Heath and Ashraf Zahedi

Children of Afghanistan

A young boy and girl stand among makeshift tents in an unofficial refugee camp on the Qharga Road in Kabul, Afghanistan, where families live who have fled the fighting in Helmund and Kandahar provinces. Photo by Beth Wald, 2009.

Introduction

JENNIFER HEATH

"War is not healthy for children and other living things" is a truism that has been ignored from the beginning of human life on our planet.[1] And nowhere, in the past forty years, has it been truer than in Afghanistan, whose children endure poverty, social inequality, invasion, civil war, occupation, displacement, and untold atrocities. Afghanistan's wars, like all wars, have been fought on the backs of the innocent. Its rehabilitation depends on the well-being of its children. Their destiny is ours.

Having included a good deal of material about children in an earlier volume about Afghan women,[2] Ashraf Zahedi and I felt it appropriate to assemble a kind of "sequel-in-spirit" to examine in more detail what childhood and youth mean in Afghanistan. Women and children are, after all, inseparable. Although we are not experts in child development, we felt it was essential in discussions about Afghanistan to put children at the forefront of the conversation. Around 57 percent of Afghanistan's population is thought to be under the age of eighteen. One in five Afghans is a school-age child, the highest proportion of school-age children in the world.[3] No Afghan under thirty-five years old has ever known peace in her country.

There are a number of excellent books for younger readers about Afghan children, such as *Afghan Dreams: Young Voices of Afghanistan* (2008), by Tony O'Brien and Mike Sullivan, and *Kids of Kabul: Living Bravely Through a Never-Ending War* (2012), by Deborah Ellis (other titles are listed in a selected bibliography below). These give fascinating, realistic, uplifting accounts of children and their individual stories and are invaluable for broadening the global perspectives of Western youngsters. To our knowledge this is the first full-length, comprehensive book for adults devoted to Afghan children, although there are numerous excellent reports—many focusing on the plights of girls and women—from the United Nations Children's Fund (UNICEF), the

World Health Organization (WHO), Save the Children, medica mondiale, and other dedicated humanitarian organizations, as well as organizations like the Afghanistan Research and Evaluation Unit (AREU), whose exemplary work we have relied on here and in other projects.

We seek as full a picture as possible, with historical background leading to insights, observations, and narratives of children's lives in the present, as close to the ground as we can get, with comprehensive solutions and modest suggestions for social policy toward the future. Obviously, we could not cover everything. We took a holistic approach, calling on the expertise of twenty-three accomplished scholars, humanitarian workers, researchers, and journalists, most with actual, extended experience inside the country. The contributors' distinctive voices, approaches, themes, and backgrounds are meant to be layered, to coincide and converse, to reflect the intricacies, multiple truths, and rhizomic realities of children's lives in Afghanistan.

It is almost impossible to avoid a topical book about Afghanistan. Events move rapidly. News outlets and the Internet become primary sources. Regrettably, there is no dependable census and indeed figures presented in this book are by and large estimates and vary, based on methods of gathering data and for what purpose.

We have tried to assemble a book that confronts the real challenges that Afghan children and youth face, the diversities and complexities, the impacts of socioeconomic, political, and cultural factors that shape the lives of girls and boys from birth to their mid-twenties, and consider their experiences in disparate social settings. There are and always have been multiple Afghanistans: Kabul, modern, multicultural, and Western-mediated, from where we get most of our information; Herat, Kandahar, Bamiyan, Mazar-i-Sharif, and other cities with quite dissimilar attitudes and populations; and villages and towns isolated in mountains and valleys populated by people — Pashtun, Hazara, Tajik, Uzbek, and others — whose ways of life stretch back long before Islam entered Afghanistan in the seventh century CE. Still another Afghanistan is composed of the externally and internally displaced, many of whom will never be able to resettle in their ancestral homes.

As Nancy Hatch Dupree writes, "It is always dangerous to generalize about Afghanistan where the intricate geographic and cultural mosaic is so complex. It is especially foolhardy to make sweeping statements at this time when new political tiles are being inserted roughly with no smooth fit."[4]

The Way We Were

The wars that began in 1979 with the invasion of the Soviet Union[5] have impinged on every facet of Afghanistan's diverse society.[6] It seems almost impossible to recall that there was once stability. In order to offer an intimate, historical description of childhood in Afghanistan, we open this anthology with Amina Kator-Mubarez's "Before the Wars: Memories of Childhood in the Pre-Soviet Era," interviews of Afghans ranging in age from ninety-nine to sixty-four, who were fortunate to be children during peacetime.[7] Most are university-educated and from at least marginally privileged backgrounds. The eldest, called Hasib Nusratty,[8] was born during Amir Habibullah's reign. Habibullah (r. 1901–1919) is said to have begun the slow process of Westernization/modernization (even building the first golf course).[9] Briefly—for it is not possible here to give more than a quick recitation of Afghanistan's history—until Habibullah opened Afghanistan's first secondary school, Habibia, for boys, education was pretty much restricted to homeschooling, or, for most of the rural poor, no schooling.[10] (In chapter 16, "Primary and Secondary Education: Exponential Growth and Prospects for the Future," Omar Qargha gives a more complete history.)

Habibullah's son, Amanullah (r. 1919–1929), came to the throne determined to modernize Afghanistan, heavily influenced by his father-in-law and prime minister, the great intellectual Mahmud Beg Tarzi, during a period when Reza Shah in Iran and Mustafa Kemal Ataturk in Turkey were thrusting their countries into development and initiating reforms of all kinds.[11] Under Amanullah's rule, secular-based education, including the first primary school for girls, Masturat School, was established.[12] But Amanullah—whose reign was characterized by Tarzi as "a building lacking a foundation"[13]—moved too fast and was forced to abdicate. After a series of violent events, the throne was taken by Nadir Shah, who pulled back on what were seen as radical gestures suited only to a minority of liberal, urban elite. Nadir was assassinated in 1933, and his nineteen-year-old son, Zahir Shah, the last king of Afghanistan, took over. Zahir approached modernization with caution, moving the country forward, as interviewees in "Before the Wars" note, slowly, but steadily. He was overthrown in a bloodless coup by his cousin Daoud Khan in 1973, signaling the beginning of the political upheaval that led inexorably to the long wars.

Toward the end of Zahir's rule, Afghanistan boasted more than two thousand schools for boys and nearly the same number for girls, most located in and near cities. There were also *madrassas*, mosque schools,[14] but in those years, as Kator-Mubarez's interviewees point out, they did not serve radical or political agendas.

Childhood in Afghanistan, even among the elite, bore little resemblance to modern Western notions of what being a child means. In 1973, anthropologist Louis Dupree wrote:

Sub-teen boys [in Afghan non-urban society] begin to assist their fathers in the fields, or, if nomadic, learn to ride, shoot, and herd. They can no longer play freely with female counterparts. Childhood is over; adulthood begins. . . . [C]hildren have no adolescence, no transitional, educational period among their contemporaries away from their families to prepare them for the world they enter as adults. The young Afghan boy from ten to twelve (or even younger) moves directly into an adult world. Adolescence is primarily a function of a literate, pluralistic society. . . . Some Westerners remain in adolescence until past thirty, undergoing training or graduate studies to enable them to take their places in the adult world. . . . [O]nce the American child enters the public school system, he spends more time away from his nuclear family than with it. He develops new sets of interpersonal, institutional relationships, and usually these change constantly through life, whereas, on the whole, the rural Afghan child keeps the same interpersonal institutional relationships within his immediate kinship unit.

A sub-pubescent Afghan girl helps look after her younger brothers and sisters, as well as the village livestock. Before she reaches nine or ten years of age, her mother teaches her to grind wheat and corn, fetch water, cook, mend and wash clothes, make dung patties . . . a thousand other odds and ends a woman must know to be a good wife and mother.[15]

In one form or another, this traditional way of childhood continues, but nowadays warped, as traumatized Afghans maneuver the globalized world that has been forced upon them and struggle to reconstruct and rediscover themselves amid continued insecurity.

Many Afghans remember the years up to the 1979 Soviet invasion as a "Golden Era," frequently symbolized in the memories of Kabulis and other urbanites by women wearing mini-skirts while modernization progressed heartily. In some ways, it was indeed "golden," but the Western glitter belonged to a tiny element of society. Then, as now, there were cavernous gaps between rich and poor, but at least there was some stutter-step movement toward better opportunities.

With the Soviet invasion, the world for all Afghans was flipped upside down, their survival threatened or destroyed. It seemed only to get worse when the Soviets left in 1989, sparking the first phase of a civil war between factions of Mujahedin[16] vying to fill the power vacuum and bringing fresh horrors, particularly to urban areas. During the Soviet occupation, the United States (working through Pakistan with Saudi Arabian aid) armed and supported the Mujahedin.[17] But when at last the Soviets withdrew and the Cold War was officially declared ended in 1992, the USSR and the U.S. agreed to conclude military and financial aid to Afghanistan, leaving the country isolated, suffering, and helpless. A chance was ignored for the U.S. to help rebuild and thus bring stability to the country and much of the rest of the world.[18]

Meanwhile, a Sunni Islamist and Pashtun nationalist movement calling itself Taliban ("students" or "seekers") was quietly massing and training in Pakistan. In 1994, the movement took Kandahar and in 1996 it conquered Kabul, then spread out across the country. Many welcomed the Taliban as liberators and bringers of peace. Various Mujahedin fled north, where they formed the United Islamic Front for the Salvation of Afghanistan, or Northern Alliance.[19] The Taliban conducted a notorious reign of terror, at first supported by the U.S. government (again through its allies, Pakistan and Saudi Arabia), motivated by the possibility of an oil pipeline project, as well as the hope that the Taliban would "tighten the noose around Iran."[20] Thousands of girls were thrown out of schools. Boys, often orphans, were conscripted into madrassas, where by then their educations consisted mainly of blind recitations of the Qur'an and indoctrination into religious fundamentalist politics. Men as well as women were subjected to the Taliban's draconian measures. Much was forbidden, from uninhibited movement to music to books to toys to children's freedom to play. Nancy Hatch Dupree writes that children, "denied the right to play, became hard to manage and emotionally insecure. . . . Sub-teenage boys recruited by the militia were given a license to beat and berate their elders in public for being inappropriately dressed or for not attending mosques on time. This struck at deeply rooted traditions of showing respect for elders."[21]

A great deal has been written about Taliban brutality, and in this anthology, several authors necessarily hark back on it, as well as on the cruel, chaotic oppression brought by Mujahedin leaders. War plays tricks on faith and social structures, as well as on innocence and compassion. Thus, conservative and repressive attitudes quite naturally continue in Afghanistan, even as a "new" Taliban—now a catchall for drug traffickers, warlords, bandits, ideologues, the impoverished, and the unemployed—have resurged and gained strength since the invasion by U.S. and allied forces that brought the regime down in 2001.[22]

The fall of the Taliban—and the influx of billions of dollars in aid for reconstruction—at last offered hope. But by 2003, the United States had shifted its attention to Iraq, once again turning its back on Afghanistan. Promised funding for reconstruction dwindled; ravenous war profiteers expanded operations into Baghdad. Across the years, particularly in rural areas, many programs and much hope have disappeared for lack of money and security. The bloodshed, hunger, disease, exposure, lack of medical treatment, environmental degradation, and other injustices continue.[23] Corruption has multiplied, both within the Afghan government—encouraged by bribes from the U.S. Central Intelligence Agency—and beyond the Afghan government, hand-in-glove with contractors.[24] In the face of constant and convoluted conflict, Afghans seem to be in perpetual motion, displaced internally and externally, but no longer as welcome to take refuge in Pakistan, Iran, or elsewhere.[25]

In "Narratives of Afghan Childhood: Risk, Resilience, and the Experiences that Shape the Development of Afghanistan as a People and a Nation," Anne E. Brodsky's interviewees tell how all these wars—fighting in them, fleeing from them, growing up with them as continual backdrop—have molded the aspirations, daily lives, identities, and social roles of Afghan children.

Much of what Kator-Mubarez and Brodsky reveal goes unseen and unheard by Westerners, whose information comes too often from exoticized and sensationalized sources. In "Jumping Rope in Prison: The Representation of Afghan Children in Film," Teresa Cutler-Broyles considers how Afghan children are depicted and what they signify in four popular movies from India, Afghanistan, Great Britain, and the U.S. (films featuring Afghan children are listed below in a selected filmography).

Among the films Cutler-Broyles examines is *In This World*, directed by Michael Winterbottom in 2002, which looks at the desperate, perilous migrations of Afghan youngsters into Europe. We regret that space has not allowed us to explore the realities for unknown numbers of Afghan boys—some as young as twelve—wandering alone across Europe, seeking work and new lives as conditions at home have become increasingly difficult.[26]

Ties That Bind: The Family in Rebound

The family has always been the center of Afghan life. "Family bonds are normally extremely close," Nancy Hatch Dupree writes. Traditionally,

> the hierarchical structure within families leaves little room for individualism, for senior male members, the ultimate arbiters, maintain family honor and social status by ensuring all members conform to prescribed forms of acceptable behavior. Nonconformist behavior invites social ostracism and com-

munity pressure becomes a formidable control factor, even within modern urbanized settings. Males, therefore, learn to exercise their authority at an early age. Very young brothers often chastise their older, post-puberty sisters for momentarily stepping beyond the bounds of seclusion.[27]

Time and necessity have shifted and reshaped family dynamics along with the roles of women, yet, "as shaky as it is, in some instances," Dupree continues, "the family is the only stable institution available," and although "Afghanistan has changed, in many ways irreversibly . . . much is still recognizable."[28]

Dupree has been profoundly involved in Afghan life since the early 1960s.[29] In addition to her invaluable work about the family—and all that goes with it from etiquette to rhetoric to cultural heritage, preservation, and education—other scholar-practitioners have produced essential volumes, such as *Aging and Family in an Afghan Refugee Community* (1996), by Patricia Omidian, and *Culture and Customs of Afghanistan* (2005), by Hafizullah Emadi, books that are far removed from the giddy popular fare that has too often misdefined Afghan women and families.

The topic of the Afghan family merits its own comprehensive volume. While we do not deal exclusively with the family, there is no element of this book that does not somehow touch upon it.

Deborah Smith's "Love, Fear, and Discipline in Afghan Families" considers corporal punishment and is an objective report based on field studies undertaken by AREU. The chapter does not demonize the culture or judge everyday violence against children as predominantly Afghan. Verbal abuse of children, corporal punishment, and domestic violence are pervasive worldwide.[30] The Pashtu proverb *che dab nawi adab nawi*—"If there is no stick, there will be no discipline"—echoes the Western proverb "Spare the rod and spoil the child." In any book about children, it is worth examining the subject, for, among other things, corporal punishment (whether a mild spanking or a fierce beating) can determine levels of violence passed on through the family that radiate into the society with profound impacts. While corporal punishment can lead to real physical harm, escalating into abuse, particularly when the parent or authority figure is under extreme stress, the psychological harm can to some extent be mitigated, depending on the society in which the children grow up, its norms and expectations, and the internal strength of the family. However, international campaigns against corporal punishment—whether domestic, in schools, or judicial[31]—emphasize that degrading punishment violates a child's dignity and human rights, and research "now shows that violence to children, even in the form of legally sanctioned corporal punishment, increases the likelihood that they will perpetrate violence on others throughout their lives, including assaulting other children, violent teenaged crime, and ultimately domestic violence and elder abuse."[32]

Esther Hyneman's chapter, "Children Who Live with Their Mothers in Prison," describes a grim side of the Afghan family in crisis. Afghanistan is not alone in detaining children with their parents. In 2008, it was estimated that 226 children in Afghanistan were living with their incarcerated mothers, while at about the same period, the American Civil Liberties Union estimated that two hundred children were being held with their parents at one immigrant prison in the United States.[33] Hyneman writes about the harrowing effects on children living in restrictive and unhealthy conditions with mothers whose crimes may be no more than to be unwanted by husbands and family (although some have indeed committed real, even severe, offenses). The children, some born behind bars, are trapped in a kind of airless purgatory, with few hopes of normalcy in the outside world and only their incarcerated mothers to look after them.

"While marriages are linked with considerable material exchanges of cash, land, and herds," Dupree writes (and in today's economically contorted Afghanistan, high bride prices have soared astronomically),

> liaisons between close kin are designed to keep economic and political
> resources within the extended family, and serve either to perpetuate or modify
> local networks and alliances. Furthermore, in this patrilineal structure, when
> a girl moves to her husband's home, all decisions pertaining to her rights and
> duties are transferred to the husband's family. One often hears it said that a
> girl is merely a guest in the house of her parents, where she prepares for life
> in her husband's household. Although the motivation for some arranged
> marriages—child marriages, compensatory exchanges, the levirate, political
> and social accommodations—can be decidedly discriminatory, in most, close
> bonds normally flourish based on affection, mutual support, and respect.[34]

Sharifa Sharif brings child and forced marriage into focus with "Little Brides and Bridegrooms: Systemic Failure, Cultural Response." Child brides in Afghanistan are a favorite topic for the Western media, who pick many of the most extreme (and photogenic) examples as illustrations of an apparently savage, pedophilic society, and overlook the nuances of family alliances, marriage contracts, how marriages are decided, by whom, and with what results (and, as Dupree notes, not all arranged marriages are unhappy). Sharif reminds us that early marriage is a worldwide phenomenon, not restricted to Afghanistan, and she makes clear that in cultures bound by tight clan politics, neither girls nor boys have choices (this, too, can impact family violence).

Although to what extent child marriage in Afghanistan actually takes place has not been documented precisely, it continues into the twenty-first century for a myriad of reasons, and is accepted, Sharif writes, as age-old convention—despite laws against it. Ancient customs, once viable in an isolated country, particularly in highly secluded rural areas, are no longer workable nor, as the outside world has closed in on the Afghan people, should malpractices—such as the outright sale or trade of young women, some underage—any longer be tolerated by Afghans. The psychological and physical consequences are too dire.

Still, Dupree reminds us, "amidst the confusion and the ambiguities, the basic integrity of the family survives."[35] And if it can continue to do so—even somewhat redefined—then there is certainly hope for the children.

Despite customs and millennia-old traditions, despite paralyzing hardships and impossible odds, we mustn't underestimate Afghan creativity and flexibility. For instance, a group of widows—Afghanistan's most vulnerable women—have built a village within the capital city, Kabul. There are upwards of 1 million Afghan widows, whose average age is thirty-five. In 2009, there were approximately fifty thousand in Kabul, often living in abandoned buildings, many non-literate[36] and most unskilled, surviving by soliciting sex and/or begging in the streets, some with their children. On a hill in Kabul, now called Tapaye Zanabad—"the hill that women built"—hundreds of widows have been squatting for a decade, building mud houses and creating a loose community. They have formed a barebones woman's association; there is a drinking water supply and spotty electricity. The deprivation continues, Tapaye Zanabad is by no means ideal, but it is a sign of ingenuity, shifting paradigms, and the determination to endure.[37]

Survival by Any Means

Billions of dollars have been paid toward Afghanistan's reconstruction, but little has actually made it to the Afghan people, let alone to fulfill the needs of children. As of 2009, Afghanistan received only about $57 per capita from international aid.[38] Matt Waldman, former head of policy for Oxfam International in Afghanistan, reported that on average in 2008, donors spent just $7 million per day. Forty percent of aid money has funneled back into the donor countries as corporate profits and extremely high consultants' salaries. Although outside expertise is needed on numerous fronts, little money is actually spent on the Afghan workforce, where it can do the most good for the country.[39]

"It is almost impossible to determine where government policies begin and [international financial institutions] end," Bank Information Center consultant Anne Carlin writes.[40] Projects overlap or compete, and there is little oversight, despite feeble attempts by the Afghan government to glean and register the hundreds of non-governmental organizations (NGOs) that followed the U.S.-led invasion.[41] The government has almost no credibility. In January 2010, the UN reported that Afghans paid $2.5 billion in bribes to public officials during a period of twelve months, across 2009.[42]

United States economic and humanitarian aid to Afghanistan fell from $4.1 billion in 2010 to $2.5 billion in 2011 and has been steadily dropping.[43] "The humanitarian space is decreasing as communities become more insecure," Samuel Lowenberg writes. "Only 60 percent of the country is accessible to humanitarian response. For the remaining 40 percent, where the fighting is the worst, aid agencies can only guess at the problems people are facing."[44] In 2013, the *New York Times* reported a huge increase in the number of aid workers killed, making the country "by far the most dangerous place in the world for relief work." Through November "there were 237 attacks . . . with 36 people killed, 46 wounded and 96 detained or abducted. This is triple the figure for all of 2012."[45]

Meanwhile, winter after winter, deadly cold takes the lives of refugee children. In 2011/2012, there were at least one hundred confirmed deaths of Afghanistan's internally displaced persons, but funding for assistance — emergency winter supplies, winterization kits, blankets, warm clothes, tarpaulins, clothing, stoves, water, and fuel — has been elusive.[46]

It is obvious that if the lion's share of funding had not profited contractors, warlords, or corrupt government officials, more orphanages — in some cases hotbeds of Dickensian abuse — could be healthy, nurturing places for Afghanistan's 1.6 million orphans.[47] Shelters for women and girls might be more plentiful.[48] Medical programs, hospitals, and clinics might be more accessible. Skills and literacy training might be more available. Thanks to corruption, insecurity, and ongoing combat, girls' and boys' schools have closed in outlying districts, where, in any event, the Afghan government seems never to have put sufficient money or thought into hiring adequate teachers and maintaining them.[49]

These are cursory examples of how lack of funding affects Afghan children, who — as Amanda Sim demonstrates in "Confronting Child Labor," and Wahid Omar writes in "The Parakeet Boys: Performing Education in the Streets of Kabul" — must work to help feed and clothe themselves and their families.

Children have always worked in Afghanistan, but their labors before the wars were as often as not forms of apprenticeship. The 1973 International Labour Organization (ILO) Convention on Minimum Age for Admission to Employment defines child labor by age: eighteen as the minimum for performing hazardous work and fifteen for "light work." The United Nations Convention on the Rights of the Child states in Article 32 that children should be protected from "performing any work that is likely to be hazardous or to interfere with the child's education, or to be harmful to the child's health or physical, mental, spiritual, moral, or social development." As Sim notes, in Afghanistan, the Labor Code mandates the minimum working age at fifteen for non-hazardous work and eighteen for hazardous work. It is estimated that 1.2 million children perform hazardous work, 3 million children have no access to education,[50] and even very young children barely out of toddlerhood are laboring at all kinds of tasks, some extremely dangerous. The so-called "worst forms of child labor" are described in the 1999 ILO Convention as sex work and drug trafficking—booming trades among young Afghan girls and boys, with, in some cases, whole families involved.[51]

Children working on the streets are predominantly boys between the ages of eleven and fourteen. According to the 2010 Consortium for Street Children,

> there are no accurate socio-economic and demographic data in Afghanistan and . . . there are no records on the number of street children in Afghanistan, although estimates show the numbers have increased dramatically in recent years. Herat, for example, has 5,000 to 10,000 street children. Estimates in Kandahar range from 7,000 street working children to 32,000 street children. In Kabul, the estimates on street children raised from 37,500 in 2003 to 50,000 in 2007, then sharply increased in 2009 to 70,000. Aschiana Foundation estimates the number of street children in Afghanistan is 600,000.[52]

As the already inadequate sums that reach poor Afghans and their children dry up, fears have naturally grown that child labor will worsen.

One steady employer is the Taliban. With the wave of humanitarian aid in 2001, hundreds of facilities—schools, clinics, literacy and vocational training programs—were created especially for women and girls. Indeed, funding was more likely when a project was for females, often leaving ordinary men and boys to flounder unaided, inspiring Taliban recruitment. Even men with relatively temperate views, but no prospects, have increasingly joined or rejoined mercenary war- and drug-lord armies or the Taliban.

In "Child Soldiering in Afghanistan," Delphine Boutin considers the reasons Afghan children become combatants and the outcomes. While forced recruitment is pervasive, she notes, children also join armed forces voluntarily, motivated by a divided society with intolerable levels of poverty, unemployment, and inequality, as well as poor educational and vocational training systems and the breakdown of law and order.[53]

Hangama Anwari's "Legal Protection: Offering Aid and Comfort" discusses the massive obstacles facing children, particularly those at risk of exploitation and violence, who seek justice and meaningful protection in the Afghan judicial system. Discrimination against children is evident across gender, age, and class, and the government's capacity to provide assistance to those who are not able to support their families is extremely limited.

The age of criminal responsibility in Afghanistan is thirteen, but, in 2012, "Afghanistan: Child Justice Brief" reported that only 10 percent of children are registered at birth and "the majority do not know their age or date of birth. Although methods are employed to establish children's ages by criminal justice agencies, these are not always accurate. [This] makes it difficult to ensure that children in the criminal justice system are of the legal age of criminal responsibility."[54]

In some provinces, juvenile rehabilitation centers exist exclusively for boys. UNICEF reports that only 15 percent of children found in the juvenile rehabilitation centers are female. "This reflects that girls seem less likely to come into conflict with the law, given that they are restricted in movement outside their homes, and that many girls are processed in the adult system."[55]

There have been, Anwari notes, countless missed opportunities to protect children, although the Constitution of Afghanistan puts weighty value on the family. Here, she posits, ancient customs relating to the care of children could be utilized with positive results. Ongoing opposition to the Elimination of Violence Against Women Law only extends the abuse, harming children by denying their mothers human rights and by leaving the door open for early marriage and other exploitations.[56] There are a great many justified fears that, particularly as the drawdown of U.S. troops approaches, a rollback of women's and girls' rights, already under way, will proceed with impunity.

Not only are Afghans daily facing the hard work of repairing decades of psychological and physical damage, but in doing so they must resolve clashes of time and traditions. The fetishizing and imposition of one-size-fits-all Western-style democracy and Western ideals and ideas are not always necessarily appropriate for a tribal, dynastic society and can result in backlash. In Afghanistan, more often than not, tradition trumps law. Anwari's suggestion that traditions be exploited for the betterment of children's lives is more than sensible.

To Be Whole in Mind and Body

In "Children's Health: The Challenge of Survival," Steven Solter offers hope. He writes that although Afghan children have always had among the highest mortality rates in the world, the situation has actually improved since 2002. Vaccinations,[57] training of community health workers and midwives—in a country that has the highest maternal mortality ratio in the world[58]—and other vital and strategically planned activities (drawing as ever on few available resources) are, bit by bit, cutting through tremendous obstacles. Children die, Solter notes, from three major causes: pneumonia, diarrhea, and malnutrition. Measles, malaria, polio, and smallpox, important causes of the past, have not been entirely eradicated, but are much reduced (refugees crisscrossing borders can be especially susceptible). Thousands of Afghan children are also debilitated by cutaneous leishmaniasis, a disabling disease transmitted by the bite of the sand fly, which leads to disfigurement usually on the face and hands, and to social stigma, particularly for women and children.[59]

Solter notes that HIV and AIDS are not yet a major health problem for Afghan children, although UNICEF and the United Nations Office on Drugs and Crime believe that the potential is there and imminent with the marked increase of drug addiction in recent years: 7 percent of the adult population of 14 million uses narcotics. Male-to-male sex with children and intravenous drug use, transmissions from mother to child, and simple accidental punctures of children sifting through garbage littered with used syringes are among the frightening factors that contribute to children's vulnerability.[60]

With profound poverty, undernutrition is widespread, made worse as agricultural fields have been strafed, the ground poisoned with weapons chemicals,[61] and sophisticated, millennia-old irrigation systems destroyed. In 2009, the worst drought in living memory affected all traditional food crops. Unsafe drinking water, lack of sanitary facilities, and fertilizers from untreated human and animal waste all contribute to Afghanistan's appalling statistics, as do harsh winters in areas that are unreachable either because of the terrain or armed combat or both. In "Food Security and Nutrition for Afghan Children," Fitsum Assefa, Annalies Borrel, and Charlotte Dufour meticulously detail the challenges brought on by lack of nutritious, vitamin-rich food (as well as knowledge of healthy infant feeding and other practices), and describe the opportunities for ameliorating the problems.

Sports are agents of socialization (along with family, religion, school, peer groups, and mass media), and teach children leadership, self-confidence, and to identify, then reach, their goals—essential skills for successful lives.

Although many organized sports impose prohibitive expenses for uniforms, equipment, or club fees, youngsters—mostly urban—have embraced them with high enthusiasm. Girls are frequently discouraged from participating, but many nonetheless excel in soccer, boxing, volleyball, or hockey. Some women, such as sprinter Robina Jalali at the Olympics, have moved beyond the local arena.[62]

Most youngsters in Afghanistan have limited time for play. Toys, such as dolls or slingshots, are useful in training rural children for future responsibilities as wives and mothers, herders and hunters. Informal games resemble those of kids worldwide: tag, blind man's bluff, stickball, hopscotch, *bujulbazi* (similar to marbles), and wrestling. And, of course, kite-flying, as Westerners learned from Khaled Hosseini's best-selling novel *The Kite Runner*, is a favorite urban sport, and though banned by the Taliban (and not much practiced when the Mujahedin were shooting up the cities), it returned quickly after the allied invasion.[63] Some of these games have traditionally been the exclusive prerogative of boys, but girls also play them in segregated groups or—if young enough—boys and girls play them together.[64]

Western children spend increasingly less time outdoors, resulting in what journalist Richard Louv calls "nature deficit disorder," which presents a wide range of behavioral problems and which he says is the outcome of parental fears, restricted access to natural areas, and growing consumption of electronic media by children. Fortunately, many Afghan children—so far—are spared the small screen, but their access to safe outdoor spaces, their opportunities to absorb and enjoy nature—perhaps the supreme healer—are constrained. Refugee camps are often composed of trash and dust (though children are endlessly flexible and can turn even the most unpleasant places into cheerful play yards). Some of the exquisite ancient gardens and parks in Herat, Kabul, and other cities have been repaired and replanted (and many historic sites and museums rebuilt), offering breathing space, cultural lodestars, transcendence, and fun. The Kabul Zoo has been reconstructed. Zoos exercise a strong benefit in that they bring legions of children into a love for wild creatures. This can, in time, help establish a population of caring and activist adults. In 2012, Afghanistan opened its first national park at the high mountain lakes of Band-e Amir to boost tourism, but not enough Afghans are cognizant of it or can afford the long journey to get there.[65]

Afghanistan's environmental damage is incalculable. Before the wars, the country was rich in biodiversity, but its fertile lands, its breadbaskets, and its wilderness are now devastated by persistent violence and the harsh weather patterns that follow. In 2002, the United Nations Environmental Programme conducted a basic research project and found that "forests, waters, soil, and wildlife were clearly in decline or on the brink of irreparable damage, and the resulting environmental degradation was endangering human health and compounding poverty."[66]

Farms and grazing lands are littered with leftover landmines and unexploded ordnance (UXO), making the outdoors especially lethal for children. Hundreds are killed or maimed every year as they help with farm chores, herd livestock, hunt, fish, stroll, play games, or simply move from one destination to another. In December 2012 alone, ten girls were killed in eastern Afghanistan when a landmine exploded while they were collecting firewood, an all too recurrent tragedy. In Kabul, roughly 85 percent of UXO victims are children. The process of dismantling the ordnance is expensive and painfully slow.[67]

Landmines are a major cause of disabilities, but there are others, such as genetic disorders sometimes caused by first-cousin marriages. In "Desperately Seeking Harun: Children with Disabilities," Lael Adams Mohib looks at how children and their families cope and follows the struggles and triumphs of several dedicated humanitarian workers.[68]

More than forty years of combat and social injustice have bred massive mental health problems for all Afghans. Mark Eggerman and Catherine Panter-Brick have conducted studies about Afghan children's mental health,[69] and in "'Life Feeds on Hope': Family Mental Health, Culture, and Resilience," they examine, among other things, "which aspects of violence and poverty are the most critical predictors of mental health status and which aspects of individual and social life best characterize the ability to overcome adversity." This is vital information if we are to help the new generation of young people to inherit Afghanistan's future.

Afghan psychologist Nahid Aziz (a founder of Rawan Online, a website focusing on psychological and mental health for Afghans)[70] and scholar Zeba Shorish-Shamley have written variously about child socialization and the nature of mental health in Afghanistan, cultural perspectives, perceived causes (such as *djinn*—spirits—and *nazar*—the evil eye),[71] attitudes, and methods of treatment.[72]

Mary MacMakin, who has lived and worked in Afghanistan since the 1960s, recalls that

> Shrines are the place for disturbed children and adolescents. I happened to
> be visiting the Jalalabad shrine years ago when an intractable thirteen-year-
> old girl was brought by her parents. The shrine had a row of little dirt-floored
> stalls where the sick were tied in or chained in if they were violent. The mul-
> lah did the healing with prayers. We returned later and the girl was "cured,"
> ready to go home.[73]

Events of the past decades have conspired to destroy young minds and souls. When parents are psychologically damaged, they cannot care properly for their children. When carnage and cruelty are all around and chronic, when families are shattered, when children are betrayed by adults, when they are mistreated, when they are unprotected, when they are left with little hope, children can break.

Education: Nurturing the Future

There are few enough comforts for the children of Afghanistan, but, in addition to family stability, the surest path to health, reconstruction, and lasting peace is education.

Throughout Afghanistan, where two-thirds of the population over the age of fifteen is non-literate, people are demanding schools. With the fall of the Taliban, schools began to open and young people returned from exile. In "Education in Transition: A Key Concern for Young Afghan Refugees," Mamiko Saito analyzes refugees' reactions as they adapt and make difficult transitions in language, culture, social patterns, and standards of education back home.

In "Primary and Secondary Education: Exponential Growth and Prospects for the Future," Omar Qargha describes the unprecedented growth in the numbers of schools built in recent decades and offers an inclusive analysis of how, in order for education to fully succeed, it must be tailored to the country's unique needs, balanced with universal modern curricula and standards.

Coeducation has been frowned upon since Afghan girls first began attending school in the 1920s. Sadly, schools and female students are under violent attack and there seems to be no end in sight. In the first six months of 2009, for example, sixteen bomb blasts took place on school premises and by fall, 80 percent of schools in southern Afghanistan were closed.[74] Even home schools—re-created in the post-Taliban era as a solution to reactions against public education for girls—have shut down. Traveling long distances to rural schools located in insecure areas presents risks parents are unwilling to take for boys or girls. The situation continues to degenerate; grand promises made with the 2001 invasion have not been kept.

Today it is thought that economic growth in developing countries results from women's empowerment and equality, but what happens when the balance is tipped the other way and boys are left behind? Gender mainstreaming in Afghan development policy and the rush to create girls' schools after the Taliban defeat often neglected boys' educational needs, a mistake considering that a nation of men ignorant of history, literature, mathematics, sciences, languages, arts, political science, and so on will continue to oppress women, even educated ones, and be unable to participate fully in the creation of a strong and peaceful civil society. As educator Sakena Yacoobi writes, the slightest ability to read not only enriches lives, but can save them, too.[75]

In refugee camps, skills can be lost within one generation: the essential knowledge of farming, for example, disappears. And the lives of boys who once apprenticed to their fathers and other male relatives have been so disrupted that many are unable to learn the skills necessary to practice a trade. Although the World Bank and the United States Agency for International Development provide some vocational training programs, they are not adequate, nor has development been sufficient—or necessarily culturally, geographically, or ecologically/sustainably appropriate—to warrant the kinds of skills training that might actually speed reconstruction and strengthen security.

A handful of valiant and trustworthy NGOs offer literacy training to young men, but funding has been more readily available for girls and women. Afghanistan's literacy rate is about 28 percent total—43.1 percent male and 12.6 percent female—and students on average have only nine years of school.[76]

"Afghanistan cannot be a viable democracy unless its populace (including children) learn to read," Sandra Cook, co-chair of the Louis and Nancy Hatch Dupree Foundation, writes of ACKU Boxed Library Extension (ABLE), a boxed library program housed in the Afghanistan Centre at Kabul University, which

> assists this goal by providing school and community libraries throughout Afghanistan. Many of the books that are distributed by ABLE are actually commissioned to Afghan authors by the ABLE editorial board, written in Dari and Pashto, and cover topics of interest to Afghans. The ABLE school libraries also contain dictionaries and other reference materials which are not written and published by ABLE.[77]

Other NGOs, like Canadian Women for Women in Afghanistan (CW4WAfghan), support community, village, and neighborhood libraries—primarily in the rural districts around Kabul—"to help reinforce literacy skills, nurture a culture of reading, and foster independent, lifelong learning." CW4WAfghan has even initiated an Afghan Women's Teen Writing Project and Teenage Writers' Workshop, and published the youngsters' poetry and prose.[78]

We felt that focusing on discussions about early childhood and primary and secondary school education might be more productive than attempting in this book to define the intricacies of higher education in Afghanistan, which has made many giant strides since the fall of the Taliban, but remains nevertheless problematic. Higher education began in Afghanistan with the establishment of Kabul University in 1932. Today, there are about thirty-eight colleges, universities, and technical institutes throughout the country in various states of organization, repair, and academic excellence, with approximately 50,000 enrolled students.[79] Much has been accomplished, but much more is needed, and ultimately depends on leadership at the Ministry of Higher Education, where, unfortunately, but not unusually, politics win over merit.[80]

Textbooks published by the University of Nebraska from 1984 and 1994, which encouraged youngsters to join the Mujahedin by using exercises illustrated with images of tanks, missiles, landmines, and other weapons, were still being used in 2001.[81] In 2012, a series of government-issue social studies textbooks for grades ten through twelve, funded by U.S. and international aid organizations, makes no mention of Afghanistan's recent history, but manages a grand jeté over forty years, leaping across the Saur Revolution, the Soviet invasion, the Mujahedin, the Taliban, and the U.S. presence. Apparently unmindful of Edmund Burke's famous warning that "those who don't know history are destined to repeat it," Afghan educators, scholars, and politicians claim they are encouraging peace and unity by pretending these events did not happen.[82]

A 2010 study by Ahmed Khalid Fahim found that modern Afghan textbooks are "male biased in texts, illustrations, and language. The textbooks portray males in active roles mostly outside home settings while females are portrayed in more passive roles such as taking care of children, looking after domestic chores and living in subordination to males."[83]

Also in 2010, the education ministry announced the publication of 40 million textbooks about Dari literature at the cost of $20 million, which journalist Nushin Arbabzadah describes as overflowing with misspellings, morality tales from the Qur'an, and trivial poetry, having "no clear structure . . . not only discriminating against girls, but disregarding boys as well . . . . the books are an accurate reflection of the ministry's intellectual poverty and cultural parochialism . . . certainly not a fair representation of the diversity, wit, and eloquence of Afghan literature."[84]

As inadequate as textbooks may be in Afghanistan, teaching styles are too frequently just as ineffectual. Louise M. Pascale has devised a method by which Afghan children can learn to read through song, and she describes her wonderful project in "Music and Literacy: A New Approach to Education." Memorization, regurgitation, drill, recitation . . . old-fashioned rote learning—which neglects art education as well—still prevails (as does the rod) in classrooms, leaving children with little room for creativity and therefore stifling critical thinking.[85] Pascale collected the songs while she was a Peace Corps volunteer in the 1960s, little realizing they would soon be in danger of extinction. She has provided an invaluable gift to the Afghan people.

Folk tales are teaching tools, too. Hoopoe Books, which bears the motto "from thinking children come thinking adults," provides children and schools with teaching stories translated into Dari and Pashto from the works of the marvelous Anglo-Afghan author Idries Shah.[86]

Participants in Brodsky's "Narratives of Afghan Childhood" (chapter 2) repeatedly emphasize education as the road to becoming fully human, the path to peace. In 2010, Amina Kator interviewed young Afghans about their hopes and dreams for the future. All of them yearned for educations and all understood that Afghanistan's fate depends on it:

> I don't let problems cause me grief. I focus solely on my studies. I study every night and sometimes when the electricity goes out, I light candles so I can continue reading. I love to read. . . . So far, it seems like education is the only answer. —Narges Mansuri, thirteen
>
> Every child needs to be educated. Right now there are so many uneducated Afghans. The government needs to provide more educational opportunities for young and old, scholarships and financial assistance. —Ghulam Asada, eighteen
>
> We need doctors, engineers, and lawyers, but we also need journalists, comedians, actors, investors, directors, singers. We need both men and women to contribute. We as Afghan youth must help Afghanistan flourish in all regards. There is so much to look forward to in life. —Bashir Said, eighteen
>
> As long as I can become as educated as possible, there will be a chance that things might get better. If not, what is the use of living this life? —Lamba Otmani, twenty-two[87]

Communicating Empowerment

Worldwide, social media has affected everything from marketing to massive political and social uprisings. The experiences and even the characters of young people everywhere are being shaped by it. And it is no different for Afghan youth who are able to access the Internet, as Lauryn Oates tells us in "Thanks God for the Twitter and the Facebook! Thanks God for That!"

All this cyber expansion has opened wide new vistas. Indeed, cellphones are even being introduced that feature an application called Ustad Mobile (Mobile Teacher) and provide national curriculum courses in both Dari and Pashto, as well as mathematics.[88]

According to Socialbakers, a market-analysis website, in 2012 Afghanistan had 397,600 Facebook users, 1.37 percent of the population. Just 2 million of Afghanistan's 30 million people have Internet access. Yet upward of 20 million Afghans are thought to have cellphones. Kabul's Nai Media Institute, which launched in January 2012 to offer diplomas in radio, television, and online broadcasting, reports that young people are rushing to study journalism, broadcasting, and media management.[89]

Although Afghan journalists—like journalists everywhere—struggle to maintain press freedoms and the right to free speech,[90] social media and the Internet offer a creative exchange of ideas. And ideas are empowering.

As are the arts. Pascale's songbook project gives credence to the fact that arts are key components of learning in any field and must not be marginalized, treated as trivial and inconsequential. Not only do arts—and history, their blood-sibling—help shape whole, creative, and *thinking* human beings, offering pleasure, beauty, grace, and knowledge, thus enabling peace, not only do they offer lessons from the past and thus innovative visions for the future, but, as historian Nancy Hatch Dupree has repeatedly emphasized, it is through culture that national identity is forged and preserved. "The fundamentals of the culture remain strong," she writes, "changed in some ways but readily recognizable as uniquely Afghan. Current expectations aim to engage various cultural elements as bonding vehicles to hasten reconstruction and strengthen peace."[91]

Young Afghans have turned enthusiastically to the visual and performing arts as forms of personal expression and unity. Joanna Sherman illustrates in "The New Storytellers of Afghanistan" that the arts (in this case theatre) provide tools to alert us to problems, expose and heal the wounds of the past and help us see them in a new light. Equally essential, the arts afford space to just be silly. All children require time to be silly (whose original meaning is "blessed"), all the more so for those who have been impacted by war.

The arts are cathartic and therapeutic, whereby the individual, the culture, and current events are reflected one against the other, serving to strengthen and make us whole. Lauryn Oates has written elsewhere about young female artists studying modernist painting, not unheard of in Afghanistan but not expected either, particularly from women and girls. Out of this have come all sorts of urgent actions, including graffiti art, courageous public expressions in a repressed society. Like poetry, an ancient and venerated art form in Afghanistan, visual art has the power to heal and to dissolve rigid certainties, a giant step toward inner and outer peace.[92]

Perhaps because Afghanistan is primarily an oral society, music and story-telling are its natural outcropping, so the re-introduction of performance has been especially successful for children and young people. In addition to Sherman's Bond Street Theatre, which has worked for years throughout Af-ghanistan, training and entertaining, there are Afghan Participatory Theatre, Mobile Mini-Circus for Children, Theatre Circus Afsâna, Parwaz Puppet Theatre, the Afghan Youth Voices Festival, No Strings International (which uses puppets to teach children to avoid landmines), and more.[93] With growing insecurity, these wonderful events and activities are shrinking in their mobility and ability to reach the hundreds of children who would benefit.

Ian Pounds personalizes his years of working with orphaned girls at the Afghan Child Education and Care Organization in "Six Epiphanies: Testa-ment to Change from Inside an Afghan Orphanage," illustrating the love and joy these brave children find every day in an environment that strives to erase the pain of the past.

And yet, outside the orphanage doors, Pounds wrote in a personal email in 2012, "things are spiraling here in Afghanistan. Jihadis are getting more brazen and trying to take more control." He began receiving death threats and has finally left Afghanistan. His story is not uncommon. Many who were giving Afghan children the benefits of their talent and enthusiasm have been forced to retreat.[94]

Do We Dare Take Responsibility for the Future of Afghan Children?

Ashraf Zahedi closes this book with "Imagining the Future," in which she considers practical actions that can be taken to improve the lot of Afghan children (and in the process the lives of the adults in charge of them) and speed the process of healing, peace, and reasonable prosperity for all Afghans. Our hope is that this book will encourage further endeavors to help Afghani-stan and that the world, particularly those who have done the most damage to the country and its people, will step up and take responsibility for the repair.

Hundreds of thousands of children die as a result of direct violence; they suffer a wide range of injuries, including rape; they are disabled and have grossly inadequate access to rehabilitation services; their health suffers as conditions for safeguarding it disappear; they suffer psychologically with post-traumatic stress disorder, depression, anxiety, and more that can lead to further violence (and in the same vein, the moral and spiritual impacts are tremendous, resulting in loss of meaning and indifference); as children in war they are at risk of losing their moral and social structures, their communities and families, and the educational opportunities which underpin their lives and give them ballast.[95]

Child advocates often remind the Afghan government that it ratified the UN Convention on the Rights of the Child in 1994. It is hard to picture exactly who, claiming to be the Afghan government during the civil war era, signed the convention or whether that signature is still considered by the powers that be to have authority. Today's government must renew that commitment.

Continued, indeed redoubled, humanitarian aid is desperately needed and will be for a long time to come. Aid costs less and returns more than fighting. What's required is a surge of teachers, medical professionals, environmentalists, organic farmers, social workers, and others—a new and progressive "peace corps"—that can facilitate healing with carefully thought-out programs and support . . . paid for by money that has been lining dishonest pockets for decades. Much has improved and can continue to improve, but Afghanistan stands on a cusp and it is possible that all the gains and all the potential could slip away.

Like Afghanistan and like children everywhere, this book is an unfinished project. We have tried to highlight the needs of Afghan children, make suggestions where appropriate for ways to solve problems, uncover the possibilities that might bring lasting change. We have also tried to illustrate the spirit and beauty that define Afghan children. Regardless of geopolitics and— chronically unsound—military strategies, we cannot turn our backs. The next steps in Afghanistan's arduous journey will be taken by its growing children, and it is vital to world peace that they be healthy and whole. Will we at last take responsibility?

Afghanistan has been called the worst place on earth to be a child. For their sakes and ours, we must not let that continue.

Notes

1. "War is not healthy for children and other living things" is a slogan from Another Mother for Peace, a grassroots, antiwar advocacy group founded in 1967 in opposition to the U.S. war in Vietnam.

2. Jennifer Heath and Ashraf Zahedi, *Land of the Unconquerable: The Lives of Contemporary Afghan Women* (Berkeley: University of California Press, 2011).

3. World Vision UK, 2012, http://www.worldvision.org.uk/what-we-do/disaster-management/afghanistan/.

4. Nancy Hatch Dupree, "The Family During Crisis in Afghanistan," *Journal of Comparative Family Studies* 35, no. 2 (Spring 2004): 311.

5. The Soviet Union invaded Afghanistan on December 24, 1979, and finally left the country in 1989, although they continued to support the communist regime in Kabul until 1992.

6. Among tribal groups are Pashtun, Tajik, Uzbek, Farsiwan, Qazilbash, Hazara, Aimaq, Moghul, Turcoman, Kirghiz, Pamiri, Baluch, Brahuis, and Nuristani. The two primary and official languages are Dari and Pashto.

7. The final piece in "Before the Wars" is from a memoir-in-progress by Wahid Omar, who contributed chapter 8 in this volume, "The Parakeet Boys: Performing Education in the Streets of Kabul."

8. Most Afghan names in this book have been changed to protect privacy or for safety.

9. For a brief history of Habibullah's reign, see Louis Dupree, *Afghanistan* (Princeton: Princeton University Press, 1980), 430–440. See also Yuri V. Gankovsky et al., Vitaly Baskakov, tr., *A History of Afghanistan* (Moscow, Russia: Progress Publishers, 1985), 231.

10. Of the Zahir Shah era (1933 to 1973), Dupree writes, "The education (or socialization other than economic activity) of the child is mainly in the hands of grandparents or . . . older uncles or aunts. Three generations of social symbiosis exist, each symbolizing various stages of the society. The grandparents represent the past and, with other elders in the villages, are the walking encyclopedias of the society. The distilled knowledge of the ages" (*Afghanistan*, 196). See also Hafizullah Emadi, *Culture and Customs of Afghanistan* (Santa Barbara, CA: Greenwood Press, 2005), 209–213.

11. Of interest: Sorab K. H. H. Katrak, *Through Amanullah's Afghanistan: A Book of Travel*, 2nd ed. (Karachi: Din Muhammad Press, 1953).

12. Dupree, *Afghanistan*, 453.

13. Shireen Khan Burki, "The Politics of *Zan* from Amanullah to Karzai," in *Land of the Unconquerable*, 45–59.

14. Dupree, *Afghanistan*, 453. *Madrassa* or *madrasah*. "Establishments of learning where the Islamic sciences are taught; a college for higher sciences." John L. Esposito, ed. *Oxford Dictionary of Islam* (Oxford: Oxford University Press, 2003), 184.

15. Dupree, *Afghanistan*, 194. For more about childrearing in Afghanistan, see Emadi, *Culture and Customs*, 177–179.

16. Mujahedin, plural of mujahid, "'one who engages in jihad.' Often translated as 'warriors of God.' Technically, the term does not have a necessary connection with war." Esposito, *Oxford Dictionary of Islam*, 213. President Ronald Reagan labeled the Afghan Mujahedin "freedom fighters." They were divided into many political parties, based on ethnicity, sectarian values, and ideologies. Today, Muslim volunteers in many countries, such as Albania, Bosnia, and Chechnya, call themselves Mujahedin.

17. Across the ten-year Soviet war, more than 1 million Afghans were killed; 1.2 million Mujahedin, government soldiers, and non-combatants were disabled; and 3 million (mostly noncombatants) were maimed or wounded. Five million Afghans, one-third of the prewar population, fled to Pakistan and Iran. Another 2 million

Afghans were displaced within the country. Internal fighting had already begun here and there in Afghanistan between the Soviet-backed regimes and anti-communist Afghans shortly before the Soviet invasion. See M. Hassan Kakar, *Afghanistan: The Soviet Invasion and the Afghan Response* (Berkeley: University of California Press, 1995), 32–50. In the 1980s, one out of two refugees worldwide was Afghan. Some 3.7 million Afghan refugees who fled the conflict in the past two decades currently live in neighboring countries. "The Cost of War in Afghanistan," American Friends Service Committee, http://www.nationalpriorities.org/auxiliary/costofwar/cost_of_war_afghani stan.pdf.

18. Soviet reconstruction aid would not have been welcomed, but even so, by then its own economy was on the brink, thanks to its Afghan adventures. In supporting the Mujahedin, the U.S. had effectively broken the USSR, but it also helped break Afghanistan.

19. It is impossible in this space to give more than a highly abridged version of Afghanistan's history and the twisted geopolitics that have led to today's events. Journalists such as Peter Marsden (*The Taliban, War, Religion and the New Order in Afghanistan*, 1998), Ahmed Rashid (*Taliban: Militant Islam, Oil and Fundamentalism in Central Asia*, 2001), Steve Coll (*Ghost Wars: The Secret History of the CIA, Afghanistan and Bin Laden, From the Soviet Invasion to September 10, 2001*, 2004), and Paul Fitzgerald and Elizabeth Gould (*Invisible History: Afghanistan's Untold Story*, 2009) are among those who have written probing, comprehensive histories peeling away the covert layers of U.S. and international collusion in Afghanistan's near destruction. The Soviet invasion (addressed in Dupree's 1980 edition of *Afghanistan*) drew hundreds of journalists into the country and inspired distinguished researchers such as Richard S. and Nancy Peabody Newell (*The Struggle for Afghanistan*, 1981).

20. Ahmed Rashid, *Taliban: Militant Islam, Oil, and Fundamentalism in Central Asia* (New Haven, CT: Yale University Press, 2000), 170–182.

21. Dupree, "The Family During Crisis," 324.

22. Even as women were barred from education and employment, their health care severely restricted and draconian laws applied (to everyone), the Taliban era brought comparative quiet and order, a respite from Mujahedin guns and rockets. Roshanak Wardak, a gynecologist and member of the Afghan parliament, described the Taliban as "well-disciplined people. In their time there was security." However, the new Taliban, she said, are very different. "They are criminals. They are thieves and they are not acceptable." Jason Burke, "I Would Never Swap My Country for All the World," *The Guardian*, September 11, 2008, http://www.guardian.co.uk/world/2008/sep11/Afghani stan.gender.

23. There are no accurate figures for the numbers of civilian casualties in Afghanistan since the United States–led invasion started in 2001, but it is estimated that 2,118 civilians were killed in 2008 alone, compared with 1,523 in 2007, the highest since the Taliban government was defeated in November 2001. Dexter Filkins, "Afghan Civilian Deaths Rose 40 Percent in 2008," *New York Times*, February 18, 2009, http://www.nytimes.com/2009/02/18/world/asia/18afghan.html. At mid-year 2010, the United Nations Assistance Mission in Afghanistan reported that the number of civilians wounded and killed increased by nearly a third in the first six months of the year, as U.S. and NATO coalition forces raised the level of military action. United Nations

Assistance Mission, Featured News, "Afghan Civilian Casualties Rise 31 Percent in First Six Months of 2010," August 10, 2010, http://unama.unmissions.org.

24. Matthew Rosenberg, "With Bags of Cash, CIA Seeks Influence in Afghanistan," *New York Times*, April 28, 2013, http://www.nytimes.com/2013/04/29/world /asia/cia-delivers-cash-to-afghan-leaders-office.html?pagewanted=all&_r=0. In 2011, there were approximately 70,000 private contractors in Kabul, outnumbering uniformed troops. Many of the groups with interests in Afghanistan also migrated into Iraq with the 2003 invasion: Halliburton, Bechtel Group, Inc., BearingPoint Group, Inc., Creative Associates International, Inc., Blackwater Security Consulting, LLC, and others. Some are the same companies operating under different names. See the Center for Public Integrity, "Windfalls of War," http://projects.publicintegrity.org /wow/bio.aspx?act=pro. For more about corruption in Afghanistan, see Stephanie Debere and Michael Sidwell, eds., *Transparency International Global Coalition Against Corruption: Annual Report 2009* (Berlin: Transparency International, 2009), 25, 30, 53. Available at http://www.transparency.org.

25. Pakistan has more than 1.6 million registered and approximately 1 million undocumented Afghan refugees. Evictions were planned for registered refugees in December 2012, but Prime Minister Raja Pervez Ashraf allowed them to stay legally through June 2013. The eviction was again extended, this time indefinitely, while a new solution was sought. Pakistan has been hosting Afghan refugees since the Soviet invasion. Refugees frequently go back and forth, from Pakistan to Afghanistan, for numerous reasons, often maintaining family in both countries. As of 2009, nearly 1 million Afghans were refugees in Iran, with few rights and little justice. About 100,000 were forcibly deported in 2007. Nevertheless, for numerous reasons, many refugees find Iran a safe haven. See Rod Nordland, "For Afghan Refugees in Iran, Painful Contradictions," *New York Times*, November 20, 2013, http://www.nytimes.com /2013/11/21/world/asia/for-afghan-refugees-in-iran-painful-contradictions.html.

26. For more, see Caroline Brothers, "Afghan Youths Seek a New Life in Europe," *New York Times*, August 28, 2009, http://www.nytimes.com/2009/08/28/world/asia /28afghankids.html. See also Anderson Cooper, *60 Minutes*, CBS News, May 19, 2013, http://www.cbsnews.com/video/watch/?id=50147163n, and Anderson Cooper, "Swedish Doctor: Afghan Boys Are Traumatized," *CBS News*, May 19, 2013, http:// www.cbsnews.com/video/watch/?id=50147174n.

27. Dupree, "The Family During Crisis," 312.

28. Ibid., 329.

29. Many Afghan women have returned from exile to advocate for women and children. Some non-Afghan women also have settled in Afghanistan to develop humanitarian programs and follow in the footsteps of U.S./American women such as Nancy Hatch Dupree (http://www.dupreefoundation.org) and Mary MacMakin (http://www.afzenda.com), who have worked virtually nonstop in Afghanistan on its behalf since the 1960s.

30. Corporal punishment of minors within domestic settings is lawful in all fifty of the United States. It has been officially outlawed in only thirty-two countries. Corporal punishment in school has been outlawed in Canada, Kenya, Korea, South Africa, New Zealand, and nearly all of Europe. It remains legal in some parts of the world, including nineteen of the United States. Global Initiative to End All Corporal Pun-

ishment of Children, http://www.endcorporalpunishment.org/pages/progress/pro hib_states.html.

31. Lucien X. Lombardo and Karen A. Polonko, "A Comparative Analysis of the Corporal Punishment of Children: An Exploration of Human Rights and U.S. Law," *International Journal of Comparative and Applied Criminal Justice* 29, no. 2 (Fall 2005).

32. Ibid.

33. Child Rights International Network, "Afghanistan: Children in Prison with Mothers," Associated Press, August 4, 2008, http://www.crin.org/resources/infodetail .asp?id=18035, and "ACLU Challenges Illegal Detention of Immigrant Children Held in Prison-Like Conditions," American Civil Liberties Union, March 6, 2007, http:// www.aclu.org/immigrants-rights/aclu-challenges-illegal-detention-immigrant-chil dren-held-prison-conditions. Of interest: Rickie Solinger, Paula C. Johnson, Mar- tha L. Raimon, Tina Reynolds, and Ruby C. Tapia, eds., *Interrupted Life: Experiences of Incarcerated Women in the United States* (Berkeley: University of California Press, 2010).

34. Dupree, "The Family During Crisis," 313. See also Emadi, *Culture and Customs,* 172–177.

35. Dupree, "The Family During Crisis," 329.

36. Throughout this book, we have chosen to use the term non-literate, rather than illiterate, which, as scholar and renowned Afghanistan expert Louis Dupree noted, has pejorative overtones. Although Afghans have a magnificent history of literature, the majority of its population cannot read or write. Nevertheless, there is a vibrant, essen- tial oral tradition. Afghan educator Wahid Omar concurs, adding, "The word illiterate is pejorative in the sense that it limits the ability to comprehend/interpret knowledge to the written form. Oral culture is *not* considered a form of knowledge by pundits of 'literacy' and this is why the term 'non-literate' replaced 'illiterate' in academia. For many anthropologists, non-literate means the inability to read and write, but it does *not* connote the inability to comprehend/interpret knowledge. Scholars in oral tradi- tions today are using the term 'non-literate,' because the term 'illiterate' is so loaded with negative connotations" (personal correspondence, November 2012).

37. Joshua Parlow, "Afghan Widows Form Community on Kabul Hill," *Washing- ton Post,* August 15, 2011, http://www.washingtonpost.com/world/asia-pacific/afghan -widows-form-community-on-kabul-hill/2011/08/02/gIQA35KtFJ_story.html.

38. As opposed, for example, to Bosnia, at $679, and East Timor, at $333, per capita.

39. Matt Waldman, "Falling Short: Aid Effectiveness in Afghanistan" (Kabul: Agency Coordinating Body for Afghan Relief, March 2008), 1, 3. Waldman goes on to say that from 2001 to 2008, the United States had appropriated $127 billion for the war in Afghanistan, with the U.S. military spending nearly $100 million a day in the country, some $36 billion a year.

40. Anne Carlin, "Rush to Re-engagement in Afghanistan" (Washington, D.C.: Bank Information Center, December 2003), 10. Available at http://www.bicusa.org /en/Article.1007.aspx. Also of interest: Susanne Koelbl, "The Aid Swindle," *Der Spiegel Online International,* April 5, 2005, https://www.spiegel.de/internationalspie gel/0,1518,348597,00.html.

41. In an interview with David Barsamian of Alternative Radio, Indian author and activist Arundhati Roy made the point that "NGOs have a complicated space in neoliberal politics. They are supposed to mop up the anger. Even when they are

doing good work, they are supposed to maintain the status quo." "India: The World's Largest Democracy," *International Socialist Review* 86 (November–December 2012): 18. An audio version of the interview can be heard at http://www.alternativeradio.org /collections/spk_arundhati-roy/products/roya017.

42. "Corruption, Not Insecurity, Biggest Concern for Afghans—UN Report," UN News Centre, January 19, 2010, http://www.un.org/apps/news/story.asp?NewsID= 33519, and "NGOs Form 'Parallel' Government in Afghanistan: Minister," Afghan News, April 20, 2005, http://www.afghanemb-canada.net/en/newsbulletin/2005 /april/20/index.php.

43. Amie Ferris-Rotman, "Afghan Child Labour Fears Grow as Aid Dries Up," Reuters, February 7, 2012, http://www.reuters.com/article/2012/02/07/us-af ghanistan-children-idUSTRE81611020120207.

44. Samuel Lowenberg, "Afghanistan's Hidden Health Issue," *The Lancet* 174, Issue 9700 (October 31, 2009): 1487–1488.

45. Rod Nordland, "Attacks Rise on Aid Workers in Afghanistan," *New York Times*, December 2, 2013, http://www.nytimes.com/2013/12/03/world/asia/attacks -rise/on-aid-workers-in-afghanistan.html.

46. Rod Nordland, "Afghan Refugee Children Perish in Harsh Winter," *New York Times*, May 9, 2012, http://www.nytimes.com/2012/05/10/world/asia/winter-killed -at-least-100-afghan-refugee-children-study-estimates.html?_r=0; Rod Nordland, "Deadly Bite of Winter Returns to the Ill-Prepared Refugee Camps of Kabul," *New York Times*, December 30, 2012, 11; and Amnesty International, Open Letter to the Government of Afghanistan, the United Nations, Other Humanitarian Organisations, and International Donors, "The Critical Need for Winter Assistances and Longer Term Solutions for Internally Displaced Persons in Afghanistan," October 19, 2012, http://www.amnesty.org/en/news/afghanistan-urgent-assistance-needed -avoid-deaths-among-displaced-during-cold-2012-10-19.

47. Marnie Gustavson, "Appeal for Support to Orphanages," PARSA (Spring 2011), www.parsajournal.com. The 1.6 million figure is approximate: UNICEF Statistics, Afghanistan, http://www.unicef.org/infobycountry/afghanistan_statistics.html.

48. Shirkat Gah, Amnesty International, "Takeover of Women's Shelters," February 14, 2011; and Khaleej Times, "Afghanistan Defends Takeover of Women's Shelters," February 15, 2011, http://www.shirkatgah.org/publications/Newsheet-2011-03 -11.pdf.

49. Qualified teachers are reluctant to relocate from the cities, and few benefits and incentives have been offered, such as hardship pay or transportation.

50. Ministry of Labor, Social Affairs, Martyrs and Disabled: http://www.molsa md.gov.af/en; Saljad, "6 Million Afghan Children Living in Critical Conditions: Officials," Khaama Press, May 31, 2012, http://www.khaama.com/6-million-afghan -children-in-critical-living-conditions-officials-518.

51. International Labour Organization, "Child Labour," http://www.ilo.org/glo bal/standards/subjects-covered-by-international-labour-standards/child-labour/lang —en/index.htm; Office of the United Nations High Commissioner for Human Rights, "Convention on the Rights of the Child," http://www2.ohchr.org/english /law/crc.htm. For more on child sex work in Afghanistan, see Alisa Tang, "Selling Sex in Afghanistan: Portraits of Sex Workers in Kabul," in *Land of the Unconquerable*, 154– 161. Of interest: Graham Bowley, "Afghan Boys Eke Living Amid Peril at Gorge,"

New York Times, October 14, 2012, http://www.nytimes.com/2012/10/14/world/asia
/afghan-boys-eke-living-amid-peril-at-gorge.html.

52. Consortium for Street Children, NGO Shadow Report for the United Nations
Committee on the Rights of the Child, 5th Session: Afghanistan, August/September 2010, http://www.crin.org/docs/Afghanistan_CSC_CRC_Report.pdf, 2. See also
Alexandra Reihing, "Child Labor in Afghanistan," *Policy Innovations* (June 20, 2007),
http://www.policyinnovations.org/ideas/briefings/data/afghan_child_labor. Aschiana
is an Afghan NGO providing services and support to street-working children and
their families out of eight support centers in Kabul, Herat, Gardez, Parwan, and
Mazar-i-Sharif (http://www.aschiana.com).

53. Fortunately, children in Afghanistan, at least in rural areas, are still relatively
free of video games. Unmanned aerial vehicles (UAVS), or "drones," that have been
bombarding parts of Afghanistan and Pakistan since about 2008, killing innumerable
children, have been likened to video games, as there are no pilots inside the vehicles,
whose flight is either controlled autonomously by computers in the vehicle, or under
the remote control of a pilot on the ground or in another vehicle. There is an obvious
relationship between drones and how "rifts in our society combine with violence in the
media and in interactive video games to indiscriminately condition our nation's children to kill," Lt. Col. Dave Grossman, *On Killing: The Psychological Cost of Learning to
Kill in War and Society* (New York: Back Bay Books, 2009), xxxii.

54. "Afghanistan: Child Justice Brief," JusticeStudio, June 2012, http://justice
studio.org/CJBrief%20Afghanistan%20June%202012.pdf, 3.

55. UNICEF, *Justice for Children: The Situation of Children in Conflict with the Law
in Afghanistan*, http://www.unicef.org/media/files/Juvenile_Detention_Study_engl
.pdf, 12.

56. In May 2013, Afghan Parliamentarians, so-called "traditionalists," demanded
that the law banning violence against women be scrapped. This has been an ongoing
fight, with, for example, President Hamid Karzai endorsing the 2012 "Code of Conduct," issued by a council of clerics, which allows husbands to beat and rape their
wives. "Afghan Parliament Halts Debate on Women's Rights Law," BBC News-Asia,
May 18, 2013, http://www.bbc.co.uk/news/world-asia-22579098?print=true. See also
Massooda Jalal, "Keep the EVAW As It Is! No to Repeal or Amendment by Parliament!" Jalal Foundation, May 20, 2013, http://jalal-foundation.org. In addition, a
group of Afghan activists and university students demonstrated in front of the Parliament building in support of passing the Elimination of Violence against Women act
in the Afghan Parliament and to denounce the political gamble on women's human
rights.

57. Of interest: a film by Jill Vickers and Jody Bergedick, *Once in Afghanistan*,
recollections of female Peace Corps volunteers who traveled throughout Afghanistan
vaccinating against small pox (Dirt Road Documentaries, 2008), www.dirtroaddocu
mentaries.com.

58. Kylea Laina Liese et al., *Addressing Maternal Mortality in Afghanistan: Utilisation and Perception of Community Midwives in Three Provinces* (London: Merlin, 2010),
5. See also *The State of the World's Midwifery*, http://www.unfpa.org/sowmy/resources
/docs/background_papers/44_CampbellF_Afghanistan.PDF. In addition to—indeed,
in advance of—the efforts of the Afghan Ministry of Public Health, in 2004, Pashtoon
Azfar (the director of Afghanistan's Institute of Health Sciences and yet another ex-

ample of the amazing work Afghan women do for their country) founded the Afghan Midwives Association, which was accepted into the International Midwives Confederation in 2006.

59. World Health Organization, "World Health Organization Action in Afghanistan Aims to Control Debilitating Leishmaniasis," 2004, http://www.who.int/media centre/news/releases/2004/pr55/en/.

60. UNODC, "Drug Use in Afghanistan: 2009 Survey," http://www.unodc.org /documents/data-and-analysis/Studies/Afghan-Drug-Survey-2009-Executive-Sum mary-web.pdf, 6.

61. Widespread field studies have been conducted to determine radiation in soil, plants, and human urine from depleted uranium used in precision weapons. In 2002, the Uranium Medical Research Center found Afghans "with acute symptoms of radiation poisoning, along with chronic symptoms of internal uranium contamination, including congenital problems." Some subjects had concentrations of 400 to 2,000 percent above that for normal populations. Doug Westerman, "Depleted Uranium—Far Worse than 9/11: Depleted Uranium Dust—Public Health Disaster for the People of Iraq and Afghanistan," Global Research, May 3, 2005, http://www.globalresearch.ca /index.php?context=va&aid=2374. In May 2009, there were reports of severe chemical burns possibly attributable to white phosphorus, a flammable material used by combatants to illuminate targets or create smoke. Jason Straziuso and Rahim Faiez, "Concerns White Phosphorus Used in Afghan Battle," *ABC News*, May 20, 2009, http://abcnews .go.com/International/wireStory ?id=7549697.

62. Cornelia Walther, "Promoting Girls' Empowerment through Sport in Afghanistan," UNICEF, http://www.unicef.org/infobycountry/afghanistan_53276.html; and Sandra Harwitt, "Rabina Jalali Chases Dream for Afghan Girls," ESPN.com, November 24, 2011, http://espn.go.com/blog/high-school/girl/tag/_/name/girls-sports -in-afghanistan.

63. Dupree, *Afghanistan*, 210–213. See also Emadi, *Culture and Customs*, 156–162.

64. In 1973, Dupree wrote that "boys do not play war games like Western children's Cowboy and Indians, Cops and Robbers . . . At an age when American boys, for example, receive their first air guns, an Afghan tribal boy gets a rifle and is taught by his father to use it properly. War in Afghan society relates to the family, tribal, kinblood honor, and is not an amorphous, ill-defined, loosely implemented ideology with built-in contradictions . . . , but is an immediate face-to-face confrontation with a real, nearby enemy. . . . Afghans do not play at war; they make war within the strictures of their cultural patterns" (*Afghanistan*, 211).

65. "Afghanistan's First National Park Aims to Attract Tourists," October 23, 2012, http://www.bbc.co.uk/news/world-asia-20053089; Frédéric Bobin, "Inside the Kabul Zoo: A Sign of Kabul's Future?" July 4, 2011, http://www.time.com/time/world /article/0,8599,2080818,00.html.

66. "UNEP in Afghanistan: Laying the Foundations for Sustainable Development," United Nations Environmental Programme, January 2009, http://www.unep .org/pdf/UNEP_in_Afghanistan.pdf. Unfortunately, not enough has been written about environmental destruction in Afghanistan. Canadian Women for Women Afghanistan (CW4WAfghan) is perhaps the first and certainly among few NGOs trying to promote responsible behavior within the NGO community toward the environment. They have introduced a Green Policy at their country office in Kabul and hosted

a Going Green workshop for NGOs in 2013. http://www.cw4wafghan.ca/NewsRe
lease-GreenPolicy2013.

67. "Fragile Footsteps: Children and Landmines," Save the Children, undated,
http://www.savethechildren.org/publications/reports/landmines.pdf; Neamatollah
Nojumi, Dyan Mazurana, and Elizabeth Stites, *After the Taliban: Life and Security
in Rural Afghanistan* (Lanham, MD: Rowman & Littlefield, 2009), 38–40; Masoud
Popalzai, "Landmine Kills 10 Girls Collecting Firewood," CNN, December 21, 2012,
http://www.cnn.com/2012/12/17/world/asia/afghanistan-girls-landmine/index.html.
Of interest: Oliver Englehart, "The Minefields of Afghanistan," *New York Times*,
November 17, 2010, http://video.nytimes.com/video/2009/11/18/opinion/124746574
2545/the-minefields-of-afghanistan.html?emc=etal. Also of interest, Roots of Peace,
an international non-profit that removes landmines and returns land to agriculture:
http://rootsofpeace.org.

68. For a fascinating history, see Mary MacMakin, "Women with Disabilities:
Recollections from Across the Decades," in *Land of the Unconquerable*, 200–211.

69. See, for example, Catherine Panter-Brick, Mark Eggerman, Viani Gonzalez,
and Sarah Safdar, "Violence, Suffering, and Mental Health in Afghanistan: A School-
based Survey," *The Lancet* (August 21, 2009), www.thelancet.com; and Catherine
Panter-Brick, Anna Goodman, Wietse Tol, and Mark Eggerman, "Mental Health
and Childhood Adversities: A Longitudinal Study in Kabul, Afghanistan," *Journal of
the American Academy of Child & Adolescent Psychiatry* 50, no. 4 (April 2011).

70. Rawan Online, April 2012, http://en.rawanonline.com.

71. Djinn are creatures, parallel to human beings but made out of fire instead of
clay, known in popular belief in pre-Islamic Arabia and mentioned numerous times
in the Qur'an. In folk religion, they are invoked for magical purposes and often held
responsible for miraculous or unusual events as well as for a wide range of illnesses.
Nazar (in Arabic *nathar*) means "gaze" or "looking." Nazar is not in itself evil, which
only comes when there is evil intention behind the look, such as envy. Many peoples
of various cultures believe the "evil eye" comes from looking enviously at someone or
something and therefore causing hurt, damage, destruction, or illness.

72. Nahid Aziz, "Psychological Impacts of War: Human Rights and Mental
Health," *Land of the Unconquerable*, 229–243; Zeba Shorish-Shamley, *The Self and
Other in Afghan Cosmology: Concepts of Health and Illness among the Afghan Refugees*,
unpublished PhD dissertation, University of Wisconsin, Madison, 1991; Nahid Aziz,
"The Psychological Well-Being of Afghan Children," unpublished paper, December
2011.

73. Personal correspondence, July 24, 2011.

74. In 2008, 256 schools were assaulted, up from 236 in 2007. In November 2008,
fifteen female students were assaulted in Kandahar. Two were blinded and two injured.
Afghan girls are not alone. In October 2012, fifteen-year-old Pakistani student Malala
Yusafzai, in the Swat Valley, was attacked by Taliban and survived. Robert Mackey,
"Pakistani Activist, 15, Is Shot by Taliban," *New York Times*, October 9, 2012. See
UNICEF, "UNICEF Condemns Attacks on Schools in Afghanistan," United Nations
Children's Fund, November 14, 2008, http://www.unicef.org/emerg/afghanistan
46387.html; and "Lessons in Terror: Attacks on Education in Afghanistan," *Human
Rights Watch* 18, no. 6 (C) (July 2006), http://www.hrw.org/reports/2006/afghani

stan0706/afghanistan0706web.pdf. See also Marit Glad, "Knowledge on Fire: Attacks on Education in Afghanistan: Risks and Measures for Successful Mitigation" (study conducted by CARE on behalf of the World Bank and the Ministry of Education, November 2009), http://care.ca/ckfinder/userfiles/files/Knowledge_on_fireattacks _%20schools.pdf.

75. There is no Dari word for "gender." Among people for whom the family means everything, the economic, political, and social lives of men and women cannot be disentangled; Sakena Yacoobi, "Empowering Women through Education: Recipe for Success" in *Land of the Unconquerable*, 309–320. See also Afghan Institute of Learning: http://www.afghaninstituteoflearning.org/index.html.

76. The online CIA World Factbook is updated weekly. CIA World Factbook, https://www.cia.gov/library/publications/the-world-factbook/geos/xx.html, April 2012.

77. Personal correspondence, December 2012. For more information about the ABLE program: http://www.dupreefoundation.org/able.htm.

78. Http://www.cw4wafghan.ca/resources/resources-librarianship-afghanistan. See also Canadian Women for Women in Afghanistan, http://www.cw4wafghan.ca /resources/resources-librarianship-afghanistan. Of interest, Hands Around the Library–Libraries around the World: http://www.handsaroundthelibrary.com/li braries-around-the-world.

79. "Academic Destinations: Afghanistan," *Chronicle of Higher Education*, January 29, 2013, http://chronicle.com/academicDestination/Afghanistan/67.

80. For more about higher education and training educators in Afghanistan, see retired Lewis and Clark College Professor Zaher Wahab, "Dispatches from Afghanistan: Thoughts About Education, War and the Future of Afghanistan from a Professor of Teacher Education," a blog begun in 2009: http://dispatchesfromafghanistan .tumblr.com.

81. This was part of a covert effort by the United States to incite resistance to the Soviet occupation. For more information about the Thomas Gouttierre and CIA textbook scandals, see "Soviet Era Textbook Still Controversial," *Lincoln Journal Star*, Nebraska, September 23, 2007, http://journalstar.com/special-section/news/article_4968 e56a-c346-5a18-9798-2b78c5544b58.html.

82. Kevin Sieff, "New Afghan Textbooks Omit Past 40 Years: Goal Is to Steer Clear of Incendiary Themes, Build a Sense of Unity," *Washington Post/Arizona Daily Star*, February 6, 2012, http://azstarnet.com/news/world/new-afghan-textbooks-omit -past-yrs/article_909a59cd-ae1f-5f41-8818-7b019170fe4c.html.

83. Ahmed Khalid Fahim, *Gender Issues and Textbooks: Gender Bias in Pashto Primary School Textbooks in Afghanistan*, April 2010, Master's Thesis, Karlstads Universitet, Karlstad, Sweden, http://www.academia.edu/1762564/Gender_Issues_and_Text books, 2.

84. Nushin Arbabzadah, "Afghan Schoolbooks Teach Their Students Little of Value or Relevance," *The Guardian*, November 27, 2010, http://www.guardian.co.uk /commentisfree/2010/nov/27/afghan-school-books-irrelevant/print#skiplinks.

85. Of interest, Fran Smith, "Why Arts Education Is Crucial, and Who's Doing It Best," Edutopia, January 28, 2009, http://www.edutopia.org/arts-music-curriculum -child-development. For further ideas on how to succeed with education in Afghani-

stan, see Wahid Omar, "From Storytelling to Community Development: Jaghori, Afghanistan," in Rickie Solinger, Madeline Fox, and Kayhan Irani, eds., *Telling Stories to Change the World* (New York: Routledge, 2008), 193–200.

86. Http://booksforafghanistan.org/bfa. Also, Joshua Partlow, "Afghan Students Learn to Read With Folktales," *Washington Post*, December 11, 2011, http://www.washingtonpost.com/world/asia_pacific/afghan-students-learn-to-read-with-folk-tales/2011/12/08/gIQAFX8HoO_story.html. Idries Shah (June 16, 1924–November 23, 1996) was an author and teacher in the Sufi tradition who wrote on topics ranging from psychology and spirituality to travelogues and culture studies.

87. Amina Kator, "Hopes and Dreams: Interviews with Young Afghans," in *Land of the Unconquerable*, 357–365.

88. "Afghan Women Educated through Cellphones," Dawn.com Sci Tech, November 14, 2012, http://dawn.com/2012/11/14/afghan-women-educated-through-cell phones.

89. Http://www.socialbakers.com/facebook-statistics/afghanistan; "Afghan Social Media War Steps Up With New Campaign," Reuters, July 22, 2012, http://www.reuters.com/article/2012/07/22/net-us-afghanistan-media-idUSBRE86L08P20120722; "Young Afghans Rush to Study Media," USAID-Afghanistan, May 3, 2012, http://afghanistan.usaid.gov/en/USAID/Article/2700/Young_Afghans_Rush_to_Study_Media. Of interest: Aunohita Mojumdar, "From Both Sides of the Mic: Women and the Media," in *Land of the Unconquerable*, 321–332.

90. According to Reporters Without Borders—which originally lauded press freedom as "one of the few achievements since the fall of the Taliban, though it remains fragile . . . targeted by religious conservatives"—in 2007, the number of female students in Herat, for example, dropped from 70 percent to 30 percent in journalism. Reporters without Borders/Reporters sans Frontières, "Press Freedom Barometer," December 2005, http://en.rsf.org/. In July 2012, a revised media law significantly tightened the Afghan government's grip over the fledgling but lively Afghan press corps, and limited foreign programming. Amie Ferris-Rotman, "New Afghan Law Ignites Fear Over Shrinking Press Freedoms," Reuters, July 1, 2012, http://www.reuters.com/article/2012/07/01/afghanistan-media-law-idUSL3E8HR4R120120701. Journalists worldwide are increasingly under the gun.

91. Nancy Hatch Dupree, "Cultural Heritage & National Identity in Afghanistan," *Third World Quarterly* 23, no. 5 (2002): 977–989.

92. Emma Graham-Harrison, "Art in the Streets of Kabul," *The Guardian*, February 24, 2012, http://www.guardian.co.uk/world/2012/feb/24/graffiti-street-art-kabul; Lauryn Oates, "First Women's Art Exhibit Opens in Afghanistan," *Herizons* (Winter 2009): 13; Lauryn Oates, "Painting Their Way into the Public World: Women and the Visual Arts," in *Land of the Unconquerable*, 333–341; Zuzanna Olszewska, "A Hidden Discourse: Afghanistan's Women Poets, in *Land of the Unconquerable*, 342–354.

93. Afghan Participatory Theatre: http://www.eurasianet.org/node/63553; Afghan Mobile Mini-Circus: http://www.afghanmmcc.org; Theatre Circus Afsâna: http://soundcentralfestival.com/383392/artists/theatre-circus-afs-na; Parwaz Puppet Theatre: http://www.youtube.com/watch?v=dcbxoeXbCks; Afghan Youth Voices Festival: http://www.afghanyouthvoices.com; No Strings International: http://www.nostrings.org.uk.

94. "I have been teaching orphan girls in Afghanistan as a volunteer for four years.

. . . I have tried to empower them. I do not try to change them. I only try to remind them who they are as human beings. But now . . . I can no longer go to their school and teach. Why? People in the Karzai government want to close our school because we teach girls music. Why?" Excerpted from a speech given by Ian Pounds in Kabul, October 14, 2012. Of interest: https://www.youtube.com/watch?v=1_96uhCbiQA and https://www.youtube.com/watch?v=iutOj8ogpA4.

95. Of interest, Joanna Santa Barbara, "Impact of War on Children and Imperative to End War," *Croatian Medical Journal* 7, No. 6 (December 2006), http://www.ncbi .nlm.nih.gov/pmc/articles/PMC2080482.

Master Afghan musician Ustad Ghulam Hussein teaching or entertaining three young girls in 1945. Unknown photographer; courtesy of Louise Pascale and *Qu Qu Qu Barg-e-Chinaar: Children's Songs from Afghanistan*.

Students studying outside their cargo-crate classrooms in Paghman while their new school, built by a Japanese aid organization, is under construction. Photo by Sheryl Shapiro, 2003.

PART 1

THE WAY WE WERE;
THE WAY WE'RE SEEN

CHAPTER 1

Before the Wars:
Memories of Childhood in the Pre-Soviet Era

AMINA KATOR-MUBAREZ

Editors' Note: *We open with excerpts of interviews conducted and translated by Amina Kator-Mubarez in 2012 of Afghans about their childhoods before the 1979 Soviet invasion.¹ Most were children during Zahir Shah's long reign (1933–1973). These men and women—whose names have been changed—range in background and in age, from fifty-five to ninety-nine. The interviews took place in Afghanistan and the United States. We added a segment of a memoir-in-progress by Wahid Omar (see chapter 8, "The Parakeet Boys: Performing Education in the Streets of Kabul").*

In many ways, these interviews display universal commonalities of childhood, youth, and young adulthood. Yet some also illustrate how war can situate the mind on fear and horror, trumping memories of stability, calm, and well-being. Some interviewees seem to rush quickly past their childhoods to emphasize the hardships they experienced. Suffering and hardship, we know, can breed further suffering and hardship, perpetuating a seemingly endless cycle of violence and abuse.

These vivid recollections help remind us, too, that much has not changed in Afghanistan: families are still close; siblings are still expected to be responsible for one another and older boys still expected to support the family when needs arise; childhood mortality still rages; early and forced marriages still take place; nepotism, privilege, and class division still dominate the society.

Hasib Nusratty, Age Ninety-Nine

I am an ethnic Tajik, born and raised in Kabul. I had an extremely privileged upbringing; my father served as the secretary general to King Habibullah.² At the time, it was customary for wealthy men to have several wives so long as the man treated them equally.³ My mother was my father's third wife. I have four sisters and six brothers. All but two have passed away. My parents really encouraged us to pursue education and actually helped pave the way for one of the first primary schools in Afghanistan. One of my sisters eventually became a famous poet, another became a principal at Nazo Ana secondary school,[4] and the other a nurse. I was homeschooled until I was nine. After that, I went to Darul Malimeen and to Habibia College.[5]

I think perhaps my most vivid childhood memory was my [1933] graduation at Habibia, where I witnessed the assassination of King Nadir Shah.[6] I was about seventeen years old and that traumatic experience still haunts me. I vividly remember shaking hands with him and his son and returning to my seat when he was shot. There was chaos in the auditorium. I remember the Hazara boy who killed him and how several of Nadir Shah's bodyguards jumped on the boy and beat him mercilessly.[7] I would have to say now that I understand why a Hazara would have wanted Nadir Shah dead. He was extremely oppressive toward Shi'ites and ethnic minorities and persecuted them terribly. My family happened to be an exception, because of our tremendous wealth and the fact that we kept our religious leaning discreet (we were Shi'ites).

My family was progressive and open-minded. They encouraged education and yet were moderate practicing Muslims. There wasn't that dogmatic religion then as there is now. No Afghan imposed his or her religiosity on another Afghan, and there was a lot of autonomy in self-expression and religious tolerance, especially under Prime Minister Daoud Khan.[8] Under Zahir Shah, there was much more adherence to religious observance, where women wore *chadari*. But even during the king's time, radical Islam was not practiced. Wearing the chadari was the cultural norm, but, again, no one imposed their religiosity on anyone.

I went on to complete my bachelor's in law from Kabul University and was granted a scholarship from the United States government to obtain my master's in public administration from the University of Maryland. After completion, I returned to Afghanistan during the Communist regime and served as advisor to the Ministry of Justice under Hafizullah Amin.[9] I went on to publish several books and currently live in the United States. I think my childhood was exceptional, because even during Zahir Shah's time, the majority of Afghans were working in agriculture. I happened to be among the select few who had amenities others could only dream of. I am grateful as I know that was why I was able to achieve what I did. I wish more opportunities were given to Afghans. Unfortunately, there was always a visible display of the disparity of wealth in Afghanistan and that continues to this day.

Palwan Yusuf, Age Seventy-Five

I am an ethnic Tajik, born and raised in Kabul in the 1940s. My father died when I was seventeen, and since I was the eldest of eight siblings, I had to be the man of the house. I never went to school, because I had to support my family, so my siblings could pursue their educations. Because my father and grandfather were wrestlers, I chose that profession. I started wrestling at fifteen and continued until I was twenty-five. I earned a lot of money, because I was a strong fighter and rarely lost. During my youth, I was extremely dangerous and constantly brawling. I had a short temper. I have broken nearly every bone in my body at one point or another. Fighting for me was the only escape, a way to maintain my honor and the respect of the community. I bootstrapped my family out of poverty by fighting and resorting to other [drug] dealings.

Growing up in Kabul was dangerous. I had to be on the lookout so that I would not get killed by my wrestling opponents. There was no one else to support my siblings. I carried a five-inch knife for protection. I never got involved in the government and received little benefit from it. I was more of a rebel than anything else. I was similar to my father and always wanted to be *kaka* (brotherly) like him—meaning that he was courageous and never afraid of death. He was among those proud, generous, and brave boys of Kabul, who had humility and fought for the helpless and poor. He was also dangerous and had a somewhat reckless lifestyle. He did not care about material possessions and spent his money on family and friends.

I was also a vigilante, in the sense that I never went to the police if someone was troubling my family, friends, or me. I took the law into my own hands and beat the culprit to a pulp so that he would never commit the crime again. I grew up as a Shi'ite, but in all honesty, we were never religious. I encouraged my sisters to be educated, independent, and self-sufficient. During the Soviet occupation, I remained neutral, neither supporting the Mujahedin nor the Communists. Both sides were too extreme. During the civil war, we were forced to flee to Pakistan for about six months. The conditions in the refugee camps in Peshawar were so unbearable we decided to return to Afghanistan. In Kabul, Gulbuddin Hekmatyar's *tanzim* (militia)[10] was launching rockets on civilian homes. Luckily, our house was not struck, but many others were and many people were killed. As horrible as the civil war was, life under the Taliban was far worse. I remember restraining myself from killing Talib men who came to our house forcing us to go to the mosque to pray and making my sons and me grow beards, as well as preventing my daughters and wife from working or going to school. I felt like a broken man.

I was thrilled that America intervened in ousting the Taliban. The situation has improved drastically by comparison. My children can at least go to school and work and earn a living, but my hope is that they can leave this country soon to have a better life. I am old and will not leave. Afghanistan is part of me and I want to be buried nowhere else.

Tareq Waism, Age Seventy-Five

I am an ethnic Hazara, who grew up in Bamiyan near Ghorband Valley under Zahir Shah. My father was a farmer and my mother was a housewife. I have nine siblings and grew up extremely impoverished. I finished seventh grade, but because of our impoverished living conditions, I was forced to drop out of school to help my father with ploughing and tending the livestock. I remember the huge disparity in wealth that existed under Zahir Shah. We struggled merely to survive, while others had privileges and luxuries my family could only dream of. I vividly remember my father's dejected expression as we walked home after a hard day's labor in the fields. He never expressed it, but I knew he wanted a better life for his children, so when I turned fourteen, we relocated to Kabul. He eventually got into the carpentry business and opened his own little shop. He refused to let us work with him and demanded we go to school. I remember being beaten after staying out late flying kites with my brothers. Although my father was a wonderful man, he had a lethal temper and the lashes we received for getting poor grades and behaving mischievously will always be etched in my memory. Now that I reminisce about my childhood, I know I deserved the punishments.

My biggest regret is that I never took school seriously and deceived my father that I was attending. I was more of an entrepreneur, always looking for ways to make money. I am rather ashamed to admit that I became a notorious hashish dealer at seventeen. That business was extremely lucrative. I was always getting into brawls because of my risky lifestyle choice. I made every effort to be as discreet as possible, so my father was completely oblivious to my dealings. After I got married, I abandoned that life and became a teacher. I wanted to earn money the right way.

I guess I would have to say that despite all the hardship during my childhood, I have very fond memories. I miss the nonchalant years and how unpretentious life was.

Zahir Asefi, Age Seventy-Five

I am an ethnic Uzbek, born during Zahir Shah's rule. I remember how peaceful life was. Although my family's economic situation was not great, we were content. The only qualm I have is the limited access to schools and universities for regular Afghans. Special treatment was given to the Mohammadzai tribe.[11] The prominent government positions were reserved for the king's family. However, even that changed over time, as more opportunities were granted for people to earn positions of power and prestige. There was relative tolerance for opposition and people had a sense of autonomy in being able to express their thoughts and concerns.

I grew up in the district of Chilsitoon in Kabul, and our socioeconomic situation was decent. My father was a government employee, but his meager salary meant we only had basic necessities. The most he could afford was a two-bedroom apartment for our family of six. We had limited access to healthcare facilities, and I remember my eyes burning from the smoke in our house, because firewood was our only source of heat. Although he was a hard worker, my father was never promoted. He did not have special connections and was not a relative of Zahir Shah.

Despite the economic hardship, we never felt inferior. Everyone in our neighborhood had a similar economic situation. We helped each other during hard times and celebrated during joyous occasions. There was a sense of community and belonging. I never felt disconnected or disenfranchised. I was taught to have pride. My father refused to succumb to corrupt and immoral means of making money. He rejected many opportunities that might have drastically improved our socioeconomic living conditions. He was a man of integrity and honor and his good name meant more than all the money in the world. At the time I resented him for it, but I realize why his principle was precious to him, and have myself rejected such a lifestyle and instead became a teacher.

Laila Hassani, Age Seventy

I was born in Murat Khani (one of the oldest districts in Kabul) during Zahir Shah's time and am an ethnic Tajik, with four brothers and four sisters. I had a twin sister who died of pneumonia when we were three. We often played in the rain even though my mother would beat us for it.

My father died when I was seven. His sudden loss completely debilitated my once strong-willed mother. My sixteen-year-old brother took financial responsibility by managing my father's lucrative grocery. He dropped out of school to run the market so the rest of us did not have to work and could concentrate solely on our studies. He abandoned his aspirations to travel abroad and attend aviation school in order to give us the opportunity for better lives. I am heavily indebted to him for his sacrifice.

I have the fondest memories of our beige-colored, seven-bedroom house. We had two Hazara servants to help with daily chores. I referred to one of them as Bebe Gul, though that wasn't her real name but a term of endearment, as she became a second mother to me. She would beautifully braid my long silky hair and sing me songs at bedtime. My mother was never affectionate and became even more reclusive after my father's death. I remember her staring out of her bedroom window as though she were anticipating something or someone that never came. Bebe Gul assured me it wasn't my fault that my mother never gave us attention and that gave me some solace.

Bebe Gul got all of us ready and walked us to school. I made sure she held my hand. Despite the hard labor she did inside our house, with washing, cleaning, and cooking, her hands were incredibly gentle and smooth. I always found comfort in holding her hand. At the time Hazaras were heavily discriminated against, treated as inferiors; however, because we were also Shi'ite—most Hazaras are Shi'ites—my brother did not treat Bebe Gul and the other servants harshly. The last beautiful memory I have of my childhood and Bebe Gul is during my graduation ceremony at Kabul University when I received my bachelor's in Dari literature. She was beaming and tears streamed down her face. My friends were appalled that she was there, as it was not common for Hazaras to attend such ceremonies, but I didn't care. The two most important people in the world were there: my oldest brother and Bebe Gul.

Bebe Gul passed away shortly after. It was unbearable. I suffered from such severe depression I lost patches of hair and weighed a mere ninety pounds. Her loss was more profound than that of my twin sister and father combined. It took me years to recover.

I am tired of being deceived by promises of a better future. Now that my hair is gray and my vision nearly gone, I just want to rest my head and meet my God.

Ramin Rahimi, Age Seventy

I am an ethnic Tajik born and raised in Kabul in a middle-class family. I was fortunate to have extremely supportive parents who pushed my ten siblings and me to attend school and become successful. We had a beautiful house and two cars, which was very rare at the time. I had a healthy and open relationship with my parents and never felt I needed to hide anything from them. Although I was extremely focused on my studies, I was also social and loquacious. I was the family jokester and always managed to get myself out of altercations with other boys through comedy. I was never a fighter. I wanted to be on good terms with everybody.

My family was extremely open minded and even in Zahir Shah's time, when women wore chadari, I remember my father teasing my sisters about it. I also personally disliked the chadari and felt that women should be independent and have the freedom to wear it or not. I wanted my sisters and mother to do as they wished. Although my family was liberal, we were discreet about it. Social norms in Afghanistan make it difficult to be truly liberal. For example, when people bought alcoholic beverages from the store, they referred to it as "medicine," rather than actually calling it by its name. There was still a taboo about drinking publicly since Afghanistan is an Islamic country.

After I received my bachelor's in education from Kabul University, I was eager to travel abroad. I always felt out of place and suffocated in Afghanistan. So in 1974, when I was accepted for a scholarship to Boston University to earn my master's in curriculum, I seized the opportunity. Although I wanted to remain in the U.S., I felt obliged to return to Afghanistan after my mother fell ill. I became chairman for the Curriculum Department at the Ministry of Education. Although there was a lot of bribery and corruption during Daoud Khan's time, there were tremendous improvements with regard to opportunities for ethnic minorities.

Nevertheless, I still felt stifled and after a year I returned to America. I have been here ever since and travel periodically to visit my family. My wife is American; my independence and freedom is paramount (even as a man). I would never be happy living in Afghanistan. I've been liberal since childhood and have not changed at all.

Maghol Jan, Age Seventy

I am an ethnic Pashtun and grew up in northern Baghlan Province, the youngest of four. My siblings are now all deceased. My father was the mayor of Pul-e Khumri and we had a lot of land and livestock. We were forbidden from going to school, because it was seen as shameful and culturally unacceptable. My father beat my mother constantly. She was sharp-tongued and rejected his lewd behavior, considering he had several mistresses. I don't really remember having a childhood. I was married off when I was fourteen. As early as six years old, the majority of the household responsibilities fell on my sister and me. There was a stream that ran in our backyard where we would fetch water for drinking and cooking and wash our clothes.

When I got married, I moved with my husband's family to Narin. He was much older than I, but he treated me well and was a good man. He had been educated in Kabul and returned to Baghlan after completing his studies. He dressed stylishly and was progressive. Although my father was opposed to education, my husband was open-minded and actually built the first primary school for girls in Narin. Although he encouraged me to go to school, too, I had my first child at fifteen and then eleven more, so was never able to continue with my studies. There was no such thing as contraception. But considering that there was no guarantee your children would survive to adulthood, you had to take precautionary measures and have as many children as possible in hopes that some would make it.

Life changed drastically for me with the Soviet occupation. After my husband joined [Hekmatyar's] Hezb-e Islami tanzim, he transformed from a broad-minded individual into a radicalized and conservative Islamist. The first indication was when he grew a beard and began wearing *paran tumban* (traditional clothing for Afghan men) instead of his trendy suits. He also became verbally and physically abusive to me and the children. He then forced the students' curriculum to be changed in the primary school so that the children were to read only the Qur'an. He also beat anyone who played any sort of music and began forcing all his sons to pray at the mosque five times daily. Life became unbearable, as his erratic and violent behavior increased. It was difficult for me to witness my husband's transformation from an affable, handsome young man to an abusive chauvinist. I do not like to recall that period in my life but instead try to remember the first years of our marriage, to preserve those blissful years and forget the man he became.

After relocating to Pakistan, we went to America. My husband was disgusted by the immoral behavior he witnessed in the U.S. and swore to return to Afghanistan as soon as he got the chance. He seized the opportunity in 2001 after the defeat of the Taliban and has been living in Narin ever since. I still live in America with my children. I absolutely love the independence I have here and would never trade it for anything in the world.

Haroon Alemy, Age Sixty-Five

My family is from Herat. I do not like to refer to myself as one ethnicity. We are all Afghans—not Tajik, Pashtun, Hazara—just Afghan. I have fond memories of my childhood. Although we were not wealthy, we had enough to keep us alive. My mother was a teacher and my father was a farmer. We moved to Kabul with my five siblings when I was about ten years old.

Halfway into completing my engineering degree from Kabul University, I worked at the Ministry of Interior under Daoud Khan. During that time, people earned decent salaries and corruption was not nearly as rampant as under the Hamid Karzai government. People had a sense of loyalty and wanted to not only improve their own living conditions, but help bring progress and development to Afghanistan. You had to register with the army when you were twenty-one. Young people were willing and even eager to join. It was seen as a prideful thing. Times were much calmer and less stressful. Today, trust has completely eroded among Afghans and even family members are secretive with one another. Until the Communists took over, Afghans looked out for one another and were true brothers.

Even at an early age, I was extremely religious, although my family was not. I chose to pray and go to the mosque and did not like when my sisters wanted to wear revealing clothing. My parents were not as strict with my siblings as I was. I am even like that now with my own children. When Babrak Karmal[12] came to power, I was one who rose up against his regime. The vision that Communists had for Afghanistan was immoral and against Islam. Daoud Khan was progressive, but he was keen on having people *slowly* adjust toward modernity. The Communists, on the other hand, wanted to shove it down our throats. They forced women to wear short skirts and engage in lewd behavior. We were disparaged for praying or growing our beards. As an Afghan man, I felt that my religion and honor were jeopardized. Therefore, I joined the Hezb-e Islami tanzim and served under Gulbuddin Hekmatyar. Now, mind you, that tanzim was not the same as it is today. We fought as brothers and there was no discrimination along ethnic lines. I am really a Tajik, but not once do I remember being discriminated against. I personally was taught under Hekmatyar, and I still admire him as a true Islamic leader. It is difficult for me to believe the accusations against him because once you know a person intimately and in a positive note, it is difficult to alter that perception.

In any case, when the Soviets invaded, I was forced to drop out of school and was arrested on charges of treason. I was sent to Pul-e-Charki Prison where I was imprisoned for nearly three years.

I do not discuss my experience with many people as it brings back painful memories. All my fingernails and toenails were ripped out and I was constantly given electrical shocks in order to get me to confess my crime of treason. I was saved by the will of God when an inmate offered to help me escape. After that, I developed a learning disability and continue to suffer from severe migraines. It was traumatic, but if you were to ask me to repeat it again for the sake of my religion, I would not hesitate to do it again. Life without religion has no meaning.

Tahmina Amanzai, Age Sixty-Four

I was born in Kunduz, Afghanistan. My father moved to Kabul when I was three. He was wealthy and had a lot of land in Kabul and Kunduz. My father married my mother after his previous wife died. I have one full sister and eight half-brothers and sisters. My childhood memories were wonderful when my mother was alive. She loved my sister and me very much. She sang lullabies to us and when I had nightmares she lay with me until I fell asleep. Her voice was gentle and to this day comforts me.

She made rag dolls for my sister and me. She spent hours stuffing the dolls and sewing them, making many clothes for them, humming softly as she worked. She also loved my half-brothers and sisters and treated us all equally. She never went to school, but learned to read and write from her parents. She and my dad taught us Qur'an and helped us with our homework.

My dad had a horse buggy. Our driver, Kaka Ahmed, took us to school every day except Fridays. Friday is a holiday in Afghanistan [like Sunday in Christian-majority countries]. We also had a maid who helped my mom with housecleaning and cooking. She was a very kind lady named Shah Bebe, whose hands were always painted with henna. Her long brown hair was always braided. Her husband worked as a farmer on our lands. She had two young daughters and they lived with us. Our house had two stories, with seven bedrooms and one large living room. Across the yard, we had two storage rooms and two rooms for Shah Bebe and her family.

My best friend was named Rukhshana. She was a bubbly girl, always smiling. We played with the dolls my mother made for hours on end. We also played Afghan games like *juz bazi* (four square) and *cheshem putakan* (hide and seek) and competed in jumping rope sometimes until our feet throbbed.

My mom died of stomach cancer when I was nine. I became so severely depressed I did not attend school for nearly a year. My dad married a year after my mom passed away thinking we needed another motherly figure to care for us. It was hard for me to accept my stepmother, who was cold and made us feel like outcasts. The situation got so bad that my sister and I moved in with our oldest half-brother, who was married and had children and lived in a different district in Kabul. He never let us think about the past and tried hard to keep us happy. My sister and I transferred from our previous school and

Kindergarten class in Puli-kumri. The little girl, the province governor's daughter, dances the *atan*, a national dance, wearing a traditional costume in the colors of the Afghan flag: black, red, and green. Photo by Donna Chen Haunch, ca. 1967; courtesy of Sam Chen.

finally graduated from high school. We went to Kabul University, where my sister pursued a law degree and I studied Dari literature.

My childhood was similar to that of other privileged children in Afghanistan. We were pampered and sheltered from the outside world. My life did in many ways turn upside down when my mother passed away. I loved my father but he was not as affectionate and compassionate as my mother. I have precious memories of a time when life was free of worries and problems.

Wahid Omar, Age Fifty-Five

The old Istiqlal high school in Kabul, originally built in the 1920s, was located in front of the king's palace. My father also graduated from Istiqlal, where French discipline prevailed.

The first day of classes, the school's director, Mr. Hadi Naim, drinking coffee and smoking French Gauloises, stood in front of the main gate wearing an impeccable suit, shiny shoes, and short haircut. At his side, during the first day of the semester, was an impressively large man with a mustache, holding a pair of sharp scissors. He was called the Monster Barber and his job was to make sure every student entering the school had short hair. No one could escape his meticulous screening. We could be John Lennon during the winter months when schools were on break, but during the school year, we were all transformed against our will into Kojaks.

At the front gate, along with Mr. Naim and the Monster Barber, there were buckets of water filled with rose stems. Every morning, on their way to class, each teacher picked a fresh rose stick from the bucket to use as a supplementary learning device when we were too loud or didn't know the answers. Discipline was hard and sometimes very cruel. One spring day in sixth grade, Zahir Shah's youngest son, Mir Wais, wrote, "The religious studies teacher is a donkey" on the board. When the teacher entered the room and read his new title, his face turned many colors. "Who did this?" he demanded, but, of course, no one dared tell on the king's son and Mir Wais was not about to confess. As a result, with the exception of the king's son, we were all beaten on the hand ten times with a fresh rose stick.

Madam Mangi, our French teacher, was also unforgettable. To our young eyes, she was almost an extraterrestrial being in a miniskirt, with her bumpy chest, generous hips, green eyes, dark hair, and white skin. She must have been in her mid-twenties. She was the admiration of the entire school and provocative, attracting many comments and whistles from the boys. With her big smile, she managed to get her way for a long time until one day . . .

We were sitting in our French lab class in a room with a big movie screen, chairs on both sides of the room, and an old desk supporting a heavy Super-8 camera. After the film, Madame Mangi gave us a written assignment. After fifteen minutes, she moved along the right side of the room to evaluate the assignments and while she was leaning on the table, her miniskirt lifted and the spectacular scenery made all the boys salivate like dogs with their heads at floor level trying to see as much as they could. The same commotion took place when Madame moved to the left side of the room, and as Mir Wais leaned in to look even more closely, his head touched the teacher's private parts. Madame Mangi whipped around and slapped the king's son with so much force he fell on the ground and broke his watch. Madame wept as she ran to the director's office to complain about Mir Wais's behavior. We heard later that the school director shrugged, *à la française*, having no idea how he could discipline the king's son. From that day on, alas, Madame Mangi never wore a miniskirt in school again, and we all cursed the prince.

Disciplining ordinary Afghan students was another story. The school had zero tolerance for insubordination and students' strikes. It was customary for universities to extend their strikes to local schools in order to create a larger movement. The punishment for initiating or disturbing the status quo was fifty strikes with a rose bush. I still shiver remembering one of our tenth-grade classmates who received this punishment in front of the whole class. Two maintenance staff forced the student to lie on his desk, took off his shoes and socks, and immobilized him. The school supervisor beat him with the rose stick and with each strike, our classmate screamed so hard his voice is still alive in my memory. Rose bushes are associated with peace, love, and compassion, but they give me the *chair de poule* (goose-flesh).[13]

Notes

1. In December 1979, the Soviet Union invaded Afghanistan, provoking a nine-year war.

2. Habibullah Khan (1872–1919) was Emir of Afghanistan from 1901 until 1919. He was born in Samarkand, Uzbekistan, the eldest son of the Emir Abdur Rahman Khan.

3. The Qur'an limits the number of wives a man can marry simultaneously to four. Many modern Islamic nations have either outlawed or regulated polygamy, but it continues to be legal in Afghanistan.

4. Nazo Ana high schools are girls' schools located in Kabul and Kandahar. The schools are named after Nazo Tokhi, known mostly as Nazo Ana or Nazoo Anaa (1651–1717), a prominent Pashtun female poet. As the mother of the tribal chief Mir Wais (1673–1715), founder of the Hotaki Dynasty, Nazo Tokhi is sometimes called "Mother of the Afghan Nation."

5. It is believed that when Habibullah came to power, 98 percent of Afghans were non-literate. Habibullah laid the foundation for Afghanistan's modern education system. Habibia College, the first all-boys secondary school, was founded in 1904. The school housed Afghanistan's first, modest, public library (http://www.afghan-web.com/bios/detail/dhabib.html).

6. Mohammed Nadir Shah (1883–1933) was king of Afghanistan from 1929 until his assassination in 1933. He served under Amanullah Khan (1919–1933) until his exile after disagreements with the king. In 1923, Amanullah Khan was overthrown and sent into exile by Habibullah Kalakani. Nadir Khan returned and in 1929 captured and executed Kalakani. Nadir Khan was visiting a high-school graduation when he was assassinated by Abdul Khaliq, an ethnic Hazara. Nadir Shah was succeeded by his nineteen-year-old son, Mohammed Zahir Shah. Zahir Shah (1914–2007) was the last king of Afghanistan, ousted by a coup in 1973. Following his return from exile in 2002, his position as ruler was not reinstated, but he was given the title "Father of the Nation." http://en.wikipedia.org/wiki/Mohammed_Zahir_Shah-cite_note-Britannica-2.

7. The Hazara compose the third-largest ethnic group in Afghanistan, about 9 percent of the total population. They live in central Afghanistan, and in Pakistan and Iran. They are overwhelmingly Shi'ite Muslims, whereas the dominant group,

the Pashtuns in Afghanistan, are Sunni (https://www.cia.gov/library/publications/the -world-factbook). The persecution of Hazara people dates back to the sixteenth century, with Babur from Kabulistan. It is reported that during the reign of Emir Abdur Rahman (1880–1901), thousands of Hazaras were killed, expelled, and enslaved. The Hazara, often treated as the servant class, were victims of genocide by the Sunni Taliban and Al Qaeda. Although their condition has improved since the fall of the Taliban in 2001, reports of ill treatment in Pakistan and Iran persist (http://en.wikipedia.org /wiki/Persecution_of_Hazara_people).

8. Sardar Mohammed Daoud Khan (1909–1978) was prime minister of Afghanistan from 1953 to 1963, and later became the president of Afghanistan. He overthrew the monarchy of his first cousin Mohammed Zahir Shah and declared himself the first president of Afghanistan in 1973, and ruled until his assassination in 1978 during the Saur Revolution.

9. Hafizullah Amin (1929–1979) was an Afghan politician and statesman, a leader in the Saur Revolution, which overthrew Daoud Khan. Amin ruled Afghanistan for about three months and was assassinated by the Soviets during the invasion in 1979.

10. Gulbuddin Hekmatyar (b. 1947) is an Afghan Mujahedin, founder and leader of the Hezb-e Islami political party and paramilitary—tanzim—group. Hekmatyar was a rebel military commander during the Soviet war and a key figure in the civil war that followed the Soviet withdrawal, and as a result is sometimes called "the Butcher of Kabul." He was prime minister of Afghanistan from 1993 to 1994, and again briefly in 1996.

11. The Mohammadzai referenced here are a prominent group of Pashtun tribes belonging to the Barakzai branch of the Durrani confederacy, primarily centered around Kandahar, Kabul, and Ghazni, whose members included Zahir Shah and Daoud Khan.

12. Babrak Karmal (1929–1996) was born Sultan Hussein and was general secretary of the People's Democratic Party from 1979 to 1986, installed by the Soviets following their invasion. He was deposed by the Soviets, replaced by Mohammad Najibullah, and exiled to Moscow. In 1991, he returned to Afghanistan, where he helped in the overthrow of Najibullah and later died of liver cancer.

13. In an email on December 28, 2012, Omar, an educator teaching Afghan educators at Kabul University, wrote: "Unfortunately despite all the training in the world, corporal punishment is still practiced in Afghan schools. What we need to change is the system of hierarchy characteristic of tribal societies. Students are not valued and they are at the bottom of everything, everywhere. Families raise their kids with the stick. The local Mullah teaches the Qur'an with a stick."

CHAPTER 2

Narratives of Afghan Childhood: Risk, Resilience, and the Experiences That Shape the Development of Afghanistan as a People and a Nation

ANNE E. BRODSKY

How am I different than my Pakistani classmates? They don't see by their own eyes what we have seen in Afghanistan. They don't have to care because they haven't suffered. [Pakistani girls] don't have equality, but they also don't have knowledge.
FARESHTA, 15; LAHORE, PAKISTAN; WINTER 2002[1]

When Afghans and foreigners speak of the future of Afghanistan, a realistic vision must take into account the innumerable forces at play in the country. These range from the global (e.g., Pakistan, the United States, Al Qaeda, China; global economics; radical Islam; climate change) to the national (e.g., Afghaniyat; Pashtunwali;[2] ethnicity, language, region; the Taliban) to the personal (e.g., family; village; experiences; education; resources; values).[3] All of these forces, independently and jointly, create a milieu, and act to potentiate and constrain a people and a country in the present and future.

While it is impossible to isolate any one influence from its milieu, this chapter will focus on one type of force, Afghan childhood experiences. Childhood is a critical period in human development.[4] Ting and Chui eloquently state: "As the wheel of life turns, people pick up new social roles and face a new reality. But however important these life events are . . . by no means do they erase the influence of childhood experience."[5] The narratives of adults and children below make it clear that Afghan developmental experiences are especially influenced by Afghanistan's forty-plus-year[6] history of civil and social unrest, dislocation, foreign intervention, and war.

Early childhood experiences are critical in the development of many basic psychosocial, cognitive, and behavioral abilities.[7] Some researchers find that late preschool and early school-aged children, influenced by the socialization of family members and school, are already beginning to form complex social and political understandings of the larger world.[8] Others argue that it is not until early adolescence that children are cognitively mature enough to develop these more sophisticated understandings.[9]

Despite decades of sociological and psychological research,[10] we still cannot predict the relative weight, direction, and impact of single and collective childhood experiences on later attitudes, behaviors, and outcomes. It is clear, though, that these developmental forces have their impact not only when they occur, but on the individual (autobiographical) and collective (historical) memories held by a population.[11] And although both are important, autobiographical memories, experienced in the first person, have a potentially stronger resonance than the collective memories learned only indirectly in childhood.[12]

This chapter draws on 225 interviews, most conducted in Dari with English translation, with Afghan women, men, and children living in Pakistan and Afghanistan. The majority of the interviews took place between July 2001 and August 2003, with members, supporters, students, teachers, or aid recipients of RAWA, the Revolutionary Association of the Women of Afghanistan, a women's humanitarian and political organization that provides social and humanitarian assistance while advocating for peace, women's basic rights, and secular democracy.[13] Twenty-three additional interviews were conducted in the summers of 2006 and 2007 with the employees, clients, family, and friends of employees of two independent women's organizations that run violence shelters and other humanitarian activities in Afghanistan. These interviews make up a research program exploring the risks to and resilience of Afghan women and girls before, during, and after Taliban rule.[14] For this chapter, those portions of the interviews that focused on childhood (childbirth to age eighteen) were extracted and coded for content. Sixty-eight interviews (fifty from the 2001–2003 data; eighteen from 2006–2007) contained 245 distinct narratives of childhood. These interviewees ranged in age from thirteen to eighty-five, meaning their childhoods spanned the rule of Habibullah Khan (1901–1919) through Zahir Shah (1933–1973), three pre-Soviet presidents (1973–1978), the Soviet occupation and war (1979–1989), Mohammad Najibullah's short post-Soviet presidency (1989–1992), the civil war (1992–1994), the Taliban (1995–2001), and the Karzai government (2002–current writing). Participants had diverse Afghan ethnic backgrounds (e.g., Pashtun, Tajik, Hazara, Uzbek), varied in level of Islamic observance, and ranged from having no formal education to post-graduate degrees. Those interviewees who talked about childhood did not differ from the larger data set in any obvious ways.

In the quotes below, these Afghan adults and children share recollected and current narratives of childhood before and during (unfortunately, there is still no "after") war in Afghanistan and shed light on the experiences that have shaped and continue to shape the development of Afghanistan as a country and Afghans as a people. Narratives of trauma, hardship, and loss, as well as adaptation, triumph, and joy, provide insights into the strength, resilience, and resistance necessary to survive in Afghanistan, as well as into how childhood experiences may shape the development of each individual, and of Afghanistan as a nation.

Early Childhood

The smallest proportion of childhood narratives came from participants' earliest years. This echoes many scientific theories of social and political development,[15] as well as the fact that very early childhood is often lost to later recollection. However, those early stories, recalled by both children and adults, were striking for the presence of war and social unrest, and their potential impact on later development.

These earliest recollections came, not surprisingly, from parents, not children. While these are not the same as childhood autobiographical memories, they paint a picture of children's earliest days that is important for comprehending the context of many Afghan childhoods. Najla, a RAWA member I interviewed in a Pakistani refugee camp in 2002, described the birth and early months of her daughter, at a village front in the anti-Soviet war in the early 1980s:

> I was on the war front for two years with eight other women. As a woman who had lived most of her life in that village, I couldn't not be part of this movement. I was married at the front. The night I gave birth was a terrible night. They [the Soviets] had continuous bombing we could hear in our front. A few months later there was a dark night and it was raining very hard. At 2 a.m., the watchman gave the sign that there was a danger and we all woke up. Soviet soldiers had scattered throughout our front and our village. The men asked us to leave the area. I had my daughter who was two months old and two other women were pregnant, so we left and went to another village that night.
>
> In the morning there were many killed from both sides. The next day they [the men] asked us to leave for Pakistan. It was difficult. We did not want to. We kept insisting, "If you die we want to die too. We are not any better than you." But they said, "Your presence will create more problems, especially with children, so you better leave." And so the next day I left for Pakistan . . .[16]

Another recollection of early childhood came from Parwana, a politically active woman of the same era. Parwana had already spent five months in prison for anti-Soviet activities before she had children, but was unsure what would happen when, after the birth of her daughter, Soviet authorities found political tracts that she had written. The Soviets investigated for six months before imprisoning Parwana and her nearly one-year-old daughter for two more years. When I talked to her daughter, Donyaa, who by 2002 was a politically active twenty-year-old, she didn't have personal memories to add to her mother's story. Even if Donyaa didn't have clear memories of this time, the knowledge of her early childhood years, passed down through her mother, have likely impacted her ideas about Afghan history and politics.

In 2002, Manizha, a RAWA member living in poor conditions in Quetta, Pakistan, compared memories of her own childhood under Zahir Shah with her preschool children's lives as refugees of the Taliban:

> I spent my childhood in a country without war. We had quite a good life, which is not the case for my children. Many mornings my children have only bread and tea. But still when I compare them with others, they are very lucky. I have seen two-year-old children coming to our house to beg for bread, and they come with not enough clothes in this cold winter. When I see them, I think my children have lots of opportunities for food, shelter, education.

Although everyone I was able to interview, by definition, had survived up to that point, it's important to remember that not every Afghan child lived through the conditions of their childhood. In 2007, I spoke with Ghezal, a married woman in her early twenties, along with her mother, Nafisa. We met in their Kabul apartment, where they had lived through scarcity and rocket attacks during the civil war and a different sort of violence and trauma during the Taliban regime. While Nafisa answered most of my questions, Ghezal chimed in with a childhood story of a little sister, who didn't make it:

> Q: Did you stay in this apartment during the whole civil war?
> A: [Nafisa, in tears] Just behind this block [of buildings] the whole floor was destroyed by rocket. All the windows were shattered. She [Ghezal] screamed, I remember it. We thought this building also was destroyed.
> Q: But your family was safe?
> A: [Nafisa] Yes, thanks god.
> [Ghezal] One of my little sisters died. She was two years old. She got sick when security was bad and so we couldn't do anything. I remember those

days, we took her to the pharmacy, but there was no medicine, no doctor, no facility. In twenty-four hours she died because of lack of medicine for diarrhea . . .

School Age

In case we should need a reminder that being school-age and going to school are two different things in Afghanistan, Shaila's story about her excitement to start school should suffice. I met with Shaila in Pakistan in 2001. She was then in her late twenties, and I asked about her early memories of Afghanistan, before she and her family fled the Soviets. She described her first day in the new village school, the first freestanding school ever built there, and how excited she was to sit with her cousin by the classroom window. Through the window she remembered seeing a water wheel turning in a nearby creek. When the two girls returned to their new school for the second day of class, it had been bombed. Her first day of school in Afghanistan was also her last. Luckily for Shaila, she was eventually able to attend, as well as teach in, Afghan refugee schools in Pakistan.

Although much attention has been rightfully paid to the educational tragedies that have befallen Afghan girls, particularly under the Taliban, a large percentage of Afghan boys have been denied an education as well. Ali's story is one example. By the time I met him in Pakistan in 2002, the twenty-eight-year-old had been a fighter all his life. Before Ali was even big enough to shoot a Kalashnikov, he joined his uncles to fight the Soviets and continued into his teenage years. By his late teens he was involved in the civil war, and in his early twenties he joined the Taliban, where he reveled in the power to beat and torture his enemies. When I met him, he was a trusted RAWA supporter and bodyguard. I asked about his military and political journey, and his story turned to his childhood and education:

> After the Soviet invasion, my involvement in the resistance put me far from education. But I had extreme interest. Often when kids my age earned a little money, they bought cookies and candy and fruit, but I always bought a pen and my father got angry. My father didn't want me to get education. I remember people coming to our village and writing the names of [school-aged] boys. I always gave my name but my father crossed it out. When I saw other boys going to school I always cried. I regretted so much that [I couldn't] read and write.
>
> Later when I had opportunity of learning, I wasn't able to get much;

when people talk about the Internet, I know I can't even write properly. But when I think about my age and all I've seen in life and that I've learned even this much, it makes me happy. Today if anything happened I would have been able to write a letter, let others know what happened and when I think about such examples it makes me happy.

When someone doesn't have education and knowledge they don't know themselves as a human being; they don't treat others as human beings; they don't have human values. And unfortunately most of those years I did not know those issues . . . Now I can think and decide about the future. Now I can see good from bad.

Ali wasn't the only Afghan man I spoke to whose education was disrupted by family and war. Yusof, an intellectual-looking twenty-one-year-old who made it to university before he dropped out to be a full-time RAWA supporter,[17] told a related story of childhood education:

My mother, who was a RAWA member, sent me away to RAWA school when I was very young. During one summer vacation when I was about thirteen my uncle decided to take me to some Mujahedin headquarters for a visit. At first it was a very enjoyable trip in the mountains. There I saw many weapons and became interested in learning about them. My uncle and the other men saw my interest and ability in math and decided to keep me there because many of the soldiers were illiterate so they needed boys like me who could do missile calculations. I had watched some Arnold Schwarzenegger movies and wanted to be like that and I learned quickly.

After I had been a year in that military camp my mother intervened. She said, "I don't want my child to be an aggressive, violent, stubborn man." My uncle argued that I would become a resistance fighter, a good man, and a military expert. He said this path would make me a servant of the people. But my mother replied, "To become a military expert is ok, but at thirteen he should concentrate on subjects. A person needs to learn peace first from science, history, politics, then he can learn war. If first you teach a child war they become violent. Bullets need to go to the proper place; only through education do you know the true enemies of your people."

So at fourteen I returned to RAWA schools and my education. But I was a changed boy. I was more mature. I understood more of what was happening around me. I had seen dead bodies. And I was very much interested in learning about politics. I started listening to the news, and reading books on politics and reading the history of different movements, political views, religion.[18]

Two decades earlier, during the rule of Zahir Shah, another mother also stood up for what she thought was right to ensure her child's education, as Jooma Gul described in 2002:

> Q: Was your mother educated? Did she want her daughter to be educated? A: No, she wasn't, but she was the first in the family to want me to get an education. Early in my life we lived in villages and provinces because of my father's job. There was no school for girls so my mother hired a tutor. Then she put me in the boys' school. Many relatives disagreed, but from grades four to twelve, my mother never budged. There were a few other girls, but it was very rare for an uneducated woman to give such importance to education.[19]

As these stories show, education in Afghanistan, and particularly during times of war and unrest, has presented unique challenges to what many of us in the West are able to view as a routine part of childhood. One of the simplest, but most profound, illustrations of this was shared by Fareshta, a fifteen-year-old girl living in a RAWA hostel[20] while she attended a Pakistani secondary school during the Taliban era. I asked Fareshta and some of the other girls what it was like to be a child refugee:

> From birth to now we have never seen freedom. We are refugees in another country. We want our country to be free. We study in a foreign school. It is hard to sing someone else's national anthem.

Although the Taliban era is synonymous with educational losses in Afghanistan, it was not the only period that presented extreme hardships for children's education and life in general. Zeyba, whom I interviewed in a Kabul women's shelter where she worked as night staff, described the best period of her life as the eight years she was able to attend school. Her school was bombed during the Saur coup in April 1978,[21] and the social unrest that followed ended her hopes for an education. Salima, a twenty-something RAWA member, told me of the difficulties she faced as a teenager in Kabul during the civil war. This was a time when *jihadi* commanders were notorious for kidnapping and raping girls and women or following them home and demanding, at gunpoint, to marry them. There was an infamous story at the time, retold by many interviewees, of Naheed, a young Kabuli woman, who threw herself off the balcony of her family's apartment to escape being married to such a commander. In this context, Salima's efforts to go to school take on another meaning:

I used to go to school with four other neighbor girls. There was a Hezb-e Wahdat[22] check post at the end of the street that we had to go past to get to school. The men always looked at us in a way that we were afraid that one day something would happen. Our school started at 1 p.m., so we tried to go past them at noon [when they were] eating and distracted. Finally my mother put ladders on either side of the back wall between my house and the neighbor's house. That way we could walk to school, avoiding the check-point. Each day my mother would put the ladders back up [when] we were to come home from school.[23]

Salima eventually left school and Afghanistan, giving up her dreams of college and a professional career. After years as a refugee in Pakistan, she returned to Kabul as a young adult and was part of the group of RAWA members who secretly filmed the Taliban's 1999 public execution of Zarmina, an Afghan woman accused of killing her husband.[24] Salima reported that one of the most heartbreaking things she saw there were the children who witnessed the execution while they sold food and drinks to the assembled crowd of (voluntary and forced) spectators.[25] As a child of war herself, she no doubt wondered how this next generation of children would cope with their experiences.

Salima's mother is not the only example of a family member, moved by war, unrest, and later the Taliban anti-education edicts, to become defiantly eager to make sure his or her child received an education. Another striking example was an elderly grandfather who was living, with his large extended family, in a squatter's camp at the edge of a middle-class neighborhood in Rawalpindi, Pakistan. He described his love of Afghanistan and of Islam and his belief that the Taliban were destroying both. While he was too old to fight against the Taliban or their edicts, he told me that his act of resistance was to allow the girls and women in his family to be educated in Pakistan, because no one, and especially not the Taliban, was going to tell him how to treat the women in his family.

The stories I heard of Afghan childhood also made it clear that for too many children education was the least of their childhood worries. Sakinah was thirty-six years old, non-literate, and the mother of nine children ranging in age from three to twenty-one when I met her in a women's shelter in 2006. She looked a decade or two older, due in part to her mutilated face. The story she told of her husband's domestic violence and the disfigurement and scars she bore as a result were so horrific that it was difficult to fathom how any human being could do this to another, let alone how she could have lived through it. Sakinah's exploitation began in 1978, in the last days before the Soviet invasion, when she was eight years old. Her father, fearing the rumors that government soldiers were kidnapping young girls, and needing money, sold her to be the second wife of a man he didn't know, and then left for Iran with the rest of the family. From that point on, Sakinah's childhood, her human rights, and—multiple times—nearly her life were over as her husband spent the next twenty years using every form of physical abuse (imaginable and unfathomable) against her.

Unfortunately, stories like Sakinah's are not isolated incidents. It wasn't just the shelter clients who dealt with such problems, but the staff as well. Zeyba, the shelter night-staff person introduced above, told of her sister's husband, who in 2007 sold her fourteen-year-old niece into marriage and was getting ready to sell his younger daughter next. As Zeyba lamented, "This is in *our* neighborhood, *our* relatives. There are lots of problems."

The End of Childhood

Marriage marks the end of most childhoods in Afghanistan. With a legal marriage age of sixteen for girls and eighteen for boys, and a multitude of families who ignore the law and marry their children earlier, childhood comes to an early end for many. Numerous participants who came of age from the 1950s into the 1970s and 1980s, and particularly those from educated, urban families, told marriage stories that would not be unusual in much of modern Western history.[26] In the narratives after the early 1980s, however, marriage for many Afghan young women and men becomes a choice between the lesser of two evils.

The stories of girls sold into marriage, as told above, are certainly repugnant, but so too is the choice, faced by some poor families, between the whole family starving and sacrificing one child so that the others might live. In this scenario, one can find it indefensible that it is often the most vulnerable girl who is sacrificed, but in other narratives, the choices, still appalling, are more nuanced. One such choice was described by Omira, who was working as a cook at a women's organization in Herat when I spoke with her in the summer of 2006. Omira described how her life changed overnight when her husband, a government hydroelectric project engineer, was killed with three coworkers by Mujahedin attempting to cripple a Communist government project. With his death, she and their six children lost their income, home, and protection against the mounting civil war. She explained:

> I was very happy with my husband, but when he was martyred my life was bitter. They [jihadi commanders] were taking widows by force to marry

them and also girls and we had no man to protect us. And then my [oldest] daughter got married, I made her. She was eleven years. She was very young and me myself, I wasn't very old. But because she had no father and the situation was dangerous, I asked her and she agreed, she was happy. [After that,] my son-in-law—he was from the relatives of my husband—was taking care of me and also my daughter. I was taking care of my children by working, just staying with them.

Q: Why did your daughter marry instead of you remarrying a man to protect the family?

A: As you know, when a widow gets married with someone else, the brother of the husband will get the children from the widow. Because I liked my children, I didn't want to be parted from them, so I didn't want to get remarried but worked to support my children.

While girls and women are undoubtedly the first victims of forced and early marriages, it's also the case that boys and young men, particularly if they have strong older brothers, uncles, or fathers, are also parties to forced, coerced, or otherwise involuntary marriages. In the story above, for instance, it is not clear how the young male relative, who was drawn into marriage to protect the honor of his family, felt. Some of these marriages may be ultimately successful and happy, but others may end up as did the union described to me by a RAWA member. When one of her elder male relatives died, the man's seventeen-year-old nephew was drafted to marry his uncle's widowed fourth wife, because a family member needed to care for this woman. Now he expresses his "discontent" with this marriage to a woman thirty-four years his senior by beating her and being cruel to his stepchildren. Meanwhile, she is blamed for his violence, because as a widow, she could have, by tradition (but not necessarily realistically), refused the marriage.

While some young people have no choice, some of the girls and women I spoke to described conscious compromises and calculations they made when faced with pressure to marry. One example is Khadija, a woman in her late thirties who was the eldest daughter of a rural, land-owning family. Her mother was uneducated and uninterested in education, but she described her father, with only a sixth-grade education himself, as encouraging both his sons and daughters in school. Unlike many of my participants, Khadija and her family had positive experiences during the Soviet occupation, moving to the city and enjoying an increased standard of living through her father's government job. When the Soviets were defeated, the family returned to their rural roots and, shortly after, Khadija learned that she was engaged. She explained the series of calculations that followed:

I was in fifth grade when I was engaged. He was a relative and "Uncle" [to me]. And one day father said, "Don't call him uncle, he's your fiancé." For one week I was hospitalized, because I wanted to commit suicide.

Q: Do you remember what most upset you?

A: I'm too young and too small and that man is too big and kind of strange. He was ten years older.

Q: Then what happened?

A: I didn't complete eleventh grade, but got married. After getting married it got better, I was happy.

Q: Was it your choice to get married in eleventh grade?

A: . . . During the time of the engagement so many others were coming to [propose] and the situation [was bad], so I decided to get married to get rid of the [worse suitors]. Nine months later I had children.

Salma gives another example of the calculations made by Afghan teens within the context of war and social unrest. By the time we talked, she was an unhappy, thirty-something, college-educated, third wife of a man at least twice her age. While on the positive side, her marriage allowed her the freedom to use her education in a full-time job, she described her personal life as a self-inflicted penance for not listening to her father when she was a teenager:

I was always very interested in education and my father wanted me to graduate from medical school and be a doctor. Then during the war, it was very bad. I was going to school and the Mujahedin were firing on the schools; sometimes they threatened my father not to let your daughters go to school. They didn't like girls to go to school and even were killing teachers. The problem of school was hard on me, every night they were coming and threatening my father.

I [also] had many people who wanted to marry me. Some were Mujahedin and threatening by force that they'd take me. A relative came as a suitor, but my father didn't agree. I was a little bit agreed to this suitor because he was in Kabul and the situation in Kabul was better to complete my education. I said, "I have to get married with this one because of the chance to complete my education." My father was not ready to agree. Then he saw that I was happy with this engagement and my mother also, so he accepted. But always he was saying, "I'm not happy and I'm predicting that it won't have a good future."

We went to Kabul and got married. I was in eleventh grade and admitted to school. And that was my dream, to complete my school and university. And I was not caring of my husband or family or life. I didn't know the objective of life together as husband and wife. I was sixteen. He was twenty-eight and he agreed with me to continue my study. We were together for about three months. After that [he changed] . . .

Over the next five years, Salma ultimately finished university, but her husband became an addict and descended so far into violence and mental illness that her father had to help her gain a divorce and take her back home with him. Although she refused all other engagements for several more years, her father became ill and told her that he would not forgive her if he died and she wasn't remarried. Finally, her father said: "I told you before not to get engaged and you didn't have experience, and this time I'm telling you [about] a good man. He can protect you and provide anything you want in your life." She ultimately gave in to her father and became the third wife of a man she admits is very good to her, but for whom she can rally no feelings. So two decades later, as a (rare) college-educated woman in a (less rare) loveless marriage, she is living, for better and for worse, with the choices she felt compelled to make as a teenager.

While interviewing politically active women, it was not unusual to hear about the remarkable and risky decisions made by resilient Afghan women living in a country that often has disdain for women who leave the house, let alone who speak up and demand their rights. It became quite clear that the West's image of Afghan women as burqa-shrouded victims was wholly inaccurate; incalculable Afghan women fight daily for their very survival. Nonetheless, I was stunned by the story I heard from a shy sixteen- or seventeen-year-old (she didn't know her age) who could barely make eye contact as she narrated her tale in Pashto at the women's shelter where she resided:

Q: How did you come to be here?
A: It was my bad luck. Before, I lived in a far village with my mother and a lot-older brother who has two wives. I have three more sisters and brothers. All are older than me. My oldest brother engaged me with that man when I was small and I don't know if my father gave permission or not. My mother didn't agree. My brother wanted me engaged for money. I had no power, but I was not happy to be given. Nobody was discussing with me any issue. *[Translator, who is shelter staff, interjects that her brother is addicted to opium and would also gain drugs for her marriage.]*
   My heart was very tired to feel very upset, sad, nervous. Three days after I was informed [of the marriage], I planned to run away from home and one night I just cut my hair. My mother was at my sister's house, where she stays

when she [was] working on the opium fields. I left early in the morning, walked thirty minutes to the bazaar, took a car an hour to Herat, then took a bus across the country to Kabul. God was kind on me and everybody was like dumb and blind. No one was seeing me.

When my mother and brother found out I was gone they fought and my brother beat her very much. My mother thought he had taken me already to [marry] and he accused her of selling me to someone else or hiding me from the wedding.

Q: When you cut your hair, what was your plan?

A: I cut it because I knew I could not get out as a girl. I wanted to be like a boy. I wore the outgrown clothes of my two-years-older brother.

Q: Where did you get the money for the car and bus?

A: Because I was embroidering, people were giving me money. Also I had earrings from a small part of the opium field I worked. I had bought earrings with that money and I sold those in the bazaar.

Q: Why did you decide to go to Kabul?

A: I went there because maybe they wouldn't find me. And also to be truthful, I had planned that I would go to Pakistan and find Naghma, the [pop] singer. But I couldn't do that. I didn't reach anywhere but prison in Kabul.

Not knowing what to do once she arrived in Kabul, Laila's strange behavior and small size for a boy attracted attention and she was eventually arrested and admitted she was a girl. After being detained and sent to court, they returned her to Herat, to the women's shelter where I met her. Here she had been detained for four months, both for her safety against the brother and the fiancé, and because she had nowhere else to go. I asked what she thought now of her decision to flee her forced marriage:

It's a problem for me . . . I don't have another way. As much as I think, there is no other solution. I have no hope. And now I think it was like a dream, how did I do that?

The Wheel of Life Keeps Turning

In every time and place, individuals and generations grow up shaped by the experiences of their childhoods. The Afghans I spoke with were shaped by childhoods split nearly equally between forty years of relative peace and forty years of unrest and war. During these years, as in other places and other generations, Afghanistan has struggled over what the future will look like and what defines progress. An older generation is shaped by childhood memories, such as Ghezal's mother Nafisa's:

> Q: In your youth, what was it like to grow up as a girl?
> A: It was very good during Zahir Shah. There was no fighting, it was very peaceful. There was not sorrow at all. There were no schools [in my village]. I studied twelve years in a mosque.[27] For girls, there was freedom. Men were not that narrow-minded like now. My marriage was a love marriage. We were cousins. He was different. Open-minded, because he was educated. There were many uneducated men, but I didn't like them. My mother was also supporting this idea. She told me, "I want my daughter to get married to a person who is educated and will really look after her."

Meanwhile, a younger generation continues to be shaped by the experiences of social and political upheaval, war and loss. These battles are not only for their country, but also for their hearts and minds. All sides in the Afghan struggle recognize the power of youth—RAWA, the Soviets and Afghan Communists, the Jihadi parties, and the Taliban. In the summer of 2006, Salma described another example:

> During the Soviet period, the Soviets managed the schools.
> There were some political subjects, some organizations, and special meetings to attract the girls and boys. They knew that the children are the makers of the future of Afghanistan.

I asked some of my younger interviewees how they thought the civil war and Taliban eras had impacted them and their country. Some, like Aatifa, a nineteen-year-old who was one of my Kabul-based translators in 2007, described how meaningful change post-Taliban could be slow and difficult:

> Q: When the Taliban actually left, what happened?
> A: The [early] days were like days of happiness and joys. The people, the boys, were playing music in the streets, everyone was clapping and dancing. The music was so loud because for five years no music, and suddenly loud music on the street. And everyone was happy.
> Q: And women were out too?
> A: Yeah. For the first six months, I had the burqa because I got used to [it]. When I didn't wear the burqa I was feeling strange. And then my father told me I didn't need it anymore. But [it was] my habit. Since for five years, we

had to hide our face, suddenly to open your face for boys, they really enjoy looking to the girls. (Laughs.) Later on [they got used to it] . . .

The five years changed [some of] the boys. Especially those boys who were, like, sixteen when the Taliban came and are now grown-up. They change their minds. Still they are like dark mind, "Don't wear this; don't wear this."

Q: Why do you think they were so affected?

A: They were trained like that. Especially some of the religious subjects they were taught in school changed their mind. Islam is a very nice religion. But some of the interpretation is wrong. It is not the same in the Holy Qur'an, the way they are using. For example, my cousin, they taught him that when you shape [pluck] an eyebrow, it is a sin. He came and said, "It is a big sin, believe me. God will not forgive you. Don't do it." And my father became angry and said, "Why are you following such stupid things? It is not a sin."

. . . Sometimes when I don't have my scarf and my cousin comes, my brother says, "Where is your scarf?" And if my father hears, [he] becomes angry and says, "While I am alive you don't have this right to tell her [what to do]."

Others, like Ghezal, described their fathers and husbands as becoming more conservative in the Taliban era, but already saw positive changes:

Q: You said many men changed under the Taliban, are they changing back or is it permanent?

A: Yes, they are changing and becoming better.

Q: What is helping change them?

A: During Karzai's presidency they see that schools are open and girls go to school so they are also changing themselves. I can see the changes in my father and brother-in-law. My father is now saying that my younger sister when grown-up can work in NGO, no problem.

Rafiq, an eighteen-year-old RAWA supporter, had grown up in an activist, secular family, fighting against successive eras of violence and oppression. He took a political, hopeful tone as he summed up how individual and generational experience, family and peer socialization, and the wheels of life impact a life and a country:

In Afghanistan, a boy is born in an Islamic family, so the boy naturally gets taught Islam every day and his mind is made so that he can't take such stand that is different than others. But I'm not like him . . . For me, the equality of women with men is the most important factor in a society or country because with [only] half the people you can't progress.

One day—and I strongly believe in this day—we will have full equality between men and women. The day will come that people will say that "our grandfathers were so ignorant to ignore a fact that is so obvious" . . . this is just a matter of time.[28]

While global forces exert their prolonged influence on Afghanistan, Afghans themselves strive to develop as individuals, families, generations, and as a nation. As the wheel of life keeps turning, Afghanistan's collective national outcome will be shaped by many forces, not the least of which is a battle for hearts, minds, and the autobiographical and collective memories of Afghan childhoods.

Notes

1. In order to protect participants, all names are pseudonyms. Due to page limitations, some quotes have been edited for clarity and brevity. Unless needed to combine two thoughts, ellipses were not added when words were removed or sentences combined. Although all words are important, these edits do not change the meaning of the quotes as would be understood by readers of English.

2. Both refer to "essential" elements of Afghan culture: Afghaniyat is a shared Afghan culture, and Pashtunwali a set of informal codes originating in Pashtun culture that is often shared across Afghan ethnic groups and tribes.

3. These span from what Urie Bronfenbrenner (*The Ecology of Human Development: Experiments by Nature and Design*, Cambridge, MA: Harvard University Press, 1979) called the macrosystem, through the historical chronosystem, to the individual ontological system (Jay Belsky, "Child Maltreatment: An Ecological Integration," *American Psychologist*, 35: 320–335). For these and other forces impacting Afghanistan, see Anne E. Brodsky, *With All Our Strength: The Revolutionary Association of the Women of Afghanistan* (New York: Routledge, 2003); Louis Dupree, *Afghanistan* (Oxford: Oxford University Press, 1997); Larry P. Goodson, *Afghanistan's Endless War: State Failure, Regional Politics, and the Rise of the Taliban* (Seattle: University of Washington Press, 2001); Ahmed Rashid, *Taliban: Militant Islam, Oil, and Fundamentalism in Central Asia* (New Haven: Yale University Press, 2000); and *Descent into Chaos: How the War Against Islamic Extremism Is Being Lost in Pakistan, Afghanistan and Central Asia* (Noida, India: Penguin, 2008); Mir Hekmatullah Sadat, "Hyphenating Afghaniyat (Afghan-ness) in the Afghan Diaspora," *Journal of Muslim Minority Affairs*, 28 (3) (2008): 329–342, doi:10.1080/13602000802547898.

4. Glen H. Elder, Jr., "The Life Course as Developmental Theory," *Child Development*, 69 (1) (1998): 1–12; Erik H. Erikson, *Childhood and Society*, 2nd ed. (New York: W. W. Norton and Co., 1963).

5. Kwok-fai Ting and Catherine C. H. Chiu, "Materialistic Values in Hong Kong

and Guangzhou: A Comparative Analysis of Two Chinese Societies," *Sociological Spectrum* 20 (1) (2000): 15–40, doi: 10.1080/027321700280017, 34.

6. The reign of Zahir Shah (1933–1973), which sparked unrest and dissatisfaction on both the left and the right, is recalled fondly by many Afghans as the last period of stability and normalcy in Afghanistan. Brodsky, *With All Our Strength*.

7. See, for example, Erik H. Erikson, *Childhood and Society*; Jean Piaget and Barbel Inhelder, *The Psychology of the Child* (New York: Basic Books, Inc., 1969).

8. Margaret M. Braungart and Richard G. Braungart, "The Life-Course Development of Left- and Right-Wing Youth Activist Leaders from the 1960s," *Political Psychology*, 11 (2) (1990): 243–282; Robert Coles, *The Political Life of Children* (Boston: Atlantic Monthly Press, 1986).

9. Braungart and Braungart, "Life Course Development of Left- and Right-Wing Youth Activist Leaders from the 1960s"; Karl Mannheim, "The Problem of Generations," in K. Mannheim, *Essays on the Sociology of Knowledge*, P. Kecskemeti, ed. (London: Routledge and Kegan Paul LTD, 1952); Howard Schuman and Jacqueline Scott, "Generations and Collective Memories," *American Sociological Review* 54 (3) (1989): 359–381.

10. Braungart and Braungart, "Life Course Development of Left- and Right-Wing Youth Activist Leaders from the 1960s"; Elder, "The Life Course as Developmental Theory"; Erikson, *Childhood and Society*; Mannheim, *Essays on the Sociology of Knowledge*.

11. Braungart and Braungart, "Life Course Development of Left- and Right-wing Youth Activist Leaders from the 1960s"; Mannheim, *Essays on the Sociology of Knowledge*; Schuman and Scott, "Generations and Collective Memories."

12. Schuman and Scott, "Generations and Collective Memories."

13. Brodsky, *With All Our Strength*.

14. Anne E. Brodsky, "Multiple Psychological Sense of Community in Afghan Context: Exploring Commitment and Sacrifice in an Underground Resistance Community," *American Journal of Community Psychology* 44 (2009): 176–187; Anne E. Brodsky, Elena Welsh, Amy Carrillo, Gitika Talwar, and Tamra Butler, "Between Synergy and Conflict: Balancing the Processes of Organizational and Individual Resilience in an Afghan Women's Community," *American Journal of Community Psychology* 47(3) (2011): 217–235; Anne E. Brodsky, G. Talwar, E. Welsh, J. Scheibler, P. Backer, G. Portnoy, A. Carrillo, and E. Kline, "The Hope in Her Eyes: The Role of Children in Afghan Women's Resilience," *American Journal of Orthopsychiatry* 82(3) (2012), 358–366; and Anne E. Brodsky, Galina Portnoy, Jill Scheibler, Elena Welsh, Gitika Talwar, and Amy Carrillo, "Beyond پ اب (the ABCs): Education, Community and Feminism in Afghanistan," *Journal of Community Psychology* 40(1) (2012): 159–181.

15. Schuman and Scott, "Generations and Collective Memories."

16. Brodsky, *With All Our Strength*, 60–62.

17. For more on the balance and compromises of formal and informal education within RAWA, see Brodsky et al., "Between Synergy and Conflict," and Brodsky et al., "Beyond پ اب (the ABCs)."

18. Brodsky, *With All Our Strength*, 212–213.

19. Brodsky et al., "Between Synergy and Conflict," 225–226.

20. Boarding facilities for secondary and post-secondary school students (British).

21. During the Saur coup, the Afghan community parties overthrew Daoud

Khan's presidency, killing him and his family, leading to the first in a series of communist presidents, and creating conditions that led to the December 1979 Soviet invasion. Martin Ewans, *Afghanistan: A New History* (Richmond, Surrey, England: Curzon Press, 2001).

22. One of the parties that was a combatant in the anti-Soviet and civil war.

23. Brodsky, *With All Our Strength*, 21–22.

24. For more about Zarmina's execution and RAWA's documentation of it, see Brodsky, *With All Our Strength*, 1–20.

25. Brodsky, *With All Our Strength*.

26. Some married after family and friends recommended the match and they met each other and agreed (i.e., blind date). Some met in school or through political activities and fell in love, and then sought and received their families' approval (i.e., "Mr. Jones, I'd like your permission to marry your daughter"); some were *in each other's name*, meaning there had been a promise to marry made by their parents or other relatives from birth, but they still decided on their own that they agreed with the match (i.e., "Our families knew each other, we practically grew up together and we were high school sweethearts"); some unions benefitted the political, economic, or social well-being of the couple and the families (e.g., "William Clay Ford, grandson of the founder of Ford Motor Company, weds Martha Park Firestone, granddaughter of the tire company magnate, Akron," *Life Magazine* 7, July 1947).

27. *Madrassas* are the form of mosque school that is now familiar due to their role in radicalizing the Taliban and other religious fundamentalists. While this has led to a negative association, historically mosques provided basic and advanced religious and Arabic training to Afghan boys and girls, and in areas without other educational opportunities, sometimes provided basic Dari literacy, and a setting for other secular schooling.

28. Brodsky et al., "Between Synergy and Conflict," 232.

CHAPTER 3

Jumping Rope in Prison: The Representation of Afghan Children in Film

TERESA CUTLER-BROYLES

From the beginning we become the captives of an unexpected light.
JASON ELLIOT, *AN UNEXPECTED LIGHT: TRAVELS IN AFGHANISTAN*

One of the most beautiful and potent scenes in the 2006 Bollywood film *Kabul Express*[1] occurs eight minutes in: the camera peers from a slightly low angle at a string of ragged, broken buildings in Kabul, Afghanistan, as a tank rolls by. Silhouetted in the foreground, black against the yellow/brown/orange shattered structures and a deep blue sky, is a child crouched and waving as the tank passes on the road. A sudden cessation of all non-diegetic sound occurs as the tank rolls on and the child's hand drops. This silence, emblematic of the ruin in which the child sits, is powerful counterpoint to the weight of life under conditions represented by the passing tank, and is only relieved when the non-diegetic music begins, reminiscent of a woman wailing somewhere offscreen. The scene ends quickly and the film moves on, and the child is left behind, unseen and unheard by the camera or by us, as the story and the main characters take shape.

Evocative in many ways, this short scene gives us much to think about. The confluence of image and silence, with the subsequent addition of music both alien and haunting to Western audiences, speaks volumes for what Afghan children signify in a number of films made both inside and outside the country. The scene is simple, but its simplicity hides a more complex issue as it positions this child in physical space very much the same way Afghan children tend to be positioned representationally in film. Unlike Western films, which often use children as props and in service to the story itself,[2] films that either feature Afghan children or are set in Afghanistan use children as multivalent signifiers. Typically foregrounded against destruction, they are liminal figures existing in the space between light and dark. They function as doorways through which we can, if we look closely enough, see both past and future. And as carriers of Afghan identity,[3] they embody both hope and despair. Understanding this mélange of meaning is crucial in understanding the messages these images convey.

This work is an exploration of images of Afghan children in a select few films, and how those images carry meaning for an American scholar. I examine four films that feature Afghan children, and in analyzing the space these children hold, I hope to understand what is at stake in the way they are represented. My goal is not to rate the films against some measure of quality, proffering unassailable truths about them, or to try to make definitive statements about the realities of Afghan film, Afghan society, or Afghan culture. Simply, I examine the way children are placed—against what backdrops both actual and metaphorical they are foregrounded—in a country rich with import.[4] In this endeavor I hope to uncover some of the forces at work in the meaning-making that occurs when an Afghan child walks onscreen.

Unlike many films about and set in Afghanistan in which children are ubiquitous, *Kabul Express* depicts children in relatively few scenes. Because of this relative infrequency, the liminal status of children in *Kabul Express* is more apparent; the smallest figures on the screen are imbued with possibly the most significant meanings throughout. The plot—two Indian journalists seek to interview a member of the Taliban after the invasion in 2001 by the United States and its allies—does not need children to help tell its story, making their presence that much more important.

The second time we see a child is just moments after the first, when one of the journalists films a young boy helping an adult pull a trailer loaded with a burned-out car along a bombed-out street, a reminder that in a country that has seen decades of conflict and various invasions, normalcy is relative. Another child watches the journalist, becoming the focal point when the camera centers him in the frame. Moments later it is revealed that he has only one leg. In a cinematically striking shot, this young boy stands casually and meets the gaze of the camera without flinching, easily balanced on one leg while his crutch rests unneeded against his side. Echoing his fractured body, the ruin and destruction behind him function as counterpoint and reminder, as if we needed one, that the past and future both are fraught with peril. In fact, I would argue that this boy stands in for the country at this moment, potent proof that the past exists as present in today's Afghanistan. When the journalists leave, the boy is forgotten—a symbolism more than ironic—and as with the first instance in which a child is left behind as instruments of war pass by, the symbolism of the boy's subsequent absence is perhaps unintended by the filmmakers. Nonetheless it is worthy of note. As children go, so goes the country.

The next time we see children is less deliberately poignant yet no less important to note. The journalists come into a village in which *buzkashi*[5] is being played, a traditional game in Afghanistan that involves many men on horseback and a goat carcass. The children in this scene are part of the larger crowd that watches the game, cheering and running after the spectacle of dead goat and yelling men. Symbolism here is in the eye of the viewer: Western audiences—despite the violence their children see daily on television—are likely to be shocked by the violence of the game and appalled that children are exposed to such a thing. This reaction needs to be tempered by an awareness of the reality of the daily violence in these children's lives, and when measured against this background—both metaphoric in the extra-textual knowledge viewers have of the presence of war, and visibly present in the mise-en-scène of crumbling walls and bombed-out buildings—this game becomes something entirely different. Buzkashi is a symbol of Afghanistan and in playing it, these men perform part of their historically based identity as Afghans. Children's identity as Afghanistan's future is solidified while they watch from the sidelines, eager to take their place in both local game and global space, and their participation here is symbolic of a renewal of Afghan identity, as well as representative of how filmic Afghan children's lives are played out in the space between what was and what will be.

The 2007 film *The Kite Runner*[6] is an entirely different kind of story, and its representations of children reflect this yet continue the underlying themes. Unlike *Kabul Express*, which uses Afghan children judiciously to convey particular meanings at moments in the stories of (foreign) adults, *The Kite Runner*'s children are integral to its plot and are the vehicle for this film's meaning-making. Images of children fill the screen from the opening credits through the end, woven into the very fabric of the story itself. As such they fulfill the same role as the children in *Kabul Express*: they carry Afghan identity into a future shaped by the past, and offer glimpses along the way of the tragedy (stark reality) of today.

The film starts in the present in the United States and moves quickly to the past, to an Afghanistan not yet in the shambles we are conditioned to expect. As a Western audience we have been taught to think of Afghanistan as war-torn, destroyed, and therefore this pre-Soviet-invasion movie version of the country seems somehow unreal. Our extra-textual knowledge of what is to come shadows our viewing pleasure; we know that the children who take center frame are doomed to either death or disruption, as is the city they inhabit. Against this looming future of destruction and despair, even their play becomes significant, no less full of import than the business of politics. In fact, one of the first scenes involves the two main young male characters carrying a kite through the city of Kabul as they discuss the upcoming kite-flying contest and the merits of the various competitors. This scene is overlaid with the voice of an adult male discussing political issues, the nation of Afghanistan, the nature of democracy, and what it means to be Afghan. In the parlance of film structure, then, this scene equates the boys' play with the nation's sense of itself. The boys become Afghanistan, their play becomes deadly serious as a marker of identity, and they fill the same space as the children in *Kabul Express*; not only are they representative of Afghan identity, they are both past and future but never present.

In *The Kite Runner*, though a story of failed friendship and redemption rather than of the devastations of war, the reality of looming death and destruction informs our viewing. Within the story itself the young boys know nothing of the upcoming turmoil that will tear them and their country apart. But as viewers we know the boys' innocence is doomed and in our hearts they become shadows of what was, long before the actualities of their situation destroy their lives in the film itself. They are, in other words, never simply boys playing with kites: they are Afghanistan searching for itself. As with the children in *Kabul Express*, these two kite-flyers are liminal figures. We watch as they live their lives in the moment between light and darkness, their laughter echoing through the emptiness between the past they once inhabited and the future they cannot yet see. When the Soviet tanks arrive, we are filled with both dread and a morbid sense of fulfilled expectation. We knew all along the boys' lives were doomed; Afghan children in film are rarely allowed happiness. Symbols need to carry weight, and this weight is visible in even the lightest scenes.[7]

One of the boys escapes with his father, the other is trapped in war-torn Afghanistan, and the film's timeframe shifts to our near-past/almost-present. Afghan children at this point take on a distance, viewed through our protagonist's eyes as he returns to his birthplace and to the fears and bullies he ran from. For the most part the children he encounters are orphans who live amidst rubble, and, similar to the children in *Kabul Express*, are doorways into the horrors of the past while they embody the difficult if not impossible path to the future. As liminal figures they are simultaneously heavy with import and empty vessels awaiting meaning. When our protagonist finally faces his fears and stands up to the bully, he does so as a necessary rite of passage in service to his saving of a young boy who stands in for all Afghan children, and by extension Afghanistan itself. Deliverance comes from outside, and childhood becomes not only a liminal state but one that can be returned to—and escaped from. This theme is made manifest in the movie *In This World.*[8]

In This World opens on adults but within moments offers us children in droves. Refugees in the Afghan Shamshato refugee camp[9] inside the border of Pakistan, they gather to look at the camera, they laugh, they hide, they play; to a casual viewer these more playful images are less weighty than those in the earlier examined films, and carry less meaning. Yet as is characteristic of the way Afghan children often appear in film, the mise-en-scène sends a different message. Backdropped by ruin, poverty, and despair, these children are physically outside the borders of the nation they are positioned by filmic convention to represent. They are both Afghan and nation-less, escaping the past and not yet moving toward the future.

In This World mimics documentary style by its use of cues that we, as knowledgeable moviegoers, know to look for: text across the screen gives us locations; a voiceover gives us information about the images we see; maps give us animated lines moving from place to place; a handheld camera shakes, simulating the feel of following in the footsteps of real people; and unscripted acting provides the finishing touch. These elements give the film a verisimilitude not uncommon in films about Afghanistan, though in this case they are utilized to the extreme.

The film follows two boys, one of whom we have seen in the refugee camp in an early scene, on a hazardous journey from Afghanistan to London. After making deals with smugglers and family members, they set out, placing their trust in a series of men who are portrayed such that we—if not the two boys—sense imminent danger from the start. They traverse mountains and hide in dingy rooms, they are stalked by both authorities and those in whose care they end up, and are finally captured and forced to return to their starting point. Immediately they stage a second attempt, endure much the same ordeals, and finally are locked into a vehicle to cross the last borders into the promised land. The mixed success of their venture wrenches the heart.

A significant theme in this film is the dissolution of the distance between childhood and adulthood. While the transition from child to adult of course occurs, sometimes forcibly, in other films about Afghanistan—in terms of *innocence* in *Osama*, explored below, and *time* in *The Kite Runner*, for instance—in *In This World* the transition is no longer a process but a concurrent moment of identity. The boys inhabit two types of liminal space, one between child and adult, another between Afghan and other. The camera follows these characters as they cross borders in ways children in the other three films examined cannot. Both geography and identity become merely conveniences, or inconveniences, and self becomes slippery.

In *Osama*,[10] this slippage of identity occurs more blatantly as a young girl reluctantly takes on the persona of a young boy. *Osama* exudes symbolism in stark, unyielding images and is relentless in its ruthless portrayal of Afghan children. In the first scene a handheld camera, lending a documentary feel to the story, focuses on a young boy in the midst of what seems like hundreds of other children in the streets of rubble-strewn Kabul during the Taliban regime. Against this destruction and repression, so complete as to be incomprehensible to a Western audience, children cannot seem anything but helpless and endangered. As embodiments of Afghanistan itself they demonstrate the fragility of both the present and any hope for the future, while existing in a nameless space between innocence and awareness. Yet they confound us; we expect children to be innocent, but none can be innocent in such a landscape. Compounding our discomfort, the young boy the camera follows periodically breaks the fourth wall and looks directly at us, a technique that draws us in and produces an immediacy that does not let us out of its grip. We become helpless voyeurs and watch as the main character, a young girl, arrives onscreen only to be quickly transformed into a boy by her mother and grandmother. The elder woman cuts the girl's hair as she sleeps, telling a story that becomes a motif throughout the film. In a sing-song voice she speaks of boys and girls who change form, becoming the other. This story, retold several times in slightly different ways, and this girl's transformation, are indicative of how the liminal status of children functions in this film. Boys and girls are both, and they are neither. They are everything and nothing, powerful and helpless. And the boy who used to be a girl is finally given a name—Osama—and ventures into the world on the strength of a tenuously constructed, repeated tale.

Images of children are everywhere in this film. They run, play, fight, study, tease, bathe, laugh, scream, and fill the screen from start to finish. In filmic language this tells us they are the most important and by extension the most powerful characters, and yet they are concurrently the least powerful figures in the unfolding events. Woven into the meanings of the way children signify in this film, then, is film technique itself. We know, through years of film watching that have made us experts, that import and significance are accorded to the images that fill our sight when we watch a screen, so we know that these images tell us more than the story they are trapped within. Meaning builds upon meaning, and is never as simple as it at first appears. The juxtaposition of the understood power of images of children, and their real powerlessness, creates the tension, the liminal space, in which all Afghan children reside.

The repetition of the grandmother's tale of transformation is an important one. It draws on hundreds of years of Afghan social history and a specific practice known as *bacha posh*: girls dressing as boys to provide them with more freedom and offer their families more opportunity and status. In itself this is not unusual in Afghanistan, and the change in gender offers the young girl hope that, in transforming, she will become powerful.[11] For a short while it works, but when Osama is found out and punished, this power slips away. As with other Afghan children in film, she becomes a sublime signifier of both ends of the paradox in which she has figured. Power is shown to be just as ephemeral as childhood, just as easily lost and as quickly subsumed into the liminal space wherein it becomes its opposite.

This film could be the focus of its own independent analysis, so rich are its images and representations. I want to mention only one last element I have until this point elided: this story is about a young girl, perhaps the most vulnerable of people in Afghanistan. I will leave to others the in-depth analysis of how she signifies as a result of her gender except to note that, in accordance with my notion that Afghan children in film represent Afghanistan, and that the liminal status of the nation is reflected and made apparent in the liminal status of these children, this girl in this film is especially suited to such a task.

Conquered populations are often figured as feminine and their conquerors as male in the language of imperialism and colonialism, both in literature and in film. Afghanistan, in this film embodied by a female main character, shifts and becomes male, a metaphoric transformation of identity that perhaps prefigures a movement by the country itself out of decades of conflict. Osama the boy/girl embodies the frail hope that Afghanistan can transform itself, that it is indeed unconquerable. If we follow this reasoning to the end of the film, however, we are presented with a bleak outcome: the boy is routed, the girl is restored and married against her will to an elderly man who becomes both savior and jailer. The girl with no name is chained to her identity, finally, as female, a destiny that is perhaps inevitable in the context of the story and that asks the question: Can she—can the country—transform into something new? The film seems to answer this question in the negative.

And yet.

A recurring, slow-motion image in this film offers hope. Three times the girl sees herself as if in a dream, jumping rope at moments of great danger and fear, and this repetition tells an experienced film-going audience to pay attention; as with all symbols, repetition augments its potency. In a story of powerlessness in the midst of an attempt to transform, this dream jumping stands out and begs for an interpretation. In the first occurrence she has been chased into her home by a group of Taliban; she peers outside for one last moment to see herself jumping in the rain in a metaphoric defiance of the threat. In the second she has been captured and is in jail, and she sees herself through the cell bars as though through a screen, again in defiance of the very real jail

in which she sits. The third and last time—and the last scene of the movie—
is potentially more significant still. We see her behind bars, dressed as a boy,
jumping rope as though in defiance of her actual state of postcoital captivity.
The difference is she does not see herself.

We are handed no interpretation of what this image signifies. Are we to
understand this in what would fit our own, Western filmic conventions? That
no matter the chains, no matter the jails, this girl—and perhaps Afghanistan—will gain strength and when an opportunity arises will break free and
fulfill all the hopes and potential visible only through the screen? Seen in this
way, children become potentiality itself, each of them a part, as in a mosaic,
of the whole that is Afghanistan, and when the opportunity presents itself,
they and the nation will burst forth en masse, powerful and ready to take on
the world they cannot yet envision.

Perhaps. But perhaps that is too ambitious a reading of this film, and perhaps the girl's slow-motion dream jumping is nothing more than a symbol
for her captivity, a way to represent her innocence and her status as child despite all that happens around and to her. In either case, she becomes another
Afghan child who as liminal figure is both less and more than she appears.

Each of these movies has figured Afghan children as conduits for meaning,
and the easy interpretation is this: it is only in escaping to become something
they are not that they, and therefore by extension Afghanistan itself, will survive. The harder message is that these children, as representative of the nation,
exist in a space that calls for multilayered understandings, and anything less
is missing the larger point.

Afghan children in these films are more than they appear. Each stares outward from the frame, their position onscreen and in the world embodying all
the contradictions of the country itself, transcending the past and embodying
the potential in the space between what is and what will be. They are powerful, and they are vulnerable, but they are never absent.

Notes

1. Kabir Khan (director), *Kabul Express*. India: Yash Raj Films, 2006.

2. Unless they are stories about children themselves; in this case children become
less prop than they do subject, yet tend not to carry meanings much beyond the bounds
of the film itself.

3. In formulating this idea I was inspired in part by Lina Khatib's *Filming the
Modern Middle East: Politics in the Cinemas of Hollywood and the Arab World* (London:
I.B. Tauris, 2008) and her discussion of gendered tools of nationalism. Khatib explores
how women in both Hollywood and Arab cinemas are metaphors for nation, and how

these cinemas utilize gender to strengthen national identities (104). Her project is quite different from mine, and we examine images and representations for far different reasons, yet I credit her work for being part of the process through which I arrived at my examination of Afghan children as representative of the nation of Afghanistan.

4. Afghanistan has loomed large in world affairs for many years. It is a space in which constant strife, humanitarian concerns, armies from countries around the world, and media coverage converge, often against Afghans' express desires, and certainly against their best interests in many cases. As a space of meaning it is ripe with possibilities; film makes the most of this potential.

5. Buzkashi is an ancient game—thought to be the father of polo—in which both participants and observers sometimes die; it was banned by the Taliban during their ban on all things non-Islamic and has experienced a resurgence since 2001 as Afghanistan's national sport.

6. Marc Foster (director), *The Kite Runner*. Based on the novel of the same name by Khaled Hosseini (2003). United States: Dreamworks, Sidney Kimmel Entertainment, Participant Productions, et al., 2007.

7. Many more events occur in these young boys' lives before the Soviets arrive. To explore those events gives too much of the story away, and while it might add something to my analysis in terms of what happens to one of the boys and how that action echoes what the world is doing to Afghanistan, to make that actually fit my analysis would require convolutions that would change my own terms. When Afghans mete out violence on other Afghans, this speaks to a different issue than those I speak to here.

8. Michael Winterbottom (director), *In This World*. United Kingdom: Film Consortium, British Broadcasting Corporation, 2002.

9. This camp is quite famous for being a base for Gulbuddin Hekmatyar, aka the "Butcher of Kabul," and his Hezb-e Islami party, which espoused violent, armed conflict as a path to power.

10. Siddiq Barmak (director), *Osama*. Afghanistan: Barmak Film, LeBrocquy, Fraser Productions, 2003.

11. Bacha posh is a long-established and accepted, if not often discussed, practice in Afghanistan. Typically these girls have no choice and their response to being forced to dress as a boy varies from reluctant acquiescence to eager acceptance. When they reach puberty, they switch back to dressing as girls, and a younger sister will often take their place as the "boy" of the family. Another film that explores this practice, to much more optimistic ends, is the 2001 Iranian film *Baran*, directed by Majid Majidi. The reverse practice, or *bacha bazi*, of dressing boys as girls, is as long a tradition and has been the subject of more media attention. Bacha bazi boys are considered status symbols of a sort, and powerful men in Afghan society often have more than one at their beck and call, to be used as the men desire.

The young family of Suliman in the Kohistan district of Fariyab Province. Photo by UNICEF/Valerie Gatchel, 2003; courtesy of Fitsum Assefa.

PART 2

TIES THAT BIND:
THE FAMILY IN REBOUND

CHAPTER 4

Love, Fear, and Discipline in Afghan Families

DEBORAH J. SMITH

In 2006, the Afghanistan Research and Evaluation Unit (AREU) launched a broad research project investigating the changing nature of family dynamics in Afghanistan, particularly how family structure and changing gender and generational roles and relations impact on levels of violence within the family. Studies attempted to assess what types of family violence are seen as appropriate and legitimate by the community as a group, women as a group, and men as a group, among different generations and individual men and women. The research aimed to identify and understand key stress factors or individual and societal characteristics related to violence and acceptance of violence among family members.[1]

Data for this study—purely qualitative in nature—were collected across rural and urban areas in four Afghan provinces: Bamiyan, Herat, Kabul, and Nangarhar. The research did not attempt to investigate extreme or unusual cases of violence; rather it is concerned with the more "normal" forms of violence that are part of people's day-to-day lives, i.e., "everyday violence."[2] The most common forms of violence identified were slapping, verbal abuse, punching, kicking, and hitting with thin sticks and shoes.

Physical violence was found to exist in varying degrees within all sixty-one case study families. It is safe to assume that most, if not all, children in these families and, most likely, in the wider community, experience violence in the family to varying degrees. It must be noted that the research teams also witnessed a great deal of love, affection, and care by parents and other adults in the family toward children. Likewise, parents reported their deep concerns and high expectations for their children's future.

Parents' Hopes and Aspirations

Examining parents' hopes and aspirations for their children[3] and the roles the children are expected to play in the family enhances understanding of adults' motivations for discipline, violent or not. Violent behavior is often motivated by feelings of love and concern. The vast majority of parents had high hopes for their children's futures and almost without exception believed their lives would be better than their own. They cited more opportunities for education, that there would be no further war or the need to migrate, and that Afghanistan would develop.[4] They expected their children to play a role in their communities' and country's development. It was more commonly expressed that Afghanistan's progress would enable sons, rather than daughters, to find good jobs and have greater material wealth than their parents. However, several parents—not necessarily in families where women were already working—discussed their desires for their daughters to find good jobs. Mainly, parents'—particularly mothers'—hopes for their daughters' futures were related to successful marriages. The hope among mothers was that their daughters' husbands would not have more than one wife and that they be economically secure.

Older women described how they had been burdened with many difficulties and problems and both expected and hoped their daughters would have better lives. A few believed their daughters were destined for lives like their own. Bakhat Bibi,[5] an older woman in a relatively poor household in Herat, said, "The daughter wears the mother's shoes. I think they will live like me and suffer as I have suffered in my life."

On a more positive note, a small number of women recounted how they'd had good lives and good marriages and hoped their daughters would too. Some expressed the opinion that there was a general improvement in women's lives over time, that their own lives had been better than their mothers' and that they expected their daughters' lives to be better still.[6]

The most commonly expressed aspiration for children by parents across the eight research sites was that their children, both boys and girls, should go to school and be well educated.[7] Parents, virtually without exception, want their children to be educated and hold formal schooling in high regard. It is not lack of desire for education that prevents people from sending their children to school. Instead, livelihood and the availability of suitable schools are the major hindering factors. Improved material well-being and adults' own experiences of being non-literate are motivating factors, and education is also seen as causing children to eventually become better parents themselves, giving an all-round greater knowledge about how to behave as an adult.

Some people have expectations for their children that go beyond the culturally prescribed norms for gendered behavior and roles, and often reported that their greater awareness of the benefits of education came from what they had seen and learned in other countries when they had migrated.[8] Some women who were not allowed to attend school say they now feel bitter toward their parents. Malika, from a relatively wealthy family, and whose husband, brother-in-law, and sister-in-law are educated, said, "She [my mother] would say . . . 'You are girls and you will get married and go to other people's houses' . . . I tell my mother I will never forgive her for not letting us go to school." With the help of her own children, Malika is learning to read and write, partly motivated by her desire to help them with their homework.

Despite desires of most parents to ensure their children an education, certain factors present obstacles. For girls, the largest obstacles are related to the norms of sex segregation and female seclusion. Girls' access is rarely restricted because family members do not perceive education for girls as desirable; instead, obstacles are located in more practical considerations of social behavioral norms: for example, lack of high schools specifically for girls in rural areas, traveling long distances to school, and lack of women teachers. Girls above a certain age are sometimes also prevented from attaining a complete education. Nazifa in Kabul, a non-literate woman in a poor household, explained that

> it was not our custom for girls to go to school and when one family follows those roles and customs in our area, other families will also do the same; otherwise people will say lots of bad things behind their backs. And because of that, my father didn't let us go to school.

Nevertheless, some of those the research team spoke with had already challenged these norms of gendered behavior and had supported their daughters in completing their schooling.

Children's Roles and Responsibilities in the Family

Boys and girls in most, if not all, households in the four provinces where the research was conducted have paid and/or unpaid work responsibilities. Daughters are expected to undertake domestic work, but some mothers reported doing their best to lighten their daughters' workload to enable them to concentrate on their studies.

While there is some evidence that boys assist their mothers or aunts with domestic work if they do not have sisters or sisters old enough to take on these roles, mainly boys' unpaid household responsibilities include collecting water, bushes, or wood for fuel; running errands; or taking care of animals. In some cases, boys work with their fathers in shops when not in school.[9]

Some children combine work and school, while others are taken out of school altogether in order to work full-time and support their families or engage in unpaid domestic work. Significant numbers of families find survival difficult without the contributions of children's labor. Children play a large role in domestic and other subsistence work within households. It was often stressed that girls have to perform domestic duties not only to contribute to the household, but also as a process of training them to become good wives, daughters-in-law, and mothers. Ensuring that children fulfill these roles was discussed by respondents as a reason for disciplining the children, at times violently. Despite the necessity, real or perceived, of children's work, many families do manage to balance children's paid and unpaid work with their attendance at school, demonstrating how, while immediate survival has to take precedence, many parents nevertheless do not lose sight of their children's futures.

Different Family Members' Roles and Responsibilities for Bringing Up Children

Respondents often quite clearly defined ideal gender roles: men as the family breadwinners and women undertaking the domestic work. However, roles were far less clear about bringing up children in all areas beyond what comes under economically supporting children or doing domestic work for children, such as discipline, providing advice and guidance, caregiving, and so forth. When research teams discussed who in the family is responsible for bringing up and disciplining the children, answers were roughly split between two perspectives across all research sites. First, that both parents had an equal responsibility; and second, that mothers had more responsibility, mostly because they are at home more than fathers, though fathers still had a role to play. More men discussed their roles and responsibilities toward children than women. It was more unusual for women to say that men and women had equal responsibility. This can be explained in part by women seeing themselves as doing more day-to-day work maintaining children, whereas men thought more of the advice and guidance they might give. What is important is that men see themselves as having a very large role to play in raising their children beyond providing for their material needs. It was never said that women had any *natural* qualities that would make them more suitable caretakers of children than men, who expressed an ideal of being equally responsible for bringing up children, although in reality this did not always transfer into how much actual childcare work was done. Saleema, a young woman in Jalalabad, spoke of the care her husband shows toward their son as exceptional:

> I am eighteen years old and I have one son, whose name is Manon; he is very cute and I love him. My husband is also happy and loves him. When my husband comes home at night, my son knows that he is his father and he hugs him and sometimes he sleeps with his son, so both of us are very happy.

A father of eight from rural Kabul told the research team how he plays a large role in the day-to-day work of caring for his children:

> I love my children and I serve them myself because my wife is a little sick and she cannot hear also. So I usually wash their faces in the morning and I prepare water for them. Also I think that those people who think women should do all the work in the house are wrong.

Beyond mothers and fathers, paternal grandmothers were reported to have the largest role to play, particularly in terms of taking care of and nurturing children; sons said that their mothers did nothing except look after their children. Daughters-in-law reported their mothers-in-law helping a lot when their children were small, often taking young children to sleep with them. Paternal grandfathers were also reported to play a significant role, although this was discussed less often. Some people said simply that all adults in the family are responsible for the children.

What Is Accepted, Who Is Beaten, and Who Has the Right to Be Violent

Beating [children] is very common, but it isn't the correct way.
It is 100 percent wrong.
OLDER WOMAN IN URBAN HERAT

Che dab nawi adab nawi. *(If there is no stick, there will be no discipline.)*
PASHTU PROVERB

In both rural and urban areas of all four provinces researched, corporal punishment is accepted as a normal way to parent children. Using violence to discipline children is commonplace. Slapping, ear-pulling, verbal abuse, kicking, punching, and beating with sticks or electricity cables were identified as accepted in response to "naughty behavior."[10] Beating with thin sticks (canes) and slapping children were the most commonly reported punishments, except in Nangarhar, where there was a much stronger emphasis on slapping children and using weapons was mentioned far less overall. Punching and kicking children and throwing stones at them were commonly discussed.

Verbal abuse was not as much discussed, but this is related more to it being seen as less important by respondents or not worth mentioning when they were asked how they discipline their children. People stressed that verbal abuse was commonplace, particularly for women. Some verbal abuse was particularly severe, with, for example, a middle-aged man in Bamiyan telling his children he would bury them in the graveyard and an older woman in rural Kabul reporting that her daughter-in-law tells her children their father has gone to Iran and died. Threats of violence were used, too; for example, a middle-aged man from rural Bamiyan, who is not particularly physically violent to his children, said he threatened to tie up and beat his daughter until she couldn't move because she had fought with the neighbor's daughter.[11]

The most common behaviors for which beating children is perceived as acceptable range from sexual impropriety[12] (particularly for girls, but also for boys) and theft to fighting with other children inside or outside the family, not engaging in productive work, being noisy, making a mess, getting clothes dirty, not doing housework correctly, and refusing to go to school or study after school. Children making noise and running around is often not tolerated. Behavior that is perceived to damage the family's reputation was, for many people, particularly intolerable. Being naughty in front of guests— which might include trying to disturb an adult when they are talking to a guest, or generally playing around in front of a guest—for some parents was the only time they reported hitting their children. Not doing housework correctly was discussed most often as a reason mothers were violent toward their daughters.

Violence toward children as a form of discipline or punishment can begin from a very early age. A rural Herati woman in her mid-twenties with three small children said:

When my son throws water and wastes it, because we bring it with difficulty [I beat him], or I beat him when he makes everything messy or when he makes his clothes dirty . . . My first son is three years old and the second son is small.[13]

An indication of the severity of violence toward children was the fears people held that punishment could seriously injure or even kill them. A woman in Kabul suggested that people shouldn't punch their children, as they may kill them by mistake. A younger man cited medical costs as one reason not to beat girls (and women) too much, "because we are poor and are not able to afford it." Baserat, a father of three from rural Herat, advised people that they could "beat the children with a cane, because the cane causes a lot of pain, but doesn't disable them." One mother from urban Nangarhar said she beat her daughter around the head and for some years her daughter complained of headaches, so she decided not to beat her children on the head anymore. An elderly woman from urban Kabul spoke of how she beat her daughter around the mouth until she bled.

These examples illustrate the severity of violence that children may experience. But it should be noted that inflicting high levels of pain on children or beating people just short of breaking their bones is not generally seen as acceptable.

People were keen to stress that the same types of corporal punishment are used to discipline girl and boy children. Likewise, they emphasized that boys and girls are treated equally when it comes to discipline more generally. Nevertheless, on the whole it was repeated that boys are beaten more often, the rationale being that boys are "naughtier" and have more opportunity to be naughty than girls. A few young women argued that girls are beaten more.[14] Girl and boy children are, to a certain degree, punished for different types of behaviors, with boys being more commonly punished for fighting or not studying and girls for not performing household duties properly.

As with all aspects of family violence studied in this research, men are perceived as having more rights to be violent.[15] Maternal and paternal uncles, older brothers, fathers, and grandfathers are all seen to be entitled to violently punish children. Younger brothers also have a right to be violent to their sisters. However, it was said that sons-in-law did not have a right to beat the children of their in-laws.

These rights or entitlements to be violent to children in the family come with responsibilities. A young woman from Nangarhar argued that it is acceptable for her brother-in-law to beat her children because he cares for them and shows them affection. Brothers are seen to have a particular responsibility to discipline their sisters and police their behavior to ensure they behave in the correct gender-ascribed manner. Shakila in Kabul City explained the rights her son, Shakib, an unmarried college student, has over her daughters:

> My son does not let his sisters wear short clothes when they want to go to school or outside; if they do not accept he beats them. A few days ago, my daughter was baking *bolani* (a stuffed pastry), when my son went into the kitchen and took one. My daughter started shouting and threw out the pot of oil in which she was cooking. My son took a cable and beat my daughter very hard until her feet and hands were black. I said, "Good, beat her because she disrespected you." If today she disrespects her brother, in the future when she goes to her husband's house she will do this with her in-law's family. My son dislikes arguments; he wants others to listen to whatever he says, otherwise he will become angry.

Older brothers also have a right to beat their younger brothers. One man from rural Bamiyan reported that his brother, who is fifteen years older, had beaten him when he was a child and that he was grateful, for the beating must have been for his benefit. Whereas men from a young age have rights to be violent to a wide range of children in their families, women are generally seen as only entitled to be violent to their own children, boys and girls, and to their grandchildren, but not to their co-wives' children. A few exceptions allowed girls to beat their young sisters and, even more rarely, sisters-in-law could punish each other's children.

A woman in rural Kabul said, "A mother has the right to beat her daughters because she gave birth to them, but she doesn't have the right to beat her daughter-in-law." A young woman in Bamiyan explained that the community would condemn a woman who beats her daughter-in-law.

Despite a general agreement among respondents that violence to children in their communities is commonplace, there is also recognition of the harm that physical violence does to children. Not only is short- and long-term physical damage recognized, but so too are the detrimental psychological effects that violence can have on children. Some people related stories of how parents had killed or disabled their children accidentally. Less notable effects of physical violence were also highlighted. Beating children will make them "lose their intelligence," "lose their confidence," or suffer chronic headaches as adults. Two women recognized that long-term violence toward their daughters could make them perpetual victims of violence. One man from rural Bamiyan stated that children "should be beaten, but not so much that they sustain trauma spiritually or physically."

Ideals versus the Reality

Perspectives vary as to what morally correct punishment for children should be. There is also frequently a disjuncture between what people say at different times and how they behave. Community discourses regarding the acceptability of corporal punishment fall into three categories: corporal punishment only as a last resort; corporal punishment as altogether acceptable; all forms of violence to children as unacceptable.

The most common viewpoint expressed by people from all socioeconomic and demographic groups is that corporal punishment should be used as a form of discipline only if verbal warnings have not worked. Some older men in rural Kabul stated that a child should be warned two or three times before they are hit or beaten with a stick. Others expressed the opinion that advice is always best, but if that doesn't work or the children have done something very wrong, they should be slapped. "Beating makes children worse," said one young woman from urban Nangarhar:

> If they do something really bad it is fair to slap them across the face to scare them and ensure they won't repeat the mistake, but at first they should be advised; if they understand their mistakes then they shouldn't be beaten. Children are like flowers. If they are beaten it will affect their health and their minds and they won't be able to learn anything.

There are certain types of behavior that were seen as so deviant—such as stealing, smoking, or gambling—that extreme violence would be the only applicable punishment. Although likely not an everyday event for most families (and therefore not discussed much), perceived sexual impropriety was considered deserving of the most severe punishments. A group of older women in urban Bamiyan argued that it is acceptable to severely beat their daughters "so that she wouldn't be able to get up" for "talking and joking with strange men." Another woman argued that death is the ultimate punishment for this behavior on the part of children, boys and girls. Indeed, people expressed their concerns regarding the potential for not only their daughters to behave in a manner that could bring shame on the family, but also their sons. Some older women in Kabul expressed the opinion that a mother, father, or brother could kill a woman if she had a relationship with a man, although there was disagreement when another woman said it would be better if the parents married the young woman to the man she loves.

A fewer number of respondents expressed the opinion that corporal punishment is an acceptable and effective way to discipline children for a far wider range of behaviors. Some said that it is good to punish children, using violence, for more normal everyday behavior such as being noisy, fighting with other children, and not doing domestic work or not doing it properly. An old man in rural Nangarhar said, "The blessing of those beatings is that some of our youth are educated now."

Across all the provinces, ensuring that children study hard and attend school was extremely important for all those parents the research team spoke with. For those who viewed violence to children as an appropriate form of punishment, this was an area in which they thought it appropriate to beat children—in order to "encourage" them to study. Most of those who expressed a positive opinion of corporal punishment stressed that children should only be slapped or beaten with a small stick and that they should not be injured.

Despite violence to children being obviously prevalent in these communities, a significant number of respondents in all the provinces held the opinion that adults in the family should not be violent. Violence, some said, doesn't necessarily make children behave or become better adults. Normalization of violence to children prevents it from having the desired effect of making them realize they have done something wrong and, as one young woman said, "can make them worse."

Yet there is disjuncture between people's opinions on the rights and wrongs of violence toward children and how they actually behave. Some claim they are against beating children, yet other family members report that they in fact do. Not everyone in the same family agrees on the best way to discipline children or on the appropriateness of using corporal punishment. There are sharp disagreements: for example, the men in the family are opposed to violence, but the women think that children need to be beaten to be well disciplined; the women in the family disagree on how to punish children; there are physical fights and conflicts between co-wives or wives and mothers-in-law.

There is uncertainty about the best ways to discipline children and large contradictions, indeed internal struggles, between people's abstract opinions and how they actually behave toward their children.

Fear and a Lack of Alternatives

Corporal punishment continues to be widely used despite opinions that it is not good for children and a generalized knowledge of its negative consequences and lack of effectiveness. There are two dominant and interrelated motivations for this: parents' fears for their children's futures, and the idea that keeping children frightened of adults makes them behave well. Parents are extremely frightened of their children not growing into good, useful, moral adults. For virtually all the parents, ensuring that their children studied hard and got a good education was uppermost in their concerns. Since violence has been used as the primary way to discipline children for so long, many adult family members are frightened of not using corporal punishment, worried that this will lead to their children not behaving correctly or not becoming the adults they want them to be. The common, if not universal, assumption is that in order to discipline children, the children should be frightened. Nevertheless, it can also be clearly seen that many parents simply do not want to be violent to their children and often regret it later. This regret does not just relate to corporal punishment or more controlled violence, but also to violence to children on the part of adults when they feel stressed, frustrated, or angry. Parents are looking for (though perhaps not actively) alternative ways to discipline their children.

People are willing to find other means of disciplining their children, but beyond "advice," it was rare that people provided other examples of how they disciplined their children. However, a few suggestions were made for alternatives, such as sending a child to collect grass for the cow during a rain (making it a more arduous chore). A man in Jalalabad told how his young daughter wanted to follow her mother to the clinic and was crying and wouldn't stay in the house. Instead of hitting her, he explained how he just held on to her until she calmed down and her mother was out of sight. Another alternative offered was to give children money to encourage them to behave and do their work properly. This, said one young woman in Herat city, is particularly beneficial for boys "for their future; it will teach them to earn money."

In addition to children's misbehavior, perceptions of dishonoring the family or the general daily frustration of adults, such as economic stress, joblessness, and cramped living conditions, were identified as potential causes of stress and frustration. (Women's frustrations with their family relationships were also highlighted as a particular cause of violence toward children in the family.) But it is more important to find reasons why people are violent to children when they feel stressed or frustrated. Awareness of stress management techniques is lacking, and violence to children remains accepted—though not acceptable to all—so people are likely to continue expressing feelings of rage or anger through violence.

A more general change in attitude is needed. Violence to children needs to be conceptualized not only as unacceptable, but also as dishonorable and something to be avoided at all costs, something that is not tolerated by the community.

Key to understanding violence to children in the family is conceptualizing the difference between violence being accepted (as commonplace, normal behavior in most families) versus being perceived as acceptable (morally good behavior on the part of adults toward children). While it is unusual for the community to condemn its members for "everyday violence" to children, many interviewed recognized the harm violence to children can cause and felt it was not the best way.

It is often assumed that the arena of the family is the hardest space to enter in order to overcome violence to children.[16] But this does not preclude people being willing to discuss violence toward children in their families and communities. Throughout this study, it was evident that in a comfortable environment, with researchers who were trusted, men and women of different backgrounds were willing to discuss violence to children in general, as well as particular acts of violence they perpetrated on their own children.

Ways Forward

Any program working to tackle violence toward children must first recognize that there is a general awareness in the communities of the negative consequences of violence to children, and an awareness that violence is not necessarily the best way to discipline or encourage children. Sensitization campaigns should therefore focus on informing people about alternative parenting skills.

- These alternative parenting skills should be designed by organizations working in this field in close collaboration with different communities, in order to ensure that such alternatives are appropriate for the many different Afghan contexts and would be adopted by the different types of Afghan families and communities. It should be ensured, therefore, that alternative non-violent parenting skills should be applicable to each particular Afghan family context.[17]
- Alternative parenting skills need to be transferred, taught, and discussed in communities directly. Influential people within the community would likely be the best to do this, including elders (both male and female), mullahs, community health workers, or teachers.
- The research identified individuals in the community who were particularly opposed to violence to children. These individuals could also be identified by programs aiming to overcome violence to children in the family and

used to spread messages of alternative parenting skills and knowledge of the harm that violence to children causes.

- Programs need to encourage communities to intervene and support those who are violent to children in their efforts to stop the behavior.
- Programs and campaigns need to encourage the community to make a generalized judgment that violence to children will not be accepted in their communities. (Even when people are stressed or feeling frustrated, they are less likely to lash out against children if this behavior does not go ignored or is not accepted as normal in the community.) Enhancing stress management skills and building a greater awareness of the effects of stress in the family would also greatly help to curb violence to children in the family.[18]

Notes

This essay, published in 2008, was originally an issues paper for the Afghanistan Research and Evaluation Unit (AREU), an independent research institute headquartered in Kabul. It was edited and abridged by Jennifer Heath for this book with the kind permission of AREU.

AREU's mission is to inform and influence policy and practice through conducting high-quality, policy-relevant research and actively disseminating the results, and to promote a culture of research and learning. To achieve its mission, AREU engages with policymakers, civil society, researchers, and students to promote their use of AREU's research and its library, to strengthen their research capacity, and to create opportunities for analysis, reflection, and debate. As an impartial Afghanistan-based voice dedicated to research excellence, AREU aspires to contribute to the development of inclusive and transparent policymaking processes, driven by the priorities of the Afghan people, which give rise to better informed policies and programs that improve Afghan lives. AREU was established in 2002 by the assistance community working in Afghanistan and has a board of directors with representation from donors, the United Nations, and other multilateral agencies, and non-governmental organizations. www.areu.org.af.

1. For research methodology, see Deborah J. Smith, "Love, Fear, and Discipline: Everyday Violence toward Children in Afghan Families," Afghanistan Evaluation and Research Unit, February 2008, Section 2, Methodology, 7. For a description of research sites, see Context I: Research Sites, 13.

2. For analytical clarity, violence directed at children in the family is divided into two categories: violence used as a form of discipline or punishment; and violence due to anger, stress, or frustration on the part of the perpetrator. In reality there may be much overlap. Violence toward children is considered here to include "all corporal punishment, and all other cruel, inhuman or degrading acts toward children," as defined in the United Nations Secretary General's Report on Violence Against Children, 2006, www.unicef.org/violencestudy/reports.html, 6. Examples of extreme or more unusual

forms of violence identified include shooting at children, tying them up, washing them in cold water outside during winter, and public humiliation.

3. Children throughout this discussion are those considered to be children by the community, mainly unmarried girls and boys under sixteen.

4. Since 2006, when this research was conducted, there has been a resurgence of the Taliban, and with deepening security concerns, many non-governmental agencies, particularly those working in rural areas, but also those in the cities, have disappeared. Funds have been reduced and many school and health projects have been halted.

5. All names have been changed.

6. For more detailed discussions, see Deborah J. Smith, "Decisions, Desires and Diversity: Marriage Practices in Afghanistan," AREU, February 2009, http://areu .org.af/EditionDetails.aspx?EditionId-35&ContentId=7&ParentId=7, and Deborah J. Smith, "Between Choice and Force: Marriage Practices in Afghanistan," in Jennifer Heath and Ashraf Zahedi, eds., *Land of the Unconquerable: The Lives of Contemporary Afghan Women* (Berkeley: University of California Press, 2011), 162–176.

7. This supports findings from Pamela Hunte, "Looking Beyond the School Walls: Household Decision-Making and School Enrolment in Afghanistan," AREU Briefing Paper, March 2006, http://www.areu.org.af/Uploads/EditionPdfs/607E -Looking%20Beyond%20the%20School%20Walls-BP-print.pdf.

8. Hunte, "Looking Beyond the School Walls," 3. See also chapter 15 in this volume, Mamiko Saito, "Education in Transition: A Key Concern for Young Afghan Returnees."

9. For further information about child labor, please see chapter 7 in this volume, Amanda Sim, "Confronting Child Labor," abridged from Amanda Sim, "Confronting Child Labour in Afghanistan," AREU Briefing Paper, May 2009, http://www.areu .org.af/Uploads/EditionPdfs/925E-Confronting%20Child%20Labour-BP-print.pdf.

10. The use of electricity cables was rarely discussed outside urban and rural areas of Kabul and Herat.

11. Not only was little difference found between the types of punishments against children in different provinces, but little difference was found between rural and urban areas or between poorer and wealthier households.

12. In the Afghan context, sexual impropriety may include such acts as smiling or talking to a member of the opposite sex who is not a member of the immediate family.

13. Corporal punishment being used against children as young as two or three is supported by statements made by others across different research sites.

14. Young men felt strongest that they were punished more often, and their opinion is likely to be based on their own experiences of violence. It is likely that many men are unaware of the levels of violence that girls receive from their mothers in the house, which would explain why it is only women who report higher levels of violence being directed toward girls. Other perceptions around girls being weak, pitiable, or more easily frightened led to some people, predominantly older men, saying that they do not beat girls as hard as they beat boys.

15. There exists a difference between people perceiving someone in the family to have a *right*, as in an entitlement, to beat a child, and perceiving violence on the part of that person to be morally just or acceptable. E.g., a woman argues she has the right to beat her children and grandchildren and, if she wants, to kill her own children. How-

ever, this does not necessarily mean she thinks killing her children is a morally correct thing for a mother to do.

16. This is clearly expressed in the United Nations Secretary General's Report on Violence against Children: challenging violence against children is most difficult in the context of the family in all its forms. There is a reluctance to intervene in what is still perceived in most societies as a "private sphere."

17. Alternative parenting skills and methods for disciplining children were discussed with stakeholders (the vast majority being Afghan themselves) during working group discussions at a conference in Kabul, organized by AREU, and at workshops in Bamiyan, Herat, and Nangarhar organized by the Afghan Independent Human Rights Commission in partnership with AREU. Suggestions were made as to what forms of nonviolent parenting would be applicable for the Afghan context.

18. While this research did not focus on Afghanistan's national-level policy in regard to violence toward children in the family, and hence does not offer corresponding policy recommendations, the author would also strongly recommend changes in the law to specifically outlaw violence to children in the family. Afghanistan became a "state party" to the United Nations Convention on the Rights of the Child on 27 April 1994, but the provisions of the convention have not been codified in Afghan law. The convention holds that state parties "shall take all appropriate legislative, administrative, social and educational measures to protect the child from all forms of physical or mental violence, injury or abuse, neglect or negligent treatment, maltreatment or exploitation, including sexual abuse, while in the care of parent(s), legal guardian(s) or any other person who has the care of the child" (Article 19:1); "shall take all effective and appropriate measures with a view to abolishing traditional practices prejudicial to the health of children" (Article 24:3); "shall ensure that: (a) No child shall be subjected to torture or other cruel, inhuman or degrading treatment or punishment" (Article 37); and "shall take all appropriate measures to promote physical and psychological recovery and social reintegration of a child victim of: any form of neglect, exploitation, or abuse; torture or any other form of cruel, inhuman or degrading treatment or punishment; or armed conflicts. Such recovery and reintegration shall take place in an environment which fosters the health, self-respect and dignity of the child" (Article 39) (U.N. General Assembly, Document A/RES/44/25 [12 December 1989]). For a fuller discussion of these issues, see Global Initiative to End All Corporal Punishment for Children (2006), Ending Legalised Violence Against Children.

CHAPTER 5

Children Who Live with Their Mothers in Prison

ESTHER HYNEMAN

In 2009, I was in the nursery of Badam Bagh, then a new women's prison in Kabul. The prison held about 100 prisoners and sixty-five children—babies in cradles, toddlers teetering in tiny walkers, children as old as thirteen running around. Suddenly an eleven-year-old boy rushed up to my translator: "Please help me," he pleaded in Dari. "I have to get out of here."

As a matter of fact, we—Women for Afghan Women (WAW)—were planning to get him out. We hoped to move this boy, Mortazar, and all children over five who were living with their mothers in the Kabul prison, into a residence (eventually called the Children's Support Center [CSC]). I told him this; I promised help was coming, but he didn't seem to believe me and wandered away. Maybe he couldn't wait another minute, and who could blame him. His mother was serving sixteen years for murdering her stepson, and for years Mortazar and his three siblings had been jerked between prison and orphanages. WAW was waiting for a grant from the European Commission to open the residence, and I needed to figure out how many would be eligible for admission.[1]

This wasn't easy. In a country where the majority of people are non-literate, where birth records may never have existed or may be buried in the rubble left by decades of war and chaos, the actual age of children is often in doubt. I also hoped to get some sense of who these children were, how damaged they might be after having spent much of their lives confined to prisons and orphanages.[2] In the months before WAW received the money and could start preparing the facility, I was afraid Mortazar had been sent back to the orphanage and we wouldn't be able to get him out. But readers can stop worrying. He's thriving in the Kabul CSC, the first residence/educational center WAW opened in late 2009 for children over five who were living with their mothers in the Kabul prison.[3]

We first discovered that children live with mothers in prison in Afghanistan in 2003, when we visited the women's prison in Kandahar, where conditions can only be described as inhuman. But that was not long after the fall of the Taliban regime in 2001, when much of Afghanistan was in ruins. By 2008, when our first Family Guidance Centers (FGCs)[4] were flourishing in Kabul and Mazar, when reconstruction was transforming Kabul into a real if shabby city complete with computer stores and Internet cafes, WAW executive director Manizha Naderi decided it was time to take another look at the prisons, and I, as a WAW board member, made a visit to the notorious prison outside Kabul, Pul-e-Charki. A massive fortress-like structure brooding over a treeless plain, Pul-e-Charki was built in the 1970s but looked like a relic from the Middle Ages. Now spruced up and housing only male prisoners, it was then a home for female inmates as well, a filthy, stinking place pulsating with pain and rage.[5]

There were no cells or bars in the women's side of Pul-e-Charki. Instead, large rooms with bunk beds and a crude stove were home for twelve to fourteen inmates and their kids. The toilets were holes in a concrete floor that was crusted with feces. The prisoners graciously arranged mats for me on the floors of their cold and damp dormitory-like rooms so we could sit together and talk. Children were batting each other around, imitating, said the prison director, the behavior of the adult inmates. Guards said the children earned money by doing chores. The single classroom was dark and dank and reeked of mold. Teachers from the Afghan Women's Educational Council (AWEC) trudged there several times a week to teach literacy to women and children, but learning could not happen in such a place. There were no government allotments for children's food, clothing, beds, or blankets, so mothers and other inmates shared whatever they received. Some necessities came from donors, non-governmental organizations (NGOs), and the few family members who visited female inmates there.

The children are from one of the poorest countries in the world, from wretched personal backgrounds defined by community and family violence, a society traumatized by war, social chaos, and continued insecurity. Having to spend years in prison is just one more insult to their already battered psyches.

The Problem

The fact that children are confined to prisons anywhere probably comes as a shock to most people in the United States, as it did to WAW members visiting the Kandahar prison. Before writing the proposal for a grant to open the

CSC, we wrote a concept paper that called the practice of having children live in prison with their mothers inhumane. Then we discovered that in most countries of the world, developed and undeveloped countries alike, it is accepted as the enlightened way to go. Since the 1990s, for example, children born to women in prisons in Mexico City have been *required* to stay with their mothers until they're six.[6] When we wrote the actual proposal a few months later, we referred to the U.S. as one of the few countries where this humane practice is rarely permitted.

But how humane is it? Developed countries try to create nurseries where professional caretakers provide a relatively healthy environment. Medical care is supposed to be available at all times. In 2009, when I was doing research in preparation for the WAW CSC, I calculated that children in European prisons were transferred out—to families, foster homes, orphanages—at the average age of three.[7] This policy allows them to bond with their parent during the early years of life, which psychologists the world over regard as crucial to the development of trust, self-esteem, and the ability to love. Some claim the presence of their children improves the often-fragile mental condition of the mothers, and maybe it does, but if the children are damaged by living in prison, how can the policy be defended? Some feminists believe the enforced separation of mothers and babies is one more form of violence against women and an abuse of our power over children.[8]

Surely when the policy applies to children beyond a certain age, negatives outweigh the positives: confinement to one location; lack of exposure to the outside world and to variety;[9] the society of women who are angry, maybe violent, often depressed; exposure to women of dubious character, to sexual activity among the prisoners and often prisoners and guards. In fact, some experts say children of parents who have been sentenced to prison are six times more likely than other youth to land in prison at some point in their own lives, and the situation may be worse for those who have lived in prison with incarcerated mothers.[10] And then, the cruel trauma of eventually being wrested from the mother and sent who knows where. When we weigh the pros against the cons, we do not arrive at a policy we can be confident about (except that fewer mothers of children should be sentenced to prison to begin with). Ideas about what is right and wrong, or just better or worse for the children, crumble like stale bread, one after the other.

All children pay heavily for the crimes of their incarcerated parents, wherever they live in the world. But children of incarcerated mothers in Afghanistan, recently named the most dangerous country in the world for women by gender experts, may be among the most vulnerable of all.[11] For in Afghanistan, unemployment is rampant, poverty dire, children often have to support widowed mothers and orphaned siblings, millions aren't in school because there is no school in or near their village, or there's a school but no teacher. In some prisons there is a makeshift school, but children rarely attend it.

In Afghanistan, the stigma inevitably attached to these children makes matters worse. Many children in Afghan prisons are strangers and embarrassments to their families, who often reject them as juvenile embodiments of the mother's crime, emblems of the family's shame, especially if they're the result of rape or adultery, even if the mother is innocent or has been sentenced to prison for a non-crime like running away from abuse.[12]

WAW shelters have received hundreds of underage females who are not the children of convicted women but who have been forced into marriage, grossly inappropriate marriages at that, who have been sold, beaten, starved, tortured. Right now, we are caring for a fourteen-year-old girl who was given in *baad*[13] at the age of three and raped by her husband's uncle when she was ten. The rape tore her vagina, which had to be repaired by a doctor. She told her caseworker that no one in the hospital, not even the doctor, asked her what caused her injuries. At ten she was married. Within two years her husband divorced her, and she was married off to the brother of the rapist. Beaten and regularly ridiculed, she finally escaped with the help of a neighbor and made it to WAW's FGC. The husband is involved with the Taliban, and family members are armed and dangerous. About two years ago, a thirteen-year-old girl, who had been forced into marriage, was found locked in a room for five months because she refused to earn money for her in-laws by becoming a prostitute. They had pulled out her fingernails and prodded her with electrified wires and hot pokers; her body was raw from bruises. She may never recover mentally.[14]

Mothers in prison know these horrors only too well, and not from TV or articles in newspapers. They have experienced them personally and witnessed them in their own families. No wonder many have tried to protect their children by keeping them in prison. From Badam Bagh, where she was serving a term for kidnapping, Jamila[15] begged us to take her three children into the CSC although they were living with her family, not in prison. The family had not let them visit her for two and a half years or allowed them to attend school, which was just a few blocks from their house. The children were their servants. Jamila was afraid they'd force the oldest girl into marriage.

Moreover, there's no tradition of foster care in Afghanistan. Mothers fear that families who take these children in may abuse them, subject them to domestic enslavement and other forms of maltreatment, traffic them for labor and/or sex. While boys are also trafficked and abused around the world, far more girls than boys suffer such fates, especially in Afghanistan.[16]

National orphanages are not a solution even though many children of mothers in prison are shifted in and out of them. They are jammed full, but not necessarily with orphans, even those who fit the Afghan definition of the term. Families, especially poor families or those from areas that lack schools, wangle their children into orphanages hoping they'll be taken care of and get an education to boot. NGO reports have claimed that mismanagement in the national facilities often results in their running out of money before the end of their fiscal year and closing down in the middle of winter, forcing the children out at the worst possible time. They document substandard conditions in public orphanages—no clean water, no heat in winter months, poor and meager food, and rampant corruption: donated goods are sold; children are abused; girls are raped and even prostituted. In 2009, parents in Badam Bagh told this writer that when children over seven years old were evicted from some prisons in conformity with the new law, they ended up living with siblings, many of whom were still children themselves.[17] After the Kabul CSC opened, NGO, ministry, and prison officials in several provinces begged WAW executive director Manizha Naderi to take children from prisons in their provinces because conditions in them were unfit for human life.[18]

Despite the hazards of sending children back to their villages and families, when we asked UNICEF in Afghanistan[19] at meetings in 2009 and 2010 to support our plan to open a residence for those in Badam Bagh and even partner with us, the agency flatly refused. Their position: all children in orphanages and prisons should be sent back to their villages because Afghanistan is a family-oriented society. "Even though the country that awards its highest value to the family awards the lowest to females?" we asked. "Even though most families and villages don't want them? Even though there are no schools in most rural communities? Who would pay for the army of social workers needed to monitor these children? Who would train them? Who would oversee them?"

Huge areas of Afghanistan are barely accessible, and some are controlled by insurgents, who do not take kindly to individuals working for the government. Many monitors, especially those who are poor and underpaid, might pocket their salaries and write reports on children they never saw. Well-meaning but apparently misguided, UNICEF had no answers to these questions. They had made up their collective mind, they told me, and could not be swayed.

Women for Afghan Women's Children's Support Centers: Mostly Pluses

In 2009, the Afghan Ministry of Labor, Social Affairs, Martyrs, and Disabled (MoLSAMD)—overwhelmed by the claims on its limited resources of millions of children and adults at risk from poverty, abuse, and other social diseases—decided to evict children over seven from the prisons. Officials might have been moved by concern for their welfare, but mothers in Badam Bagh wrote MoLSAMD to protest. They did not want their children sent to orphanages or to their families. They asked MoLSAMD to come up with a solution they could accept. MoLSAMD did not have one, but WAW did.

"There is now an oasis for some of these kids. In a quiet neighborhood . . . Women for Afghan Women . . . has created a fairy-tale home, the Children's Support Center, with [sixty-six] children currently in residence."[20] To accommodate the growing population of children living in prison, since it opened in late 2009, the Kabul CSC has twice had to move from its original facility to larger quarters. It now consists of three buildings—a dormitory for boys, one for girls, and a building for offices and classrooms. In mid-2011, WAW opened a CSC in Mazar-i-Sharif, which today houses and educates sixty-six children from prisons in Balkh, Jawzjan, Samangan, Sar-e-Pul, and Faryab, and a center in Kunduz, which now cares for sixty-five children from prisons in Kunduz, Takhar, and Badakhshan. Education, starting with an accelerated learning program, and mental health are the focal points.

Children arrive at the centers in a rage, sometimes a murderous rage. They suffer from anxiety, depression, obsession, and plain fear. They go on crying jags, withdraw, won't cooperate, disrespect teachers, destroy office and personal property, lie, swear, steal, and fight. But this behavior changes fast. The questions are how and why.

Surely their transformation to civility begins with the innate resilience of the children themselves. And leaving the hated prison is a major factor; many resist returning even for one day a month to visit their mothers. Lovely little Gulabo had to be pried from the tree she wrapped herself around whenever it was time to board the bus, and she cried hysterically all the way to Badam Bagh. She was haunted by memories of her life there and afraid we'd abandon her. Ahmad Zia, a seven-year-old boy in the Mazar CSC, said,

> I don't have exact information about the crime, but I know my mother, who committed adultery, can be jailed, and I also went with her. I love my mother. I hated life in prison. I was always hoping that someday they will get me out. After one year, they took me to WAW's Children's Support Center

in Mazar, and I have been living there for months. I used to be illiterate, but now I am in school. I learned during my first four months here.[21]

Another boy told his mother, "They made me human there."

In fact, the children have been starving for education, not necessarily for the subject matter although most know if they can't read and write, they are doomed to poverty and hardship and perhaps crime. Their enthusiasm for school suggests that being deprived of education maximized their feelings of shame and unworthiness as children of prisoners. Put pencils in their hands and books in their book bags, sit them in a classroom, praise them when they make progress, and they become different beings, self-confident. They have hope for their futures. They have value.

The CSC facilities themselves contribute to the transformation. Children emerge in rags from months or years of confinement in prisons that are squalid, freezing cold, or sweltering, with broken plumbing or no electricity, most lacking basic services. Their mothers and WAW caseworkers have told them where they're going, but they are bewildered. What do they know about boarding schools? Depending on where the prison is, they have a short or long trip in a van, maybe across a province before they arrive at the center, a place they could not have imagined, especially those who have been in prison since infancy. It is bright and cheerful, designed for children, immaculate, supplied with books, a small library, a computer room, classrooms, a dining room where kids eat three solid meals a day prepared by a good cook, entertainment areas, staff offices, a playground, vans to transport them on trips to the prison to visit mothers. There are caretakers on duty in the CSCs twenty-four hours a day, and they accompany the children to and from school. All children are clean and well dressed and look like any kids in the world on the way to school, with big book bags jammed with required school materials hanging off their backs.

Trained teachers teach children who are not ready to enter public school in the CSC accelerated learning classes (which use the Ministry of Education curriculum) until they pass public school entrance exams. Because in Afghanistan there are far too few public schools to accommodate the number of students enrolled, the Afghan class day is divided into two sessions. So kids in Afghanistan attend school for about four hours a day. Therefore, CSC teachers supplement their education with English and computer skills classes, tutoring sessions, and help with homework. A full-time psychologist works with kids in groups and individually.

To find out what goes on in the CSC from the student-resident's point of view, I went directly to a former resident for information: Nilab Nusrat, an eighteen-year-old girl who spent three years in the Kabul CSC and who is now on a four-year full scholarship at the Putney School in Vermont.[22]

Nilab had a lot to say:

> When they first arrive, the children aren't like the kids who have been there for a while. They're disrespectful and cause lots of problems. Then they become very friendly. They say to other kids, if I make mistakes, please let me know. All of them have experienced bad abuse and this transformation is wonderful. The kids are from different ethnicities, but unlike adults, they don't fight over that, Tajiks against Pashtuns. We become brother and sister. Forget Tajik, Hazara. We need to be a family. You can teach me Pashto, I will teach you Dari. Older kids, the ones there longer, are the leaders and want the newer children to become the next leaders.
>
> The way they talk, how polite they are; they are not like other kids in Afghanistan. They're very friendly, like families should be. When I went to my aunt's house for a visit, I noticed that my cousins are very bad by comparison.
>
> Children who have been in the CSC for a while have learned a lot about good behavior from the staff and from each other. If new arrivals make mistakes, other children scold them. All the children are role models, even younger ones are leaders for each other. When some feel very upset and sad, others say to them, sometimes we feel very sad too, but you should play games, study, play with us. They say very mature things.

Nilab first met Mortazar's older sister Nargis in a WAW shelter before the CSC opened.[23] Nargis wouldn't talk to anyone. WAW put her in a private school a few blocks away with two younger clients, but she was ashamed because she was in a class with little kids. When the FGC director heard this, she transferred Nargis to public school, where she was in a higher grade. Six months later, the CSC opened and she settled in. Once there, she changed. Teachers talked to her about being withdrawn. She sat in accelerated learning classes and went to a private English language course. Now she is in the seventh grade and wants to take the exam to skip a grade. She studies. She wears beautiful clothes her mother gets for her.[24] She is serious, says Nilab, "but not as serious as I am.[25] She doesn't try hard in her studies, but she is friendly with other kids. The CSC is a very friendly place for everyone."

All the children love Sikander Halimi, the CSC full-time psychologist and father figure, whose program includes individual and group therapy, storytelling, drama, drawing, games, supervised play—a grab bag of techniques developed by child psychologists the world over. Nilab emphasized his methods: his group and private sessions, how he consults the children about what they want to study in the winter when public schools are closed, how he listens, always speaks the truth, never says negative things to students or demands that they do something. When kids first arrive and cry a lot, he never scolds them. Two six-year-old boys fought all the time. Finally other boys their age said, don't you remember, Sikander told us not to fight. And they stopped.[26]

Fawzia was also in the WAW shelter with Nilab and Nargis, but unlike them, she had been a shelter client. She had been raped in her village when she was five years old. When her father, a non-literate peasant from Badakhshan, brought her to us via a two-day rickety bus ride, he sat down on the concrete in the FGC courtyard and cried, "I want justice for my daughter."

It took a few years for Fawzia to emerge from her shell, leave rage behind, stop fighting everyone, and begin to study. We feared she might never transcend the trauma or thrive in school, but she has done both. Her intelligence is intact; she is the top student in CSC and public school classes. She always has a book and notebook in her hand, and she has become popular. She goes home on vacations, and her father visits her regularly. He is overcome with pride for his daughter, the first person in his family who can read and write.

Shahbibi Halimi, who manages the Kabul facility with an iron fist and profound empathy for her charges, said that when the children behave badly, they often come to the administration and say, "I am so sorry," and they don't do it again. Newcomers learn to imitate the behavior of children who have lived in the CSC for a while and no longer behave like budding criminals. One mother asked us to take her fifteen-year-old son, although he was not living in prison. She said he had behavior problems, was using drugs. In the CSC, teachers and Sikander worked with him, and his behavior changed—180 degrees, said Shahbibi. After one year in the residence, he went to work as a logistics person in an office. He recently married and invited all the CSC staff to the wedding. Of course Shahbibi was there.

Our teachers and caretakers struggle with the children's behavior when they first arrive. But after four to six months in our accelerated learning program, they are ready to attend public school. They become focused on education and progress so quickly that we struggle only to satisfy their hunger to learn.

The Big Minus: Sending the Children to
Their Mothers and Whatever Awaits Them

When a mother is being released, CSC staff deliver her child or children to the prison. Most students don't want to leave the CSC, and many mothers don't want to take their children then because they have no way of supporting them. Most are not literate and have no income-generating skills. Many families reject them because they have been convicted of adultery and other moral crimes. They are pariahs who lack the wherewithal to start over. Some are forced to resume their criminal lives, so their children are also in trouble. An officer in the prison told me in 2009 that many end up on the streets, where they eventually die violent deaths—although there are no statistics to verify this claim.

So many mothers bring the children back to the CSC until they figure out a solution.

During CSC's first year, five mothers were released from prison; eighteen were released the second year. All together, we returned fifty-five children to them. Of those, seventeen children have come back. Some had no place to live; others returned to villages that lack schools.

Letting the children go, sending them back to what may be an unhealthy, even toxic, environment—children who have made extraordinary progress in a short time—is the negative of an otherwise inspired endeavor, a negative that hangs like a cloud over the project, the big minus. The children have learned a new way of living. They've been visiting their mothers in prison all along; some have grown to be their parents' advisors.

As compensation for their crime, Gulabo's father wanted to give her as payment to the family he and his wife injured (a baad transaction). When his wife refused, he smashed her over the head with a boulder in the prison yard, and she has never been the same. Beautiful Gulabo says, "I hate my face because I look like my father." When her damaged, erratic mother left prison, Gulabo was brought to her. We do not know where they are or how they are doing. She haunts my mind.

Shukria's mother, who was convicted of prostitution, had forced Shukria to sell her body when she was seven or eight years old and was one of the only mothers who did not want her daughter in the CSC. To protect Shukria, now eighteen, from being forced into prostitution again when her mother leaves prison, WAW petitioned the court to award us temporary custody and won. Meanwhile, Shukria was accepted into the Putney School in Vermont and WAW raised money for the tuition. But the consular section of the U.S. Embassy in Kabul has denied her three applications for a visa on the grounds that once in the U.S., she would apply for political asylum rather than return to Afghanistan (to a mother who had prostituted her!).

But WAW cannot become a guardian for all children at risk. We send most into the arms of loving mothers, but even the loving mother may lack the psychological and material resources and the opportunities to turn her life around or protect herself and her children from abuse. Few people in the developed world can fathom the almost insurmountable odds against a woman, especially an ex-convict, establishing an independent life in Afghanistan. And how far the lessons the children have learned in the CSC will go to protect them is anyone's guess. We do not have the money or staff to monitor them when they leave, and the number of children leaving the CSC increases each year. Once their mothers leave prison and the children rejoin them, sometimes less than a year after arriving, we do not know whether they regress or hold on to the progress they've made.

Throughout our years in Afghanistan, we have walked a trail with prominent markers. Problem A pointed to problem B, which pointed to problem C: violence against individual women and girls led us to create Family Guidance Centers and shelters; clients' stories of hellish conditions led us to open the CSCs, which led us to create Transitional Houses for mothers transitioning from the safety of prison into lives fraught with danger. We have now opened four of these residences where women can develop the resources they need to lead independent lives, eventually support themselves and their children, perhaps live communally for safety.[27] Some may become role models, examples to women who have everything to be afraid of until they discover their own power, which is potentially enormous if now still dormant.

Coda

Unfortunately, much of what I have written in this chapter will feed the widespread view of Afghanistan as a country locked permanently in a medieval time warp, brutally misogynist and cruel to children, especially female children. People express their disgust with this unfortunate country in crude comments tacked on to articles they read that accentuate its worst aspects and omit the positives. "Some countries are just bent that way, no matter how many wars you start or money you spend, it wouldn't make much difference. Prior to 9/11, Afghanistan was stuck in 1810, ten years later they have moved up slightly to 1811. In fifty years' time, they would still be stuck in the 19th century. Give it up. . . ."[28]

A few comparisons might soften that view, comparisons even with countries like the United States, where statistics on child abuse, domestic violence, and the murder of women by intimates, on government and corporate corruption, may be far lower than Afghanistan's but are surely reprehensible in a country that should do much better. The chief point I want readers to take with them after reading about these Afghan children and the CSCs is something most do not know but should think about before they decide on the U.S. role in that country. It's this: there has been progress in Afghanistan, progress in many areas, but especially toward human rights for women and children. Progress despite enormous odds, despite what talking heads and media addicted to sensationalism have been telling you. Progress in what is actually a brief time: ten years to rebuild a shattered country from the ground up, to turn around a culture that had been lagging behind the modern world to begin with and was then deprived of education, music, books, everything necessary for freedom to flourish. During the same time, the great New York City struggled to rebuild just the World Trade Center.

When you factor in what Afghanistan has endured for almost a half century, this progress compares favorably with progress women have made in many developed countries. Most Swiss men may not have treated women the way some Afghan men treat them, but unlike Afghanistan, which gave suffrage to women in 1965, the Swiss didn't give women the vote until 1971, and then some cantons resisted until 1990.

The more than fourteen shelters operating in Afghanistan are a concrete sign of progress.[29] So is the help, the access to justice, Women for Afghan Women and other women's rights NGOs gain for thousands of women and girls each year. With more donations and grants we could help more. Add the Law on the Elimination of Violence Against Women, written by courageous Afghan women's rights activists and signed by Karzai in 2009,[30] and include WAWs, CSCs, and Transitional Houses for women leaving prison. The clamor in the U.S. to leave Afghanistan may be based on economic issues and war weariness, but it is often bolstered by the erroneous belief that no progress has taken place or will ever take place there. Take WAW's word for it: progress has happened because the people want it. It will continue to happen as long as security is maintained and women's rights workers, like WAW's 470 staff members, all of them local Afghans, all of them risking their lives to gain better lives for their fellow citizens, can continue their work in safety.

Despite the hardships they have suffered, the children I have written about in this chapter are exactly like the children in the U.S. They may not start from the same point, but given the chance, they study the same subjects, watch the same cartoons and movies, dance to similar music, obsess over computers, try to outsmart adults in the same ways. They are not living in 1811. They are seeds planted in soil worked up in the twenty-first century; they are the future of Afghanistan and the world.

Notes

1. Many things have changed since this essay was written several years ago. WAW has now opened three Children's Support Centers in three provinces. When a fourth opens in Herat in early 2014, WAW will be taking almost every child over five years old out of all prisons in Afghanistan. Children remain in the Jalalabad prison because the road from the Kabul CSC to the prison, where they would have to visit their mothers every month, is infested with Taliban and very dangerous. The boy Mortazar (now a strapping young man) and his siblings left the CSC to live with their mother when Karzai granted her a pardon and she was released from prison.

2. In Afghanistan, an orphan is a child without a father, a definition that illuminates the status of women in the country and is consistent with the law that divorced mothers must hand over to the ex-husband all male children when they're seven and female children when they're nine. Many divorced mothers never see their children again.

3. For more about the legal protection of children and women in Afghanistan, see chapter 10, Hangama Anwari, "Legal Protection: Offering Aid and Comfort," in this volume.

4. WAW's Family Guidance Centers, now in nine provinces, provide counseling, family mediation, and legal representation in court to women/girls who have experienced human rights abuses of all kinds.

5. I once stood in the sleet in a prison courtyard watching workers on the men's side shovel slimy food from vats in the bed of a pickup truck into pails teetering on the concrete below. It was hit or miss with the food.

6. In the early 1990s, Mexico City decided that children born in prison should stay with their mothers until they were six rather than being turned over to relatives or foster parents. The children are allowed to leave on weekends and holidays to visit relatives. James C. McKinley Jr., "Mexico City Kids Share Moms' Prison Existence," *Chicago Tribune*, February 6, 2008, http://articles.chicagotribune.com/2008-02-06 /features/0802040112_1_prison-mothers-jungle-gym. For more on the pros and cons of children living with mothers in prison, see "Children Living in Prison With a Parent," Prison Fellowship International, http://www.pfi.org/cjr/human-rights/vulner able-populations/children-in-prison/living-with-parents; and Oliver Robertson, *Children Imprisoned by Circumstance*, Quaker United Nations Office, Human Rights and Refugees publications, April 2008, http://www.quno.org/geneva/pdf/humanrights /women-in-prison/200804childrenImprisonedByCircumstance-English.pdf.

7. To calculate that average, I relied on figures published in Marlene Alejos, "Babies and Small Children Residing in Prisons," Quaker United Nations Office, March 2005, and information in an array of articles on policies in individual countries. Very likely policies in some of those countries have changed since that time. Whether children should live with their mothers in prison, how long they should remain there, where they should go when they leave, what causes the greatest damage to their psy-

ches—bonding with mothers and then being taken from them or being denied the opportunity to bond—are questions that cannot be answered definitively.

8. Sheila Kitzinger, "Mothers and Babies in Prison," http://www.sheilakitzinger .com/Prisons.htm. Sheila Kitzinger is a birth activist who campaigns for women, providing the information they need to make choices about childbirth. She is honorary professor at Thames Valley University, where she teaches the master's in midwifery in the Wolfson School of Health Sciences.

9. Some prisons allow children to visit relatives. The school in the otherwise-squalid Jalalabad women's prison is quite attractive, but guards said it rarely sees students. We were not there long enough to verify this unwelcome information, but one seven-year-old girl, who was born in the prison and who had never been outside its narrow confines, told me she knew what a school actually looks like because she had seen one on TV.

10. Zadock Angira, "Kenya: Hundreds of Children Under Four Live in Prison With Their Mothers," All Africa, February 2012, http://allafrica.com/stories/2012 02220081.html.

11. Two hundred and thirteen gender experts from five continents ranked countries by overall perceptions of danger as well as by six risks: health threats, sexual violence, non-sexual violence, cultural or religious factors, lack of access to resources, and trafficking. "Afghanistan emerged as the most dangerous country for women overall and worst in three of the six risk categories: health, non-sexual violence and lack of access to economic resources." "Afghanistan 'Most Dangerous Place for Women': Survey Says War-Torn Nation Worst Place for Women While Congo, Which Has 'Horrific Levels of Rape,' Is Ranked Second," Al-Jazeera, June 15, 2011, http://www.aljazeera .com/news/asia/2011/06/201161582525243992.html.

12. Many women are in prison for having committed adultery (the crime of *zena*), which can earn the couple a seven-year sentence. The male may not be sentenced or may bribe his way out of jail. Many women who are raped are re-victimized. They are usually assumed to be guilty of having attracted the man or consented anyway—a view that dominated the U.S. judiciary system until the women's movement set the record straight. The Afghan woman will be released from prison if she agrees to marry the rapist, provided that he agrees as well. In any case, a woman who is in prison for a moral crime has shamed the family, and the child of this illicit act will bear the brunt.

13. A now-illegal but still widespread custom that requires one family to hand over a piece of property to a family it has injured as restitution for the crime and to cleanse the bad blood. Since girls are considered property, they are often the payment. The transfer of the young girl(s) is usually permanent. She will be married to a man in the new family and often treated like a slave.

14. Graham Bowley, "Three In-laws of Afghan Girl 15 Are Held in Her Torture," *New York Times*, Asia Pacific, January 2, 2012; Jawad Sukhanyar, "The Road to Recovery for Sahar Gul," *New York Times*, June 2, 2012. We thought she would never recover mentally, but after almost two years in a WAW facility, Sahar Gul is well on her way to recovery. Early in 2013, the perpetrators of this heinous crime were illegally released from prison. Kimberly Motley, a lawyer in Afghanistan who was working with WAW on the case, petitioned the Supreme Court of Afghanistan to return the guilty family members to prison. The court found mostly in our favor.

15. Some names have been changed to protect the subjects.

16. This information has a variety of sources: seven years of experience with underage girls who have sought refuge in WAW shelters, the backgrounds of children gathered by staff in WAW's Children's Support Center, discussions with their mothers in prison and with the head of Badam Bagh.

17. Rod Nordland, "Orphans' Defender Jostles With Afghan Corruption," *New York Times*, December 31, 2011. See also http://wikileaks.org/cable/2009/11/09KA BUL3811.html.

18. We do not want the information in this paragraph to poison the reader's mind against Afghanistan. Conditions in public orphanages the world over have often been scandalously substandard. Further, NGOs in Afghanistan such as PARSA, led by Marnie Gustavson, have been working for several years to improve conditions in orphanages in Afghanistan. And according to Wikileaks cables, Deputy Minister Wasil Noor (Ministry of Social Affairs) has been determined to provide acceptable care for the children. WAW's experiences with Minister Noor over the years have always been productive and supportive, and we trust his intentions, if not the ministry's capacity in terms of finances and staff, to make all necessary improvements.

19. At meetings in the UNICEF headquarters in 2009 and 2010.

20. Elizabeth Rubin, "Studio Kabul," *New York Times*, October 21, 2010, http://www .nytimes.com/2010/10/24/magazine/24SoapOpera-t.html?_r=1&pagewanted=all.

21. Told to WAW intern Christina Vargas in an interview at the CSC in the summer of 2011.

22. WAW brought Nilab to New York City to speak at our tenth anniversary gala in October 2011. She received a standing ovation; there wasn't a dry eye in the house when she spoke about her life experiences. WAW knew that a few years earlier Putney had accepted a boy from Afghanistan, so we approached them about Nilab and brought her there for an interview. She was accepted immediately and is thriving.

23. Zarafshan, the director of Badam Bagh, pleaded with us to take Nargis out of the prison because she was afraid of what would happen to her there. She wouldn't specify, but she suggested that it was sexual, and I surmised she worried about a possible seduction by a female prisoner. The CSC hadn't opened yet, but we took her into the shelter. Then Zarafshan begged me to take Nilab to the shelter as well. Nilab was living with her mother's relatives, who didn't like her or her siblings and wouldn't let them attend school.

24. When her mother was released from prison, she worked in a hospital while living at the new WAW Transitional House in Kabul. At her request, her four children (among them, Mortazar) remained in the CSC. The family is now living together somewhere in Kabul.

25. Few kids anywhere in the world are as driven as Nilab to succeed in school and after. Nargis can probably do better, but the comparison may be unfair.

26. Sikander is not a licensed child psychologist. Such professionals are few and far between in Afghanistan, where colleges and universities were closed for years and all books were burned by the Taliban. Shahbibi Halimi, his mother and the gifted manager of the CSC, convinced us to try him out. He's wonderful with children, she said, and she was right.

27. Women who live alone in Afghanistan are soon marked as prostitutes and suffer the consequences of that identity—most likely death. Women with children have a somewhat easier time.

28. Comment by Zorroremade at end of DATABLOG, "10 Years in Afghanistan: The Data Showing How the Country Has Changed," *The Guardian*, October 7, 2011, http://www.guardian.co.uk/news/datablog/2011/jun/23/afghanistan-war-data.

29. The first battered women's shelters did not open in the U.S. until 1972.

30. See "Monitoring the Implementation of the Elimination of Violence Against Women Law," Womankind Worldwide: Afghan Woman's Network, http://www.womankind.org.uk/what-we-do/where-we-work/afghanistan/womankind-projects/afghan-womens-network/.

CHAPTER 6

Little Brides and Bridegrooms:
Systemic Failure, Cultural Response

SHARIFA SHARIF

All around the world, children, especially girls, lose their childhoods, dreams, hopes, and health to marriages contracted by their parents in exchange for money, honor, or other girls. A report by Girls Not Brides, an initiative of the Elders Foundation, indicates that every year, worldwide, ten million girls under the age of eighteen are married. One in seven is married before her fifteenth birthday, sometimes as young as eight or nine.[1] The results are early pregnancies, pervasive domestic violence, and other factors that put young women's lives and well-beings at risk.

Researchers and human rights organizations reveal shocking statistics about multifaceted abuses of child marriages in Africa, Asia, and Latin America, with higher percentages in South Asia, the Middle East, and sub-Saharan Africa.[2] Most of these marriages take place in the name of religion, culture, customs, family and tribal relations, geographical and historical conditions, or economic hardship. Although no dominant factor can be identified, each society and country has created arbitrary discourse and justification for underage marriage.

In Afghanistan, child marriage is widespread, despite the international commitment to ensuring human rights and constitutional law determining the marriage ages of sixteen for girls and eighteen for boys.[3] According to a United Nations Population Fund (UNFPA) report, "Escaping Child Marriage in Afghanistan," recent surveys estimate that about 46 percent of Afghan women are married by age eighteen and 15 percent before age fifteen. In a 2004 paper, medica mondiale, a German NGO concerned with women's health, reported that they "found no research and very little data to document the extent of the practice of child marriage in Afghanistan. Marriages generally are not recorded in this country. Consequently, there are many questions we can't answer: we don't know the average age of Afghans at marriage, or why some places have many child marriages and others few, or whether the incidence of child marriage is increasing or declining. We don't know if it is equally prevalent among all social groups and ethnicities."[4]

According to the Afghanistan Independent Human Rights Commission, between 60 and 80 percent of all marriages in Afghanistan are forced.[5] A standard definition for forced marriage is when "one or both of the partners do not give free or valid consent to the marriage."[6] Often in traditional societies, a girl's silence is perceived as agreement, though it may be a reflection of fear and/or the girls' and boys' desire to please their families.

Girls are usually the focal point of discussions, but forced marriages of boys are also not uncommon, though unfortunately, there is little available information. Like girls, many boys are engaged and married to their cousins without their consent through casual agreements between their fathers and uncles. Researcher Deborah J. Smith writes that young men or boys who feel forced into marriage often take their frustration and anger out on their wives and/or are led to want to take second wives. And even when they "don't necessarily object to the woman who was selected for them . . . [they are] averse to the timing of the marriage, which can interfere with their educations or apprenticeships."[7]

In the aftermath of nearly three decades of political instability and unspeakable war crimes, beginning with the 1979 invasion by the Soviet Union, Afghan children are unprecedentedly vulnerable to all forms of social, cultural, and economic abuse. Child labor, child trafficking, child and forced marriages, and sexual exploitation, particularly of boys, are recurring news from Afghanistan. A diversified social, economic, cultural, religious, and political force binds parents, largely fathers or other male guardians, to marry off their underage children, while religious beliefs pertaining to supervision and control of women's sexuality provides a justification.

History and Political Perspective

Since its independence from the British Empire in 1919, Afghanistan has witnessed political upheavals that have swung from social liberalism to religious fanaticism. The gendered aspects of these upheavals have had lasting impact on the status of Afghan women, the effects of which can be observed to this day. The contested history of social liberalism and gender reforms in Afghanistan have been examined by many scholars including Mohammad Hashim Kamali, Senzil Nawid, Hafizullah Emadi, and Valentine Moghadam.[8]

The first phase of modernization was introduced by King Amanullah

(r. 1919–1929), who legalized the age of marriage to sixteen for girls and eighteen for boys and was forced into exile for his progressive initiatives. Well aware of the risks, Amanullah's successors, Nadir Shah (r. 1929–1933) and his son, Zahir Shah (r. 1933–1973), acted more cautiously and conservatively with regard to women's rights, but nonetheless forged moderate, steady progress on women's education, justice, and voting rights.[9] Mohammed Daoud Khan,[10] Zahir's cousin, who served as his prime minister from 1953 to 1963, launched somewhat more ambitious programs for women's rights, encouraging unveiling and employment partly in response to the demands for women's progress embedded in economic packages presented by the United States and the Soviet Union.[11] Schools and educational programs that included women were well funded, but again, child marriage, forced marriage, and domestic violence remained beyond the superpowers' demands and outside the official Afghan judiciary and legal framework. When laws were violated, the government took no action, and in any case, most laws were exercised only in the cities and among the educated elite.

Nevertheless, with relatively effective central government, education was extending beyond urban limits and influencing popular customs by spreading information and presenting better alternatives to families. Although parents were not punished for marrying their under-age girls, they were criticized by the ever-widening circles of educated men and women in their communities. Meanwhile, urban working women and girls were slowly becoming national role models, and young men from remote districts who came to study at Kabul University—the only university in Afghanistan at the time—began preferring to marry capable and educated women.[12]

The People's Democratic Party of Afghanistan (PDPA) took over the country in 1978, in a coup known as the Saur Revolution, and radicalized the legal rights of girls' marriage, not only by determining marital age, but by restricting the amount of the bride price (in Arabic: *mahr*; in Pashto: *walwar*; in Dari: *toyana*). The majority of the Afghan population denounced the laws of the communist regime as cultural violations, un-Islamic and disruptive to customary family values. The Soviet Union invaded in 1979, and as the war against them wound on for a decade, girls became increasingly vulnerable and families became more and more protective and controlling.

Girls were targets of rape, torture, and kidnapping, acts that, among other things, meant families were shamed and dishonored. Parents were desperate to care for their daughters, as well as to rid themselves of the sources of potential disgrace, and thus married them off as early as possible. However, marrying off sons or finding suitably matched partners for daughters became progressively difficult as boys were expected to fight, either with the Mujahedin or the government. If they were not at war, young men fled the country in search of work. Mujahedin commanders, armed and rich with funds from the United States and Saudi Arabia, bullied villagers to wed their young daughters, frequently as second and third wives. Villagers were caught between opposing forces—Soviet troops and the communist government during the day and Mujahedin at night—and for safety's sake hurried to marry off their daughters as soon as they passed the ages of ten or twelve. Roya, a fifteen-year-old girl from an educated family, was forced to marry a Mujahid commander. Her father, an educated and modern man, was himself vulnerable to the commanders' assaults. Often fathers who rejected commanders' proposals were targets of attacks and ambush.[13]

When Roya's husband was killed two years later, she was married to her younger brother-in-law. Levirate marriage is customary in Afghanistan, whereby the brother of a deceased man is obliged to marry his brother's widow, and the widow is obliged to marry her deceased husband's brother, regardless of age.[14] Here again, neither girl nor boy is given a choice.

After the Soviet withdrawal in 1989, forced marriages, rape, and kidnapping grew more vicious as a civil war between Mujahedin commanders raged through the cities and by 1992 reached the capital, Kabul, where the PDPA government of Mohammad Najibullah was overthrown. Many families living in Kabul with girls over ten either sent them to relatives in Pakistan or Iran or married them off. The custom of child marriage, which had been slowly changing—especially in communist-ruled Kabul—became a survival mechanism, shifting from cultural ignorance to cultural obligation. The ruling Mujahedin now adopted a political strategy of traditional and religious codes.

This pattern of religious extremism and cultural chauvinism further expanded with the takeover in 1996 of the Taliban, the Sunni Islamist group calling itself "students" or "seekers." They legalized violence against women and forcefully implemented it. Unemployment, poverty, the destruction of family properties, including farms, vineyards, and orchards, compelled even urban-educated Afghans to rely on their daughters as potential last resorts for security and survival. A married girl was one less mouth to feed and she brought cash and security, particularly if the husband was an Afghan expatriate living in the West.[15]

The Taliban exploited strict and fanatical interpretations of religious codes, justifying and encouraging underage marriage with references to the Prophet Muhammad's marriage to Aisha, the nine-year-old daughter of his closest companion.[16] The majority of Taliban fighters were boys as young as fourteen who had been trained in Islamic schools in Pakistan, were now settled inside Afghanistan holding military and administrative jobs, and needed young wives.

In 2001, the U.S. and its allies defeated the Taliban, and in 2002, brought Hamid Karzai to power as president on the condition of democratizing and ensuring women's equal and human rights. The establishment of the Ministry of Women's Affairs and the Afghanistan Independent Human Rights Commission, along with various non-governmental organizations (NGOs) promoting justice and equality for women, has created a framework for confronting violence against women and girls on the public social agenda. Stories of child marriage have been widely published in news and social media outlets. It is unclear whether child marriage has increased during the present government, but it seems not to have diminished, despite laws against it.

Tribal Patterns

Afghanistan is largely a tribal society. Tribal connections dominate most social relations and practices among the majority of the population, particularly the dominant Pashtun tribes, although underage marriage is by no means restricted to Pashtuns.[17] Pashtuns adhere to an ancient code of conduct called Pashtunwali that is pre-Islamic and has as its core values *badal* (revenge or exchange), *melmastia* (hospitality), and *nanawatai* (giving refuge to anyone, including one's enemies). Pashtunwali can vary somewhat from region to region and is variously practiced by other ethnic groups. Complex tribal cultures and religious renditions have provided a justifiable discourse for underage marriage of children, particularly girls. Tribal rivalry over land and women has created a profound need for extended families with many male members. The more children, the bigger the clan. The younger the bride and bridegroom, the stronger their chances of reproducing for many years. Girls' most desirable reproductive age is considered to be under twenty.

Marriage between cousins is culturally and religiously acceptable and, in many cases, facilitates child marriages. It allows extended families to retain their wealth, land, and property. Wealth is transferred to and carried by the woman through her dowry and whatever she may inherit after her husband's death. It is expected that cousins of similar ages in the extended families of siblings, especially brothers, will marry to strengthen relations. Uncles with unmarried sons have the primary and normative position to marry their nieces to their sons. Marrying a daughter to someone outside the family can be considered an offense among some tribes and has often led to long-term interfamilial enmities. Cousin marriages are usually arranged by casual agreements between their parents and uncles without the children's knowledge, even before they are born. Boy and girl infants are sometimes called "married" by their parents, and breaking the promise of marriage entails rejections, shame, and ultimately animosity.

The absence of a strong central government and application of the law are still among the factors that have encouraged continuation of tribal social rules in most parts of Afghanistan. Baad, the practice of giving a girl in marriage for the purpose of resolving a long-term enmity between tribes, continues. In the case of murder or another offense, the offended family agrees to end the feud in exchange for land, money, or a young girl to any male member of the family regardless of her age.[18] Badal, a core value of Pashtunwali, includes exchanging women between families in marriage. In the vast majority of cases it is two daughters of roughly the same age who are exchanged as wives for their brothers. Exchanges are also made by fathers of their own daughters to get new wives, often of girls of considerably different ages.[19]

Cultural Patterns

In addition to Pashtunwali and its variations, Afghans base their cultural and social patterns on the fundamentals of Islam, founded on interpretations of the Qur'an or the Hadith (sayings of the Prophet). As with all religions, Muslim interpretations can be subjective, and shaped by historical, geographical, and economic realities, as well as tribal conditions.

Marriage is a blend of cultural and religious practice. Its ceremonial details vary with region and ethnicity. But the religious component of *nikah* (marriage ceremony) and the requirement of virginity remains the same across Islamic societies. A girl's desirability for marriage is based on her sexual and reproductive capacity, her chastity, and her physical beauty. Honor and ownership of girls and women belongs to fathers and brothers, who control and dictate their lives. Unmarried girls are a liability to their families, vulnerable to social labeling of immodesty and impurity. Early marriage ensures against any violations.

While sex outside marriage is forbidden for both men and women in Islam, men are not appraised for virginity. Yet, in a study conducted by the Afghanistan Research and Evaluation Unit (AREU), "cases were found in which a family's fear that their sons would engage in sexually or romantically deviant behavior led them to marry their sons to girls the boys did not want or at a time when the sons did not want to get married."[20]

Islam condemns premarital and extramarital sex and discourages celibacy and monasticism.[21] Marriage is encouraged as a sacred and spiritual bond that enables the believer to attain the highest form of righteousness. Scholar Haideh Moghissi suggests that the Prophet Muhammad considered marriage as "half" the religion of Islam. And "marriage shields men from promiscuity, adultery, fornication, homosexuality; and is commendable even for a person who has a strong will to control his sexual desire, who has no wish to have children, and who feels that marriage will keep him away from his devotion to Allah."[22]

Among Afghans, the boys' parents are responsible for the costs of the wedding and the mahr. But the dowry the bride brings to her husband's home normally equals the value of the bride price. It includes clothing, bedding, and household utensils, and its quality can influence the treatment and status accorded the bride in her husband's home. A majority of her trousseau is embroidered, woven, and tailored by the girl, in cooperation with her female relatives and friends, and its quality is important to the prestige of both families.[23] It is the fulfillment of parental responsibility and status to send a bride into the house to lavishly celebrate a son's wedding. Grown, unmarried sons indicate parental negligence or financial incapability. Unmarried daughters bring shame to the family and are susceptible to complex cultural and social reproach. The girls' parents establish the value of the bride, that is, the amount of the bride price, which is determined by the desirable qualities of virginity, physical beauty, health, and her good reputation. If she is over twenty, she is considered outdated and expired, subject to derogatory terms such as "rotten," "decayed," or "spoiled." Everyone wants to avoid reaching that stage.

Youth and physical beauty do not determine a boy's value, but his masculinity and financial strength do. As in Western cultures, the received wisdom is that men don't become undesirable with age, but grow wiser and often more powerful through a lifetime of accumulated wealth.

Islam allows men to marry up to but not exceeding four wives, and this in turn is permitted in Afghanistan, according to civil law.[24] Often, when the first wife has reached the end of her childbearing years, men seek younger brides, not only for sex but as fresh, energetic reproductive resources. But while the Qur'an instructs Muslim men to "live with [their wives] on a footing of kindness and equity," unfortunately, this is rare, indeed, almost humanly impossible.[25]

Consequences of Child Marriage

According to Girls Not Brides, "Child brides face high risks of death and injury due to early sexual activity and childbearing. Girls under fifteen are five times more likely to die in childbirth than women in their twenties. Yet child brides are less likely to be in control of when and how many children they have."[26]

Afghanistan has been called the worst place on earth to be born (or to raise a child) for many reasons, not least the often dire complications when underage women give birth. Women under the age of fourteen are four times more likely than physically mature women to lose their lives in childbirth. This accounts for much of the high maternal mortality rate—whereby about one out of eleven Afghan women lose their lives during pregnancy or giving birth.[27]

In addition to increasing the risks of maternal mortality, child marriage prevents many children, boys and girls, from enjoying the fundamental right to pursue education. As was slowly becoming evident before the wars, education can offer a remedy to underage marriage and its destructive impact on children's health and family life.

And child brides are more likely to be victims of domestic violence and abuse. According to an Afghanistan Research and Evaluation Unit (AREU) report, young men, forced into questionable marriages, themselves often underage, are also vulnerable to domestic violence, taking out their frustrations on their wives.[28]

Economic Factors

Economics has been cited as one of the major influences on child marriages worldwide.[29] In Afghanistan, while child marriage is not limited to low-income families, poverty is the primary driving force.[30] Even before the wars, the majority of Afghanistan's population was living at or below the poverty line. One cannot deny the slow economic development taking place in Afghanistan since the fall of the Taliban in 2001, yet it largely comprises a wealthy and powerful minority controlling most of the wealth, who are in fact growing richer, while little or no infrastructure has been built that might improve the lives of the general public.[31] The economic strain that has always perpetuated child marriage remains. The deeper the economic need, the speedier the marriage. Today, despite an average annual income of $400, the bride price has increased to match the rising costs of living and the commercialized social image of the girls' families. While the bride price was once exchanged in Afghan currency, the Afghani has now been replaced by the U.S. dollar. And the expense of weddings has become so high, in 2011, the Afghan government actually sought to limit the costs but to little avail.[32]

Young men struggling to find employment, whose parents are destitute, often cannot marry, leaving the field of young girls open to older men. Among other things, the need for a paycheck has been a strong recruitment tool for the Taliban. Kenneth R. Weiss notes in the *Los Angeles Times* that

> in a sluggish agrarian economy, few young men can find legitimate employ-
> ment. Their lack of a steady income essentially closes the door to marriage in
> a society where sex outside of wedlock is forbidden. Tradition requires paying
> a dowry and staging a wedding celebration, which together cost as much as
> $5,000—three times the average annual household income.
>
> A young man can earn far more working for the Taliban than for the
> Afghan army or the police, according to Western intelligence reports and
> researchers. Planting a roadside bomb can pay 20 times more than a day's
> manual labor.[33]

Obviously, for this to change, the Afghan government and international donors must ensure that financial aid is used to generate income and employment for the majority of poor, rural Afghans. Long-term, income-generating projects must replace short-term, result-oriented mini-projects that do not last into the future.

Progressive Laws, Passive Rules

Afghan laws about marriage and family relations have always remained merely printed documents confined to legislative propaganda and implemented on selected educated urban populations.[34] Since King Amanullah's progressive programs for women's equal rights provoked the people's ire in the 1920s, central governments in Kabul have been wary and negligent about the rule of family law. Today, the problem is not merely the lack of social systems and networks, or that safe houses, shelters, and courts are failing abused women, but the government's reluctance to enforce women's rights. The rule of law is overpowered by warlords and warlordism, by continuing insecurity and civil war, which have prevented the Karzai government (weak-willed at best), and possibly any future government, from ensuring improvement in educa-tion, health, employment, and justice at the grassroots level throughout the country.

Ironically, the good news is that stories of girls who are victims of early marriages and maltreatment have made the news, worldwide, followed by outcries among international funders that may help lead to changes. The situation for boys must be further explored, as well, and meanwhile, for all children, the task is to change sad stories into happy ones.

Notes

1. Girls Not Brides: The Global Partnership to End Child Marriage, http://www.girlsnotbrides.org/, 2012, 1.

2. UNFPA, "Marrying Too Young," http://www.unfpa.org/webdav/site/global/shared/documents/publications/, 2012. According to the report, the highest percentage of underage marriages worldwide takes place in Niger and Bangladesh (75 and 66 percent, respectively).

3. Article 54 (Chapter 2) of the 2003 Constitution of the Islamic Republic of Afghanistan makes the legal marriage age of girls sixteen and of boys eighteen.

4. S. Bahgam and W. Mukhatari, "2004, Study on Child Marriage in Afghanistan," medica mondiale, May 2004, http://www.medicamondiale.org/fileadmin/content/07_Infothek/Afghanistan/Afghanistan_Child_marriage_medica_mondiale_study_2004_e.pdf.

5. UNFPA, "Escaping Child Marriage in Afghanistan," http://www.unfpa.org/public/cache/offonce/home/news/pid/12296, October 4, 2012. Afghanistan Independent Human Rights Commission, http://www.aihrc.org.af/en.

6. "Forced and Child Marriage," Stop Violence Against Women, http://www.stopvaw.org/forced_and_child_marriage.html; and United Nations "Convention on Consent to Marriage, Minimum Age for Marriage and Registration of Marriages" states that "no marriage shall be legally entered into without the full and free consent of both parties," http://www2ohchr.org/english/law/convention.htm. See also "Women's Rights Unit," Afghanistan Independent Human Rights Commission, http://www.aihrc.org.af/womenrights.htm.

7. Deborah J. Smith, "Between Choice and Force: Marriage Practices in Afghanistan," in Jennifer Heath and Ashraf Zahedi, eds., *Land of the Unconquerable: The Lives of Contemporary Afghan Women* (Berkeley: University of California Press, 2011), 168. See also Girls Not Brides, 2.

8. Mohammad Hashim Kamali, *Law in Afghanistan: A Study of Constitutions, Matrimonial Law and the Judiciary* (Netherlands: Leiden: R.J. Brill, 1985); Senzil Nawid, *Religious Responses to Social Change in Afghanistan, 1919–29: King Aman-Allah and the Afghan Ulama* (Costa Mesa: Mazda Publishing, 1999); Hafizullah Emadi, *Repression, Resistance and Women in Afghanistan* (Westport, CT: Greenwood Publishing Group, 2002); Valentine Moghadam, *Modernizing Women: Gender and Social Change in the Middle East*, 2nd ed. (Boulder, CO: Lynne Rienner Publishers, Inc., 2003).

9. Shireen Khan Burki, "The Politics of Zan from Amanullah to Karzai: Lessons for Improving Afghan Women's Status," in *Land of the Unconquerable*, 45–59.

10. Daoud Khan was dismissed by Zahir Shah in 1963. In 1973, he overthrew

Zahir in a bloodless coup, and was himself killed with his entire family in 1978 in the Saur Revolution.

11. Burki, "The Politics of Zan," 51.

12. Burki, "The Politics of Zan," 45–59.

13. Personal interview with Roya, a young woman from my ancestral village.

14. http://en.wikipedia.org/wiki/Levirate_marriage.

15. Burki, "The Politics of Zan," 45–59.

16. Aisha was the daughter of the first Caliph Abu Bakr and was the Prophet Muhammad's youngest and reputedly favorite wife. She was said to have been married to Muhammad when she was nine, but the marriage was not consummated until she reached puberty.

17. Pashtuns—variously called Pushtuns, Pakhtuns, Pukhtuns, and Pathans—are historically the dominant ruling ethnic group in Afghanistan, although they do not have a large majority. Other ethnic groups include Tajik, Turkmen, Hazara, Uzbek, Aimak, Kirghiz, Qazilbash, Balouch, Pashai, Nuristani, Guijar, and Farsiwan. For more about Pashtunwali (or Pukhtunwali), see Louis Dupree, *Afghanistan* (Princeton, NJ: Princeton University Press, 1980), 126–127.

18. "Harmful Traditional Practices and Implementation of the Law on Elimination of Violence Against Women in Afghanistan," United Nations Assistance Mission and Office of the High Commissioner for Human Rights, December 9, 2010.

19. "Afghanistan Rule of Law Project: Field Study of Informal and Customary Justice in Afghanistan and Recommendations on Improving Access to Justice and Relations Between Formal Courts and Informal Bodies," Checchi and Company Consulting, Inc., prepared for the United States Agency for International Development, June 2006, http://www.usip.org/files/file/usaid_afghanistan.pdf, 12. See also Smith, "Between Choice and Force," 170, 176.

20. Smith, "Between Choice and Force," 168–169. Of interest: Malalai Bashir, "Love Marriages in the Pashtun Society," in *Pashtun Women*, May 2013, http://pashtunwomenvp.com/index.php/2013-01-28-03-21-27/social/249-love-marriages-in-the-pashtun-society. The author writes of the romantic versus romance: "A society that adores the stories of broken hearts and unfulfilled desires, sings the songs of love and passion, admires romantic poetry and loves love, ironically, is perhaps one of the most opposing to love-marriages in today's modern world."

21. "But the Monasticism which they invented for themselves, We did not prescribe for them but only to please God therewith, but that they did not observe it with the right observance." A. J. Arberry, *The Koran Interpreted: A Translation* (New York: Simon & Schuster, 2008), 57:27.

22. Haideh Moghissi, *Feminism and Islamic Fundamentalism: The Limits of Postmodern Analysis* (London: Zed Books, 1999), 21–22.

23. Peter R. Blood, ed., *Afghanistan: A Country Study* (Washington: GPO for the Library of Congress, 2001), http://countrystudies.us/afghanistan/57.htm.

24. Many other Muslim-majority nations permit polygyny, among them Iran, Saudi Arabia, and Pakistan. See "Legal Status of Polygamy," http://en.wikipedia.org/wiki/Legal_status_of_polygamy.

25. Arberry, *The Koran Interpreted*, 4:19.

26. Girls Not Brides, http://girlsnotbrides.org, 2.

27. For further information see UNICEF, "State of the World's Children 2009"

(New York: United Nations Children's Fund, December 2009), http://www.unicefusa .org/news/publications/state-of-the-worlds-children/The_State_of_the_Worlds _Children_2009.pdf. Also see Rahim Kanani, "Rahim Kanani: Maternal Mortality in Afghanistan: A Way Forward," The Huffington Post, March 8, 2010, accessed September 12, 2011, http://www.huffingtonpost.com/rahim-kanani/maternal-mortality -in-afg_b_490107.html. See also chapter 11, Steven Solter, "Children's Health: The Challenge of Survival," chapter 11 in this volume.

28. Smith, "Between Choice and Force," 168.

29. Girls Not Brides, http://girlsnotbrides.org, 2.

30. Laila Ahmed, *Women and Gender in Islam: Historical Roots of a Modern Debate* (New Haven: Yale University Press, 1992), 52.

31. Office of the Special Inspector General for Afghanistan Reconstruction, Fiscal Year 2011, "Afghanistan Infrastructure Fund Projects Are Behind Schedule and Lack Adequate Sustainment Plans," July 30, 2012, http://www.sigar.mil/pdf/audits/2012 -07-30audit-12-12Revised.pdf.

32. See Farah Stockman, "Afghanistan Tries to Limit Excessive Wedding Day Costs," *Boston Globe*, February 6, 2011, http://www.boston.com/news/world/asia/arti cles/2011/02/06/afghanistan_tries_to_limit_excessive_wedding_day_costs/ and Rob Taylor, "Afghan Laws Banning Lavish Weddings Proving Hard to Enact," Reuters, July 29, 2012, http://www.reuters.com/article/2012/07/29/us-afganistan-weddings-id USBRE86S08I20120729.

33. The article goes on to note that this is a problem in other countries, as well, and has helped lead to uprisings in Egypt and Tunis. Kenneth R. Weiss, "Runaway Population Growth Fuels Youth-Driven Uprisings," *Los Angeles Times*, July 22, 2012, http:// www.latimes.com/news/nationworld/world/population/la-fg-population-matters2 -20120724-html,0,982753.htmlstory.

34. For more information on children and the judicial system, see chapter 10, Hangama Anwari, "Legal Protection: Offering Aid and Comfort," in this volume.

Many houses in Kabul are without running water; these neighborhoods are lined with open drainage sewers. The children are often the ones hiking up and down to central water sources to bring water back to their homes. Photo by Ginna Fleming, 2008.

A young girl sells bangles on the streets of Mazar-i-Sharif. Photo by Sheryl Shapiro, 2003.

PART 3

SURVIVAL BY ANY MEANS POSSIBLE

CHAPTER 7

Confronting Child Labor

AMANDA SIM

Child labor is an issue of growing concern in Afghanistan. According to recent estimates, one in four Afghan children aged seven to fourteen is engaged in some form of work.[1] Although poverty is an obvious contextual factor that dominates the decision making of all thirty-three rural and urban households interviewed for this study in Kabul, Herat, and Badakhshan provinces,[2] household composition and gender norms also affect the availability of labor resources, which can result in the need to send children to work.[3]

Not all poor or labor-constrained households, however, resort to using child labor. One crucial factor in household decision making about child labor is the way households weigh the costs and benefits of work versus school, which leads them to increase or limit their investment in education based on their perceptions of the potential for future returns. Poor households that send their children to school instead of work are able to justify short-term sacrifice with the prospect of long-term gains, usually in the form of secure or well-paid employment. How households evaluate the tradeoffs between work and school depends on a number of factors, including access to and quality of education, and exposure to successful role models in their social network.

Differing perceptions of risk also distinguish households that use child labor from those that do not, with the latter more attuned to and intolerant of physical and moral hazards associated with work. Study findings also point to the influence of community norms in household decisions to send children to work or school. Households often cite the behavior of others in their social circles when explaining their decision-making processes, thus suggesting that shifting community norms toward education and away from work may be one of the most powerful ways to reduce the prevalence of child labor in the long run.

An effective response to the issue of child labor in Afghanistan requires a critical analysis of the factors that influence household decision making and the nature and level of risk to which children are exposed. The target of the intervention—children at risk of work, children already engaged in work, or children in the worst forms of child labor—will determine if the approach should be oriented toward prevention, mitigation, or elimination.

Why Children Work

Poverty and deprivation dominate the existence of all households in this study. They face chronic livelihood and economic insecurity and struggle to afford basic necessities due to scarce and irregular employment, low earnings, high living costs, and debt. In the absence of an overarching social protection framework,[4] child labor is one of the strategies that some poor households use to diversify and increase income. However, not all poor households in this study responded to livelihood insecurity by sending children to work, which suggests the influence of non-economic factors. One father, interviewed in the capital city, Kabul, said, "In my mind there is no one poorer than me. If I can send my children to school, though I have economic problems, then why can't others? Everyone can do anything they want . . . no one can say I was so hopeless that I kept my children from school."

Household composition is an important factor that can influence the decision to use child labor. The study found that households in which the adult male is deceased or incapacitated by old age or illness are likely to use child labor. As gender norms prohibit their mothers from working outside the home, male children in female-headed households are particularly likely to work to compensate for the lack of an adult male income-earner. There are notable exceptions, however, of women contravening such gender norms to keep their children in school and out of work. The ability of women to contribute to household income and thereby reduce the need for children to work is highly variable and depends on individual agency, family attitudes, and community norms.

One mother interviewed has been the sole income-earner for her six-person household since the death of her husband. To keep her children in school, she has worked as a domestic servant in a neighbor's house, and expressed her fear of the backlash that may result from violating community norms around female seclusion:

> I do not want them to tell my children that I am working in other people's houses. If people say such things to them, then they will be ashamed, and

I do not want that. Their father was a big man, he was a mullah and people will not accept that his wife will make the family ashamed.

Trade-offs Between School and Work

All these households face the same challenges of poverty and insufficient labor resources. Yet not all choose to respond by using child labor. Households usually considered the question of how to most effectively allocate the use of children's time within the framework of work versus school, or a combination of both. Study findings demonstrate that households engage in a careful analysis of the costs and benefits of work versus school and increase or limit their investment in education based on the potential for returns in the short- and long-term.

Households in the study considered three main factors in evaluating the value of schooling: quality, cost, and potential for future employment. The quality of education that children were receiving in school was of grave concern to many families. Children and parents complained about poor school facilities, overcrowded classrooms, and unqualified, unmotivated, and even abusive teachers. They also expressed frustration over poor learning outcomes. As one mother in Herat city complained, "My daughter has studied up to fourth grade, but she still can't read and write, so what was the point of going to school?"

In this case, the girl herself expressed the desire to drop out of school to weave carpets with her mother. This decision was likely due to both the poor quality of education and the sense of pride and satisfaction she derived from learning a skill and contributing to the household income.[5]

One exception was the case-study village in Badakhshan, where respondents reported general satisfaction with the quality of education provided at the school. The perception among households of high-quality education, combined with the strong commitment to education among the community leadership, had a dramatic effect: almost all the children in the village were attending school on a regular basis. This example demonstrates the importance of educational quality in household decision making about work and school.

In addition to issues of quality, education's hidden costs were of concern to these poor households. While primary and secondary education are ostensibly free to all school-aged children in Afghanistan, in reality, households often incur school-related expenses such as uniforms, stationery, and even gifts for teachers in exchange for passing grades. These costs can be a huge burden to households already struggling to afford basic needs. Poor households can and do, however, find creative ways to bear the cost of school materials if they determine that the investment in education is worthwhile. Some households in the study, for instance, turned rice sacks into school bags and recycled scrap paper for school notebooks in order to ensure their children could continue their education.

Households also consider the potential for future returns on education when evaluating the choice between work and school. Families expressed greater willingness to invest in their children's education if the investment resulted in increased potential for stable, high-paid employment in the future, which would in turn benefit the rest of the household. For some households, however, the capacity to consider long-term gains was constrained by a focus on subsistence.

"It is good to learn different kinds of skills," one grandfather in Herat, whose household was engaged in child labor, said:

> It is good to even learn how to repair shoes because then you can sit in the
> street and do that work and earn 20 or 30 Afghanis to buy food. Sometimes
> having skills is more important than having an education, because with edu-
> cation you cannot find a job as quickly as when you have a skill. When you
> have a skill you can start working any time you want. For example, if a per-
> son can sit in the street and repair shoes, he is not educated, but he can sup-
> port his family.

Given the high unemployment rates in Afghanistan, many respondents were doubtful that formal education would result in greater prospects for their chil-dren. This skepticism was further compounded by the poor quality of teach-ing and learning in schools and the limited access to secondary and higher education.

Combining Work and School

Confronted with the choices between work and school, poor households weigh the costs and benefits of each in the short- and long-term and make strategic choices to maximize returns within the context of extremely limited options. Some households attempt to mitigate their risk by having some chil-dren attend school and others work, or by having their children combine work and school. By utilizing the latter strategy, children can continue to invest in their education while simultaneously learning a skill to fall back on should their education not result in secure employment.

Children who attempt to combine work and school, however, face many challenges in attendance and performance. Respondents in Herat and Kabul reported that employers did not allow children to attend school or spend time on homework, while teachers punished children who missed school or failed to complete homework due to their workload. Child respondents also reported feeling exhausted by the demands of work and school and shamed by teasing from their non-working classmates. One thirteen-year-old mechanic's apprentice in Herat left school, because his teacher was always beating him for not doing his homework. "I was working until late at night," he said. "How could I find time to study?" Unable to cope with competing demands on their time and energy and discouraged by the insensitivity of the school system to their needs, several working children in the study felt compelled to drop out of school to work full-time.

Learning as Motivation for Work

Faced with the apparent lack of concrete benefits to education in the short- or long-term, poor households may decide that their children's time is more effectively used for income generation. The opportunity cost of spending time in school is often too high to bear given poor educational quality and outcomes and the pressing need for household survival. Child labor, then, is not only a means of ensuring short-term benefit to the household in terms of increased income in the present; it is also a way for children to learn marketable skills that can support them in an uncertain future.

Respondents reported learning as an important non-economic motivation for child labor and generally preferred work activities that would impart skills—such as apprenticeships—over those that provided little opportunity for learning, such as street vending. Child labor was also described as a means of transition from childhood to adulthood, whereby children would learn vital life skills necessary for being a successful adult. A fourteen-year-old boy, who gathers and sells firewood in Badakhshan, said, "I know how to plow the land, sow the seeds, harvest . . . when my father is not at home, I am the one responsible for my household. And when there is something happening in the village, I'm invited to the meeting where the elders make decisions." Parents and children themselves viewed learning a sense of responsibility as a key positive outcome of children's work.

Keeping Children Safe and Out of Trouble

An interesting relationship between child labor and parental fears for children's safety and morals was revealed as many respondents expressed deep suspicions of free time and leisure and cited the desire to keep their children off the streets and out of trouble as one of the main reasons for sending them to work. Parents were particularly fearful of their children being exposed to negative influences and behaviors, such as smoking and drugs, or being the victim of kidnapping and other violent crime given the country's rising insecurity.

Such fears were most pronounced in the urban study sites of Kabul and Herat, whereas children were freer to enjoy recreational activities with their peers in the rural village in Badakhshan. This difference is most likely due to the close-knit nature of the rural community, where households demonstrated much greater levels of social cohesion and trust than their urban counterparts. While some households that were engaged in child labor pointed to work as a means of keeping children safe, households that chose not to use child labor emphasized the physical and moral dangers of sending children to work. For these households, school was a safe place for children to learn and play. A mother from a Kabul household engaged in child labor said, "Wahid was very naughty when he was a child. He was flying kites, climbing on walls, and getting on the roof all the time. So later, we decided to send him to work somewhere so he would not hurt himself." By contrast, a father from a Kabul household that is not engaged in child labor said, "I think people who send their children out to work are crazy, because their children learn bad things from the outside. They find bad friends who will take them the wrong way. These things have bad impact."

Girls

Decision making around the allocation of children's time is highly gendered in the Afghan context. For many households, the harm to family reputation and honor caused by girls' presence in the public sphere is a more vital consideration than the income girls could generate by working outside the home. Similarly, girls who have reached puberty are often discouraged from continuing their education due to the norm of female seclusion. Some in the study reported they saw little benefit to educating their daughters since they will marry and move out of their natal homes. "Girls have to go to their husband's house one day," a Herati father said. "If we spend money on their studies, what will we gain from it? So it's better to keep them at home to do the house chores."

Although girls may not be as likely as boys to work outside the home, they are at high risk of being deprived of their right to education and of being required to work for long hours on domestic chores in their natal or marital homes. In all research sites, girls were found to perform both paid and unpaid home-based work such as carpet-weaving and pistachio shelling. In some cases in Kabul and Badakhshan, girls were found working outside the home scavenging or tending livestock, although the backlash from their presence in the public sphere increased as they reached puberty.

Influence of Community Norms

As households do not live in isolation, decision making about child labor is greatly influenced by the attitudes and behavior of other members in the community. The power of community norms regarding work and school can be seen in the comparison between the case-study village in rural Badakhshan and the community near the Islam Qala border with Iran. In the former, school attendance is the norm for almost all village children: community leaders demonstrate commitment to education, parents report satisfaction with school quality, and as a result, the majority of children are regularly attending classes. By contrast, work is the norm in the border community of Islam Qala: children and parents alike see little value in attending the poor-quality classes at the local school and choose instead to earn income at the nearby border crossing that offers significant work opportunities.

Furthermore, the striking absence of community cohesion and organization in the Islam Qala village means that there is no community mobilization around the issues of education or child labor, and working children enjoy little community support or protection. Households in the Badakhshan village, on the other hand, cooperated to ensure that female students were accompanied by trusted male community members on the way to school, thereby allowing access despite concerns over distance and security.

The influence of strong community ties in the Badakhshan village could also have negative effects on children, however, as evidenced by the decision of the local *shura* (council) to send two children to work in order to repay their families' debts.[6] In these cases, community priorities outweighed the children's interests.

The study also found that peers and role models play a significant role in decision making about work and school. Children are extremely influenced by the actions of their peer groups and are less motivated to pursue an education if most of their friends and relatives are working. Similarly, households referenced role models in their social networks who influenced decisions to either send children to work or to school. Knowledge of positive role models who achieved professional success through education was for some households one of the main factors in their decision to educate their children. Notably, some households that refrain from child labor see themselves as positive role models for others in their community. As one respondent stated, even the emergence of a single role model from the community could create a ripple effect, changing people's perceptions of the possibility of success through education.

"What people say" had a tremendous effect on all households in the study regarding decisions on children's activities. Fear of gossip, for instance, could make a family decide to take its daughter out of school. Conversely, the enhanced status and reputation derived from being the family of an educated professional could encourage a household to invest in education. The importance of reputation and status in many Afghan communities suggests that shifting community values and norms toward education and away from work could be a key strategy to reduce child labor.

The decisions made by households to keep their children in school, put them to work, or combine the two are influenced by a complex interplay of factors, including economic necessity, household composition, quality and potential outcomes of education, and community values and norms. Strategies to reduce incidence of child labor must therefore be multifaceted, ranging from macro-level action to targeted interventions with children, households, and communities.

Children at Risk and How to Respond

Working children are exposed to a range of physical and psychosocial hazards as a result of their work. Some children in the study worked as much as twice the legally mandated hours for adults[7]—often performing physically injurious activities—and many were subject to harassment and abuse from employers or even the police, as in the case of street-working children.

While all forms of child labor entail some degree of risk, the nature and severity of risk depend on the type of work. Street-working children in urban or border areas may be at greater risk of harassment and abuse compared to children performing agricultural work in rural communities. The extent to which child labor results in severe and long-term harm to a child depends on the kind of work performed, hazards present in the workplace, and the nature of the work and home environments. For instance, an apprentice at a mechanic shop is exposed to dangerous machinery and falling objects, but may be at lower risk of long-term physical or psychosocial harm if there is proper supervision from a caring employer.

School attendance is an important factor that can mitigate the risks associated with child labor. Children who are able to combine work and school have the opportunity to attain literacy and numeracy skills, as well as gain self-esteem and life skills through peer interaction. The ability of working children to attend and perform in school is therefore one of the main factors that determines their risks of long-term harm.[8]

Due to their hidden and taboo nature, little is known about the incidence or nature of Afghan children's involvement in activities such as sex work, drug trafficking, or participation in armed conflict.[9] The activities considered to be the worst forms of child labor violate the fundamental rights of children and must be targeted by immediate elimination. International law mandates that children identified as being involved in such forms of work be immediately removed and provided the social services necessary to facilitate their recovery and reintegration.[10]

There is currently no reliable information on the extent or nature of children's involvement in these forms of child labor for Afghanistan, nor is there sufficient awareness of how to identify and respond to such cases at the local or national level. Efforts to eliminate children's involvement in the worst forms of child labor must therefore begin with awareness-raising and information-gathering by local and national state and non-state actors. It is likely that community-based, grassroots-level monitoring would be the most effective means of identifying cases. However, given the stigma associated with such activities, great care and sensitivity must be taken in order to ensure that the children's privacy and physical and psychological well-being are protected.

All the child-labor cases in this study fall into the middle categories of children at risk, including children in hazardous forms of work, working children who are denied schooling, and working children in school whose learning is compromised or who are at risk of early drop out. While the ideal would be to achieve complete elimination of all child labor, the economic and social reality in Afghanistan necessitates a more gradual approach of risk mitigation. Acknowledging that some children will continue to have to work in the short- to medium-term, interventions must seek to reduce risk and increase protection for working children. Such remedial action includes improving work conditions, ensuring access to education, and supporting children in achieving learning objectives. Some forms of work may be so hazardous to children's physical and psychosocial well-being, however, that they necessitate elimination.

Whether or not the response should be elimination or mitigation therefore depends on the specific context of the child and household. Remedial interventions must not result in legitimizing work that is harmful to the child's development. On the other hand, immediate action to remove a child from work must avoid putting the child at further risk by plunging the household into a state of extreme deprivation. All interventions to remove or mitigate harm to the child must therefore also include intensive engagement with the household—primarily parents and caregivers—in order to ensure sustainable improvement in the child's well-being.

Effective preventive measures targeting children and households at risk of engaging in child labor are necessary to reduce the incidence of child labor in Afghanistan in the long term. The households in this study that do not use child labor demonstrate unique characteristics that have enabled them to survive without sending their children to work. However, these households remain extremely vulnerable and are at high risk of engaging child labor in the event of an unforeseen shock.

A key prevention strategy is therefore to improve the resilience of these at-risk households by increasing their financial, physical, and human capital. Strengthening the livelihoods of poor and vulnerable households would help make them less likely to use child labor as a coping mechanism.

Improving access to and quality of education is another essential preventive measure. As the study findings demonstrate, children who learn from knowledgeable teachers in a participatory and learner-centered environment are more likely to stay in school instead of turning to work. Parents are also more likely to support school attendance when they can observe tangible returns on investment in education. Finally, communities play an essential role in preventing child labor. As household decision making is influenced to a large extent by prevailing norms around work and education, community-level interventions to shift attitudes and values can have a tremendous effect on reducing child labor.

The response to child labor in Afghanistan must therefore incorporate multiple levels of intervention targeted at prevention, mitigation, and elimination objectives. Using a conceptual framework that outlines appropriate action for various levels of risk enables actors to prioritize, coordinate, and sequence interventions. The recent emergence of child-labor issues onto the national agenda—as signaled by references in the Afghanistan National Development Strategy (ANDS)[11]—signifies promising political awareness and commitment. However, the response to child labor remains fractured, with little effective coordination among government, donors, and NGOs.

There is a need for a comprehensive strategy that outlines prevention, mitigation, and elimination goals and integrates the various interventions of government and implementing organizations at the national, community and household levels. Examples of coordination mechanisms such as the Child Protection Action Network (CPAN)[12] are positive steps forward. However, they must be strengthened and expanded to include actors from other related sectors in order to create the multi-sectoral response necessary for tackling child labor.

Improving Education Quality and Access

Findings from this study clearly demonstrate the influence of educational quality and access on household decisions about child labor. Improving the quality of education is crucial to preventing child labor, as households are more likely to keep their children in school and out of work if they perceive positive learning outcomes. For children who are already working, increasing access to education is an important remedial action that can protect children from full-time work, mitigate harmful effects of work, and ensure continued learning. This study suggests that girls and children from ethnic minorities face particular challenges in accessing education and require targeted support to stay in school and out of work.

Issues of educational quality and access are discussed in Afghanistan's National Education Strategic Plan (NESP). The plan specifically mentions girls, nomadic children, children with learning disabilities, preschool children, and children who have missed the first years of basic education. However, it does not discuss how to meet the particular needs of working children.[13]

Targeted interventions to provide educational services to working children have been undertaken only by a small number of NGOs—mostly in Kabul and other major cities—that offer center-based, non-formal education or accelerated learning. The establishment of such centers is an important first step toward ensuring some form of continued learning for working children. But they reach only a small number of children and are often highly dependent on donor funding, which can be unpredictable. Sustainability is also of concern: not all centers have the specific aim of preparing working children for eventual integration into the mainstream education system and in some cases may even have the opposite effect. Of course, not all working children may be able or willing to reenter the formal education system. Discussions among implementing organizations and the government of Afghanistan—particularly the Ministry of Education (MoE) and the Ministry of Labor, Social Affairs, Martyred, and Disabled (MoLSAMD)—are necessary to determine a coordinated yet flexible strategy for intervention that serves the best interests of children at risk of or already engaged in child labor.

Improving Livelihood Opportunities and Outcomes for Poor Households

Poverty caused by scarce, low-paid employment and high living costs is a crucial driver of child labor. This study found that the economic contribution of working children is in some cases essential to household survival, which means that those children are unable to stop working in order to continue (or begin) their educations. Furthermore, households that do not currently engage in child labor are at high risk of sending their children to work in the event of an unexpected shock, such as an illness or death among the adult income-earners.

Strengthening the livelihoods of poor households would therefore serve both a remedial as well as a preventive function: working children would be able to return to school or even stop work entirely in some cases, while nonworking children would be at less risk of starting work. In particular, providing adult women access to culturally appropriate employment opportunities may reduce the need for children to work, although care must be taken to ensure that the burden of household work is not displaced onto girls.

The ANDS emphasizes the importance of a "pro-poor" economic development strategy. Yet households lacking physical, human, social, and financial capital—exactly the households using and at risk of using child labor—continue to lack opportunities for skills and business development. Most microfinance, vocational training, and business-development opportunities have criteria that exclude the most vulnerable households due to concerns with investment returns. In order to reach such households, donors must be prepared for a higher level of risk and investment in time and resources. Additionally, child protection objectives such as child labor prevention and reduction have not been sufficiently mainstreamed into economic and community development activities in Afghanistan. Given the strong link between livelihood and child protection outcomes, the government, donors, and NGOs are missing important opportunities to increase child well-being through household-level economic strengthening interventions.

Engage Communities in Changing Norms and Attitudes toward Child Labor

Comparative findings from the case studies—rural Badakhshan and the Islam Qala border community in Herat, in particular—demonstrate the importance of a cohesive, aware, and mobilized community for reducing and regulating child labor. Investing in strong community networks of community leaders, elders, teachers, employers, and household members is crucial to understanding and responding to child labor, especially as most child labor is hidden in the home or the informal economy.

Community members—with their intimate knowledge of local norms, resources, and needs—are best placed to identify hazardous forms of child labor, particularly the worst forms that are too taboo for outsiders to uncover. Community members can also play an important role in monitoring school attendance and engaging households whose children are excluded or marginalized because of their work.[14]

Communities can provide social safety nets for vulnerable households in the absence of effective social protection by the state. Poor households with strong social networks may therefore be able to cope with unforeseen shocks without turning to child labor. By contrast, in communities where there is little social cohesion and the norm for children is work rather than school (as in the case of the Islam Qala border community), households are more likely to engage in child labor.

The power of community norms suggests that shifting community values from work to school would significantly reduce child labor, and increase school attendance. Positive role models, particularly from poor households that have found ways to keep their children out of work, have an important role to play in achieving such transformations.

Strengthen the Policy, Legal, and Regulatory Environment for Reducing Child Labor

A supportive political, institutional, legal, and regulatory environment is necessary for achieving sustainable reductions in child labor. There are positive signs of increased political commitment and momentum around the issue, as demonstrated by its inclusion in the ANDS, National Employment Policy and Strategy, and National Strategy for Children at Risk. The ratification of the International Labor Organization (ILO) Convention on Worst Forms of

Child Labor and the ILO Convention on Minimum Age of Employment is also an important legal development that will signal Afghanistan's commitment to addressing child labor.[15]

The policy, legal, and regulatory frameworks governing child labor, however, remain flawed, as they do not adequately address the informal sector, where the majority of children in Afghanistan work. The Afghan Labor Code sets a minimum age for employment and establishes a maximum number of working hours for workers under eighteen, but does not define the terms "light" and "hazardous" work.

Furthermore, there is no mention of the mechanisms through which these provisions will be monitored or how workplaces will be regulated. Given the prevalence of child labor in the informal sector, community-based mechanisms as described above are likely to be the most effective means of monitoring and protection. There are still, however, little to no linkages between communities and the CPANs, which exist primarily at the national and provincial levels. The government of Afghanistan, with MoLSAMD taking the lead in close collaboration with MoE, must demonstrate more effective leadership in policy setting and stakeholder coordination around child labor and develop a strategy for intervention at the national, provincial, district, and community levels.

An effective response to child labor must address the complex interaction of economic and social factors that influence household decision making. Interventions must be multi-sectoral and coordinated to achieve prevention, mitigation, and elimination objectives in the short, medium, and long terms. They must also build upon and reinforce positive community values and role models that promote the physical, emotional, and intellectual well-being of children. Given that household and community vulnerability to the use of child labor varies according to local context, interventions must be tailored to the specific dynamics of each economic, sociocultural, and educational environment to achieve the greatest impact.

Efforts to reduce child labor cannot be isolated from the broader context of chronic poverty and insecurity in Afghanistan. As demonstrated by this study, the interaction among poverty, conflict, crime, and weak rule of law has a tangible impact on children's ability to learn, play, and grow into healthy and productive adults. Only within a peaceful and thriving Afghanistan can children and families fulfill their hopes for a brighter future.

Notes

This essay, written in 2009, was originally a briefing paper for the Afghanistan Research and Evaluation Unit (AREU), an independent research institute headquartered in Kabul, Afghanistan, and edited and abridged for this book by Jennifer Heath with the kind permission of AREU.

AREU's mission is to inform and influence policy and practice through conducting high-quality, policy-relevant research and actively disseminating the results, and to promote a culture of research and learning. To achieve its mission, AREU engages with policymakers, civil society, researchers, and students to promote their use of AREU's research and its library, to strengthen their research capacity, and to create opportunities for analysis, reflection, and debate. As an impartial Afghanistan-based voice dedicated to research excellence, AREU aspires to contribute to the development of inclusive and transparent policymaking processes, driven by the priorities of the Afghan people, which give rise to better-informed policies and programs that improve Afghan lives. AREU was established in 2002 by the assistance community working in Afghanistan and has a board of directors with representation from donors, the United Nations, and other multilateral agencies, and non-governmental organizations. www.areu.org.af.

1. Islamic Republic of Afghanistan and UNICEF, "Best Estimates of Social Indicators of Children in Afghanistan 1990–2005" (Kabul: UNICEF, 2006).

2. Interviews took place in Kabul province in Kabul city and the peri-urban community in Paghman; in Herat province, Herat city, and a community near the Islam Qala border with Iran; and in a rural village in Badakhshan province. For more detailed analysis and findings from each research site, refer to the Kabul, Badakhshan, and Herat case studies at www.areu.org.af.

3. The question of how to define child labor is subject to ongoing debate. There are two general approaches to defining child labor, the first guided by the International Labor Organization (ILO) Convention on Minimum Age for Admission to Employment (1973) and the second by the United Nations Convention on the Rights of the Child (1990). As the title of the ILO Convention on Minimum Age implies, its definition of child labor is driven exclusively by age, with eighteen years set as the minimum age for performing hazardous work and fifteen for "light work." The Convention on the Rights of the Child takes a more conditional approach, stating in Article 32 that children should be protected from "performing any work that is likely to be hazardous or to interfere with the child's education, or to be harmful to the child's health or physical, mental, spiritual, moral, or social development."

4. In Afghanistan, the Labor Code adopts a minimum-age approach, which mandates the minimum working age as fifteen for non-hazardous work and eighteen for hazardous work. For the purposes of this study, the term "child labor" refers to paid or unpaid work performed by children under the age of fourteen as well as hazardous work performed by children aged fifteen to eighteen. The so-called "worst forms of child labor" described in the 1999 ILO Convention, which include armed conflict, prostitution, and drug trafficking, are unequivocally defined as child labor regardless of age.

5. See Amanda Sim and Marie-Louise Høilund-Carlsen, the case of Shafiqa in

"Factors Influencing Decisions to Use Child Labor: A Case Study of Poor Households in Herat," Afghanistan Research and Evaluation Unit, 2008.

6. See Pamela Hunte and Anastasiya Hozyainova, "Factors Influencing Decisions to Use Child Labour: A Case Study of Poor Households in Rural Badakhshan," Afghanistan Research and Evaluation Unit, 2008.

7. The maximum number of legally mandated workdays per week is six, with restrictions placed on night and holiday work. A typical work week is forty hours for a full-time employee. But if an employer is responding to a seasonal production increase, the work week may extend up to a reasonable increase as dictated by that industry—typically not beyond fifty hours per week for a reasonable period of time (http://irc.nacubo.org/countries/Pages/Afghanistan.aspx).

8. Furio Rosati and Schott Lyon, "Tackling Child Labour: Policy Options for Achieving Sustainable Reductions in Children at Work" (Rome: Understanding Children's Work, 2006).

9. International Labour Organization, *Concerning the Prohibition and Immediate Action for the Elimination of the Worst Forms of Child Labor*, Convention Number 182 (1999). Studies by ActionAid Afghanistan on child labor in the border areas of Islam Qala in Herat province and Torkham in Nanqarhar province, as well as in Kandahar, met similar challenges in uncovering incidence for high-risk work and hazards such as sexual abuse.

10. In 2010 Afghanistan ratified both the ILO Convention on Minimum Age of Employment and the ILO Convention on Worst Forms of Child Labor.

11. *Afghanistan National Development Strategy 1387–1391 (2008–2013): A Strategy for Security, Governance, Economic Growth and Poverty Reduction*, http://www.undp.org.af/publications/KeyDocuments/ANDS_Full_Eng.pdf, 33.

12. The CPAN is a network of child protection organizations facilitated by UNICEF and the MoLSAMD. There are currently CPANs in twenty-eight of Afghanistan's thirty-four provinces, and a national-level CPAN in Kabul. For an updated report, see Wasil Noor Muhmad, "High Level Meeting On Cooperation for Child Rights in the Asia Pacific Region, November 4–6, 2010," Child Protection System, Prevention And Response to Child Protection In Afghanistan (Beijing, China), http://www.unicef.org/eapro/DM_shanghi_CPAN_meeting.pdf.

13. For current NESP review and report for mainstreaming the principle of inclusion, which emphasizes the need for educational systems to meet the varied needs of all children, particularly marginalized or excluded groups, including working children, see http://www.gtz.de/de/dokumente/en-verbesserung-grundbildung-afghanistan.pdf.

14. One of the roles of School Management Committees established by community-based education providers, for instance, is monitoring and following up on student absenteeism.

15. Interview with ILO Afghanistan Programme, August 2008.

CHAPTER 8

The Parakeet Boys:
Performing Education in the Streets of Kabul

WAHID OMAR

Since 2001 and the fall of the Taliban, Kabul, Afghanistan, has transformed from a ghost town, perforated by millions of bullets, into a dusty city consumed by construction sites, polluting generators and cars, and an increasing population. Rebuilding the streets of Kabul, its sewage system, and other infrastructure is a formidable task that will take many years and require the mobilization of many resources. Although signs of progress are only beginning to benefit most Afghans, one very vulnerable section of the population is still struggling to survive: street children.

According to Engineer Mohammad Yousef, founder of Aschiana, an Afghan non-governmental organization (NGO) designed to help working street children,[1] more than 50,000 children in Kabul are working the streets, begging, burning incense for tips to protect passersby against the evil eye, washing cars, selling chewing gum or eggs, collecting paper or aluminum cans from garbage around the city, and working as slave labor in many trades. According to UNICEF, many street children in the capital city, Kabul, and other urban areas are in danger of contracting the HIV/AIDS virus,[2] because they eventually get involved with selling and using drugs. Some efforts are made to help these street kids regain their dignity and reclaim their stolen childhoods, but in general they are outcast, looked down upon, and dependent on what little charity is available. Most of these children, according to Xinhuanet,[3] are stripped of their basic human rights, completely unaware of such niceties as, for instance, International Children's Day. Although the conditions in which they work are deplorable, children are still able to provide meager incomes for their families. This essay is a salute to the street children of Afghanistan and an attempt to understand how Afghan children, through the art of performance and the dynamics between orality and literacy, are not only able to preserve their cultural heritage but also to improve their literacy skills.

Strangely enough, some of these children working the streets for a few Afghanis are in fact the repository of thousands of years of literature and poetry, the guardians of ancient traditions and customs. They awaken early in the morning, leave their families, study at school, and work part-time in the streets of Kabul. As Jack Goody wrote: "The whole process of removing the children from the family, placing them under special authorities, can be roughly described as one of 'decontextualization,' formalization; for schools inevitably place an emphasis on the 'unnatural,' 'non-oral,' 'decontextualized' process of repetition, copying, verbatim memory."[4] It is within this framework that, as we shall see, some street children of Afghanistan operate as agents of change with transformative powers.

The Streets as Training Grounds

Each day at work in the streets of the capital city is an opportunity to earn money, as well as increase the ability to learn classical poetry with precision; and thus the streets of Kabul become the practicum training that supplements academic training at school. Moreover, they fill the "narration sickness" that Paulo Freire described in the setting of formalized schooling:

> A careful analysis of the teacher-student relationship at any level, inside or outside the school, reveals its fundamentally *narrative* character. This relationship involves a narrating Subject (the teacher) and patient, listening objects (the students). The contents, whether values or empirical dimensions of reality, tend in the process of being narrated to become lifeless and petrified. Education is suffering from narration sickness.[5]

Before entering the heart of this essay, it is appropriate to define what the terms "orality" and "literacy" mean and how they are understood among academics and non-academics. It is first important to reiterate that the distinction between oral literature versus written literature is losing ground among scholars and authors, such as Paul Zumthor, William Foley, Ruth Finnegan, Dell Hymes, and Walter Ong,[6] who have sufficiently proven the fluidity between the two fields. In the English language, the primary connotation of "literature" has changed from its fourteenth-century meaning of "polite learning through reading" to "imaginative forms of writing." But in Afghanistan, where oral tradition is still the major form of cultural expression and literacy is the domain of a minority, literature—while referring to production of literary works—still retains its connotation of "literary culture." Writing emphasizes the relationship between literature and manners—both of which are called *adab*.[7] Because Dari, the lingua franca of Afghanistan, was the ceremonial language of the royal court from the first Afghan kingdom,[8] it has influenced literature (oral and written), as well as customs in Afghanistan, one way or another. When Afghans greet each other, a series of long formulas[9] are used in order to comply with cultural etiquette (good manners), the legacy of great Afghan people. Manners and customs of the Afghan people were transmitted orally and recorded by classical authors such as the Persian lyric poet Hafez (1325/1326–1389/1390 CE). Today, when students write papers at any grade level, in schools or universities, one third of their writing is dedicated to aesthetic form rather than content, and redundancy is an unknown word.

Afghan oral tradition is a vast subject, present and constant in everyday Afghan life: in addition to folklore and stories told everywhere by nearly everyone of every class, Afghans use poetry in political, historical, religious, and literary discussions to justify and give weight to arguments and opinions. Classical poets and scholars, such as Hafez, Rumi (1207–1273), Firdausi (934–1020), Jami (1414–1492), Ansari (1175–1260), and others, are venerated among educated and non-educated Afghans alike. Afghanistan has an extremely rich repertoire of oral traditions, including a large body of special performance forms: legends, stories, epics (written and oral) on one hand; and a body of short conversational forms, such as proverbs, riddles, sayings, fables, poems, popular beliefs, eulogies, sermons, and songs on the other. All are representative of the country's cultural richness. As Richard Bauman writes, cultural performances tend to be the most prominent performance contexts within any community, and the most challenging job for students of performance is to establish continuity between scheduled public cultural performances and the spontaneous, unscheduled optional performance contexts of everyday life.[10] Cultural performances, calendrical events, and everyday speech performances are abundant in the Afghan nation. For example, proverbs are used as fixed formulas, feeding thought patterns that represent collective wisdom, the art of good speech, and good manners. Everywhere, every day, in literate and non-literate circles, short narratives and their moral lessons are used to illustrate and legitimize an opinion. Oral traditions are collective, shared understandings, and serve as matrices to build communities. They also represent authority and agency. In a semi-primary oral culture such as Afghanistan, it is perfectly logical and acceptable to use proverbs, classical poetry, or other oral forms of expression to justify and/or reinforce an opinion. Stories, proverbs, poems, or any other oral genre are memorized, repeated, and become fixed in the library of thoughts, to be retrieved at the right moment and in the right place, regardless of one's social, economic, or political status, and delivered through the art of performance.[11]

No doubt performance involves a dynamic between orality and literacy. It is fruitful to discuss the differences between reading a particular scene in silence privately, and watching and hearing it performed. How much does the performance mode—reading versus watching—change the scene? How much and in what ways does it modify the act of reception? A salient example of the instability of the notion of receiver/audience is undeniably demonstrated by a group of Afghan street children whom I call "The Parakeet Boys." It is through this discourse of instability that these street children find their ways and educate themselves in order to become versed in classical poetry and increase their chances of escaping poverty.

Decades of war and uncertainty have made fortune telling quite a lucrative business among the Afghans.[12] A few children,[13] between the ages of nine and twelve, use parakeets as fortune tellers in order to support themselves and their families. After attending free public school[14] in the morning, the Parakeet Boys start their self-practicum training by waiting for customers under the shade of trees. Ironically, some place themselves in front of the Ministry of Communications in Kabul. Each boy has one cage with a pair of parakeets in it, and a shoebox located outside the cage filled with folded papers. The birds will be the initial performers and the stakeholders of the self-practicum training. The folded papers are photocopies of Hafez's poetry, which will be used for prognostication and divination.[15] Each paper comes from a different page of a printed copy of the original text.

Once a customer pays the price (usually five Afghanis, the equivalent of ten cents), one of the boys takes a parakeet[16] out of the cage, and the trained bird goes directly to the shoebox, picks up a folded paper, and lets it drop on the ground. Meanwhile, the Parakeet Boy asks the fortune seeker to make a wish and recite the following formula in his heart:

Ay Hafez Sherazi! Tu kashefi har razi
Ma talebe yak falem
Bar ma benoma raze
(Oh, Hafez from Shiraz, you are the explorer of secrets
I am seeking my fortune
Please tell me my secret.)[17]

By this time, a crowd of curious people, the audience (not just mere disengaged bystanders), including the fortune seeker, has gathered around the cage, the shoebox, and the boys. The piece of paper is picked up from the ground carefully, as if it was the most precious gift containing magical words, and offered to the seeker, who must read his fortune and the answer from Hafez aloud.[18] If the fortune seeker is non-literate, then a member of the audience or one of the Parakeet Boys will volunteer and read a magical paper bearing a poem like this:

ARISE, oh Cup-bearer, rise! and bring
To lips that are thirsting the bowl they praise,
For it seemed that love was an easy thing,
But my feet have fallen on difficult ways.
I have prayed the wind o'er my heart to fling
The fragrance of musk in her hair that sleeps
In the night of her hair—yet no fragrance stays
The tears of my heart's blood, my sad heart weeps.
   Hear the Tavern-keeper who counsels you:
"With wine, with red wine your prayer carpet dye!"
There was never a traveler like him but knew
The ways of the road and the hostelry.
Where shall I rest, when the still night through,
Beyond thy gateway, oh Heart of my heart,
The bells of the camels lament and cry:
"Bind up thy burden again and depart!"
   The waves run high, night is clouded with fears,
And eddying whirlpools clash and roar;
How shall my drowning voice strike their ears
Whose light-freighted vessels have reached the shore?
I sought mine own; the unsparing years
Have brought me mine own, a dishonored name.
What cloak shall cover my misery o'er
When each jesting mouth has rehearsed my shame!
Oh Hafez, seeking an end to strife,
Hold fast in thy mind what the wise have writ:
"If at last thou attain the desire of thy life,
Cast the world aside, yea, abandon it!"[19]

To the fortune seeker this great poem might answer any of his/her wishes because the poem is subject to interpretation, as all forms of poetry are. It would be unjust to the profession of fortune telling if any speculation were made as to what the poem might mean for the fortune seeker. Suffice it to say that there are many ingredients in the poem, such as wine, cup-bearer, tavern-keeper, "Heart of my heart," "seeking an end to strife," or attaining life's desires, that allow for myriad interpretations depending on the question.

Although the boys are literate, they do not dare read Hafez's poetry, a task requiring special skills of diction that is reserved for much older people. Instead, they listen carefully to each verse to familiarize themselves with classical poetry and good diction, something that they will probably carry into adulthood. They listen carefully, internalizing and memorizing each poetic line, as would any professional storyteller. Instead of reading from the text, the Parakeet Boys learn classical poetry by listening repeatedly, as if, like storytellers, they were memorizing the words, sounds, nuances, rhythms, and meanings of the text. As Jack Goody notes:

> Most people find difficulties in verbatim recall from long term storage unless they adopt explicit rehearsal procedures. Learning by heart is a very deliberate process of repeating sequences several times until one has them correct. This can be done relatively easily by reading a text, turning away the eyes, repeating as much of the content as possible, then returning to the text to correct what was remembered and continuing from the corrected section.[20]

The audience, too, listens attentively and corrects any mispronunciations. From a performance point of view, the text ceases to be the original. In this peculiar performance, the boys serve as instruments to externalize the fortune of the seeker by using the parakeets, symbols of innocence and neutrality. The boys, the shoebox, and the parakeets are the original performers,[21] but then the fortune seeker becomes not only the new performer but also the voice of a written text, even though the new version will be different. Here the performer/seeker, the witnessing audience, the boys, and the parakeets become the "larger audience" and may interact with each other. The audience generally praises the seeker and wishes him or her good luck. In this example, the receiver is both the audience and the reader, as well as the voice of a medieval text, making it hard to separate the notions of receiver, reader, performer, and writer. The Parakeet Boys are exposed to this multiple discourse, which will develop not only their performance abilities but also their academic skills, since classical poetry is part of the Afghan school curriculum. They re-create the memorized poem in their classrooms where as formal students they excel in reading classical poetry and in the art of "rhapsodizing," thus re-creating knowledge. As Goody writes:

I have spoken of the growth of knowledge by the search, the quest, the journey, the sojourn in the woods, all common themes of oral recitation. I am concerned to stress that oral cultures are not simply incessant reduplications of the same things, the model of perfect reproduction, a pre-literate photocopier. There is some change in knowledge, sometimes perceived as growth by the actors.[22]

Toward a Parakeet School

Indeed, the Parakeet Boys of the streets of Kabul are re-creating knowledge, as well as enriching their skills as students. Despite the many training efforts by the international community, the preferred method in Afghan schools is still teacher-centered. In a tribal society where hierarchy is valued in all aspects of life, it is a great challenge to introduce student-centered approaches. The Parakeet Boys learn poetry in their classrooms through the voice of the teacher in boring, static, and motionless lectures, where there is no interaction among pupils. They are limited to Freire's "narrative sickness," from which they need to free themselves:

> Narration (with the teacher as narrator) leads the students to memorize mechanically the narrated content. Worse yet, it turns them into "containers," into "receptacles" to be "filled" by the teacher. The more completely she fills the receptacles, the better a teacher she is. The more meekly the receptacles permit themselves to be filled, the better students they are.[23]

The streets of Kabul are where the Parakeet Boys find solace and push back the narration sickness in order to become self-filling receptacles. They interact with the audience, the voice of Hafez, and the parakeets, undoubtedly creating a learner-centered environment where knowledge is tried and transformed, thus giving the Parakeet Boys agency and power. The disconnected teaching within the classroom is "supplemented" by the dynamic and transformational power of the street. The international community is working tirelessly to increase children's literacy skills through formal teacher-training programs with top-down approaches. Nevertheless, it would also be worth looking directly into informal settings, such as a street performance, to try to discover where we can connect informally with formal education. A "Parakeet School" for "Parakeet Boys" would surely be an effective work-study setting for some Afghan street children.

What could be the rationale for such a utopic idea? Many schools and students in Afghanistan today are facing great challenges, such as a dearth of teachers, outdated teaching methods, lack of infrastructure, and unfriendly and unaccommodating study environments, as well as lack of administrative skills and leadership. These problems will take many years to repair. Time might not be on the side of the current student population, especially street children who are in their age of development. With the challenges described above, including home environments that are not conducive to studying and financial difficulties at home, these street children are profoundly vulnerable. Many will drop out of school, beg in the streets of the capital city, or become involved in illicit activities, evolving later into much more serious problems for Afghan society.

With an aviary as its central focus, the Parakeet School could offer an opportunity to use and train easily domesticated birds to provide an income for these street children, to nurture a love for birds and ornithology, and to increase the children's knowledge of classical poetry and the art of good diction. Although the Afghan government[24] and various conservatives would likely categorize the Parakeet Boys and fortune telling as superstitious beliefs, we need to revisit the value of these traditional practices. The Parakeet School could act as a bird sanctuary, preserving many different species and educating other children through field trip visits.[25] The success of butterfly pavilions across the United States in supporting education is a model that can be duplicated in many different projects and permutations. The Parakeet School could generate a steady income from these visits and extend its programs to benefit many other children of all classes and circumstances. It may seem far-fetched, but creating an inspired connection between poetry, birds, fortune telling, and education would improve the lives of many street children in Afghanistan, providing them with opportunities for becoming well-developed, imaginative human beings who can help transform their own lives and the future of Afghanistan.

Notes

1. In 1995, Engineer Mohammad Yousef founded the internationally acclaimed NGO called Aschiana (The Nest). To date, according to its own reports, Aschiana has helped more than 50,000 children and young adults. "Engineer" is a common Afghan honorific, indicating someone who is educated and has studied engineering.

2. Leslie Knott, "Children at Risk of Contracting AIDS in Afghanistan," UNICEF, http://www.unicef.org/infobycountry/afghanistan_46717.html.

3. Faird Behbud and Chen Xin, "War Weary Afghan Children Long for Peace,

Schooling," Xinhuanet, June 1, 2012, http://news.xinhuanet.com/english/indepth/20 12-06/01/c_131626134.htm.

4. Jack Goody, *The Interface Between the Written and the Oral: Studies in Literacy, the Family, Culture and the State* (New York: Cambridge University Press, 1987), 184–185.

5. Paulo Friere, *Pedagogy of the Oppressed* (London: The Continuum International Publishing Group Inc., 2010), 71–72.

6. See Paul Zumthor, *Oral Poetry*, trans. Kathryn Murphy-Judy (Minneapolis: University of Minnesota Press, 1990); John Miles Foley, *How to Read an Oral Poem* (Urbana: University of Illinois Press, 2002); Ruth Finnegan, *Oral Poetry: Its Nature, Significance, and Context* (Cambridge: Cambridge University Press, 2002); Dell Hymes, "Models of Interactions of Language and Social Life," in John J. Gumperz and Dell Hymes, eds. *Directions in Sociolinguistics* (New York: Holt, Rinehart and Winston, 1972) 35–71; and Walter J. Ong, *Orality and Literacy* (London: Routledge, 1988).

7. The word *adab* is not fully translatable from Arabic to English. It encompasses all the good things a Muslim must do. Adab linguistically means to invite people for food. The Arabic word *Ma'duba* is derived from the word *adab*, and means to invite all or many people for all types of food, or a gathering around a table. Adab hence includes all that is good: every noble characteristic, habit, or trait that is included within the scope of adab.

Adab is natural, it isn't really taught, or learned, but it is naturally developed. Children acquire adab from their parents, students from their teachers, the young from the elders. We may have much knowledge but lack adab and we may have much adab but lack knowledge; but it is adab that holds the greater value and importance. In today's society, where parents, teachers, and elders are no longer given their correct honors, respect, or rights, basic manners have made a swift exit, whilst we compete for glory, knowledge, or worldly gain (http://adabinislam.wordpress.com/adab/).

8. The first kingdom of Afghanistan was established in 1709 by Mir Wais Hotaki, and the last king was Zahir Shah, who ruled from 1933 to 1973. It was during the reign of Sultan Mahmud of Ghazna (971–1030) that Dari became the favorite language of the court.

9. A more detailed list of these formulas can be found in Mohammad Ali Raonaq, *A Manual for Spoken Dari in Afghanistan*, trans. Wahid Omar (Kabul: Danish Press, 2008).

10. Richard Bauman, *Verbal Art as Performance* (Long Grove, Illinois: Waveland Press, Inc., 1984), 28.

11. Charles Briggs in *Competence in Performance* (Philadelphia: University of Pennsylvania Press, 1988) shows that in Hispanic America, elders are free to use proverbs more than younger people because they are knowledgeable authorities. Similarly, in Afghanistan, mostly elders use proverbs and sayings in their everyday speech and transmit them to younger generations. Through repetition, proverbs become a frame of reference understood by everybody and become part of culture and performance.

12. There are many other forms of fortune telling in Afghanistan, such as readings through tea leaves, Quranic verses, palms, astrology, and pigeons. For more details please see Wahid Omar, *Afghanistan: A Nation in Performance, A Comparative Study Between Medieval France and Contemporary Afghanistan* (Saarbrücken, Germany: VDM Publishing, Verlag Dr. Müller, 2010).

13. I have observed and documented four children involved in this profession. There may, however, be more around the city and other provinces.

14. All public schools and universities are free of charge for Afghan students according to the Afghan Constitution.

15. In the Afghan and Iranian traditions, only Hafez among many poets is used to read someone's fortune. This is because the poems are crafted in such a way that they can be interpreted easily to answer any question, wish, or inquiry.

16. The boys always keep two birds in case one of them becomes capricious and refuses to leave the cage.

17. There are many different versions of this formula, since they are sourced in oral traditions. A list can be found at http://hafezdivan.blogpars.com.

18. It is said in the Afghan oral traditions that Hafez can sometimes be moody and scold the fortune seeker with very negative poems. This negativity can also turn up if the fortune seeker is not satisfied with his fortune and repeatedly demands a new reading.

19. This poem is the first ode in the compilations of Hafez poetry and was translated by Gertrude Lowthian Bell in 1897 and accessed at the Poet Seers website, edited by Abichal Watkins and Tejvan Pettinger, http://www.poetseers.org/the_poetseers /hafiz/h_p/arise/, where further Hafez translations can be found.

20. Goody, *The Interface Between the Written and the Oral*, 177.

21. Animals and objects can be considered as performers since, according to Bauman, the term "performance" has been used to convey a dual sense of "artistic": *action* (the doing of folklore) and artistic *event* (the performance situation, involving performer, art form, audience, and setting), both of which are basic to the developing performance approach (*Verbal Art as Performance*, 4).

22. Goody, *The Interface Between the Written and the Oral*, 155.

23. Freire, *Pedagogy of the Oppressed*, 71–72.

24. Since 2009, Afghan media outlets such as Tolo, Ariana, and the Afghan National Television have been conducting a campaign against the art of fortune telling by broadcasting programs ridiculing those who practice it. They present fortune tellers as "illiterate" fabricators of superstitious beliefs and anti-Islamists who are using religion for their own personal gain. They accuse them of falsely interpreting the words of the Qur'an and advise the public not to patronize or believe fortune tellers, while, ironically, these same "journalists" offer their own versions of the "true" meaning of Quranic verses, without caveat.

25. According to Wikipedia, "List of Birds in Afghanistan," the avifauna of Afghanistan includes a total of 499 species. Many suffer for lack of habitat, thanks to deforestation and other hazards created by more than three decades of war (http:// en.wikipedia.org/wiki/List_of_birds_of_Afghanistan).

Child Soldiering in Afghanistan

DELPHINE BOUTIN

*Afghanistan's situation was so that all people from fifteen years old
to eighty had to fight.*

MORTAZA, FORMER CHILD SOLDIER IN AFGHANISTAN, TALKING
ABOUT THE POLITICAL INSTABILITY AFTER THE SOVIETS LEFT

Little is known about the history of child soldiers in Afghanistan, although
it is believed that the exploitation of children as combatants has been prevalent throughout the country's ongoing conflict of the past more than forty
years.[1] Since the late nineties, Afghan children are known to have been fighting with all forms of armed groups. Unfortunately, international organizations
or researchers have, until recently, demonstrated little interest in the issue.[2]
The groundbreaking report by Graça Machel, drawing global attention to the
devastating impact on children of armed conflict, did not emerge until about
fifteen years ago.[3]

The United Nations defines a child soldier as:

> any person below eighteen years of age who is, or who has been, recruited
> or used by an armed force or armed group in any capacity, including but not
> limited to children, boys and girls, used as fighters, cooks, porters, spies or
> for sexual purposes. It does not only refer to a child who is taking, or has
> taken, a direct part in hostilities.[4]

In Afghanistan the number of actual and former child soldiers is estimated at
around 8,000,[5] but that figure may not be accurate, due in part to mass dis-
placements and turmoil caused by armed conflict, which make it more complex to register people and accumulate precise data.[6] Who are these child
soldiers? Why do some children become involved in armed conflict? How is

soldiering harmful to them? How have Disarmament, Demobilization, and Reintegration (DDR) programs helped them?

The Use of Children in Armed Groups

Even if there are no precise statistics on Afghan child soldiers, several reports attest to the severity of the problem. Since the fall of the communist Najibullah regime in 1992, many children have taken a direct part in hostilities, particularly along the Afghanistan-Pakistan border. The military use of Afghan children is not limited to participation in combat, but includes laying mines and explosives and the performance of a wide range of supportive tasks, such as scouting; spying; and acting as decoys, couriers, or guards. In some cases, children have been trained in foreign countries (mainly Pakistan) to undertake suicide missions or have been forcibly involved in the insurgency when, unbeknownst to them, explosives were hidden in their bags or clothing.[7] In January 2011, Afghanistan's National Directorate of Security asserted that more than 80 percent of the 112 would-be suicide bombers detained in the country in 2010 were boys aged between thirteen and seventeen.[8] Although the overwhelming majority of Afghan child soldiers is male, between fourteen and eighteen years old, some girls or younger children are also implicated in the Afghan armed conflict. Beautiful young boys and girls can be snatched from the streets or sold by their families to armed groups and rebels. Afghan girls have been reportedly forced into marriages with fighters in factional and clan-based militias and armed groups.[9] In many cases, adolescent girls are recruited by armed groups to perform the same military functions as their male counterparts.[10] Girls may even be preferred to boys by warlords because they are likely to raise little or no suspicion.[11] They are also recruited for performing domestic tasks or for providing sexual services. In Afghanistan, male children are also recruited for sexual purposes. In recent years, warlords have returned to an ancient practice of using young boys for sex and entertainment. Ownership of young boys, the *"bacha bazi* or *bacha bereesh* (boy play or boy without a beard), who are trained to sing and dance and provide sexual favors, has become a sign of prestige."[12]

Many groups stand to benefit from exploiting children as soldiers. Armed opposition forces (such as Haqqani network, Hezb-e Islami, Jamat Sunat al-Dawa Salafia), as well as the Afghan National Security Forces, including the Afghan National Police,[13] use children as soldiers. Only the Taliban publically opposes the use of minor children as soldiers, claiming to rely only on volunteer adult recruitment. However, the secretary-general of the United

Nations, Ban Ki-moon, stated in April 2011 that there were numerous in-dications that the Taliban have in fact been actively recruiting child soldiers under eighteen.[14]

Children are not necessarily used as a last resort. Government armies, rebels, paramilitaries, and other militarized groups use children as soldiers because they are convenient, cheap, easily manipulated, and obedient. Their small size is considered an advantage: they are often exploited as "cannon fodder" by their leaders, who force them to the front lines or to minefields ahead of older troops. Children are not fully aware of the dangers, have un-formed notions of right and wrong, and are not burdened with domestic re-sponsibilities, according to military commanders interviewed in a 2007 report by Susan Tiefenbrun. Adolescents reportedly have a sense of their own om-nipotence and "view themselves as invulnerable to harm and injury."[15] The dif-ferentiation of tasks between children and adults indicates that they are com-plementary. In addition, it is easy to train children to use modern weapons. While a child may lack the physical capacity of an adult, light, user-friendly weapons and small arms require little instruction and are easy for children to use and carry. Rising numbers of small arms circulate illegally among armed groups in Afghanistan: a Small Arms Survey report in 2003 estimates the number of uncontrolled small arms to be 1.5 to 10 million.[16] Additionally, armed groups seek children for political advantage. According to Vincent Ntuda Ebode, using children as combatants is a war strategy that provokes fear and powerlessness within populations.[17] It is particularly frightening for communities to see their own children turning weapons against them. More-over, enrolling children at an early age is the best way to ensure a future elec-toral base, as they are easy to manipulate.

Thus, warlords do not hesitate to abduct children from their homes, schools, or communities. Many forcibly recruited children—street children or orphans—belong to economically and socially disadvantaged groups or to minorities (Hazaras, Tajiks, Uzbeks, Turkmen, Nuristanis, Baluchis, or Bra-huis).[18] The lack of protective community or family structures increases these children's exposure. Widespread displacement due to ongoing conflict also exacerbates the children's vulnerability. Thousands of Afghan families have been forced to flee their homes due to fighting and economic hardships.[19] While large numbers of the internally displaced remain "invisible" because of ongoing hostilities and access constraints, the secretary-general's Report on Children and Armed Conflict noted a correlation between high levels of dis-placement and child recruitment.[20] According to the report, forced recruit-ment of children by armed groups is "prevalent in areas with high concen-trations of returnees or internally displaced persons." Forced enrollment into armed forces is only one mode of conscription. Sometimes joining an armed faction is a deliberate choice.

Voluntary and Coerced Enrollment to Armed Groups

Children have often been portrayed as passive innocents whom adults have forced and intimidated into soldiering. In fact, most children go to war willingly. Research has identified that those who become child soldiers are overwhelmingly found living in conflict zones in the first place.[21] War itself creates the environment for child soldiering. In the long-running Afghan conflict, children rapidly become acclimated to fighting; it has become the normal, everyday background to their lives. War also creates other conditions that work against children's peaceful well-being.

In recent years, Afghanistan has consistently ranked near the bottom of the Human Development Index,[22] with more than one-third of Afghans living in extreme poverty.[23] Afghan children are growing up in a deeply divided society with intolerable levels of poverty. Worldwide, poverty is a common denominator in the recruitment of child soldiers. Armed conflict has also exacerbated the socioeconomic hardship of many Afghan families due to displacement, the death of one or several family members, or the loss of livelihood. In peacetime, Afghan children have traditionally contributed to household incomes, working in all kinds of jobs—some of which were apprenticeships for learning vital skills—often side-by-side with fathers, uncles, or brothers.[24] But in these desperate times, boys have frequently had to become the heads of households to support their widowed mothers and younger siblings.[25] Gauss Rashid, deputy minister of the Afghan Ministry of Labor, Social Affairs, Martyrs, and Disabled (MoLSAMD), stated in 2003 that "there are over two million child-headed households and widows struggling to earn a daily livelihood."[26] Forming into armed militias is one of the ways to become family breadwinners. Not all poor children become child soldiers. Poverty can create a general vulnerability to recruitment but it is not the only factor.

Lack of employment opportunities or educative options provided by the society can also push a child to join armed groups. Illicit activities (the Afghan economy is dominated by the informal sector), high levels of unemployment (estimated at 35 percent in 2008 by the CIA *World Fact Book*), and drug trafficking are increasing due in large part to government corruption.[27] The unprecedented large inflows of international aid (international donors are financing more than half of the government budget) and the pressures to have rapid and visible results (by spending money quickly) have raised the political corruption. Government corruption, in-service delivery and regulation, and the lack of funding for ordinary people are exacerbated by the corruption of contractors.[28] Only about 20 percent of donor funds reach the Afghan people. Most of the aid has neglected Afghans' needs and preferences and is limited to urban areas.[29] In this context, entering armed groups offers children access to competencies, options, and support that they have been unable to obtain in civilian life. Military groups can provide access to otherwise nonexistent benefits such as physical protection, housing, food, medical care, or opportunity for employment (be it formal employment in the army or police or an informal source of financial income via armed groups).[30]

In addition, education cannot necessarily be seen as a serious alternative to work or soldiering. Despite recent progress in school enrollment,[31] the quality of educational and vocational training systems remains poor, often due to the lack of infrastructure, the destruction and damage to schools, and the significant aggregate loss of teachers, who do not wish to work in rural schools or who lack qualifications.[32] Besides, abductions from school are common and can take many forms, from kidnapping to brainwashing. Textbooks "filled with violent images and militant Islamic teachings" were still used in 2001.[33] Many children are recruited from *madrassas* (schools) run by political Islamists.[34] Many of these schools are legitimate, serving poor students with few alternative educational opportunities. But some of the madrassas have independent sources of income and are linked to religious sects and political factions like the Taliban in order to train children for political and military activities.[35] By indoctrinating vulnerable children with political and/or martyrdom ideologies, the madrassa system ensures new recruits to fill the ranks of all armed groups.[36]

Family environment, community, friends, and peer groups hold considerable influence over the choices a child makes. For some, military life seems normal, when parents, siblings, or other family members are involved, particularly if this is combined with religious, ethnic, or ideological elements.[37] Studies in, for example, Colombia and Sri Lanka reveal a high correlation between the decision to join armed groups and an abusive and/or exploitive domestic situation, especially for girls, who, like boys, protect themselves from domestic exploitation and abuse by choosing to enroll in military groups.[38] The peer group is another major influence on adolescents, who are still constructing their identities. Friends already enrolled can encourage and pressure a young person to join up. As with the other factors identified, this does not mean that all young people in a group will join the conflict, but the pressure to get involved can be greater.

Joining the struggle is also a way for children to honor their ideological beliefs and political opinions. In a country where martyrdom has deep cultural roots and is often glorified, children may learn to feel the willingness to die for a noble and just cause. By definition, a martyr is "one who voluntarily suffers death rather than deny his religion by words or deeds; such action is afforded special, institutionalized recognition in most major religions of the world."[39] Martyrdom is thus viewed as an achieved religious status. A higher purpose can justify violence, and combatants honored as *shahid* (martyr in Arabic) are idealized, thus creating a strong attraction, particularly for adolescent children, to join the struggle.

For instance, Rachel Brett and Margaret McCallin suggest that "the cult of martyrdom" plays a particular role in relation to recruitment and occasional training of adolescents in Palestinian territories for suicide attacks.[40] As in Palestine and other countries worldwide, Afghan children may see themselves as protagonists of their ideologies' successes and can see fighting and being ready to die for the cause as a way to gain respect and honors.[41] The political context in which young people grow up is, of course, relevant in influencing their perceptions, as shown by the testimony of Ali, ten years old when he chose to fight among the Tajik forces of Ismail Khan (former Mujahedin commander and former governor of Herat province) in Herat:

> If I wanted to live under the Taliban there was no enjoyment in our life because the Taliban regime was following a racist policy. We had no choice except fighting [against] the Taliban. There was hope that if I fight the Taliban and if I kick them out there would be a better life for the rest of my family, even if I were killed . . . I fought for the sake of my belief and for Islam. It was our Islamic duty to fight against infidelity.[42]

The factors explaining why a child has chosen to join are myriad and this essay cannot provide an exhaustive list. These situations are often combined to drive children into armed militias. The decision depends on the individual's unique and precise combination of factors. And, as we've seen, how "voluntary" the child soldiers' participation might be is questionable. "Volunteering" is generally defined as not being abducted or conscripted. However, children are often deliberately misled by romanticized descriptions of "working conditions." Many volunteer children believe that they will be able to leave when they want, only to find that once in, they are unable to flee from their predicament.

What Future for These Children?

Whether they were forced or "volunteered," the effect of their experiences is profound, life-changing, even devastating for these youngsters. Although undoubtedly harmful for children, little is known about the long-term effects of soldiering. Subject to ill treatment and sexual exploitation, they are often also forced to commit terrible atrocities, including rape or murder, and are subjected to brutal initiation and punishment rituals, hard labor, cruel training regimes and torture, drugs, and alcohol. Over and above the dangers of actual combat, child soldiers can become physically deformed or disabled by war wounds or landmines.[43] They are victimized by malnutrition, exposed to all kinds of weather and unsanitary living conditions that can cause skin diseases (such as the deforming cutaneous leishmaniasis) and/or respiratory infections.[44] Despite low reported prevalence rates, experts warn that armed conflict exacerbates risk factors (like intravenous drug use, the displacement of people, or the lack of hygiene) contributing to the spread of HIV/AIDS in Afghanistan.[45]

In the aftermath of conflict, children may encounter exclusion or rejection by their families or communities. Problems of social isolation or social reintegration are not unusual, as communities tend to stigmatize former child soldiers. This stigmatization often takes the form of fear (that the ex–child soldiers will fall again into violent patterns) or resentment (for the special support these children receive during the reintegration programs). Girls and bacha bereesh in particular are often stigmatized as having had inappropriate sexual involvement, limiting their future opportunities for employment and/or marriage. The human capital loss due to time away from schooling and employment is another impact of armed group participation and also contributes to marginalization and inactivity. Facing social and economic marginalization, many former child soldiers resort to crime, prostitution, and/or opium drug use to cope and survive. Drug dependency in Afghanistan, notably to opiates such as heroin, opium, and opioid painkillers, continues to increase across the country. With widespread and easy access to relatively low-cost drugs, more and more Afghan citizens, including a reported 60,000 children under the age of fifteen, are becoming drug-addicted.[46] Little is done to halt this phenomenon. Despite short-term interventions, such as a number of generic health and drug treatment services in Kandahar financed by the government of Canada through the United Nations Office on Drugs and Crime (UNODC), no long-term policies have yet been implemented to help drug-addicted children.[47]

Former child soldiers have often been depicted by media as "damaged

goods," violent and beyond rehabilitation.[48] During the 2007 Paris Child Soldiering Conference, French foreign minister Philippe Douste-Blazy qualified them as "a time bomb that threatens stability and growth."[49] However,
the dominant view of "lost children" can be excessive. One particularity of
Afghan underage soldiers (compared to child soldiers from other regions in
the world) is that most are conscripted for short periods of time (two or three
months) before returning to their communities. This "occasional soldiering"
leads Afghan NGOs to presume that Afghan children are less psychologically
or physically damaged than underage soldiers in other countries.[50] Likewise, a
growing body of ethnographic and psychological studies is finding that rather
than being traumatized, former child soldiers, who had regularly served in
armed groups worldwide, exhibit considerable resilience, mostly thanks to
Disarmament, Demobilization, and Reintegration (DDR) programs.[51] Two
parallel and separate DDR initiatives are running in Afghanistan. The first,
Afghanistan's New Beginnings Program (ANBP), was launched in April
2003 and implemented by the Afghan government and the United Nations
Assistance Mission to Afghanistan (UNAMA). This program aimed to dis-
arm, demobilize, and reintegrate former soldiers who were over eighteen at
the time of demobilization. To date, the efficacy of the ANBP's DDR program is partial and excludes children. Program evaluations focus on outputs,
claiming, for instance, significant achievements in the numbers of weapons
collected by the ANBP disarmament component.[52] Nearly 100,000 weapons
had been collected at the end of 2010.[53] However, some militias either held
on to caches of weapons or disarmed more slowly than others. According to
Steven Zyck, the disarmament component of the ANBP program has led to
social fragmentation and threatens the country's cohesion because it contributes to a common thought that some militias have been disarmed while the
international community has permitted the rearming of others (in particular
some community self-defense initiatives of the Pashtun-dominated south).[54]

The second program, designed and led by UNICEF, is targeting "minors
associated with the fighting forces," but contains no disarmament component.
UNICEF's Demobilization and Reintegration (DR) initiative includes two
objectives: first to demobilize underage ex-soldiers and provide them with
shelter and care.[55] According to the United Nations, 8,000 child soldiers have
been demobilized throughout Afghanistan.[56]

The second objective is to offer information but also one year of vocational
training and hands-on skills (including those related to farming), clothes
(each individual received a *salwar kameez*, the traditional shirt and trousers),
food aid, literacy assistance, emergency employment, health facilities, and
psychosocial support to facilitate their return and reintegration to civil society.

As of June 2007, reintegration support was being provided to 5,000 former child soldiers and more than 7,000 other war-affected and at-risk children.[57]

The Afghan process of reintegration is quite complex yet also limited because of the absence of coordination and collaboration between the ANBP and UNICEF, which pursue the same objectives. Potential benefits of financial resources and technical assistance were wasted because of duplication of effort in the two programs.[58] Rehabilitation centers are not numerous enough to absorb the increasing number of former child soldiers referred by parents and armed groups.[59] The absence of a comprehensive needs assessment, the lack of qualified staff and financial resources, the growing levels of insecurity, the lack of commitment on the part of key commanders, and the inadequate support from the Afghan Ministry of Defense make it difficult to implement the DR process in all areas and for all Afghan armed groups.[60] Due to the difficult and lengthy process of identifying, contracting, and implementing NGO partners, the demobilization phase was delayed and applied in fewer regions than initially planned, with little regard to how objectives were met in assisting children to make the transition back into their communities. In some cases, demobilization started without reintegration partners in place, discouraging participants from starting with vocational training courses. The separation between the two programs appears to be inefficient, as several NGOs stated that many youth participants would prefer to be part of the adult program because of the more comprehensive reintegration options and access to microcredit schemes offered by the ANBP.[61]

Because the reintegration process fosters ineffective and culturally inappropriate livelihoods, former combatants are vulnerable to remobilization. The weak Afghan economy has posed difficulties for ex-combatants seeking to make the transition into civilian life. The DDR process did not provide for the monitoring of potential recruitment or re-recruitment of children, according to the 2008 United Nations Secretary-General's Report on Children and Armed Conflict in Afghanistan.[62] Mostly due to economic incentives, some children reportedly returned to their former commanders, or joined local police forces or the Afghan army.[63] Thus, the Afghan DDR programs seem to have had limited successes.

Yet some progress has been made to reduce the use of children as soldiers. In 2011, Afghanistan signed a formal agreement with the United Nations to end the recruitment of children into the country's police forces, as well as place a ban on the use of young boys as sex slaves. Nevertheless, all things considered—from culture to corruption—it seems doubtful that much progress will be made in the near future to stop the use of children as soldiers in Afghanistan.

Notes

The chapter epigraph comes from Rachel Brett and Irma Specht, *Young Soldiers—Why They Choose to Fight* (London: Lynne Rienner Publishers for International Labour Organization, 2004), 32.

1. For instance, Human Rights Watch interviewed 3,000 Afghans in 2003. They found that more than 30 percent of them had participated in military activities as children. Jo Becker, *Children as Weapons of War*, Human Rights Watch Report (New York: HRW, 2004), 8, http://www.unhcr.org/refworld/pdfid/402ba6d44.pdf. "Under Soviet occupation, boys were trained to be spies and to identify and lead Soviet troops to the homes of Mujahedin leaders." Jo Boyden, Jo de Berry, Thomas Feeny, and Jason Hart, *Children Affected by Armed Conflict in South Asia: A Review of Trends and Issues Identified through Secondary Research*, Refugee Studies Center, Working Paper no. 7 (Oxford: RSC, 2002), 46, http://www.rsc.ox.ac.uk/publications/working-papers/RSC workingpaper7.pdf.

2. There are two main reasons why so little interest was demonstrated before the 1990s. First, international attention was focused on the military use of children in Somalia or in Bosnia and Herzegovina during this period, while very little was reported about the conflicts in Afghanistan. Second, the difficulty of access in war zones and the relatively slow spread of information before the end of the 1980s explain the lack of information and documentation on the issue of Afghan child soldiers.

3. Graça Machel, *The Impact of Armed Conflict on Children* (New York: UNICEF, 1996), http://www.unicef.org/graca/a51-306_en.pdf.

4. UNICEF, *Paris Principles and Guidelines on Children Associated with Armed Forces or Armed Groups*, United Nations, February 2007, http://www.un.org/children /conflict/_documents/parisprinciples/ParisPrinciples_EN.pdf.

5. UNICEF, *Afghanistan—Country in Crisis: Measures to Help Victims of War*, United Nations, 2003, http://www.unicef.org/emerg/afghanistan/index_9028.html. Figures come from a UNICEF field assessment on the situation of child soldiers. See UNICEF, *UNICEF Humanitarian Action: Afghanistan Donor Update 23*, ReliefWeb, September 23, 2003, http://wwww.reliefweb.int/w/Rwb.nsf/0/8fa0690d36b0ab6ac12 56daa003a3099?OpenDocument.

6. The difficulties are exacerbated by inadequate official definition, poor birth registration systems, and lack of age verification. In many regions in Afghanistan, especially those with weak administrative systems, identifying the age of some recruits is complicated. People may not know how old they are or have any documentation of their births. For these reasons, figures concerning child soldiers in Afghanistan must be regarded as provisional.

7. For example, in April 2009, a young boy transported an improvised explosive device, which prematurely detonated fifteen meters from the governor's office in Samangan province. Subsequent investigations indicated that the improvised explosive device had been planted without the knowledge of the boy. Watch List on Children and Armed Conflict, *Setting the Right Priorities: Protecting Children Affected by Armed Conflict in Afghanistan* (New York: Watch List Publications, June 2010), 32, http://watchlist.org/reports/pdf/Afghanistan%20Report%202010.pdf.

In another June 2011 case, a young girl was used as a suicide bomber in the Char China District of Afghanistan, http://www.twitter.com/childreninwar.

8. "Baby Fighters on Frontline of Afghan War," *Daily Times* (Pakistan), February 9, 2011, http://www.dailytimes.com.pk/default.asp?page=2011\02\09\story_9-2 -2011_pg14_10.

9. Coalition to Stop the Use of Child Soldiers, *Child Soldiers: Global Report 2004* (London: Coalition to Stop the Use of Child Soldiers, 2004), 21, http://www.child -soldiers.org/global_report_reader.php?id=281.

See also Anne E. Brodsky, "Centuries of Threat, Centuries of Resistance: The Lessons of Afghan Women's Resilience," in Jennifer Heath and Ashraf Zahedi, eds., *Land of the Unconquerable: The Lives of Contemporary Afghan Women* (Berkeley: University of California Press, 2011), 80.

10. For some time, scholars did not distinguish between girl and boy soldiers. Although it has become clear that girls fight and perform the same functions as boys in an armed group, no figures or details are yet available, especially in Afghanistan, where girls and women are officially excluded from participating in military activities. Afghan history gives us examples of the role of women (of varying ages) on the front lines, willing, for instance, to be Mujahedin during the Soviet occupation. See, for example, the story of Najla, who spent two years on a front line in eastern Afghanistan, participating actively in "cleaning and loading weapons, sewing face masks to protect against poison gas, providing medical care, teaching literacy classes, and taking part in military operations trainings." In Brodsky, "Centuries of Threat, Centuries of Resistance," 79. For more information, see Anne E. Brodsky, *With All Our Strength: The Revolutionary Association of the Women of Afghanistan* (New York: Routledge, 2003).

11. Michael Wessells, *Child Soldiers, from Violence to Protection* (Harvard University Press, 2006).

12. The bacha bereesh—generally between fourteen and eighteen years old and dressed in women's clothing—is paraded out to dance at parties and weddings and is sometimes sexually abused. The practice of Afghan men taking boys as sexual partners antedates the arrival of Islam. This five-thousand-year-old tradition, although dormant under the Taliban regime (1996-2001), was prevalent in Afghanistan before World War I, because women were not allowed to participate in public entertainment. The practice has reemerged with the United States and allied occupation and is now popular among anti-government armed groups. "The quality of the bacha bazi reflects on the power of the party's host; the stronger the stable of dancing boys, the more respected the man." *Examination of and Recommendations for Fighting Human Trafficking Boys* (Hope for Boys Project, 2010), 13, http://hopeforboysproject.com /uploads/7/2/7/4/7274208/whitepaperlayout3.pdf.

13. "The policy of the Government is officially not to recruit children under eighteen years of age, and there are some measures in place to verify the minimum age of recruits at the provincial and training camp levels. However, interviews with victims, government officials, and other sources confirmed that children were still recruited and used by Afghan National Security Forces. It is of concern that local-level Afghan National Police offices also confirmed that recruitment campaigns have taken place in school compounds. Insufficient age verification procedures, extremely low levels

of birth registration in the country, opportunities to manipulate age in the national identity document, and the drive to increase troop levels within the Afghan National Army and the Afghan National Police have led to under-age recruitment." United Nations Security Council, *Report of the Secretary-General on Children and Armed Conflict in Afghanistan*, 3, 2011, S/2011/55, http://www.unhcr.org/refworld/docid/4d6238044 .html.

14. United Nations Security Council, *Report of the Secretary-General on Children and Armed Conflict for the Recruitment and the Use of Children under the Age of Eighteen Years*, no. A/65/820-S/2011/250 (New York: UNSC, April 23, 2011), http://www .un.org/children/conflict/_documents/S2011250.pdf.

15. Susan Tiefenbrun, "Child Soldiers, Slavery and the Trafficking of Children," *Fordham International Law Journal*, 1, no. 2 (New York: Fordham University School of Law, 2007): 19, http://ir.lawnet.fordham.edu/cgi/viewcontent.cgi?article=2091& context=ilj.

16. *Small Arms Survey 2003: Development Denied* (Cambridge, England: Cambridge University Press, 2003). Eleven years after this report, the numbers have surely increased.

17. Note that even if Ebode focuses on sub-Saharan countries, these mechanisms can easily be applied to Afghanistan. Joseph Vincent Ntuda Ebode, "Les enfants soldats dans les crises africaines: entre logique militaire et stratégies politiques," *Guerres mondiales et conflits contemporains*, no. 222 (February 2006), 111-119, http://www.cairn .info/revue-guerres-mondiales-et-conflits-contemporains-2006-2-page-111.htm.

18. Afghanistan has fifty-five ethnic groups who speak forty-five languages. Since the Taliban era (1996-2001), we have seen an "ethnicization" of Afghan politics. Indeed, Taliban, mostly Pashtuns, ruled as the authority, while Tajiks and other minority groups such as Hazaras or Uzbeks had no representation in any government in Kabul. For instance, Nigel Allan points out that "twenty-six out of twenty-seven members of the Taliban government's leadership were Pashtuns; many of them were determined to bring the various ethnic groups of Afghanistan under traditional Pashtun conservative rural culture." Nigel Allan, "Defining Place and People in Afghanistan," *Post-Soviet Geography and Economics* 42, no. 8 (2002): 545-560.

19. Interviews and group discussions conducted with more than seven hundred Afghans report that approximately three in four people, including children, asserted that they were forced to leave their homes at some point during the conflict. Of these, 41 percent were internally displaced, 42 percent were externally displaced, and 17 percent were both internally and externally displaced. Many individuals were displaced multiple times, moving from one place to another in search of security, only to be forced to flee again months or years later or after having returned home. At the end of January 2011, 309,000 people remained internally displaced due to armed conflict, human rights abuses, and other generalized violence. Oxfam, *The Cost of the War: Afghan Experiences of Conflict, 1978-2009* (London: Oxfam, 2009), http://www.oxfam.org.uk /resources/policy/conflict_disasters/downloads/the-cost-of-war-afghanistan.pdf; International Displacement Monitoring Center, *Afghanistan: Need to Minimise New Displacement and Increase Protection for Recently Displaced in Remote Areas* (Geneva: IDMC, April 2011), http://www.internal-displacement.org/8025708F004BE3B1/(ht tpInfoFiles)/8C20C57891906F4FC125786F003978FE/$file/Afghanistan_Over view_April2011.pdf.

20. United Nations Security Council, *Report of the Secretary-General on Children and Armed Conflict in Afghanistan*, no. S/2008/695 (New York: UNSC, November 10, 2008), http://daccess-dds-ny.un.org/doc/UNDOC/GEN/N08/534/13/PDF/N085 3413.pdf?OpenElement; Watch List on Children and Armed Conflict, *Setting the Right Priorities: Protecting Children Affected by Armed Conflict in Afghanistan* (New York: Watch List on Children and Armed Conflict, June 2010), http://protectingeducation .org/sites/default/files/documents/unsc_afghanistan_report_2008.pdf.

21. Alice Schmidt, "Volunteer Child Soldiers as Reality: A Development Issue for Africa," *New School Economic Review*, 2, no. 1 (2007): 49–76, http://www.newscho oljournal.com/files/NSER02/49-76.pdf.

22. In 2010, Afghanistan ranks 155th out of the 169 countries evaluated, http:// hdr.undp.org/en/statistics/.

23. In 2008, 36 percent of Afghans were living with less than 1$25 PPA. The World Bank, http://data.worldbank.org/country/afghanistan.

24. One of the dominant features in Afghan culture is that, as in many other poor societies, "survival depends primarily on cooperation and mutual support within the kin group. . . . Contributing to the family is prized much more highly than making one's own way in the world. Anybody in receipt of a regular income is duty-bound to contribute to the common family fund; dereliction of this duty is despised, and for the vast majority of Afghans, is unthinkable. If a family member cannot contribute because he or she is disabled, this has an important bearing on their status in the family." Peter Coleridge, "Development, Cultural Values and Disability: The Example of Afghanistan," in Emma Stone, ed., *Disability and Development: Learning from Action and Research on Disability in the Majority World* (Leeds: The Disability Press, 1999), 149–167, http://www.leeds.ac.uk/disability-studies/archiveuk/stone/chapter%2010 .pdf.

25. According to Girardet and Walter, more than half a million Afghan children lost one parent during the last three decades due to the conflict. Edward Girardet and Jonathan Walter, eds., *Crosslines Essential Field Guides to Humanitarian and Conflict Zones: Afghanistan*, 3rd ed. (Geneva: Crosslines Publications, 2005), http://www .essentialfieldguides.com/BOOKS/EFG3rdEditionEXCERPT.pdf. Twelve percent of Afghan children were orphans in 2003. UNICEF, *Children on the Brink 2004: A Joint Report of New Orphan Estimates and a Framework for Action* (New York: UNICEF, 2004), 11, http://data.unaids.org/publications/External-Documents/unicef_children onthebrink2004_en.pdf. See also Kona Swapna, *Child Soldiers in Afghanistan*, IPCS special report no. 44 (New Delhi: IPCS Publications, 2007), 2, http://www.ipcs.org /pdf_file/issue/100752309IPCS-Special-Report-44.pdf.

26. Integrated Regional Information Network (IRIN), "Afghanistan: Eight Thousand Children under Arms Look for a Future," December 1, 2003, http://www.irin news.org/InDepthMain.aspx?InDepthId=24&ReportId=66989&Country=Yes.

27. CIA, *World Fact Book*, 2008, https://www.cia.gov/library/publications/the -world-factbook/fields/2129.html; United Nations Office on Drugs and Crime, *Fighting Corruption in Afghanistan: A Road Map for Strategy and Action: Draft for Discussion*, February 16 (New York: United Nations, 2007), 4–9, http://www.unodc.org/pdf/afg /anti_corruption_roadmap.pdf; USAID, *Assessment of Corruption in Afghanistan, January 15, 2009–March 1, 2009* (New York: United Nations, 2009), 4–11, http://pdf.usaid .gov/pdf_docs/PNADO248.pdf.

28. Susanne Koelbl, "The Aid Swindle," *Der Spiegel* Online International, April 5, 2005, http://www.spiegel.de/international/spiegel/0,1518,348597,00.html.

29. Matt Waldman, *Falling Short: Aid Effectiveness in Afghanistan* (Kabul: Agency Coordinating Body for Afghan Relief, March 2008), 1, 3; Gayle Tzemach Lemmon, "Extending the Horizon for Women's Aid Projects in Afghanistan," *New York Times*, August 15, 2009, http://www.nytimes.com/2009/08/15/business/global/15mall.html ?pagewanted=all.

For more information on the embezzlement of aid in Afghanistan, see the 52-minute documentary *Afghanistan: On the Dollar Trail*, directed by Paul Moreira in 2009. This documentary follows the money trail from Europe to Kabul in order to track down how the estimated US$18 billion given by developed countries as reconstruction aid has been used, http://vimeo.com/9388088.

30. Rachel Brett, "Adolescents Volunteering for Armed Forces or Armed Groups," *International Review of the Red Cross, Current Issues and Comments* 85, no. 852 (December 1, 2003), 857–866, http://www.icrc.org/eng/assets/files/other/irrc_852_brett.pdf.

31. Enrollment rates for primary school children (aged six to nine) increased nationwide by about 40 percent between 2005 and 2007/08 (The World Bank, http://data.worldbank.org/country/Afghanistan).

32. According to the Afghan Ministry of Education, around 80 percent of teachers have not completed their high-school or post-secondary educations. OSI, "Afghanistan: Education in a War Zone," Transitions Online, February 13, 2009, http://www.soros.org/initiatives/esp/articles_publications/articles/afghanistan_20090213.

33. These textbooks, published from 1984 to 1994 at the University of Nebraska, encouraged youngsters to fight by using exercises illustrated by pictures and drawings of tanks, missiles, landmines, and other weapons. For more information about the Thomas Gouttierre and CIA textbook scandals, see "Soviet Era Textbook Still Controversial," *Lincoln Journal Star*, September 23, 2007, http://journalstar.com/special -section/news/article_4968e56a-c346-5a18-9798-2b78c5544b58.html.

34. The madrassa system includes any type of educational institution, whether Islamic schools, other religious schools, or secular institutions. They have existed for centuries.

35. Some documents report that madrassas sponsored by networks supporting the Taliban close periodically for holidays and send young students for military service—presented as a form of *jihad* (holy war) and therefore part of the students' religious obligation and education. Scott Peterson, "Child Soldiers for Taliban? Unlikely," *Christian Science Monitor*, December 1999, http://www.csmonitor.com/1999/1206 /pls3.html. See also Ahmed Rashid, *Taliban: Militant Islam, Oil and Fundamentalism in Central Asia* (New Haven: Yale University Press, 2000); or William Maley, *Afghanistan and the Taliban, Fundamentalist Reborn?* (London: C. Hurst & Co, 1999). Until its defeat in 2001, the Taliban recruited young boys from madrassas. However, uncertainty still remains about the proportion of under-eighteens who actually participated in combat. Vera Chrobok, *Demobilizing and Reintegrating Afghanistan's Young Soldiers: A Review and Assessment of Program Planning and Implementation*, Bonn International Center for Conversion, Paper 42 (Bonn: BICC, 2005), 16, http://www.bicc.de/up loads/pdf/publications/papers/paper42/paper42.pdf.

36. Ahmed Rashid, *Taliban*, 56.

37. The following testimony of an Afghan child is eloquent: "In the education of

the Koran in the mosques the *mullah*s [name commonly given to local Islamic clerics or mosque leaders] all the time tell the boys that they have to participate in the holy war and help to liberate their country in order to come to Paradise. Many boys want to participate as soon as possible. Also the mothers want their sons to fight for their country. My mother has always encouraged me." From Jo de Berry, *Children Affected by Armed Conflict in Afghanistan*, Refugee Studies Center (Oxford: 2001), 34, http://www.rsc.ox.ac.uk/pdfs/workshop-conference-research-reports/CAAC%20Afghanistan%20final%20report.pdf. See also Human Rights Watch, *World Report 2009* (New York: HRW, 2009), http://www.hrw.org/world-report-2009.

38. Brett, "Adolescents Volunteering for Armed Forces or Armed Groups," 862.

39. Encyclopaedia Britannica online, http://www.britannica.com/EBchecked/topic/367142/martyr.

40. Rachel Brett and Margaret McCallin, *Children the Invisible Soldiers* (Stockholm: Rädda Barnen, Swedish Save the Children, 1996), 64. Joining armed forces motivated by ideological commitment is not limited to this region of the world. Examples of children or youth worldwide fighting for ideological reasons are numerous. See, for instance, the child participants in the wars in Mozambique and Angola, the young *guerilleros* fighting in Colombia to free their country from Spain in the nineteenth century, the Catholics in Northern Ireland, who are thought to have taught their children to be fighters, and many others throughout history worldwide.

41. Ashraf Zahedi, "State Ideology and the Status of Iranian War Widows," *International Feminist Journal of Politics* 8, no. 2 (2006): 267–286.

42. Brett and Specht, *Young Soldiers—Why They Choose to Fight*, 28–29.

43. According to Peter Coleridge, one million Afghan children have conflict-related disabilities, many caused by exploding landmines. Child soldiers are in general the most vulnerable to conflict-related disability. They are particularly exposed to landmines: they are often used to explore known minefields and thus can be killed or permanently disabled from landmine detonations. Peter Coleridge, *Disability in Afghanistan* (Islamabad: UNDP/UNOPS Comprehensive Disabled Afghans' Programme, 1999).

44. While leishmaniasis and other communicable diseases occur commonly throughout Afghanistan, this skin disease is particularly dire among soldiers, including children, due to unsanitary living conditions. Tami Tamashiro, "Impact of Conflict on Children's Health and Disability," in *Background Paper for the Education for All Global Monitoring Report 2011: The Hidden Crisis: Armed Conflict and Education*, no. 2001/ED/EFA/MRT/PI/35 (Paris: United Nations Educational, Scientific and Cultural Organization Publishing, June 2010), http://unesdoc.unesco.org/images/0019/001907/190712e.pdf.

45. UNAIDS and WHO have registered one to two thousand Afghans, including children, living with HIV. Official numbers are, however, likely to underestimate the situation due to stigmatization, low levels of surveillance and testing in the country, and taboo on the modes of transmission (including male-on-male sex, often with children, and intravenous drug use). Leslie Knott, "Children at Risk of Contracting HIV/AIDS in Afghanistan," December 1, 2008, http://www.unicef.org/infobycountry/afghanistan_46717.html; The World Bank, *HIV/AIDS in Afghanistan* (Washington, DC: The World Bank Publishing, August 2008), http://siteresources.worldbank.org/SOUTHASIAEXT/Resources/223546-1192413140459/4281804-1231540815570

/5730961-1235157256443/HIVAIDSbriefAF.pdf; Watch List on Children and Armed Conflict, *Setting the Right Priorities: Protecting Children Affected by Armed Conflict in Afghanistan.*

46. These figures include former child soldiers, although accurate statistics are difficult to collect. United Nations Office on Drugs and Crime, *Afghanistan, Drug Use Survey 2005* (Kabul: UNDC, November 2005), http://www.unodc.org/pdf/afg/2005 AfghanistanDrugUseSurvey.pdf.

47. United Nations Office on Drugs and Crime, *Afghanistan, Drug Use Survey 2010, Assessment of Drug Use Levels and Associated High Risk Behaviours amongst the Prison Population of Sarpoza Prison, Kandahar* (Vienna: UNDC, June 2010), http://www.unodc.org/documents/afghanistan/Prison_Reform/SPDUS_Full_Report_130 710_new_cover.pdf.

48. Michael Wessels, "Child Soldiers: The Destruction of Innocence," *Global Dialogue* 1, no. 2 (Autumn 1999), http://www.worlddialogue.org/content.php?id=45.

49. BBC News, "Child Soldiers as a Time Bomb," February 5, 2007, http://news.bbc.co.uk/2/hi/6330503.stm.

50. Chrobok, *Demobilizing and Reintegrating Afghanistan's Young Soldiers*, 18.

51. Neil Boothby, Jennifer Crawford, and Jason Halperin, "Mozambique Child Soldier Life Outcome Study: Lessons Learned in Rehabilitation and Reintegration Efforts," *Global Public Health* 1, no. 1 (February 2006): 87–107, https://childprotection.wikischolars.columbia.edu/file/view/Boothby+Crawford+%26+Halperin_Mozambique+Child+Soldiers.pdf.

See also Susan Shepler, *Conflicted Childhoods: Fighting Over Child Soldiers in Sierra Leone* (Berkeley: University of California, 2005); and Michael Wessells, *Child Soldiers: From Violence to Protection* (Cambridge: Harvard University Press, 2006).

52. Caroline Hartzell, *Special Report: Missed Opportunities: The Impact of DDR on SSR in Afghanistan*, SR-270 (Washington, DC: United Nations of Peace Publishing, April 2011), http://www.usip.org/files/resources/SR270-Missed_Opportunities.pdf.

53. Afghanistan's New Beginning Programme, "Introduction to ANBP," September 16, 2010, http://www.anbp.af.undp.org/homepage/index.php?option=com_conte nt&view=article&id=2:afghanistans-new-beginnings-programme&Itemid=2.

54. Steven Zyck, "Former Combatant Reintegration and Fragmentation in Contemporary Afghanistan," *Conflict, Security and Development* 9, no. 1 (April 2009): 111–131.

55. All minors associated with the fighting forces, regardless of their actual combatant status, are accepted in the DR program. Officially, to enter the program, children "should not be any older than eighteen years of age at the time of demobilization, they should be part of a military unit with a formal command structure, they should have been involved in activities that are directly related to that unit, and they should have served in a military unit for a period of at least six months." However, the program accepts a larger number of war-affected Afghan youth. Chrobok, *Demobilizing and Reintegrating Afghanistan's Young Soldiers*, 31–32.

56. United Nations of Peace, *Special Report: Missed Opportunities: The Impact of DDR on SSR in Afghanistan*, SR-270, April 2011, http://www.usip.org/files/resources /SR270-Missed_Opportunities.pdf.

57. Ibid.

58. Such as creation of parallel computer databases, uncoordinated negotiations

with the same regional commanders, the offer of similar training options for both youth and adults.

59. Vera Chrobok, "Démobilisation et réintégration des jeunes soldats afghans: examen et évaluation de la planification et de la mise en œuvre des programmes," in Yvan Conoir and Gerard Verna, eds., *DDR, Désarmer, démobiliser et réintégrer* (Laval: Presse de l'Université de Laval, 2006).

60. Antonio Giustozzi, "Bureaucratic Facade and Political Realities in Afghanistan," *Conflict, Security and Development* 8, no. 2 (2008): 169–192; Michael Bhatia, "The Future of the Mujahideen: Legitimacy, Legacy and Demobilisation in Post-Bonn Afghanistan," *International Peacekeeping* 14, no. 1 (2007): 90–107.

61. Chrobok, *Demobilizing and Reintegrating Afghanistan's Young Soldiers*, 56.

62. United Nations Security Council, *Report of the Secretary-General on Children and Armed Conflict in Afghanistan.*

63. Zyck, "Former Combatant Reintegration and Fragmentation in Contemporary Afghanistan"; Chrobok, *Demobilizing and Reintegrating Afghanistan's Young Soldiers*, 54.

CHAPTER 10

Legal Protection: Offering Aid and Comfort

HANGAMA ANWARI

Preventing, responding to, and addressing violence against children requires a legal framework. Such a framework must first reflect the real needs of and concerns about issues related to the protection of children, and it should be comprehensive and responsive. In addition, the legal framework should be understood by stakeholders and beneficiaries and respected by duty bearers. For children to be protected against violence, the established legal framework must also be backed up by adequate resources and accompanied by supporting documents, such as policies and action plans.

Background

Around 57 percent of Afghanistan's population is under the age of eighteen. Afghanistan has the highest proportion of school-age children in the world. One in five Afghans is a school-age child.[1] Statistics vary but generally show that child marriage is counted as 43 percent and child labor as 24 percent, and birth registration of children below the age of five is only 6 percent. Eight thousand children are living in institutions, and the number of children associated with armed groups and armed forces who were demobilized between 2003 and 2005 is around 7,444.[2] These statistics illustrate the overall vulnerability of children and describe the urgency to provide children of different ages, genders, and ethnicities with protection. Most of the children in the above mentioned groups are victims of violence and/or targeted to be victims of violence by various groups, including their own families, communities, and duty bearers.

Children must be legally protected against sexual exploitation, trafficking, child labor, unlawful imprisonment, recruitment, or forced conscription by armed groups, as well as harmful traditional practices, such as early marriage. Afghan law should also target children who are uniquely vulnerable to violence, such as those living without parental care, in conflict with the law, and/or in armed conflict.

The Term "Legal Protection of Children"

The goal of the legal protection of children should be to ensure that children—defined by the United Nations Convention on the Rights of the Child[3] as all persons under the age of eighteen—are best served and protected by justice systems, including the security and social welfare sectors. The Convention specifically aims at ensuring full application of international norms and standards for all children who come into contact with justice and related systems as victims, witnesses, and alleged offenders, or for other reasons where judicial, state administrative, or non-state adjudicatory intervention is needed, for example, regarding their care, custody, or protection. The best interests of the child must be given primary consideration, guaranteeing fair and equal treatment of every child, free from all discrimination, advancing the rights of the child to express his or her views freely and to be heard. Every child must be protected from abuse, exploitation, and violence, treated with dignity and compassion, their legal guarantees respected and safeguarded in all processes. The prevention of conflict with the law is a crucial element of any juvenile justice policy, while depriving children's liberty should be a measure of last resort and for the shortest appropriate period of time, so that all rule-of-law efforts must mainstream children's issues.

Children encounter the justice system when they are in conflict with the law or as parties to a judicial process, such as in custody arrangements, or because they are victims of violence. If the Afghan rule of law is not improved and the legal system does not provide clear standards of legal protection, more children, in all categories, will be vulnerable. While arguments presented here take the overall situation of children in the Afghan legal system into account, due to limited space, I will focus on three major issues.

Children in Conflict with the Law

Article 8 of the Juvenile Code of Afghanistan states that "confinement of a child should be a last resort for rehabilitation and reeducation of the child."[4] Life imprisonment is not allowed for children. According to the Juvenile

Code, from arrest to completion of trial no child can be detained for more than forty days. Yet children suspected or accused of having committed any offense are often detained far longer.[5] Beijing Rule 19.1 also states that "the placement of a juvenile in an institution shall always be a disposition of last resort and for the minimum necessary period."[6] Nevertheless, a recent report published by Terre des Hommes (TDH), a Swiss non-governmental organization (NGO), shows that formal alternatives to detention are not used extensively by Afghan juvenile courts. One of the measures cited as an alternative to detention is the use of open juvenile rehabilitation centers (JRCs).

> As of December 18, 2009 there were no children housed at the only open JRC in Afghanistan. In fact, two months prior there were only seven juveniles held at the open JRC in Kabul. Ideally, juveniles who do not pose a significant threat to society should be sentenced to open JRCs as opposed to closed JRCs. The idea for the open JRC is that juveniles are allowed to go to school and/or work during the day and are expected to report back to the JRC at night in order to complete their sentence. While the open JRC represents a formal alternative to detention, it is clearly being under-utilized by the court.[7]

The report goes on to say that the response from judges was that transportation is limited to and from the open JRC. Clearly, some type of funding or programming needs to be put in place that allows juveniles to be sentenced to the open JRC.[8]

Moreover, the data produced by TDH shows an alarming increase in the number of children detained. "As of December 2009, there were six hundred children in conflict with the law in Afghanistan, representing eighty girls and five hundred and twenty boys. This number represents nearly a 30 percent increase from the four hundred and fifty-five juveniles who were reported as being detained in January 2008."[9]

Girls in conflict with the law are more vulnerable than boys. No clear data on the imprisonment of girls is available—their numbers can't be verified, as they are often detained in women's prisons, where the juvenile code does not apply. In addition, studies conducted by United Nations Children's Fund (UNICEF), the Afghanistan Independent Human Rights Center (AIHRC), and United Nations Office on Drugs and Crime (UNODC) reveal that girls are more likely to be detained for so-called "moral" crimes, such as running away, adultery—defined in Afghanistan as the engagement in any consensual sexual activity outside of marriage[10]—and often kidnapping charges, where the victim is usually considered to be the perpetrator. According to a

UNICEF/AIHRC report, at least 56 percent of females were charged with so-called "moral offences," including running away from home or adultery/sodomy. These included many cases where the girl was clearly a victim of abuse:

> The cases for which females were prosecuted were significantly different. . . . A fourteen-year-old girl was sold by her stepfather for marriage to an eighty-year-old man for $2000. She was then sold on to another man for $5000. When the man had sexual intercourse with her, she went into a coma and was transferred to hospital where police began to investigate the case. She was transferred after three days to the prosecution office and then to a rehabilitation centre. She remained there for three-and-a-half months with the judge insisting she should marry the man. Only after intervention of the Afghanistan Independent Human Rights Commission and the Child Protection Action Network was she finally released from illegal detention.[11]

A report produced by TDH states:

> When questioning twenty-two judges who have presided over cases involving children in conflict with the law, Article 130 was the jurisprudence cited in the criminalization of moral crimes. Article 130 of the Islamic Republic of Afghanistan Constitution states that, "In cases under consideration, the courts shall apply provisions of this Constitution as well as other laws. If there is no provision in the Constitution or other laws about a case, the courts shall, in pursuance of Hanafi jurisprudence [one of four accepted schools of Islamic law], and, within the limits set by this Constitution, rule in a way that attains justice in the best manner."[12]

This leaves girl children in a difficult situation whereby they might not even benefit from the provisions of the juvenile code, which insists on the best interests of the child in all matters affecting them.

TDH also points to the fact that from the total number of children interviewed in juvenile rehabilitation centers, 45 percent reported being charged with the moral crimes of running away from home and adultery:

> Some reported running away from home to escape physical abuse at the hands of parents or spouses, and some reported running away to escape arranged marriages. Many of the kids charged with adultery claimed to have been falsely accused. In one case, a girl reported trying to go home and getting into a car with two men that she thought was a cab. The car was pulled

over by the police and she was subsequently charged and arrested for adultery, receiving a two-and-a-half-year sentence.[13]

In another case, a girl who returned home two hours late from school was charged with running away from home and received a one-year sentence.[14] Reports also indicate that girls sometimes end up in JRC because of the unavailability of options, when, after a kidnapping, the families have refused to take the children home.

The report by TDH informs us that "unfortunately, for many of the females surveyed, the detention serves more as a place of refuge due to the fact that many of their families do not want them. Some females articulated their fear of release due to the threats that they have received from their family members."[15]

According to internationally agreed-upon principles, children have a particular right to be heard in any judicial/administrative proceedings, directly, through a representative, or through an appropriate body, in a manner consistent with the procedural rules of national law. This implies, for example, that the child receives adequate information about the process, the options, and the possible consequences of these options, and also that the methodology used to question children and the context (e.g., where children are interviewed, by whom, and how) be child-friendly and adapted to the particular child. In contrast, the 2010 TDH report shows that many children interviewed reported going to court and being immediately told by judges to admit their crime: "A 17-year-old charged with pederasty and who had been beaten by police into signing a confession was told by the Primary Court Judge, to 'not speak while I am here, and don't even look at me.'" Several juveniles in the central region of Afghanistan, interviewed separately by TDH, reported being told the same thing by the same judge when going to court.[16]

The United Nations Convention Against Torture and Other Cruel, Inhuman or Degrading Treatment or Punishment defines torture as

any act by which severe pain or suffering, whether physical or mental, is intentionally inflicted on a person for such purposes as obtaining from him or a third person information or a confession, punishing him for an act he or a third person has committed or is suspected of having committed, or intimidating or coercing him or a third person, or for any reason based on discrimination of any kind, when such pain or suffering is inflicted by or at the instigation of or with the consent or acquiescence of a public official or other person acting in an official capacity.[17]

Data shows that torture and degrading punishments have been a regular part of overall procedures in dealing with Afghan children in conflict with the law. Overall, 45 percent of juveniles interviewed by TDH reported being physically abused, sometimes for weeks, by the National Security Police and prosecutors. Many showed physical signs consistent with their claims. Of these, most were boys. Only two juvenile girls reported being beaten, but many reported being intimidated by the police, who screamed at them and "called them bad names."[18]

Children in conflict with the law should be protected from any form of hardship while going through state and non-state justice processes and thereafter. Procedures must be adapted and appropriate protective measures put in place against abuse, exploitation, and violence—including sexual and gender-based violence—taking into account that the risks faced by boys and girls will differ. Torture or other cruel, inhuman, or degrading treatment or punishment (including corporal punishment) must be prohibited. Also, capital punishment and life imprisonment without possibility of release must not be imposed for offenses committed by children.

Limited human resources and minimum technical capacity of state officials to deal with their cases are two reasons for the suffering of children in conflict with the law. Most judges and prosecutors are unaware of the rules and regulations applied to children; indeed, there are few judges assigned to the juvenile court. Many NGOs with programs to train judges complain that by the time they have helped a judge improve his or her capacity in dealing with children's cases, the judge has been replaced and the training and awareness-raising sessions must begin all over again. In a voluntary test given by TDH to judges about their knowledge of due-process rights of juveniles, 46 percent had no knowledge of the United Nations Convention of the Rights of the Child. (Many thought it was a speech given by either Afghan president Hamid Karzai or United States president Barack Obama.) Fifty-three percent of the judges reported being unaware of the rights of juveniles in detention.

Sexual Exploitation of Children

Child sexual abuse (CSA) is one of the most serious violations of children's rights. The extent of the problem in Afghanistan is not known exactly, as it is difficult to obtain data on it. According to the World Health Organization (WHO), studies conducted in nineteen countries found that sexual abuse prevalence rates ranged from 7 to 34 percent among girls and 3 to 29 percent among boys.[19] However, there are clear indications that the problem is widespread and that it takes place in all spheres of life, including families, schools, workplaces, and communities. It is well known that sexual abuse has severe, lifelong consequences for children. Child sexual abuse was defined in a 2003 study conducted by Save the Children Sweden-Denmark as "the imposition of sexual acts, or acts with sexual overtones, by one or more persons on a child."[20]

Until recently it was assumed that only a small number of children were sexually abused. It was believed that most abusers were strangers or adults in positions of responsibility, and only in exceptional circumstances were parents. In fact, "abusers" come from all social classes and groups and can be either male or female, although statistically men compose the vast majority of those who sexually abuse children and adolescents. Abusers may be parents, teachers, employers, religious leaders, members of criminal gangs and networks, or people from law enforcement agencies. While evidence suggests more girls than boys are victims of sexual abuse, studies indicate many more boys than previously suspected are sexually abused as well. Sexual abuse of children and young people is a key issue of power disparity, and requires calling on and organizing boys and men in the society to protest against violence and child sexual abuse and take initiatives to create more equal gender roles and relationships.

CSA is much hidden in Afghanistan. Women's groups in particular have been speaking up against cases of sexual abuse of women and children, but any public discussion of sexuality continues to be highly taboo. No baseline data or statistics on CSA cases are available, and most of the information is from anecdotal accounts.

In addition, there are traditional precedents for "accepted" child abuse. Reports of men using young boys for sexual gratification (*bacha bazi*, or "playing with boys") are well known and talked about.[21] Traditionally, "keeping" good-looking boys adds status and prestige to a man, and adds to his image (self-created or externally imposed) of virility.[22]

Child sexual abuse is also clearly linked to child marriage, child trafficking, and child labor. Estimates suggest that one in three girls and one in ten boys are married between the ages fifteen and nineteen.[23] In the Save the Children Sweden-Denmark study, many young girls raised serious concerns about early marriage, saying that they were not prepared for getting pregnant. Their fears, though not directly voiced, could also have been about the sexual aspect of marriage.[24]

Other challenges—in addition to social taboos against public discussion of sexual abuse matters—include identification of CSA victims; reluctance of

NGOs and the Afghan government to deal with the issue as a top priority; lack of psychosocial support to the abuse victim; lack of rehabilitation support for children who may be perpetrators and commit sexual abuse on other children; and poor medical procedures, which may further violate the child's safety, with physicians insensitive to victims' needs and how to deal with the trauma the child faces. Addressing CSA in Afghanistan has exposed many key points and issues for which legal protection of children is essential. Impunity to CSA perpetrators is widespread due to weak rule and application of the law, and courts are not accessible in rural areas because of physical distance and security, which prevent traveling to court locations. Issues of honor and shame also prevent many families from seeking justice.

Legal/judicial response to CSA is low, and this is considered one reason for an increase in the number of incidents. In Afghanistan, a strong international and constitutional mandate for protecting the rights of children against violence and exploitation, including sexual exploitation and abuse, has not yet been established. Provisions of the existing criminal code in this regard are insufficient, owing to the failure of the code to explicitly recognize child sexual abuse as a distinct criminal offense and to provide a clear, comprehensive definition. Prosecutors and courts are often forced to rely on other generalized provisions in criminal law, which do not clearly define different types of sexual abuse—for example, forms of sexual harassment—but instead only speak about rape. As a result of the law's limitations, other types of sexual abuse and exploitation are left unpunished. Lack of awareness among Afghan lawyers about CSA, or specific legislation for different forms of CSA, helps explain why the problem is growing country-wide.

Child Victims of Trafficking

Trafficking in persons is a crime that can impair a personality and destroy human life. Today Afghanistan is a source-transit-and-destination country, with children being one of the large pools of potential trafficking "targets." Various human rights violations, such as forced marriage, child marriage, child abuse, and domestic violence, contribute to an environment that fosters or tolerates trafficking in persons in Afghanistan. The majority of victims interviewed for a 2008 report produced by the International Organization for Migration (IOM) were young adults or children. Thirty-five percent of the trafficked victims were under the age of eighteen.[25]

Given that Afghanistan is not a party to the United Nations' 2000 Protocol to Prevent, Suppress, and Punish Trafficking in Persons, Especially

Women and Children[26] or the South Asian Association for Regional Co-operation Convention on Preventing and Combating Trafficking in Women and Children for Prostitution,[27] and that as of 2012, Afghan law had not been finalized and no clear, binding legislations were in place, Afghan children are even more vulnerable. Poverty increases their vulnerability to trafficking, and the sale of children by their own families has become an increasing concern. According to the 2008 IOM report, three girl children, one aged four months and the others aged nine months, were sold for $40USD, $10USD, and $240USD, respectively. All the parents denied any wrongdoing, but also explained their inability to feed their children. And those who bought the children also felt they had done nothing wrong, claiming that they intended to protect the children from extreme poverty.[28]

No legal protections to prevent such actions are in place. Occasionally, and rarely, the government finds out about such cases through civil society advocacy, pays the family some amount, and gives them the child back. But there are no systematic mechanisms to protect children from sale, so, in the absence of a regular monitoring system, the wheel will continue to be reinvented with each case.

Trafficking for sexual exploitation and unlawful marriage is a common crime against girls in Afghanistan.

> Zeba is fifteen years old, originally from the Southeast region. Her parents died when she was a little child. Her cousin, Ali, took her under custody and she grew up with his family as a refugee in Pakistan. One day, Ali told Zeba that he was going to take her on a trip and she agreed. Zeba was handed to a man called Abdullah in Kabul and never saw Ali again. She was left alone with Abdullah and a woman living in his house. Abdullah later told Zeba that he spent a lot of money for her and that she was his wife now. Zeba wanted to refuse him, but was afraid that he would kill her if she did. She was not even able to communicate well with Abdullah, as he was a Dari speaker and she speaks only Pashto. Zeba was raped a number of times after the *nikka* (marriage) ceremony. Twenty days later, Zeba had a chance to talk with her neighbor who understood Pashto and told her story. While talking, the woman living in Abdullah's house came out and started beating her. The neighbor informed police and they arrested Abdullah.[29]

The link between trafficking and sexual abuse in cases related to women and children is undeniable. Afghanistan's legal framework does not properly define or provide a mechanism to tackle this problem. In another case reported in the 2008 IOM report, a different dimension of trafficking was portrayed:

A 15-year-old boy was kidnapped from Pakistan while working. He was then brought to the Northern region through the land border crossing point between Afghanistan and Pakistan by traffickers. In the destination province, he was forced to work. One day he finally escaped but got arrested by the police. The local commander took him home and made him work as a servant and perform dancing at wedding parties for his friends. He was also sexually exploited occasionally. The boy was made to wear the army uniform and accompany the commander in public. His freedom of movement was limited and the commander behaved as if the boy was his own property. He finally found a chance to run away and went back to Pakistan with IOM's assistance.[30]

There is no data describing the punishment of offenders, and the provisions of existing laws do not address the different aspects of trafficking, making it easier for the perpetrators to escape punishment.

Strategies to Strengthen the Protective Environment for Children

The government of Afghanistan does not have comprehensive child-sensitive procedures, due to lack of resources and/or political will. Services to promote children's rehabilitation and reintegration into society are not universal and therefore not necessarily available to all those who need it.

The following principles, based on international legal norms and standards, should be advocated in order to protect Afghan children from violence and exploitation:

- In all actions concerning children, whether undertaken by courts of law, administrative, or other—including non-state—authorities, the best interests of the child must be a primary consideration;
- The principle of non-discrimination that underpins the basic framework for developing child-friendly legal systems with a particular focus on gender-sensitive approaches in all interventions should be taken into consideration;
- The legal system should operate so as to protect every child from abuse, exploitation, and violence. In such a system, compassion should be given primary importance and real consideration. The child's individual dignity, special needs, interests, and privacy should be respected and protected;
- Basic procedural safeguards as set forth in relevant national and international norms and standards should be guaranteed at all stages of proceedings in state and non-state systems;

- The legal system's emphasis should be placed on prevention strategies facilitating the successful socialization and integration of children in conflict with law and child victims of violence and exploitation, including sexual exploitation and trafficking, in particular through the family, the community, peer groups, schools, vocational training, and the world of work;
- Such legal framework should ensure that children's issues are mainstreamed in all rule-of-law efforts, including (but not limited to) legislations, performance of duty bearers, national resource mobilization, national monitoring, and reporting mechanisms.

In addition, legal and overall protection of children should be systematically integrated into all national planning processes, such as national development plans, sectoral plans, poverty assessments and reduction strategies, and policies or plans of action developed by state and non-state actors, in national budget and international aid allocation and fundraising, particularly through joint and thorough assessments, development of a comprehensive rule of law strategy, and taking the best interests of the child into account.

Participation of children in matters affecting their own lives is a universal principle that needs to be taken into account in all initiatives concerning the design and implementation of programs aimed at legal protection of children.

Building a protective environment for children that will help prevent and respond to violence, abuse, and exploitation involves essential components, including:

- Strengthening government commitment and capacity to fulfill children's right to protection;
- Promoting the establishment and enforcement of adequate legislation;
- Addressing harmful attitudes, customs, and practices;
- Encouraging open discussion of child protection issues that involves media and civil society partners;
- Developing children's life skills, knowledge, and participation;
- Building capacity of families and communities;
- Providing essential services for prevention, recovery, and reintegration, including basic health, education, and protection;
- Establishing and implementing ongoing and effective monitoring, reporting, and oversight.

Notes

1. World Vision UK, 2012, http://www.worldvision.org.uk/what-we-do/disaster-management/Afghanistan.

2. UNICEF, Monitoring the Situation of Children and Women (Afghanistan MICS Report 2003), http://www.childinfo.org/files/AfghanistanMICS2003.pdf. The figure for the number of child combatants in Afghanistan is an estimate and may not be entirely accurate. See UNICEF, *Afghanistan—Country in Crisis: Measures to Help Victims of War* (United Nations, 2003), http://www.unicef.org/emerg/afghanistan/index_9028.html. Figures come from a UNICEF field assessment on the situation of child soldiers. See UNICEF, *UNICEF Humanitarian Action: Afghanistan Donor Update 23* (ReliefWeb, September 23, 2003). For more, see chapter 9 by Delphine Boutin, "Child Soldiering in Afghanistan," in this volume.

3. UNICEF defines the Convention on the Rights of the Child thus: "Built on varied legal systems and cultural traditions, the Convention is a universally agreed set of non-negotiable standards and obligations. These basic standards—also called human rights—set minimum entitlements and freedoms that should be respected by governments. They are founded on respect for the dignity and worth of each individual, regardless of race, colour, gender, language, religion, opinions, origins, wealth, birth status or ability and therefore apply to every human being everywhere. With these rights comes the obligation on both governments and individuals not to infringe on the parallel rights of others. These standards are both interdependent and indivisible; we cannot ensure some rights without—or at the expense of—other rights" (http://www.unicef.org/crc/).

4. Juvenile Code of Afghanistan, Article 8, http://www.rolafghanistan.esteri.it/NR/rdonlyres/565B6AC3-4472-4B4E-8315-9987F40E280D/0/23JuvenileLaw.pdf.

5. UNICEF and Afghanistan Independent Human Rights Commission, *Justice for Children: The Situation for Children in Conflict with the Law in Afghanistan*, http://www.unicef.org/media/files/Juvenile_Detention_Study_engl.pdf, 11.

6. Office of the United Nations High Commissioner for Human Rights, "United Nations Standard Minimum Rules for the Administration of Juvenile Justice ('The Beijing Rules')," November 29, 1985, http://www2.ohchr.org/english/law/pdf/beijingrules.pdf, 12.

7. Kimberly Cy Motley, "An Assessment of Juvenile Justice in Afghanistan" (Terre des Hommes, January 2010), http://s3.amazonaws.com/webdix/media_files/903_Tdh_Juvenile_justice_web_original.pdf, 62.

8. Ibid.

9. Ibid., 11.

10. The legal definition of adultery in Afghanistan comes from the Hanafi school of Sharia law: Adultery (Zina) is any sexual act between a man and a woman who are neither married nor have a slave/master relationship. Under the Afghan Penal Code of 1976 that is currently in force, "A person who commits adultery . . . shall be sentenced to long imprisonment." Afghan Penal Code, Art. 427, published October 7, 1976 (15 Mizzan 1355 AH) in the Official Gazette, No. 347. English translation available at: http://www.lexadin.nl/wlg/legis/nofr/oeur/lxweafg.htm.

11. UNICEF and Afghanistan Independent Human Rights Commission, *Justice for Children*, 14.

12. Motley, "An Assessment of Juvenile Justice," 18.

13. Ibid., 27.

14. Ibid., 28.

15. Ibid.

16. Ibid., 35.

17. United Nations Convention Against Torture and Other Cruel, Inhuman or Degrading Treatment or Punishment (Part I, Article 1, July 16, 1994), http://www.hrweb.org/legal/cat.html.

18. Motley, "An Assessment of Juvenile Justice," 36.

19. Karin Heissler, Background Paper on Good Practices and Priorities to Combat Sexual Abuse and Exploitation of Children in Bangladesh (Dhaka, 2001), http://www.unicef.org/evaldatabase/files/BAN_2002_801.pdf.

20. Cath Slugget and John Frederick, eds., *Mapping of Psychosocial Support for Child Sexual Abuse in Four Countries in South and Central Asia: Afghanistan, Bangladesh, Nepal and Pakistan* (Save the Children Sweden-Denmark, 2003), http://sca.savethechildren.se/upload/scs/SCA/Publications/Mapping%20of%20psychosocial%20support%20for%20girls%20and%20boys%20affect%20by%20CSA.pdf.

21. "The practice of Bacha Bazi takes place in many parts of Central and South Asia. Here, young boys are taken by military leaders and war lords and made into male sexual slaves. They are often made to dance and provide entertainment for older men. The practice has been present in these societies since ancient times. Even the ancient Greek commanders were known for such excesses." Radhika Coomaraswamy, United Nations Office of the Special Representative of the Secretary-General for Children and Armed Conflict, 64th Session of the United Nations General Assembly, Third Committee, "Promotion and Protection of the Rights of Children," October 14, 2009, http://www.un.org/children/conflict/english/14-october-2009-general-assembly.html.

22. Slugget and Frederick, *Mapping of Psychosocial Support for Child Sexual Abuse in Four Countries*, 57.

23. Legal marriage ages in Afghanistan are sixteen for girls and eighteen for boys. However, nearly 60 percent of marriages in Afghanistan involve girls below the legal age of sixteen, according to reports from the Ministry of Women's Affairs and NGOs. Some girls are married as young as nine (http://www.irinnews.org/report.aspx?reportid=28727).

24. Slugget and Frederick, *Mapping of Psychosocial Support for Child Sexual Abuse in Four Countries*, 57.

25. Katsui Kaya, "Trafficking in Persons in Afghanistan Field Survey Report" (International Organization for Migration, June 2008), http://www.iom.int/jahia/webdav/shared/shared/mainsite/activities/countries/docs/afghanistan/iom_report_trafficking_afghanistan.pdf, 31.

26. Protocol to Prevent, Suppress, and Punish Trafficking in Persons, Especially Women and Children, Supplementing the United Nations Convention Against Transnational Organized Crime (United Nations, 2000), http://www.uncjin.org/Documents/Conventions/dcatoc/final_documents_2/convention_%20traff_eng.pdf.

27. SAARC Convention on Preventing and Combating Trafficking in Women

and Children for Prostitution (Member States of the South Asian Association for Regional Cooperation, Kathmandu, January 5, 2002), http://www.saarc-sec.org/user files/conv-traffiking.pdf.

28. Kaya, "Trafficking in Persons in Afghanistan Field Survey Report," 25.

29. Ibid., 26.

30. Ibid., 28.

A young mother feeds her child in a park in the city of Jalalabad. Photo by Sam Chen, ca. 1968.

A young boy in Kabul practices using a new prosthetic leg at the Orthopedic Center of the International Committee of the Red Cross. Photo by Beth Wald, 2009.

PART 4

TO BE WHOLE IN MIND AND BODY

CHAPTER 11

Children's Health: The Challenge of Survival

STEVEN SOLTER

Surviving to the age of five has always been a challenge for Afghan children. Even before 1979, when the current sustained period of violence began with the Soviet invasion, Afghan children experienced among the highest mortality rates found anywhere. More than one-fourth of all children died by their fifth birthday. For example, during the famine in Ghor Province in the early 1970s, more than 40 percent of Afghan children with measles died, the highest case-fatality rate for measles ever recorded in the world. So it is surprising that since 2002 the health of Afghan children has greatly improved, with significantly lower mortality rates than ever before.[1] How is that possible?

Afghan children die from three major causes: pneumonia, diarrhea, and malnutrition,[2] with measles, malaria, and smallpox also having been important causes in the past. Since 2002, there has been an enormous effort by the Afghan Ministry of Public Health and its partners—donors, international agencies, and non-governmental organizations (NGOs)—to focus on these causes and thereby reduce mortality. Despite tremendous obstacles, this effort has had a significant impact not only on mortality but on awareness (especially of mothers) of key public health messages, notably the importance of immunization, exclusive breastfeeding for the first six months of life,[3] handwashing with soap, and appropriate weaning practices.

In 2010, the Afghan Ministry of Public Health and Macro International conducted a national mortality survey.[4] More than 24,000 households were visited in all 34 provinces, and families were asked about all deaths of household members during the past three years. The study estimated that the under-five mortality rate over the previous three years had been about 97 per 1,000 live births, meaning that about 10 percent of Afghan newborns did not live to their fifth birthday. But in 2006, 191 per 1,000 Afghan children died before the age of five.[5] And in 2002 the best available estimate was that 257 Afghan children per 1,000 live births did not survive to their fifth birthdays, a mortality rate of just over 25 percent.[6]

Since 2002, then, what have been the most important factors influencing child survival in Afghanistan? Four factors stand out. First, the Ministry of Public Health and donors have focused on those interventions where there was strong evidence of an impact on mortality. Rather than developing a comprehensive, but relatively expensive, package of health services that could not cover the majority of the population, they developed the "Basic Package of Health Services."[7] It could reach 70 to 80 percent of the rural population and was aimed at women and under-fives. Because Afghanistan and its donors did not have the resources to provide a comprehensive package, the ministry and its partners felt that it was more important to ensure that the great majority of Afghans had access to a few lifesaving interventions than it was to have a small fraction of the population receive a full range of health services.

The second factor was the use of NGOs: the government contracted primary health care services out to NGOs rather than providing them itself. This arrangement allowed the Ministry of Public Health to play a stewardship role, so it could focus on setting standards, coordinating all actors in the health sector, and ensuring the quality of health services rather than dissipating its limited resources on direct service delivery.

Third, in a conservative Muslim setting where women cannot generally be seen by male health care providers unless a male in the family allows it and accompanies her, it was essential to expand the workforce of trained women who can provide maternal, newborn, and child health care. More than 28,000 volunteer community health workers, half of them women, were trained, and are currently providing health education and treating sick children with diarrhea, pneumonia, and malaria in villages in all 34 provinces. More than 2,000 community midwives have been trained and assigned to rural areas, where they assist with deliveries as well as resuscitate newborns.[8] The community midwives constitute a critical new cadre of health workers. They are recruited from rural areas where there is no midwife and are then assigned to the health facility nearest their villages. Because they remain close to home, their attrition rate over the last five years, when they were first deployed, has been very low.

The United States Agency for International Development (USAID), the World Bank, and the European Union, Afghanistan's main health donors, have worked collaboratively with the Ministry of Public Health from 2002 onward. The ministry was consistent in maintaining its priorities, despite having three different ministers of health from 2002 to 2012.[9] From the beginning, the ministry insisted on focusing on mortality reduction as its highest priority even though there was considerable pressure to do more about mental health and disabilities, which were clearly also major problems.

Taking each of these factors in turn, what have we learned about the health of children in Afghanistan during the past ten years?

A Basic Package of Health Services for All Afghans

Health, of course, is much more than preventing early and unnecessary deaths. Afghan children, 80 percent of whom live in rural villages, face many other challenges, including poverty, lack of access to education (especially for girls), lack of food,[10] and facing the ravages of winter with inadequate shelter. These children also endure the stress of living in a violent land that presents urgent mental health issues, relocation of their families because of fighting, and the risk of severe disabilities (related to land mines and other causes). But the most important aspect of child health is to survive to adulthood, which Afghan children are doing more often than ever before. The situation, however, was very different in November 2001, when the Taliban were forced out of Kabul and a new minister of health took over responsibility for the well-being of children and of the entire population generally. What were the options at that time and how did the Ministry of Health, as it was called at that time, decide what to do?

Dr. Suhaila Seddiqi, selected to be the first post-Taliban minister of health (2001–2003), faced a daunting challenge in December 2001. With most health centers and hospitals destroyed or not functioning because of fighting or neglect, with most Afghan health workers dead or in exile or living as refugees in Pakistan or Iran, and with the government nearly bankrupt, she found the government health sector almost totally dependent on donor funds and international agencies. But Afghans are an incredibly proud and resilient people and resist dependency upon foreigners, especially for something as crucial as their health.

Dr. Seddiqi, a military surgeon, brought together all interested parties, including the three major donors, and urged them to reach a consensus about what to do. Over the next few months, a number of fundamental decisions were made and priorities established, with the Ministry of Health playing a facilitating role. One of the group's most important decisions was to focus the government's and donors' resources on reducing the number of women and children dying of preventable causes, rather than spreading those resources to cover a wide range of health problems and diseases. The evidence-based interventions that were identified as having the greatest potential for reducing mortality among rural women and children were brought together as the Basic Package of Health Services.

Many health interventions featured in the Basic Package of Health Services impact child mortality. These include immunization; vitamin A supplementation; case management of malaria, pneumonia, diarrhea, tuberculosis, anemia, and parasitic and other infections; nutrition interventions; promotion of hand washing with soap, maintaining clean drinking water, and use of safe latrines; and newborn interventions.[11] Healthy timing and spacing of pregnancy (through use of oral contraceptives, injectables, IUDs, and condoms) also makes a major contribution to lowering child mortality. In the 2010 Afghanistan Mortality Survey, more than one-fifth of married women reported using some method of family planning, which represents a dramatic increase from 2003, when only one in ten women were using contraception.[12]

The Basic Package of Health Services made a big difference for the health of Afghan children. It meant that every doctor, nurse, midwife, vaccinator, and community health worker dealt with the same set of interventions (although some interventions are carried out exclusively by doctors or nurses). It meant that each type of health facility was responsible for a limited set of services, using a standardized list of clearly identified medicines, supplies, and equipment,[13] and that the interventions in the package were focused specifically on reducing mortality among children under five and among women of reproductive age. As a result of the Basic Package of Health Services, most Afghan children are now being immunized against major killers, including measles and pneumococcal pneumonia, and soon most will also be immunized against rotavirus, a cause of diarrheal deaths. In addition, community health workers provide community case management of child illnesses, treating pneumonia, diarrhea, and malaria themselves at the village level.

The Basic Package also involves changing health behaviors and traditional practices such as throwing away the colostrum at birth (depriving the baby of important antibodies) or refraining from feeding an egg to a baby in the belief that doing so will prevent the child from learning to talk. Family behaviors that negatively affect children's health and nutrition stem from factors that include mothers' lack of education, early age at marriage, and lack of autonomy.[14]

NGOs Providing Health Services for Afghan Children

The health of Afghan children has benefited greatly over the years from the work of a large number of NGOs, both international and Afghan.[15] For more than two decades, from 1980 until 2002, NGOs based in Peshawar and Quetta in Pakistan supported many initiatives that benefited Afghan children, dealing with primary health care, disabilities, mental health, or immunization. After the Taliban was forced out in November 2001, many of these NGOs moved to Kabul and other Afghan cities to continue their efforts. In addition, Afghan doctors, nurses, and managers who had worked for international NGOs in Pakistan began forming their own Afghan NGOs to provide many of the same services but at lower cost, because they did not need to pay expatriates' salaries. When the Ministry of Public Health, its main donors, and international agencies realized that they had an experienced pool of medical personnel in their midst, they decided to have the NGOs, rather than the government, provide the basic health services. This was a highly unusual step, because most national ministries of health prefer to have foreign funds given directly to them and not have the money end up going to NGOs, but it was a step that would have far-reaching consequences for the health of Afghan children. As of this writing in 2012, most rural Afghan children are receiving free health care through NGOs, which in turn receive funding from one of three foreign donors: USAID, the World Bank, and the European Union. The donor funds in most cases are managed by the Ministry of Public Health, but there has been surprisingly little corruption—the money really does reach the NGOs. The secret of success has been a clearly defined and transparent process administered by Afghan managers with salaries that are high enough to allow them to support their families without depending on kickbacks.

This system supports the rural areas, but poor Afghan children living in cities (including the estimated 400,000 children under five living in Kabul) do not have access to the Basic Package of Health Services and must fend for themselves in the private sector; many are so poor that they cannot afford high fees at private clinics or expensive medicines and in effect lack access to health care. Similarly, *kuchi* (nomad)[16] children lack regular contact with the health system, as do many of those living in camps for internally displaced people. So despite the great success of the Basic Package for Health Services, it has primarily benefited rural Afghan children, rather than kuchis or the urban poor.

Community-Based Health Care for Afghan Children

With a total Afghan population of about 30 million in 2012, the number of children under five is about 6 million. Approximately 120,000 Afghan children die each year, or about 330 every day, the great majority from preventable causes. Since 80 percent of Afghans live in rural areas, an estimated

270 rural children die each day (enough to fill a jetliner), mostly at home in their villages (very few die in hospitals or health centers, where some deaths might have been prevented). What can be done to reduce this terrible, needless tragedy? The answer that Afghans came up with was to train community health workers.

Afghanistan first began training and deploying community health workers in 1977, but the Afghan government ended the program in 1978 after a pro-Soviet coup (the new Soviet advisors to the Ministry of Health didn't agree with training community health workers because it wasn't done in the Soviet Union). During the period of Soviet occupation (1979–1989), a number of NGOs based mostly in Pakistan trained community health workers who worked in Mujahedin-controlled areas of Afghanistan. But by the fall of the Taliban, there were few health workers remaining in the country.

Beginning in 2002, however, NGOs providing the Basic Package of Health Services have been recruiting, selecting, training, supplying, and supervising community health workers. There are now 28,000 volunteer community health workers delivering primary health care to Afghanistan's rural population, focusing mostly on women and children. Half are women and they work in all 34 provinces. The fact that few are literate has not been a problem, since they use pictorial checklists and learning aids to help them with their health education, diagnosis, and treatment. There is growing evidence that community health workers are having a significant impact on child health. What is the evidence?

In 2011, nearly half of all sick children in rural Afghanistan were being seen in their own homes or in their villages by community health workers rather than at health centers or hospitals. When children are seen at home, it is likely that the time between the onset of the symptoms of killer diseases such as pneumonia and diarrhea and the time when treatment is obtained will be less than if the children had to go to health centers located far from their villages.

Two-thirds of all family planning visits in rural Afghanistan are with community health workers. Contraception leads to longer birth intervals, and there is very strong evidence that babies born more than two years apart have significantly lower mortality rates than babies born less than two years apart. By contributing so much to family planning, community health workers are also contributing to lower maternal and child mortality rates. Community health workers also provide vital information to mothers about critical practices like early and exclusive breastfeeding, appropriate weaning, the need for immunization and vitamin A capsules, hand washing with soap, and so forth.

Community midwives and other skilled birth attendants (mainly physicians) are now delivering many more babies (20 percent) than was the case in 2001, when less than 5 percent were delivered by trained professionals. In addition, a number of new initiatives are likely to improve child health even more in the future. For example, Family Health Action Groups have been formed in many villages. These are groups of mothers who have been taught important health behaviors by the female community health worker of their village. These health behaviors can have a major impact. The Family Health Action Groups are expected to be role models for their friends and neighbors in the village, in such practices as breastfeeding, immunizing, and weaning their children beginning at six months of age with appropriate weaning foods, such as cooked mashed carrots, legumes (e.g., split peas, dry beans, chickpeas), and squash.

Growth promotion meetings are also beginning to happen in villages. Mothers bring their children to these meetings to be weighed each month to make sure they are gaining weight. With all the mothers gathered together, the sessions present opportunities for other child health interventions, such as health education, immunization, deworming, iron, and iodine tablets, and treatment of children with pneumonia, diarrhea, or malaria.

Community Midwives

There has been revolutionary change in the training and deployment of midwives working in rural areas. In 2001, there were very few midwives working in rural Afghanistan, but by 2012 their number had increased to more than 2,000 and hundreds more are graduating each year from a network of NGO-managed community midwifery schools located in provinces throughout the country. Babies delivered by skilled birth attendants are more likely to survive than babies delivered by traditional birth attendants, who are known as *dais* in Afghanistan. For example, midwives are trained to resuscitate newborns with difficulty breathing; dais usually have no such training. Midwives nowadays are trained to keep the baby warm after birth, to prevent hypothermia; dais don't always know to do this. So even for home deliveries, away from any health facility, a skilled birth attendant has an impact on child health and newborn mortality. But midwives have another impact as well: when pregnant Afghan women visit midwives for prenatal care, they are counseled about nutrition and avoidance of certain medicines, for the benefit of their babies.

These thousands of newly trained community midwives provide village women with a sense of empowerment; they represent a safe haven where women can be together and receive good advice about their babies, their pregnancies, and family planning.

Donors and Child Health in Afghanistan

The tremendous progress made since 2001 toward child survival would not have occurred without the enormous contribution of donors, especially "the big three"—USAID, the World Bank, and the European Union—which paid the Afghan and international NGOs to deliver the Basic Package of Health Services. Major help also comes from UNICEF (immunization, nutrition) and the World Health Organization (policy, disease control strategies). Donors from many countries have also funded hospitals (though to a much lesser extent than they have funded health centers and community-based health care) and other programs affecting child health, such as providing food to internally displaced people and those living in areas of famine and crop shortages. Many international NGOs have generously funded Afghan orphanages, centers for prosthetic limbs (for the children requiring leg or arm amputations due to land mines), and other programs benefiting children.

The main challenge now is how to maintain many of these programs as NATO and the United States anticipate withdrawing combat troops by the end of 2014 and donor funds are decreasing. How will the Afghan government and NGOs be able to sustain even a fraction of the services benefiting children when donor funds dry up?

This is hardly an unprecedented situation. Any country dependent upon massive donor support loses that support as a result of a change in geopolitical priorities. But what is different about Afghanistan compared with almost any other developing country, at least regarding child health, is the extreme nature of donor dependence. It is difficult to measure what percentage of funds going to child health come from government, but it is certainly extremely low, probably less than 5 percent. Afghans spend a great deal of money out-of-pocket for health care in the private sector, especially for medicines, as well as for transportation and private fees, but funding for programs that have the potential for major impact on mortality comes almost entirely from donors and NGOs.[17] This is true not just in urban areas but in impoverished rural areas as well—there are thousands of small shops selling medicines throughout rural Afghanistan and many local practitioners with no training but who possess a syringe and collect their fees.

What can be done when the donors leave? Some ideas regarding future strategies include the following:

- The Ministry of Public Health, working closely with remaining donors, NGOs, international agencies, and the private sector, must prioritize so that discretionary funding is used in such a way as to have the greatest chance to be sustainable in the long run and have the greatest impact on the health of Afghan children, both urban and rural.

- Public-private partnerships can be established in which private funds are used for clinics and hospitals that involve collaboration with government in some way—for example, a government hospital that is taken over by a private venture. In this sort of partnership, the private partner can make money by providing services to those who can afford them while the government's interest is being met by ensuring that a certain percentage of services are provided free to the poor.
- The government should no longer mandate that all primary health care services be free. Instead, only certain services would remain free (such as preventive care, curative care for children under five, immunization, family planning, and prenatal and postnatal care), while all other services (primarily curative care for those older than five) would be paid for. This approach would prioritize preventive services and young children, as well as pregnant women, over curative care for adults and older children. This solution would ensure that the interventions and services with the greatest public health impact would continue.
- The government could gradually shift a higher proportion of its budget to health and to meeting the needs of children. It is also possible that a future, more stable Afghanistan could attract major investments for its minerals and raw materials (especially from Chinese investors), so that Afghan government revenues as a whole would significantly increase. This may be an overly optimistic scenario given all the challenges, but it remains a possibility.

Although in 2013 there was still a great deal of donor funding pouring into Afghanistan, young children continue to face tremendous challenges. Many still must survive freezing winters with insufficient clothing, shelter, and food. Malnutrition affects their immune status, making them more vulnerable to infectious diseases of all kinds, although fortunately up until now HIV and AIDS has not become a major health problem for Afghan children. With an uncertain political future for Afghanistan, the progress in the health of Afghan children could be reversed if civil war continues or escalates in the years ahead.

Notes

I would like to acknowledge the assistance of Dr. Barbara Timmons of Management Sciences for Health in developing this chapter.

1. While there has never been a Demographic and Health Survey in Afghanistan and there are few sources of information about child health before 2002, several books and studies offer relevant background about the health system and situation: Alfred A. Buck, *Health and Disease in Rural Afghanistan*, Johns Hopkins Monographs in International Health (Baltimore, MD: York Press, 1972); Ronald W. O'Connor, ed., *Managing Health Systems in Developing Areas: Experiences from Afghanistan* (Lexington, MA: Lexington Books, Lexington, MA, 1980); Ronald W. O'Connor, ed., *Health Care in Muslim Asia: Development and Disorder in Wartime Afghanistan* (Lanham, MD: University Press of America, 1994).

2. O'Connor, *Managing Health Systems in Developing Areas*, page 181, lists the main causes of death in children under five, based on a three-province household survey carried out by Management Sciences for Health in 1977. Of the 58 under-five deaths reported, the three main causes (when a specific disease was mentioned) were diarrhea, acute respiratory infection, and measles. "Djinns" were named as the leading cause, which referred to neonatal deaths, some of which were due to tetanus.

3. Feeding infants only breast milk—without any additional food or drink, not even water—for the first six months of life is the international best practice recommended by the World Health Organization in "Exclusive Breastfeeding for Six Months Best for Babies Everywhere," January 15, 2011, http://www.who.int/media centre/news/statements/2011/breastfeeding_20110115/en/index.html.

4. Afghan Public Health Institute, Ministry of Public Health; Central Statistics Organization; ICF Macro; Indian Institute of Health Management Research; World Health Organization, *Afghanistan Mortality Survey 2010* (Calverton, MD: ICF Macro, November 2011).

5. Indian Institute of Health Management Research (IIHMR), Johns Hopkins University (JHU), Ministry of Public Health (Afghanistan), Afghanistan Health Survey 2006.

6. Linda A. Bartlett et al., "Where Giving Birth Is a Forecast of Death: Maternal Mortality in Four Districts of Afghanistan, 1999–2002," *The Lancet* 365:9462 (2005): 864–870.

7. Ministry of Public Health Islamic Republic of Afghanistan, *A Basic Package of Health Services for Afghanistan, 2005/1384* (Kabul: Ministry of Public Health, 2005), http://moph.gov.af/Content/Media/Documents/BPHS-2005-FINAL29122010 162945969.pdf.

8. *Rural Expansion of Afghanistan's Community-Based Healthcare Program: Transforming a Fragile Health System* (Cambridge, MA: Management Sciences for Health, 2006) tells the story of the development of programs to train female community health workers and community midwives between 2003 and 2006, with funding from USAID. The booklet is available at http://www.msh.org/Documents/upload/EOP _Booklet-1.pdf#search=%22REACH%22.

9. Dr. Suhaila Seddiqi, 2001–2003; Dr. S. M. Amin Fatimie, 2004–2010; Dr. Suraya Dalil, 2010–present.

10. Fitsum Assefa, Mohammed Zahir Jabarkhil, Peter Salama, and Paul Spiegel, "Malnutrition and Mortality in Kohistan District, Afghanistan, April 2001," *Journal of the American Medical Association* 286:21 (2001): 2723–2728.

11. Afghan children should receive the following immunizations: BCG (against tuberculosis), oral polio, hepatitis B, DPT (diphtheria, pertussis, and tetanus), measles, pneumococcal, HIB (against *Haemophilus influenzae* type b, which causes pneumonia and meningitis), and rotavirus (which is being newly introduced). Vitamin A supplements (200,000 IU) should be administered every six months to children between one and five years of age. Newborn interventions to address the major causes of neonatal mortality—birth asphyxia, infection, and prematurity/low birth weight—are resuscitation, treatment of newborn sepsis, and prevention of hypothermia through "kangaroo mother care," which means that the mother holds the baby skin-to-skin against her chest for warmth. This is particularly important for premature or low-birth-weight babies, who are more susceptible to cold. World Health Organization, *Kangaroo Mother Care: A Practical Guide* (Geneva: WHO, 2003).

12. *Afghanistan Mortality Survey 2010*, 59.

13. USAID-supported provinces receive technical assistance, through the Systems for Improved Access to Pharmaceuticals and Services Program, to build the capacity of the Ministry of Public Health to manage pharmaceuticals, including preventing stock-outs of essential medicines for child health.

14. Taufiq Mashal et al., "Factors Associated with the Health and Nutritional Status of Children under 5 Years of Age in Afghanistan: Family Behaviour Related to Women and Past Experience of War-Related Hardships," *BMC Public Health* 8 (2008): 301, http://www.ncbi.nlm.nih.gov/pmc/articles/PMC2551613/.

15. Dozens of foreign and Afghan NGOs deliver health services in Afghanistan. They range from well-known groups such as the Red Cross and Red Crescent societies to small, recently established NGOs. A list of seventeen NGOs that focus on children—among them Austrian, Danish, UK, and U.S. groups—is available at http://afghanistan-analyst.org/ngos/. The best-known of those include Save the Children and UNICEF.

16. The kuchis—who make up the majority of Afghanistan's internally displaced people and are among Afghanistan's poorest people—have suffered from droughts that killed their livestock and disputes over land rights. They are primarily Pashtun pastoralists from southern and eastern Afghanistan, but many have been settled in northwest Afghanistan. The largest population of kuchis now lives in the desert in southern Afghanistan (*World Directory of Minorities and Indigenous Peoples*, http://www.minorityrights.org/5444/afghanistan/kuchis.html). They are a social rather than an ethnic group who total about 2.4 million (*National Multi-sectoral Assessment of Kuchi*, 2004), of whom about 1 million have been displaced.

17. B. Sabri, S. Siddiqi, A. M. Ahmed, F. K. Kakar, and J. Perrot, "Towards Sustainable Delivery of Health Services in Afghanistan: Options for the Future," *Bulletin of the World Health Organization* 85:9 (2007), http://www.who.int/bulletin/volumes/85/9/06-036939/en/.

CHAPTER 12

Food Security and Nutrition for Afghan Children

FITSUM ASSEFA, ANNALIES BORREL,
AND CHARLOTTE DUFOUR

Despite ten years of significant investments in reconstruction and development, children in Afghanistan continue to suffer from undernutrition.[1] Its
persistence is a result of complex factors that include lack of access to high-
quality food that provides the nutrients a child needs to grow and be healthy,
a high prevalence of infectious diseases, and the significant challenges that
women and their families face in providing adequate care for infants and
young children. These factors are compounded by complex social, political,
economic, and cultural factors and continue to perpetuate poor economic and
social development.

Afghanistan is characterized by some of the worst health and nutrition
statistics in the world, ranked as the highest for the proportion of children
affected by chronic malnutrition or stunting,[2] affecting 59 percent of children
under the age of five.[3] This very high prevalence of stunting has remained persistent over the past three decades. Furthermore, today 9 percent of Afghan
children are reported to suffer from acute malnutrition or wasting[4]—nearly
four times the expected prevalence of 2.3 percent in otherwise healthy, well-
nourished populations. As in many other contexts, children under the age of
two years are much more likely to suffer from malnutrition. In Afghanistan,
the highest prevalence of stunting (70 percent) is recorded among children
two to three years old, and the highest prevalence of wasting (18.1 percent) is
recorded in children one to two years old.[5] This undoubtedly results in irreversible consequences for their survival and future development.

Malnutrition among children in Afghanistan is also characterized by deficiencies of vitamins and minerals, such as iron, iodine, and vitamin A, which
are critical for children's growth and development. More than two-thirds of
children under the age of five (70 percent) are reported to suffer from iron
and iodine deficiencies.[6] Observations suggest that disabilities exist as a result

of severe micronutrient deficiencies, including mental retardation, cretinism, neural-tube defects,[7] and blindness. Furthermore, high incidence of birth defects has been documented in hospitals in Kabul, which may suggest a high prevalence of folate deficiency,[8] likely to result from poor diets and lack of access to folate supplementation in prenatal health services. Vitamin C deficiency—also known as scurvy, which is considered nonexistent in most parts of the world—was reported in up to 10 percent of households in some rural districts in 2001. This was the highest level ever recorded globally[9] and was reported to be the cause of 7 percent of all child deaths reported in the district.[10] This extreme situation resulted from four years of drought, followed by a harsh winter and continued conflict, which led to remote districts having limited access to markets and other services. Women in those districts were not able to seek adequate health care since they could not travel long distances, because the majority of men who could accompany them had temporarily emigrated elsewhere for employment or to serve in the war.

Malnutrition contributes to locking children and their families in a vicious cycle of poverty. Malnutrition is associated with a higher risk of common childhood illnesses such as diarrhea, pneumonia, and neonatal complications, and increases the risk of mortality as a result of such diseases. According to the most recent global estimates, maternal and child undernutrition contributes to more than one-third of child deaths.[11] Therefore, such high levels of undernutrition are likely to explain the very high under-five mortality rate in Afghanistan,[12] ranked one of highest in the world.[13] Those children who survive are likely to perform poorly in school,[14] to be more vulnerable to disease later in life, and thus be less productive and earn less than adults who were not undernourished as children. For girls, the consequences are even greater: chronic undernutrition in early life, either before birth or during early childhood, can later lead to their own infants being born with low birth weight. The direct and indirect consequences of undernutrition reduce a country's gross domestic product by 2 to 3 percent.[15] Improving the fragile economy and development of Afghanistan, which has one of the lowest domestic products per capita in the Asia Pacific[16] and among the lowest human development index rankings[17] (172 among 187 countries in the world),[18] will require addressing the causes of undernutrition as an integral part of peace and development efforts.

Undernutrition: A Multifaceted Problem

The factors that lead to malnutrition in Afghanistan are undoubtedly diverse and complex. For decades, civil armed conflict and political instability have been a persistent reality for Afghanistan. The consequences have been widespread, exacerbating poverty and impeding economic opportunities for rural and urban populations. Insecurity has led to massive destruction of basic infrastructure, including roads—which impacts directly on population mobility and trade, both of which are fundamental to Afghan livelihoods and essential for the supply of food to areas facing food deficits. The combination of repeated droughts and insecurity has also led households to lose or sell essential assets, such as livestock and land, and incur large amounts of debt. During the severe drought years of 1999 to 2002, some households even reported giving their daughters in marriage as a means of debt collateral.[19] Basic health and sanitation services, such as clinics, drinking water, and sewage, were already very limited prior to the conflict, particularly in rural areas. The conflict further contributed to the deterioration and disruption of these services. Decades of war and conflict have also destroyed hundreds of schools and colleges, and many of those who are well educated have emigrated to other countries, primarily in the West, leading to a professional brain drain that exacerbates the lack of capacity for services.

Inadequate household food security, particularly in terms of having the capacity to access adequate quantity and quality of food, is one of the most fundamental underlying causes of malnutrition. An estimated 35 percent of Afghan households are reported to have inadequate caloric intake, and an estimated 46 percent of households nationally have diets that are not sufficiently diverse.[20] This may even underestimate the extent of the problem for households in remote communities, where conflict has negatively affected production, trade, and the social fabric of communities. A significant proportion of the Afghan population relies on rudimentary agriculture systems, with limited capacities to build resilience and mitigate the impacts of recurrent droughts. Harsh climates, especially severe winters, further exacerbate vulnerabilities due to limited access to markets and other livelihood opportunities for prolonged periods.

A poor overall health environment remains a significant cause of undernutrition for children. An estimated 73 percent of households still lack access to safe drinking water, and 75 percent lack access to improved sanitation.[21] Hygienic practices, such as hand washing with soap, are not widely practiced. Many households in rural communities across Afghanistan use surface and river water, including for drinking, since flowing water is generally believed to be clean regardless of potential contamination from human and animal waste. This practice is supported by an Afghan Dari proverb, "*Ba lagh lagh sag darya mordar namesha wad*," meaning, "A river is not contaminated by having a dog drink from it." Widespread seasonal epidemics of diarrheal diseases are common in Afghanistan and associated with increased levels of acute malnutrition.[22] Insufficient access to quality health services is still a determinant for poor nutrition among children, despite notable improvements in access over the past decade. In 2006, 65 percent of households had access (two hours' walking distance) to basic health care compared to 9 percent in 2000.[23] However, many households still do not have the means to make optimal use of these facilities, constrained by cost, lack of transportation, and the cultural factors that limit women accessing services for themselves and their children. The quality of care and service also needs improvement.

In Afghanistan, children's nutritional status is also directly influenced by both the physical and mental health of mothers, as well as women's sociocultural position. Women who are thin or anemic during pregnancy are more likely to have infants with low birth weight, who themselves are subsequently likely to be more malnourished than older children. At the same time, maternal undernutrition increases also mean greater risk of maternal death during childbirth. Afghanistan has the highest rate of maternal mortality in the world, with one out of every eleven women dying from pregnancy- or childbirth-related complications.[24]

A strong maternal-infant bond provided through psychosocial stimulation is essential for positive child development.[25] Breastfeeding and other care practices provide opportunities to help establish a positive attachment between caregiver and child. Unfortunately, many caregivers in Afghanistan are not in a position to provide psychosocial stimulation to their children due to their own poor mental health. Mental illness among women in Afghanistan is reported to be widespread.[26] A study estimated that 62 percent of Afghan women had experienced at least four traumatic events during the ten years preceding the study, including severe loss of access to household necessities such as food and water. The study showed that 67.7 percent of women reported suffering from symptoms of depression and 72.2 percent suffered symptoms of anxiety. Women with poor mental health themselves are less likely to be able to provide adequate care and nourishment to their children. This is further exemplified by operational research conducted in 2003, which showed that 32 percent of the severely malnourished children who were admitted for treatment into nutrition centers in Kabul during the period of 2002 to 2006 were under six months of age.[27] Typically, it is rare to see large numbers of severely malnourished children less than six months of age, since optimal breastfeeding practices protect them. However, many mothers in Afghanistan complain of "breast milk deficiency," which can often be explained by mental health problems, combined with inadequate feeding practices. For example, delayed introduction of breastfeeding caused as a result of giving foods such as ghee (clarified butter) instead of breast milk on the infant's first day,[28] or the early cessation of breastfeeding as a result of young children being given bread dipped in tea with sugar to suck on.

Childcare and behavioral practices are influenced by women's education levels and their positions in their society. It is well documented that many women in Afghanistan have limited influence and decision making on household management matters, including access to and expenditure of resources, when and where to seek health care for their children and themselves, and the types of foods that are purchased. Multiple births with limited birth spacing and large families place further strain on women's time and capacity to provide adequate care and nutrition for their children. Recent research[29] reaffirms that factors such as low education levels, early marriage, lack of maternal autonomy, and shortage of basic material needs are negatively associated with poor nutritional status of young children. Women as mothers and caregivers make extraordinary efforts to overcome these challenges. For example, those women who are capable, and permitted to, do engage in employment, such as carpet weaving. However, while these practices may supplement household income, there are potential costs to childcare practices. A qualitative study[30] showed that the prevalence of acute and chronic undernutrition was much higher among children whose mothers were engaged in carpet weaving, regardless of higher income in their families. These women were likely not able to spend time to provide adequate care or to practice breastfeeding.

Cultural taboos and traditional beliefs prevent children and mothers from consuming adequate nutrient-rich foods. Many foods are described as "hot" or "cold" (description is region-specific) and their consumption is encouraged or restricted according to certain conditions. For example, in Bamiyan, some women reported that they should not eat green vegetables during pregnancy, especially during the winter, because they are "cold," while beans were encouraged because they are "warm" and "energetic." Eggs are often not given to young children, because they are considered to "cause a speech stutter later in life."[31] Mothers-in-law have a strong influence over childcare practices, even in situations where mothers themselves have adequate knowledge and skills for good nutrition practices. A significant risk to children affecting appetite and feeding patterns is the practice, in some areas of the country, of providing narcotics, such as boiled poppy bulb, at early ages as a sedative for ailments and/or in situations where mothers need time to undertake household tasks and income-generation activities.[32]

Culture and social obligations also play a fundamental role in food security and nutrition. A central characteristic of Afghan households' resilience to crises and shocks is their belonging to extensive social and kinship networks, which are reinforced through mutual obligations and a strong sense of social responsibility. These networks are an indispensable source of support in times of hardship, as families rely on distant relatives for shelter or loans. However, these same social obligations can also incur costs for families who cannot refuse providing shelter, food, or financial support to poorer relatives, putting additional strain on households that are already food-insecure.

Addressing Nutritional Need: Successes and Challenges?

Addressing the numerous challenges related to nutrition requires tackling both the symptoms and the underlying causes of malnutrition. Given the multifaceted nature of the problems of nutrition that Afghanistan faces, addressing the challenges undoubtedly requires the engagement of professionals working in health, agriculture, education, women's affairs, and other sectors, and entails developing partnerships between government, development agencies, civil society, and the private sector. The political situation during the Taliban regime was a major constraint to building such alliances, and the absence of long-term development funding limited interventions to short-term emergency projects. Until early 2002, nutrition programs therefore focused essentially on treating children suffering from acute malnutrition, through "supplementary feeding programs" and "therapeutic feeding programs."[33] The coverage of these programs was limited to urban areas such as Kabul and Herat, and to refugee camps. Prior to 2002, despite the challenges, some increasing efforts were being made to complement the treatment of acute malnutrition with activities that address its causes. For example, in Kabul, nutrition education sessions were provided in supplementary or therapeutic feeding centers; programs designed to improve water and sanitation were targeted at neighborhoods with high rates of acute malnutrition; and efforts were made to target food-aid distributions and food-security interventions to those families at greatest risk of malnutrition. But the scale and nature of emergency programs were neither adequate nor conducive to sustainable solutions for addressing undernutrition characteristic of Afghanistan.

The post-Taliban period and the associated significant increase in development assistance provided more opportunities for longer-term integrated nutrition programs. From 2002 onwards, efforts were made to engage multiple stakeholders and sectors around "a public nutrition approach" under the leadership of the newly established Public Nutrition Department in the Ministry of Public Health (MoPH).[34] From the outset, it was necessary to put in place the appropriate policy frameworks. As a result, the first Public Nutrition Policy and Strategy (2003–2006) was elaborated through an extensive consultation process, and institutional mechanisms for multi-stakeholder engagement were established. This strategy provided a clear roadmap for multisectoral work to address the symptoms and causes of malnutrition in Afghanistan[35] and established a clear framework for other ministries, namely the Ministry of Agriculture, to complement MoPH efforts to address malnutrition.[36] The Ministry of Public Health updated the strategy in 2009 through another consultative process, which helped define the existing five-year action plan (2009–2013).[37] As that strategy focused on the Ministry of Public Health interventions, development partners working in nutrition initiated efforts to prepare a multi-sectoral Nutrition Action Framework (NAF) for the period of 2012 to 2016,[38] which compiles the nutrition-relevant interventions of multiple ministries including public health; agriculture, irrigation, and livestock; commerce and industry; education; and rehabilitation and rural development. The process of preparing the NAF raised political commitment for nutrition, and the coordination of its implementation is now placed under the responsibility and championship of the vice president, indeed, a very positive development. As of this writing in 2012, Afghanistan has put in place policy frameworks that have facilitated a broad-based approach to addressing undernutrition.

The government of Afghanistan and its partners have recognized the immense challenges, the complex causes, and the widespread nature of the problem of malnutrition, and in 2002 began addressing a number of nutrition priorities consistently. These include scaling up infant and young child feeding programs, putting in place multifaceted strategies to increase micronutrient intake, institutionalizing treatment protocols, and, most importantly, ensuring that nutrition responses are integrated and owned by multiple sectors.

The well-recognized challenges that women face impeding optimal breastfeeding and complementary feeding practices underpinned the importance of investing in this area. In 2002, the MoPH's Public Nutrition Department, with its partners, primarily invested in operational and formative research on infant and young child feeding practices to better understand factors influencing these caring practices that could be used to inform a national training program for medical and public health professionals. Since 2002, several thousand doctors and nurses have been trained to help mothers with milk deficiency acquire the skills and regain the confidence they need to breastfeed optimally. Massive campaigns, involving civil society, the media, and even religious authorities, have been implemented to promote optimal breastfeeding. In 2006, the Ministry of Agriculture, Irrigation, and Livestock (MAIL) complemented the MoPH's efforts by developing improved local complementary feeding recipes using locally available foods. For example, in Bamiyan province, a common food given to young children is *halwagak*, basically porridge cooked from wheat flour with water and oil added. This recipe was improved when mothers were encouraged to add a small amount of bean flour and mashed carrots or spinach (which are increasingly cultivated in the province), making the porridge more nutritious for young children. Nutrition education and communication behavior change was integrated into multiple sectors, not only the health sector. Tremendous efforts are still needed to ensure that this training reaches all communities. Sustaining efforts is important since changing behaviors requires not only improving skills and knowledge, but changing certain beliefs and customs. This takes time and entails working on the social environment as a whole, including with husbands, fathers, and other family members.

A second nutrition priority in Afghanistan has been to address micronutrient deficiencies, in particular iodine, iron, and vitamin A. An effective and innovative strategy to eradicate iodine deficiency has been implemented, through a Universal Salt Iodization program. Since 2002, a coalition of partners under leadership of government (MoPH and the Ministry of Commerce, in partnership with the UN, NGOs, and the salt industry) has ensured that all salt produced in Afghanistan is iodized. By 2007, Afghanistan had a capacity to produce sufficient iodized salt to meet the population's demands, which had increased largely as a result of partnership with the private sector for its production and distribution, nationwide campaigns, and extensive social mobilization implemented through radio, school, religious forums, and community structures. As a result, there were significant improvements in coverage of iodized salt from less than 1 percent in 2002 to 28 percent between 2002 and 2004; 41 percent in 2005; and 61 percent in 2007–2008.[39] Unfortunately, more recent data suggest a lower coverage (55 percent)[40] and may be indicative of more recent challenges for the importation of raw salt that has affected the availability and quality of salt for iodization.[41] However, sufficiency of sample size, and hence reliability of findings, of this survey on access to iodized salt is debated.[42]

Similar efforts have also been introduced to fortify flour with iron, folic acid, vitamin B12, zinc, and vitamin A in commercial mills. Plans are in place to scale up the fortification of flour, initiate the fortification of oil/ghee with vitamin A, and strengthen legislative frameworks to support fortification.[43] Wheat consumed in Afghanistan is predominantly milled in the many small, often remote, village mills, therefore presenting a challenge for any effective fortification strategy, since it would have to ensure adequate decentralized capacity before fortification is in place, supply fortificant mixes, and ensure quality control. Furthermore, without a system in place to monitor and ensure compliance with fortification legislation, more costly fortified products are not as competitive as those cheaper unfortified products (which are often illegally branded and advertised as fortified).

Finally, targeted iron/folic acid, vitamin A, and zinc supplementation is officially part of routine health services, but the challenge lies in ensuring a reliable supply of supplements and compliance with health protocols. The MoPH is also exploring strategies to introduce and scale up the use of micronutrient powders, which will be added at the household level during food preparation.

Strategies to supplement diets with micronutrients cannot replace the need to improve the quality of diets, which entails improving access to diverse and safe foods, and providing families with the knowledge and skills for production, storage, processing, and preparation. The Ministry of Agriculture, Irrigation, and Livestock (MAIL), is taking a lead role and, together with development partners, has been working to diversify food production through the introduction of home gardens, small-scale poultry and dairy production, and other income-generating activities such as beekeeping and honey processing. Such projects are sources of both food and income, which can then be used to buy food or meet other essential household needs, such as access to health care and education. MAIL has also been working to integrate nutrition education, including improved complementary feeding and family recipes, as part of agriculture programs around the country. In 2011 and 2012, for instance, MAIL's General Directorate for Extension, with UN support, trained more than 5,400 men and women on nutrition education. Nearly 5,000 men and women benefitted from cooking demonstrations, more than 1,200 women were trained on home-based food processing, and more than 7,500 men and women were taught gardening.[44] As a result of lessons learned from previous projects, increased awareness about nutrition issues in MAIL, and stronger leadership in the ministry, agriculture experts are increasingly realizing the importance of focusing on food production for domestic markets and are introducing more comprehensive approaches to agriculture extension that promote production of highly nutritious foods and diet diversification.

While preventive measures are a priority, retaining the capacity to treat malnutrition remains essential. Since 2002, efforts have focused on institutionalizing the treatment of acute malnutrition into routine health policies and services, by establishing therapeutic feeding centers for children with severe acute malnutrition and complications, in all major provincial hospitals. Furthermore, facilities for treatment at the community level, through the distribution of Ready-to-Use Therapeutic Foods[45] and the establishment of patient monitoring through basic health centers at district levels, have been introduced and scaled up.

Improving the quality and level of education, particularly for girls, as well as integrating nutrition education and behavioral change into school curricula, are important strategies, and the education sector has played a central role in leading these initiatives. Nutrition education is being introduced in school curricula, including strengthening the syllabi for grades one to six and training teachers on nutrition.[46] Literacy courses, including those run by the Ministry of Women's Affairs, are also potentially contributing to improving nutrition and health knowledge in the longer term. School gardens have been introduced in primary schools, with the assistance of MAIL, as a foundation for promoting healthy diets and introducing environmental education. Youth centers, where they exist, have also provided a forum to both sensitize young people and encourage them to promote nutrition in their communities. The Ministries of Education, Women's Affairs, Religious Affairs, and Youth Affairs have thus far all been engaged in efforts to address malnutrition. Finally, the Ministry of Higher Education, professional training institutes, and universities are also mobilized to gradually improve nutrition training among doctors, nurses, agronomists, and education professionals. This represents an important foundation for ensuring that professionals in all sectors, as well as youth, gain a fundamental understanding of nutrition.

Emerging, Persistent Threats and Continued Consequences

Despite all these efforts, Afghan children continue to face high levels of mortality associated with poor nutrition and growth. Furthermore, they risk not reaching their full intellectual and productive potential. Afghanistan still faces significant challenges and persistent perils. While noteworthy progress has been achieved, nutrition programs, because they are not yet fully institutionalized, continue to be restricted in scale. This is as a result of limited skilled human resource capacity, poor infrastructure, and inadequate access to basic services such as clinics and schools, as well as weak markets and continued conflict and insecurity in many parts of the country. As a consequence of persistent levels of high undernutrition, therefore, Afghanistan's economic development is likely to be negatively affected over the long term.

However, these challenges should not overshadow the immense progress that has been achieved. Nutrition is now established as a national priority, not only in the public health sector, but in other areas as well, such as agriculture, gender, trade and commerce, and education. As Afghanistan moves toward economic recovery, nutrition must now become an integral component of this broader agenda. In moving forward, it will be important that Afghanistan build on what has been achieved, particularly in terms of implementing the important policy frameworks developed to promote a multi-sectoral approach to the diverse and complex problems of malnutrition. Nutrition programs need to reflect a thorough analysis of the cultural, ethnic, and religious characteristics of Afghan societies, particularly in relation to how they affect women. Afghanistan is likely to continue to face new and emerging risks, such as political conflict, the global economic crisis, and climate change, which may continue to negatively impact children's nutrition. It is, therefore, all the more critical that Afghanistan sustains and further scales up longer-term multi-sectoral preventive programs, which contribute to improve resilience of families and communities, while simultaneously ensuring that the relevant national institutions have the capacities and plans to respond quickly and effectively to any additional nutrition risks that children face in the future.

Notes

1. Undernutrition includes being underweight for one's age, too short for one's age (stunting), dangerously thin for one's height (wasting), and deficient in vitamins and minerals (micronutrient deficiencies).

2. Stunting is technically defined as height for age minus two standard deviations from the median height for age of the standard reference population, indicating the situation of being too short for a given age.

3. UNICEF, State of the World's Children (SOWC), 2012.

4. Ibid.

5. MOPH (Ministry of Public Health) of Afghanistan, UNICEF (United Nations Children's Fund), CDC (Centers for Disease Control and Prevention), National Institute for Research on Food and Nutrition-Italy, and Tufts University, *National Nutrition Survey, Afghanistan* (2004).

6. Ibid.

7. Neural-tube defects (NTDs) are birth defects causing an opening in the spinal cord or brain that occurs very early in human development. Researchers have found that 50 to 70 percent of NTDs can be prevented when women supplement their diet with folic acid, a water-soluble B vitamin. Supplementing pregnant women with

iron combined with folic acid is the standard preventive intervention, including in Afghanistan.

8. Fitsum Assefa, personal observation/communication, 2005.

9. According to the World Health Organization, a prevalence of scurvy in more than 1 percent of the population is considered of severe public health significance.

10. Fitsum Assefa, M. Z. Jaberkhil, P. Salama, and P. Spiegel, "Malnutrition and Mortality in Kohistan District, Afghanistan," *JAMA* 286, no. 21 (April 2001): 2723-2728.

11. Robert E. Black et al., "Maternal and Child Undernutrition: Global and Regional Exposures and Health Consequences," *The Lancet* 371, no. 9608 (January 19, 2008): 243-260.

12. Under-five mortality rate in Afghanistan is 149 per 1000 live births, ranked the eleventh-highest rate globally.

13. UNICEF, State of the World's Children (SOWC), 2012.

14. Both iron and iodine are implicated in cognitive development of children in the first years of life. For example, high levels of iodine deficiency in a population, as in Afghanistan, can result in a reduction of the population's IQ by up to 10 percentage points.

15. "Repositioning Nutrition as Central to Development: A Strategy for Large Scale Action" (World Bank, Directions in Development series, 2005).

16. Estimated at $1,200 in 2009, cited on http://hdrstats.undp.org/en/indicators.

17. The HDI is a summary measure for assessing long-term progress in three basic dimensions of human development: a long and healthy life, access to knowledge, and a decent standard of living. Afghanistan's HDI value for 2011 is 0.398 — in the low human development category.

18. "Human Development Report 2011," United Nations Development Program.

19. Sue Lautze, Elizabeth Stites, Neamatollah Nojumi, and Fazal Najimi, "Qaht-e-Pool 'A cash famine' — Food Insecurity in Afghanistan 1999-2002" (London: Overseas Development Institute, 2002). Available at http://reliefweb.int/sites/reliefweb .int/files/resources/04FA28AB5FDFCE5DC1256BE6004D79D1-odi-afg-21jun .pdf.

20. "National Risk and Vulnerablity Assessment 2007/8: A Profile of Afghanistan," Icon Institute, 2009.

21. *WHO/UNICEF Joint Monitoring Project, 2008.*

22. Charlotte Dufour and Annalies Borrel, "Towards a Public Nutrition Response in Afghanistan: Evolutions in Nutritional Assessment and Response," in Adam Pain and Jacky Sutton, eds., *Reconstructing Agriculture in Afghanistan* (United Kingdom: Practical Action, 2005).

23. Ministry of Public Health, 2008.

24. UNICEF Afghanistan, factsheet, 2011.

25. "Mental Health and Psychosocial Well-Being among Children in Severe Food Shortage Situations," World Health Organization, 2006.

26. Barbara L. Cardozo, Oleg O. Bilukha, Carol A. Gotway Crawford, Irshad Shaikh, Mitchell I. Wolfe, Michael L. Gerber, and Mark Anderson, "Mental Health, Social Functioning and Disability in Postwar Afghanistan," *JAMA* (August 4, 2004): 575-584.

27. C. Bizouern, "Action contre La Faim," case study presented to 35th Standing Committee on Nutrition Session—Working Group Nutrition in Emergencies, 2008.

28. Traditionally, also, the colostrum—the first secretion from the mammary glands—is thrown away at birth, depriving the baby of important antibodies. See Steven Solter, chapter 11 in this volume, "Children's Health: The Challenge of Survival."

29. Taufiq Marshal, Takehito Takano, Keiko Nakamura, Masashi Kizuki, Shafiqullah Hemat, Masufumi Watanabe, and Kaoruko Seino, "Factors Associated with the Health and Nutritional Status of Children under Five Years of Age in Afghanistan: Family Behavior Related to Women and Past Experience of War-Related Hardships," BMC Public Health 8 (2008): 301.

30. "Breastfeeding and Weaning Beliefs and Practices, Andkhoy, Khanacharbagh, Qaramqual and Qurghan Districts, Jawzjan Province, Qualitative Study Findings," Save the Children (2003).

31. Food and Agriculture Organization of the United Nations, Report on Child Feeding Practices (unpublished), 2006.

32. "Breastfeeding and Weaning Beliefs and Practices, Andkhoy, Khanacharbagh, Qaramqual and Qurghan Districts, Jawzjan Province, Qualitative Study Findings," Save the Children (2003).

33. Supplementary Feeding Programs provide treatment for moderately acute malnutrition through a weekly distribution of fortified porridge mix; therapeutic feeding programs provide treatment for severe cases and require medical follow-up and the use of specialized therapeutic foods.

34. A long-term capacity development approach was led by Tufts University and UNICEF that focused on policy and institutional arrangements, knowledge and research, leadership and accountability systems.

35. Annalies Borrel and Peter Salama, "Public Nutrition Case-studies," Disasters (2009); Charlotte Dufour and Annalies Borrel, "Towards a Public Nutrition Response in Afghanistan: Evolutions in Nutritional Assessment and Response", in Adam Pain and Jacky Sutton, eds., Reconstructing Agriculture in Afghanistan (United Kingdom: Practical Action, 2005).

36. Ibid.; Emily J. Levitt, David L. Pelletier, Charlotte Dufour, Alice N. Pell, "Harmonizing Agriculture and Health Sector Actions to Improve Household Nutrition: Policy Experiences from Afghanistan (2002-2007)," Food Security; The Science, Sociology and Economics of Food Production and Access to Food 3, no. 3 (September 2011): 363–381.

37. Ministry of Public Health, National Public Nutrition Policy and Strategy 2010–2013, September 2009.

38. Islamic Republic of Afghanistan, Nutrition Action Framework, A multi-sectoral framework of the Ministry of Agriculture Irrigation and Livestock, Ministry of Commerce and Industry, Ministry of Education, Ministry of Public Health, and Ministry of Rehabilitation and Rural Development, April 2012.

39. According to the National Risk and Vulnerability Assessment conducted in 2005 and 2007–2008.

40. Multi Indicator Cluster Survey, Afghanistan, 2010-2011.

41. Salt extracted from the mines in northern Afghanistan is of lower quality, and it costs factories in the south a lot more to transport salt from northern Afghanistan

than from Pakistan. The recent ban of raw salt importation can result in smuggling and use of unionized salt by households and may explain the lack of progress/decline in proportion of households reported to consume iodized salt.

42. Dr. Nasiri Shah M., personal communication.

43. Islamic Republic of Afghanistan, *Nutrition Action Framework*.

44. MDG-Fund UN Joint Programme activity monitoring report, communicated by Akbar Shahristani, MDG-Fund UN Joint Programme food security coordinator, November 2012.

45. RUTF (Ready-to-Use Food) is intended specifically for the treatment of severe acute malnutrition and recommended by the World Health Organization (WHO) for home treatment of this condition. RUTF requires no preparation, no dilution in water prior to use, and no cooking, and can be consumed directly from the sachet.

46. Akbar Shahristani, personal communication, November 2012.

CHAPTER 13

Desperately Seeking Harun: Children with Disabilities

LAEL ADAMS MOHIB

In the well-known story of Moses (Musa) and Aaron (Harun), God calls upon Moses to undertake a seemingly impossible journey—confronting the Egyptian Pharaoh and freeing the Israelites from a tyrannical rule. Moses was an unlikely character to present God's case before the Pharaoh—he had a disability, a severe speech impediment that led him to live a quiet, secluded life as a shepherd. He was doubtful and had no confidence, so he pleaded with God to let his brother, Aaron, who had the gift of eloquent speech, accompany him. A verse from the Qur'an reads:

> Go to the Pharaoh! He has transgressed (the bounds). Moses said, "My Lord! Relieve my mind and ease my task for me; And loosen a note from my tongue, That they may understand my speech. Appoint for me a supporter from my people, Aaron, my brother. Confirm my strength with him and let him share my task, That we may glorify You much and much remember You. You are ever Seeing us." He said: "You are granted your request, O Moses."[1]

While Moses doubted himself, his brother helped him realize his potential as a person and shared his struggle with him.

Best- and Worst-Case Scenarios

All disabled children in Afghanistan need their own Harun to help them reach their potential as human beings or even just to improve their quality of life, whether that support comes from family, care centers, hospitals, schools, the government, or non-governmental organizations. But the reality is that, with very few facilities for assistance and treatment, and with little public awareness of the causes and nature of disabilities, in Afghanistan often the best-case scenario for a disabled child is basic care within the home from family members who do not have training or external support, but who are often overwhelmed with the financial and physical burdens of such a responsibility. As is often true for severely disabled children even in more developed countries, education and social integration for disabled Afghan children are usually luxuries. Inclusive education or home-schooling opportunities are rare and underfunded. Teachers sometimes turn disabled children away at the door, saying they cannot accommodate them in the classroom. Appropriate health care, education, or social services for special-needs children are simply not readily available or accessible in Afghanistan. Some families are able to get services from one of the approximately thirty institutions working with disabled children, primarily in the capital city Kabul, or pool their resources and efforts to care for the child within the home as best as they can afford.[2]

In the worst-case scenario, children with severe disabilities are victims of physical and mental abuse, neglect, or abandonment. Some families may regard such children as a curse or punishment from God upon the family or the mother who bore the child. Such children are unlikely to receive any therapy, treatment, or basic education. Cases have been reported of children being tied to beds or abandoned in mosques or public parks.[3] If orphaned or abandoned, they may be taken into one of the few private-care homes around the country, or placed in a government orphanage or one of the five *marastoon*s (places for the sick) run by the Afghanistan Red Crescent Society (ARCS).[4]

Though such unsettling scenarios can be found all over the world, they are too often the norm for children with disabilities in Afghanistan, a country with great need for economic, health, education, and infrastructure development. According to the United Nations' 2013 Human Development Report, Afghanistan is one of the least developed countries in the world, ranking 175 out of 187 countries with comparable development.[5] In a country where the international community is heavily engaged in an ongoing military and development campaign, funding for children with disabilities has not been a priority for most international donors. Neither is it a priority for the Afghan government, which is too weak to effectively budget and distribute the billions of foreign dollars gifted to it yearly. In Afghanistan, despite some happy endings and gradual progress, the glass more often than not looks half empty.

Ahmad's Story

Karen Dahlgren[6] and her colleague Zarmina Behroz, social workers for Children in Crisis (CIC), a British non-governmental organization (NGO), have seen both the worst- and best-case scenarios over the course of their four years working in the field of child protection services in Afghanistan. Perhaps closest to Dahlgren's heart, she says, is the case of a fifteen-year-old boy with severe cerebral palsy named Ahmad, who has become a kind of poster child illustrating the need for services for severely disabled children in Afghanistan. In October 2010, Ahmad was found abandoned in a public park in Kabul, drastically undernourished and on the verge of starvation, his body frozen into a stiff fetal position. "Ahmad's family must have hit a crisis point," surmises Susan Helseth, program manager for the United Nations Afghanistan Disability Support Program, who has been involved in Ahmad's case. "They must have thought they had no option but to abandon him. Perhaps they were turned away from hospitals. They must not have had the skills or knowledge to take care of him."[7]

Due to neglect and lack of any physiotherapy, Ahmad was nearly catatonic, unable to move or sit up on his own, speak, or eat solid foods. With no specialized government facilities or emergency plans for dealing with cases such as Ahmad's, he was placed in a government orphanage in Kabul, with no trained caregivers to provide the round-the-clock attention he needed to survive. He was discovered in a dire state by an employee for a logistics company making deliveries to the orphanage, and brought to Dahlgren and Behroz's attention at CIC. After some investigation, Behroz discovered that Ahmad had once lived at a government-funded institution in Kabul for the disabled. His records there contained only a picture with no name. It's not clear when he was given the name Ahmad. Dahlgren and Behroz visited him at the orphanage. Dahlgren remembers sitting at his side, taking his hand, and speaking to him. "Everyone in the orphanage was looking at me as though I were crazy. Even my co-worker, who has had training, said to me, 'Karen, he doesn't understand you,'" Dahlgren recalls. "I didn't know what was going on in his head, but I thought, I have to talk to him and see."[8]

They were concerned about the lack of care and even resentment the orphanage staff showed toward Ahmad. With meager salaries, no training to care for special-needs children, and no specialized facilities in the orphanage, so as to avoid changing Ahmad's diapers regularly the staff often did not feed him enough, catheterized him improperly, which blocked the flow of his urine, and isolated him. He developed bedsores and fever. They set about finding a hospital that would admit him, but the task turned out to be more difficult than imagined. He was rejected from several hospitals, even a specialized foreign-funded children's hospital, on the grounds that they were not obligated to provide the constant care he needed while undergoing treatment.

Finally, the International Committee of the Red Cross (ICRC) Orthopedic Center in Kabul agreed to treat him. Alberto Cairo, an Italian physiotherapist who has worked for ICRC in Afghanistan for the past twenty-one years, oversaw Ahmad's care and recovery, while Dr. Shakrullah Zerick treated him. Over the course of Ahmad's three months at ICRC, he "changed completely," says Cairo, who credits the boy's revival not only to proper care and physiotherapy, but to simple acts of kindness. "We smiled at him. We were kind to him," says Cairo. "He is a human being. Even a dog feels if he is loved or not."[9]

While Ahmad was in the hospital, Dahlgren and Behroz worked to find him a proper caregiver, but several worked for only a few hours before abruptly quitting: the men refused to do such work, and the women were uncomfortable caring for a pubescent boy due to cultural restrictions. Finally, one poor, jobless man, visiting his relative in the hospital, saw Ahmad and offered to be his full-time caregiver. The man, named Taki, gradually learned to understand Ahmad's sounds and signals and Ahmad learned how to ask . . . and more. One day during therapy, Ahmad took a plastic ball and put it to his mouth as if he were taking a bite from an apple, Dahlgren says — it was then that everyone understood that he could eat solid foods. With persistent therapy, the hospital staff soon realized that Ahmad could stand. They fitted him for leg braces, and soon he was walking with a walker and Taki's help.[10]

Both Dahlgren and Behroz became champions of Ahmad's case, regularly meeting face-to-face with deputies at the Afghan Ministry of Labor, Social Affairs, Martyrs, and Disabled (MoLSAMD) in an attempt to get the government to take responsibility for Ahmad and emergency cases like his. Working with Helseth and Carol Le Duc, the European Union's social protection advisor to the MoLSAMD, they brought Ahmad's story to the forefront during coordination meetings in January 2011 with government officials and members of about thirty NGOs currently working with disabled children in Afghanistan. Deputy Minister of Labor and Social Affairs Wasel Noor Mohammad promised them he would allocate funds to create an emergency care facility for abandoned disabled children within the orphanage where Ahmad was living, and fund caregivers, if they would develop a budget and proposal. They did so, but three months later, when Ahmad was discharged from the center, the deputy minister's promise had materialized into nothing more than one small room with a fresh coat of paint. Desperate, Dahlgren took Ahmad straight from the center to the deputy minister's office, demanding he take responsibility for Ahmad.[11]

But it would take several more months for the government to act on behalf of Ahmad. It may take many more years for an effective government strategy and action plan to be activated for dealing with the thousands of other emergency cases like Ahmad's. Cairo of ICRC claims that he has seen little progress in the past two decades. "Honestly," he says, "I don't expect any change in the next ten years."[12]

One of Thousands

Ahmad's story is just one among thousands. Cerebral palsy is a common disability among children in Afghanistan. ICRC, which provides services in seven locations across the country, registered nearly seven thousand new patients in 2010. Of those, nearly two thousand (nearly 30 percent) were children with cerebral palsy. Other common disabilities include mild to severe congenital disorders, such as club foot, hip dysplasia, and other birth defects leaving the child with paralysis or deformities.[13] Such disabilities arise from a range of causes, most notably the lack of adequate prenatal care for expectant mothers or treatment for easily preventable diseases. A 2011 Save the Children study ranked Afghanistan as the worst place in the world to be a mother, with high maternal mortality and malnourishment rates.[14] According to this report, one out of every eleven mothers dies during childbirth, and only four out of every five children will live to about age five. Furthermore, only 14 percent of births are attended by healthcare personnel in Afghanistan, which increases the chances of permanent damage due to complications at birth.[15] Congenital diseases are also caused by the high rate of interfamilial marriages in Afghanistan. Unions between cousins are a widely accepted and ingrained part of the culture, greatly increasing the chance that recessive genetic disorders within a family will be passed to the child.[16]

According to the 2005 National Disability Survey in Afghanistan conducted by Handicap International—the most recent account, as of 2011, of disability statistics in Afghanistan—2.7 percent of Afghans have a severe disability. When less severe disabilities are included, the percentage rises to 4.8 percent of the population. For every five households, one will include a family member with a severe disability. More than half the Afghan population is under the age of twenty-five, and most disabled Afghans are children under fourteen years old.[17]

Understanding and Coping

Sadiq Mohibi is the Afghan government's network coordinator, and co-founder of his own NGO for the disabled called Afghanistan Landmine Survivor Organization (ALSO), which works to raise awareness and lobbies for proactive disability policies within the government, coordinating activities amongst all players. Disabled from birth with a club foot (congenital talipes equinovarus), Mohibi is trying to generate public awareness about disability and reverse negative mentalities. ALSO has published a series of booklets, including *Islam and Disability* and *Outreach Magazine for Disabled Affairs*, in local languages. The booklets are meant to educate families about why disabilities occur, where to go for help, and how the family can facilitate the child's development. Many families believe that a child with a disability is a sort of divine punishment for some perceived mistake or wrongdoing in life, Mohibi says. It is very common for families to first seek spiritual remedies for their disabled child, such as visiting shrines to leave offerings.

Regardless of a family's understanding of a child's disability, most simply cannot afford the time or money to give the child conventional treatment and care. Dahlgren tells of finding, during a home visit, two mentally retarded women chained to their beds by family members who could not afford to provide them constant supervision and care. Susan Helseth notes that the orphanage staff that neglected Ahmad "aren't cold-hearted people—they are just overwhelmed by the task."[18]

"We need to educate, to raise awareness," says Mohibi. "Disabled people have rights. They need to be integrated properly."[19] One of ALSO's booklets features the story of a young girl named Kamar, who, partially paralyzed from birth, spent the first thirteen years of her life crawling before her family learned through counseling services provided by ALSO that her condition could be fixed with surgery and braces. Having undergone a surgical procedure at ICRC Orthopedic Center in Kabul in 2009, and been fitted for leg braces, Kamar is now walking and in her first year of high school.[20]

More often than not, communities and extended families unite to provide the best care possible for the child. Carol Le Duc shares several positive stories from her twenty years of experience working in child services in Afghanistan and Pakistan: "Families can be extremely supportive. The best place for almost all children is in the home. But the families need training."

She tells the story of a former male colleague who had a daughter who was paralyzed from birth. The girl's mother provided her with round-the-clock care for twenty years until she became too weak to lift her grown daughter in order to wash her, dress her, and take her to the toilet. Because the family had no other options, the girl's father took on these responsibilities himself, in addition to his full-time job.[21] Such examples of dedication and perseverance within families who struggle financially are abundant in Afghanistan.

Cairo of ICRC agrees that the problem is not the will of the family. The real battle, he believes, is educating families about what treatment or therapy options are available. Physical disabilities are "not rejected, not refused among families with disabled children," he says. "If families don't bring children here, it's not because they hide them—they just don't know that we can do something for them, or they live very far away," says Cairo. "I've never seen a case where the parent does not want to do something for the child."

But Cairo admits that in Afghan society, as in many parts of the world, the societal mentality toward individuals with disabilities has not progressed positively. Those with acquired disabilities, such as war-wounded or landmine victims, usually garner higher regard than those with congenital or mental disabilities, especially women and children. Acquired disabilities, he explains, are usually easier to understand and accept.[22]

Rural versus Urban

With 74 percent of the Afghan population dwelling in the countryside,[23] cases of disabilities are most widespread outside urban areas. Despite this, most treatment centers are located in the five major urban centers around the country—Kabul, Jalalabad, Kandahar, Mazar-i-Sharif, and Herat. Some parents bring their children from the provinces to the nearest city in search of treatment. At the ICRC Orthopedic Center in Kabul, a nine-year-old boy from the eastern province of Paktia has come to be refitted for a new prosthesis—he lost his entire leg from the pelvis down several years ago after stepping on a landmine near his house. With the prosthesis, he's been able to walk independently and attend school. His father brings him to the center in Kabul as needed for follow-up treatment.[24]

But for those rural children with disabilities whose families cannot afford to bring them to the cities, there is a widely accepted alternative approach. Community-Based Rehabilitation (CBR), implemented by the Swedish Committee for Afghanistan (SCA), has set the standard for in-home care in all regions of Afghanistan. The program mobilizes communities to identify families with disabled members, with a particular focus on women and children. "The idea is to look at the disabled person holistically," says Fiona Gall, who works for SCA as a disability advisor. In-home therapy and education is provided, with local physiotherapists working directly with the families so the care is sustainable. Employment support for adults is also a component of the program, the goal being not just physical rehabilitation but social integration.[25]

In Afghan society, the family unit is often the only means of support—physical, social, financial, or otherwise. Thus, sustainable treatment and social integration programs, such as in-home education and treatment and employment support, must be based around the family. While a family may be accepting of a child's disability, it is nevertheless limited in the care and resources it can contribute, due to poverty and lack of training. Despite difficult economic and social conditions, abandonment of children with disabilities is exceptional in Afghan society. In urban areas, it happens more frequently, as the tight-knit community structure of rural villages breaks down in the cities.

Impossible to Turn Away

At the Kabul Orthopedic Organization (KOO) in Kabul, Marsal, a young, plump mother with perfectly applied make-up wearing a black chiffon *chadari*, waits with about thirty other mothers every Saturday and Wednesday for physiotherapist Fahima Kohistani to teach them how to give therapy at home to their children with club feet. Marsal has four children—her two daughters, ages one and nine, both have club feet. She has been coming to the classes for the past seven years hoping for a miraculous cure. Though club foot and other congenital diseases cannot be cured, only treated, most families have heightened expectations. Some families lose patience with the repetitive nature of the treatments and give up. "The families want instant results," explains Dr. Kohistani.[26]

KOO is the "Afghan-ized" result of what began in 1983 in Pakistan during the Soviet war (1979–1989) as the first-ever NGO for Afghan war-disabled, the Sandy Gall Afghanistan Appeal (SGAA). Sandy Gall, a British journalist who reported from Afghanistan during the Mujahedin resistance in the 1980s, was astounded by the number of those disabled in the war—the many men, women, and children who were landmine victims, as well as *mujahid* soldiers who became amputees in battle. Gall's daughter, Fiona, still advises KOO, which is managed by Dr. Gul Makay Siawash, a physician, who was one of the few Afghan women to run for parliament in 2010. The organization quickly evolved from helping the war-wounded to providing services for a range of disabilities, and like SCA, includes an in-home education program for disabled children, which Dr. Siawash personally funded for some time.[27]

The International Red Cross, arguably the most proactive and far-reaching organization providing services for the disabled in Afghanistan since 1988, changed its policies from caring exclusively for landmine victims when the line forming at the door included more and more individuals with congenital disabilities. Initially the only children passing through their doors were those who had stepped on landmines, but that changed. "It was almost embarrassing," says Alberto Cairo. "Sometimes in front of the gate, we had fifty patients, twenty of them war victims, who we welcomed. The remaining thirty were disabled people with other pathologies and we were telling them, 'No, sorry, we cannot do anything for you.'"[28]

Jawad's Mother

In 1994, during the Afghan civil war (1992–1996), one determined woman seeking help for her young son with polio opened a new chapter in services made available to the disabled in Afghanistan. According to Cairo, Jawad's mother carried her nine-year-old son, whose legs and arm were paralyzed from polio, on her back under her blue *burqa* several miles to the doors of the ICRC Orthopedic Center, where she waited at the gate day after day until finally she was admitted. "Because of her, things changed," says Cairo. "We moved in a new direction, accepting and admitting non-war victims."[29] Fitted for a wheelchair and treated with physiotherapy, Jawad was soon independently mobile.

Two years later, during the reign of the Taliban (1996–2001), Jawad's mother, herself non-literate, returned with another request for her son—education. She had pleaded with school headmasters in her neighborhood to accept Jawad, but though they sympathized with her, they refused. At her behest, the ICRC staff members decided to privately fund a pilot home-education program. In just three months, Jawad had raced through the equivalent of two grades of coursework. Four years later, he had completed the curriculum through the twelfth grade. When he was thirteen, the ICRC employed Jawad as a database operator. After the fall of the Taliban, he worked as a translator for foreign journalists. Through these connections, he managed to secure a scholarship at a college in the United States. He has since worked as a policy analyst in Washington, DC, interned for the United States Senate, and now resides in Kabul, where he is conducting research.[30]

Jawad's story highlights the positive differences that can be made in the life of disabled children, and society and culture as a whole, if they and their families are able to access even the most fundamental treatment or equipment, and are given the most basic opportunities, such as education.

On Paper, Not Practical

Roles, responsibilities, and strategies have been delegated and outlined in the Afghanistan National Disability Action Plan 2008–2011 and the National Strategy for Children at Risk 2006, and international-standard social protection laws for disabled people were passed this year in the Afghan parliament, but these plans and laws have not been fully actualized.[31] Sadiq Mohibi, who works with the government as an advisor and coordinator, has a relatively optimistic view—"The law itself is progress," he says. "Despite this progress and development, it seems like the programs are more, but the response is less," he admits. "We have paper, but we don't see progress practically yet."[32]

Karen Dahlgren and Zarmina Behroz's push with the government to help in Ahmad's case provides a window into the situation. It is part of a larger effort at sustaining a national dialogue—a collaborative effort between foreign donors, NGOs, and government institutions—in an attempt to address urgent issues in the short term while developing a long-term, sustainable system for dealing with emergency and abandonment cases like Ahmad's in the future. The effort is an across-the-board attempt to get all players on one page, and to get progress and implementation off the page.

The Child Protection Action Networks (CPANs) are provincial-level bodies set up by the United Nations Children's Fund (UNICEF) to monitor local child protection issues and identify ways to respond to them, such as raising community awareness on the rights of children, and advocating at the national level on specific issues. CPAN meetings bring together government ministries and NGOs working in the field of child protection. Individual cases are often referred to CPANs and addressed by setting up emergency planning meetings, with a small number of individuals from different organizations involved in each case. Ahmad was one of the children whose case was put forth at a CPAN meeting. Emergency funds from CPANs were allocated to pay for Ahmad's caregivers until the government could provide funding for staff several months later. The issue of children with disabilities is generally addressed by the Kabul CPAN Social Protection Working Group, which focuses on the care of children in institutions in Kabul.[33]

Carol Le Duc describes the government as "reactive rather than proactive." She believes most of the lack of interest and action on the part of the government comes not so much from lack of funding or resourcing, but from a pervasive discomfort that such issues even exist. "There's a great deal of denial for things that aren't quite up to standard," Le Duc says. "But if we deny it, we don't provide facilities for it." Despite her frustration, she, like other workers in the field, has seized Ahmad's case as a way to raise awareness of the need. The case has "catalyzed some of the organizations to begin to think about this issue," she says.[34]

A Window of Hope

During mild summer days, the thirteen children living at the Kabul-based private care home Window of Hope—set up and funded by two Afghans living in the United Kingdom and Kabul—can be found in the garden, seeing how long they can keep a balloon afloat by batting it back and forth to each other. They may also be pushing the three children with cerebral palsy around the yard in their wheelchairs. Some days, they help the gardener tend to the tomato plants in the garden. On other days, they visit a play center in Kabul, especially equipped for disabled children, created by Anghared James, a former pediatric nurse from the UK.

When Dahlgren stops by Window of Hope on a Friday to play with the children, a nine-year-old mentally disabled boy comes dashing across the lawn and throws his arms around her in a fidgety embrace, greeting her excitedly in Dari between gulps of laughter and smiles. Several months ago, before the children relocated to a larger house, this same boy was aggressive, demanding, and distant, hardly speaking or interacting at all.

At first, the children didn't know what to do with the toys Dahlgren had brought for them. Three of the children have severe cases of cerebral palsy, one has autism, and the others have various levels of mental disabilities. They were all seriously undernourished, with daily meals consisting of bread-based soups and porridges. Three beds were jammed into one small room, and seven other children were sleeping on the floor of another room. The monthly allowance donated by the benefactors when the center was established years ago was simply no longer enough. A young woman in her twenties, who grew up in the home and now takes care of its day-to-day operation, was expending all her time and the center's resources just to keep the children clothed and fed. She has been there since she was a child, orphaned and disabled in a rocket attack on her home, and has put aside her dreams of studying to become a lawyer to look after the children and manage the center, with the part-time help of a housekeeper and cook.

Dahlgren requested that the MoLSAMD provide the Window of Hope children with a larger, government-owned building. Window of Hope is one of the few independent care homes in Kabul that takes in disabled orphans.

The thirteen children residing there have trickled in across the years, most of them left in local mosques or found abandoned by people who then brought them to the home. The government has also attempted to refer some children to the home through their social workers. Despite the pressing need, the MoLSAMD was not able to provide a larger location. Through private fundraising headed by Dahlgren, the Window of Hope was able to move to a new home. Clothes, food, and monetary donations were made in order to improve the children's nutrition and provide them toys and games to stimulate their minds. The young woman who runs the home has been given basic physiotherapy training. She helped one of the children, a seven-year-old boy with a leg deformity, learn how to walk with the aid of leg braces.

Although the Window of Hope center continues to struggle—its future teetering on uncertainty as donations ebb and flow with the goodwill of mainly international donors coming and going—it is a success story for the care of disabled children in Afghanistan. Though education for the children is a looming need, therapy sessions are only occasional, and the government was not able to make provisions to improve the center, the children do have a support system. As the young woman who runs the center says, "We're a family here."

Full Circle

Seven months after Ahmad was found abandoned in a park in critical condition, numerous organizations and individuals have helped turn his life around. During one of her routine visits to the orphanage in May 2011, Dahlgren stopped by Ahmad's room to chat with his caregiver, Taki, about a toilet-training routine for Ahmad. The room had been set up, under direction from the MoLSAMD, just for Ahmad. A small TV on a chair hummed in the background, trying to pick up a signal. Light filtered through two large, screen-less windows. Taki is now being paid with government funding and has the help of one other caregiver. Ahmad uses his own strength now to sit up in bed. Taki dresses him each morning. He smiled widely and laughed when he saw Dahlgren, who took his hand and asked him, in Dari, how he was doing.

There will be many more requirements over the years for Ahmad's care, but he now has the support that he and every other disabled child in Afghanistan need. The months of effort by Dahlgren, Behroz, Helseth, Le Duc, Mohibi, Cairo, and others have paid off, though these efforts seemed to progress in spite of the government instead of in league with the government. Just as

Moses needed his brother Aaron, disabled Afghan children need support to ensure that they are, at the very least, receiving the care required for survival, and at the most, reaching their full potential as human beings.

Notes

1. Muhammad Marmaduke Pickthall, "Surah 20, Taha," *The Meaning of the Glorious Qur'an: An Explanatory Translation* (Birmingham, UK: Islamic Dawah Centre International, 2004), 191.

2. Mohammad Sadiq Mohibi, interview, May 17, 2011.

3. Karen Dahlgren, interview, April 21, 2011.

4. Carol Le Duc, interview, April 17, 2011.

5. United Nations Human Development Report, 2010, http://hdr.undp.org/en/countries/profiles/AFG.html.

6. Karen Dahlgren no longer works for Children in Crisis. Others may also have moved on since this chapter was written.

7. Susan Helseth, interview, April 23, 2011.

8. Karen Dahlgren, interview, April 21, 2011.

9. Alberto Cairo, interview, June 5, 2011.

10. Ibid.

11. Karen Dahlgren, interview, April 21, 2011.

12. Alberto Cairo, interview, June 5, 2011.

13. ICRC internal statistics documents, loaned to me in June 2011 by Alberto Cairo. No further information available.

14. Save the Children Fund's Mother's Index, May 2011, http://www.savethechildren.org/atf/cf/%7B9def2ebe-10ae-432c-9bd0-df91d2eba74a%7D/SOWM 2011_INDEX.PDF.

15. Ibid.

16. N. C. Aizenman, "In Afghanistan, New Misgivings About an Old but Risky Practice," *Washington Post*, April 17, 2005, http://www.washingtonpost.com/wp-dyn/articles/A59531-2005Apr16.html.

17. Handicap International, Afghanistan, "National Disability Survey in Afghanistan 2005," 2006.

18. Susan Helseth, interview, April 2011.

19. Sadiq Mohibi, interview, April 2011.

20. Sadiq Mohibi, interview, May 17, 2011.

21. Carol Le Duc, interview, April 17, 2011.

22. ICRC internal statistics documents, loaned to me in June 2011 by Alberto Cairo. No further information available.

23. Central Statistics Organization, "National Risk and Vulnerability Assessment, Afghanistan," 2007/2008.

24. Alberto Cairo, interview, June 5, 2011.

25. Fiona Gall, interview, April 16, 2011.

26. Fahima Kohistani, interview, April 16, 2011.

27. Dr. Gul Makay Siawash, interview, April 16, 2011.

28. Alberto Cairo, interview, June 5, 2011.

29. Ibid.

30. Ibid.

31. Ministry of Labor, Social Affairs, Martyrs, and Disabled, "Afghanistan National Disability Action Plan 2008–2011," May 2008.

32. Sadiq Mohibi, interview, April 2011.

33. Karen Dahlgren, e-mail communication, June 19, 2011.

34. Carol Le Duc, interview, April 17, 2011.

CHAPTER 14

"Life Feeds on Hope":
Family Mental Health, Culture, and Resilience

MARK EGGERMAN AND CATHERINE PANTER-BRICK

For many outsiders, Afghanistan encapsulates the ongoing brutality of war, the misery of poverty, and the basic violation of many human rights. Violent conflict and population displacement have disrupted access to health care, steady employment, and formal education. Young Afghans grow up in environments characterized by violence, poverty, and deep-seated inequalities: they live and breathe a noxious combination of violent conflict, economic stressors, gender discrimination, ethnic divisions, and widening social gaps. In this context, risks to health are multiple and multifaceted, as well as socially produced and perpetuated.

Afghan families, however, have demonstrated a striking fortitude in coping with political, social, and economic adversity that ranges from irksome everyday stressors to traumatic life events. With state governance showing little clarity of purpose, the family has proven the only stable institution available to provide networks of support.[1] Families are the primary resource for structuring individual and collective life—and for structuring all instrumental aspects of child development, health, education, social, and economic advancement. In terms of their fortitude in facing adversity, the people of Afghanistan could be held up as a prime example of collective resilience, an everyday resilience embedded in the social contexts of family and community networks.

Some questions remain. How do these general points play out in the lives of actual people? What kinds of evidence do we look for when characterizing health and resilience? From a policy standpoint, what kinds of risks need to be addressed, and what kinds of material, social, and political resources need to be advocated?

Interdisciplinary Research

We examined these issues in the context of conducting a study designed to understand adversity, risk, and resilience in the wake of war and displacement.[2] We conducted the first systematic, longitudinal, interdisciplinary study of mental health and resilience in Afghanistan. We interviewed a large sample of eleven- to sixteen-year-olds (1,011 youth, both boys and girls), together with their principal caregivers (1,011 adults) and schoolteachers (358), in Kabul, Bamiyan, and Mazar-i-Sharif. We also tracked a small cohort (364 child-adult pairs) in Kabul over a one-year period. Our work examined which aspects of violence and poverty were the most critical predictors of mental health status, and which aspects of individual and social life best characterized the ability to overcome adversity, as expressed by Afghan youth themselves and echoed by family members.

Our large-scale survey was based in schools, which provided a safe context for in-depth interviews and the best point of contact to draw a community-level sample, to access both male and female youth and their male and female caregivers. The security situation proved very volatile; during 2004, a local NGO withdrew support for the project because the vehicle transporting the female interviewers had returned after dark; during 2006, our project office was sprayed by gunfire during riots in Kabul; during 2007, suicide bombings in Kabul had become a significant threat. Working with schools made it possible for our field team (three male and three female Dari/Pashto interviewers, one translator, and a bilingual project manager) to build trust and obtain multiple measures of mental health and social functioning. We wanted a broad picture of Afghan lives, sensitive to age, generation, socioeconomic group, ethnicity, and rural-urban location. Participants engaged well in the research: children told us this was the first time someone had ever asked them about their problems and difficulties; teachers told us this was the first time they had been asked to reflect on how children's psychological health might hamper their educational performance; and our survey provided the first-ever opportunity for some women, from conservative families, secluded at home, to visit their children's school.

Mental Health and Everyday Violence

We highlight here two main findings of the study. First, poor mental health (probable psychiatric disorders, depression, and post-traumatic stress) had four main drivers: gender, trauma exposure, caregiver well-being, and geographical area. Thus Afghan girls were two and a half times more likely to have ratings indicative of a psychiatric disorder than boys. Children who experienced five or more traumatic events were two and a half times more likely to have psychiatric ratings, and three times more likely to report post-traumatic stress, than those who reported fewer than five events. Child mental health was correlated to caregiver mental health, with the likelihood of psychiatric disorder increasing by 10 percent for each and every symptom of psychological distress reported by their caregiver. Finally, children living in Kabul were more likely to have psychiatric and post-traumatic stress ratings than those in Bamiyan or Mazar-i-Sharif.

Those findings signal that poor mental health is a significant issue for the next generation in Afghanistan: overall, one in five (22 percent) schoolchildren in Afghanistan suffered from mental health problems in the clinical range, twice the rate expected for this age group. However, the findings also signal that a majority of children managed to function quite well according to ratings given by local respondents. We concluded that one in five Afghan schoolchildren were at risk of a probable mental health disorder, but also that four in five children proved fairly resilient.

We also reached a largely unexpected conclusion: in Afghan children's lives, "everyday violence" matters just as much as "militarized violence" in the recollection of traumatic experiences. We saw that Afghan children were remarkably good at discriminating traumatic from merely stressful life events, and that most families were very good at shielding children from traumatic experiences: only 63.5 percent of children reported one or more traumatic events, and only 8.4 percent were exposed to five or more traumas in their lifetime. We also saw that trauma was not confined to acts of war: children identified life-threatening accidents, medical treatments, domestic beatings, and violence in the neighborhood as their most distressing lifetime experiences, not just war-related injury, loss of relatives, and forced displacement. It was not just war-related violence that created trauma in the lives of children, but violence at the level of family and community life, violence generated by the ongoing exposure to harsh social and economic stressors that spilled into brutality close to home.

Trauma in Context

The following two vignettes illustrate the importance of contextual, subjective, and social experiences in the recollection of traumatic experiences. They focus on why children, exposed to multiple traumatic experiences, would prioritize a single trauma in terms of psychosocial significance.

Our first example is the narrative of a sixteen-year-old girl with post-traumatic stress disorder. She described her close relatives as "martyred" (Dari: *shaheed*)—she saw firsthand the beheaded body of her grandfather "killed in a rocket attack in Kabul during the Taliban," and knew her father had also been killed in a rocket attack. Yet her most distressing lifetime event was a medical operation, to remove a lump in her right breast. She had been taken on a long bus journey to Pakistan, four months earlier, to be operated upon by unknown male surgeons. This happened just at the end of the school year and conflicted with her final-year school exams. She would now have to repeat the entire school year to pass exams—this was particularly frustrating, given her ambition to go on to university and become a medical doctor, and also very difficult to negotiate, given social pressures to marry. Her drive to complete her schooling was shaped by a sense of duty toward her parents and her wish to improve her family's financial prospects; her twenty-five-year-old brother was unemployed, living at home, and addicted to opium.

This young girl was clearly wrought by an acute sense of failure and injustice. With respect to the deaths of her father and her grandfather, she could articulate her grief in terms of the ideology of martyrdom, a cultural script of moral and social value. However, she could make no sense of a lost year of schooling, given the anxiety and fear of being taken out of school before she could get her school-leaving certificate, being of marriageable age. In her words, she had lost "all I had ever worked for." The relevant question to ask, here, is "what really matters" to ordinary people, in normal and extraordinary times, when living a life amidst uncertainty and danger?[3] Narratives give us the moral dimension of heart-wrenching experiences. In this particular case, what really mattered was the wider impact of the operation: she bore a physical, an emotional, and a social scar, due to a break in the scaffolding of her life—a post-traumatic stress linked to a rupture of meaning and a rupture of moral order.

The second example is a fourteen-year-old boy born in Kabul in 1992, when heavy fighting between Mujahedin factions over control of the capital began. He had experienced ten different frightening, violent, and/or distressing events over his lifetime. Seven of his close relatives had been killed in the wars, going back to the Communist period (1978–1992), and one of his brothers had been missing for the last sixteen years. His mother had twice attempted suicide—and had suffered a miscarriage following a severe beating by his father. In addition, the boy had been knifed in the leg in a neighborhood fight, and had also had a run-in with the police, who had beaten him and jailed him for a day. Despite all these events, the boy identified his most distressing lifetime trauma as a severe beating by his father six months earlier. He now wished "to escape from the house" and become a journalist. He was in love with a girl, his cousin, but knew this love would anger his parents if they ever found out. He expressed a desire to leave Afghanistan—to be in a place "where boys and girls can be together"—and he bluntly described the crux of his misfortune as "having been born in such a desolate, God-forsaken country." The boy was severely depressed, his trauma and depression clearly rooted in a fraught family life and macro-level sociocultural stressors.

Mental Health in Conflict Zones

We thus reached a novel insight into child mental health in conflict zones: everyday suffering in the family and community contexts matters just as much as exposure to war-related violence. Ongoing, everyday stressors—factors other than war-related violence, though linked to the social and economic upheaval of war—account for much of children's psychological distress and mental health problems. This means that we cannot focus attention solely on the most visible forms of violence, but need to understand how military, structural, and domestic violence are intertwined. Afghan communities suffer ongoing forms of violence that are not necessarily confined to war: they face *everyday and structural violence*, not just militarized violence.

We tested that insight with a follow-up survey, one year after baseline. Due to formidable logistic and security problems, however, we could only follow up with our cohort in Kabul, and even in the capital, we could only trace 64 percent of our participants (other students had left school, and due to the absence of records regarding home addresses, all their families were lost to follow-up; there was no attrition bias with respect to demographic, socioeconomic, or mental health characteristics). Again, we were surprised by two main findings.

First, over a period of a year, child and caregiver mental health had improved, for all measures except post-traumatic stress. This improvement occurred in the absence of a dedicated mental health intervention, or better political and economic security: of the 234 families in our follow-up, forty-five moved home, sixteen were threatened with eviction, fifty-one lost a wage-earner, and 178 incurred a substantial debt. Such families were able to anchor their adolescent children in school, despite incurring substantial debt, being afflicted by illness, being anxious about the surrounding violence, and confronting economic and cultural dictates to have adolescent boys earn money and adolescent girls get married. In this context of poverty and insecurity, keeping children in school was an important indicator of fortitude in the face of material and social adversity.

We concluded that "in Afghanistan, the ability of families to maintain psychosocial and material resources, and particularly to remain geographically stable, economically robust, and socially supportive enough to keep near-adolescent boys and girls in school for yet another year, may capture an important facet of resilience."[4] Adults and children alike were focusing on school as the gateway to socioeconomic advancement, to alleviate economic stressors and to maintain family unity. Anchoring children in school was a significant expression of hope and resilience in a high-risk environment.

Second, the quality of family relationships was a key predictor of psychiatric mental health difficulties and depression: domestic violence, traumatic beatings, and family conflict predicted worse outcomes, while family "harmony and unity" (Dari: *ittifaq* and *wahdat*)—local terms meaning a sense of family connectedness—predicted better outcomes. This is striking, given the context of extraordinary levels of militarized violence: participants knew of suicide bombings that had resulted in the deaths of children on a school trip, had witnessed suicide bomb attacks at bus stops/police stations, or had witnessed the aftermath of such attacks. We concluded that proximate family environments were more salient than collective violence for their ongoing impact on psychiatric and depressive burden.

This was not the case for post-traumatic stress, which did not abate over the intervening year, and for which lifetime trauma exposure trumped all other risk and protective factors. This suggests distinct pathways of risk and resilience: the quality of family relationships is central to developmental resilience, alleviating psychiatric difficulties and depression, while trauma and post-traumatic stress may be unresponsive, once manifested in the individual child. There is no one pathway of resilience, such as family support, driving all mental health outcomes, just as there is no single driver of poor mental health, such as war-related violence.

Hope and Suffering

Afghan families articulated quite clearly the material, social, and political threats to mental health, as well as the psychosocial and structural dimensions of resilience.[5] An everyday struggle for life was first and foremost expressed in terms of its material dimensions: as one father succinctly stated, "Lack of work is the root of all a man's miseries." For men, stable work and income was the root of personal dignity; an inability to contribute to their families' livelihoods was equated with a loss of honor and resulting social marginalization. For women, lack of money meant that families had to crowd together in very small residential spaces or live under tents in communal courtyards, which generated huge stressors, especially given cultural dictates on female seclusion; one woman flatly stated that she would rather go hungry than live without having her own home, meaning that she would not have to co-reside with her husband's extended family. Both adults and children spoke of a "broken economy" (Dari: *iqtisad kharab*) as the central driver of pain, violence, and misery, and viewed domestic violence as a product of the frustration, strain, and humiliation engendered by material poverty. One sixteen-year-old girl expressed this as follows: "My father's salary is not enough for us, he has *takleef asabi* [affliction of the nerves] and he beats us. . . . If he finds a decent job then maybe he will calm down." This statement is emblematic of narratives expressing economic drivers as the nexus of social suffering, with suffering engendering family-level violence and cascading from one generation to another.

The core reasons for psychosocial suffering were thus structural, regarding overwhelming economic impediments to physical, social, and emotional well-being. Another example shows how social aspirations and expectations are crushed by harsh material realities, leading, in extreme cases, to attempted suicide. An eighteen-year-old boy stated: "I'm the eldest son in my family. We've got six people in our home, and I am the only one working. . . . Because we have economic problems, my father forced me to quit school. So I swallowed rat poison after that, and I was in hospital for a week. They pumped my stomach out and I couldn't eat for nine days." The statement shows how crucial access to education is for the maintenance of hope.

The counterpoint to this discourse of suffering was a discourse of fortitude and resilience. Our thematic analyses of interviews with 1,011 children and 1,011 adults showed that families bring up their children to espouse six fundamental cultural values: religious faith, family unity and harmony, the obligation of service to family and community, perseverance or effort, good morals, and social respectability or honor. These cultural values form the basis for hope and resilience, and give families a sense of order and promise in their lives. Resilience was most clearly expressed in this short statement by a twenty-eight-year-old mother: "Life feeds on hope." Another expressed this sentiment as follows: "The only way to make life better is to be hopeful . . . If a person has hope, then he or she can work and acquire knowledge to make their life better." Simply put, Afghans put their faith in the belief that hard work and sustained effort can help them make life better. Their sense of hope is directed toward accessing the resources that will create social and economic opportunities for their family. This is "social hope"—the bedrock of resilience.

Indeed, one of the most surprising aspects of this research was the expressions of hope in the midst of everyday suffering. For children, the height of their personal and social ambitions was well demonstrated in the drawings that students produced for this study. As part of rapport-building, before implementing the survey, we asked students to draw themselves in the present and in the future. Most students drew themselves in rags and tears in the present, and as excellent doctors, remarkable engineers, and dedicated teachers in the future. We reproduce here two drawings that clearly encapsulated hardship in the present and hope for the future, and demonstrate that while Afghan children may live in poverty, they do not show a poverty of aspiration.

The drawings of a fourteen-year-old girl, who attended a school catering to vulnerable social groups (street children and war widows), provide a striking example of this hopeful orientation toward the future. She was the only breadwinner in her household, rag-picking and finding scrap plastics before and after school, for resale in a junkyard. Her severely depressed mother stated that her greatest worry in life was to see her daughter grow up—because after puberty, she would not be able to send her into the streets to work. What were the girl's aspirations for the future? The girl drew herself at a table, with a microphone, stating that she wanted to be the first female newscaster at Radio Kabul. Such high hopes, engendered by access to education, might well have been raised here to the point of illusion. Far more elaborate were the drawings of a fourteen-year-old boy, who attended an art class at his school. He drew his great hardship in the present day: he worked, outside school hours, because his father was disabled and his three brothers had been "martyred" in the war. In the future, his ambitions to be a doctor were a world away from his present circumstances: he could picture his car, briefcase, and doctor's office in striking detail. The drawing of his present life is emblematic of misery, while the drawing of his future is emblematic of dignity.

Beyond Superficial Views of Resilience

Despite the protective effect of cultural values that emphasized faith, effort, and family unity, young people also found themselves oppressed by cultural dictates governing their choices and life trajectories. "Social hope" for social and economic improvement could easily lead to social entrapment. On the one hand, Afghan cultural values fostered resilience to everyday adversity. On the other, they caused many Afghans to feel they were falling short of material

Drawings by Afghan children: "I want to be an excellent doctor in the future" (above). "I want to be a painter, newscaster, and actress" (left). Courtesy of Catherine Panter-Brick and Mark Eggerman, 2006.

and social expectations, a threat to their dignity and well-being. People suffered great psychological distress when they found themselves unable to conform to the high standards of "what makes an honorable Afghan." Failure or frustration in attaining social and cultural milestones was articulated in local idioms of stress, anxiety, and depression, or family conflicts that were debilitating and life threatening. Afghans live in a world where cultural values are necessary for survival, yet also lead to forms of oppression: thus culture is the anchor of resilience, but also an anvil of pain.

Understanding suffering on a social scale includes the consideration of structural factors that impact peoples' sense of well-being and material lives. In not fulfilling their cultural obligations, such as arranging a good marriage or securing a good job to achieve social and material status, young Afghan men and women become entrapped within a series of cultural standards that they are not always able to live up to. Afghan youth strive to bring themselves out of poverty, to work hard and obtain a good education, but simultaneously they have to provide service to their family and leave school to obey cultural directives for girls to marry and boys to provide financial support. They become entrapped within the system of cultural values that defines their lives while struggling to cope with political violence, insecurity, and the structural violence engendered by everyday social stressors. Thus, owning one's own home and holding down employment is a salient milestone in the context of forced displacement and a broken economy; getting married, begetting children, and providing service to one's family is another, given the importance of family as a social institution; accessing formal education after the forced curtailment in the Taliban regime is yet another precious goal, necessary to achieve economic and social standing in the Afghan context. Education, employment, timing of marriage, home ownership—these were key to realizing the societal blueprint of social prominence, respectability, and honor (Dari: 'izzat). For Afghans, these are the economic, social, and moral goals that underpin honor and self-respect.

Such life goals are not intrinsically different from the standard American set of "goods" and milestones that compose the normative life course of youth in the United States, the core elements of a "good enough" life. But in Afghanistan, there are huge impediments to achieving the outward manifestations of an "honorable life," given economic, social, legal, and political barriers to accessing resources and deep-seated gender and ethnic inequalities structuring resource provision. Furthermore, living an honorable or good-enough life is a family matter rather than a personal objective: families are at once the most important sources of social support, and the most important sources of social pressure, in the pursuit of culturally relevant milestones.

Policy Implications

Many forms of violence and suffering arise from structural barriers and social entrapment. If young Afghans are to become more resilient to the challenges they face, we argue that a better understanding of resource provision and social aspirations is needed, both to alleviate suffering and to foster hope-building. How young people in Afghanistan cultivate resilience could be greatly assisted by listening to their accounts of their experiences.

Afghans tell us of suffering engendered by ongoing political violence, frustration with the lack of economic momentum, a dearth of service infrastructure, poor governance, and fraught relationships played out at the family and community level. In the Afghan context, a culturally relevant mental health intervention would be a structural intervention to strengthen families and sever the insidious linkages between political insecurity, economic instability, domestic crowding, and domestic violence that threaten well-being. These efforts would provide structural, social, and economic resources to families who struggle with everyday stressors. To accomplish this requires efforts to revitalize the economy in order to give dignity to men; providing better housing and reducing overcrowding, which would make families feel more secure and alleviate considerable stressors for women; and, in schools, increasing the quality of education to help children thrive in an environment they greatly value, and, in particular, paying teachers a decent wage so that they would not be compelled to hold down two jobs.

Policies that address the "structural" determinants of resilience would enhance a sense of safety, a sense of coherence, a sense of moral order, a sense of hope, and a sense of family connectedness—all of which are essential elements of intervention efforts and principles at the heart of mental health and psychosocial resilience. While specialized psychotherapy is needed for individuals with trauma-related problems, such as post-traumatic stress disorder, resource provision is needed to strengthen and revitalize communities, providing psychosocial support to individuals and families whose major problems are not solely the consequence of trauma. What is important is concerted action to address the structural causes that debilitate well-being.[6]

Finally, our work leads us to emphasize an important ethical issue inherent in intervention efforts to "build hope" in humanitarian areas. In Afghanistan, a program of massive refugee repatriation promised hope to returnees, but largely disappointed their expectations. A massive Back to School campaign was launched in 2001, after the fall of the Taliban regime, to provide hope for children and their families in the form of state-sponsored free education. But searching for hope brings disillusionment in societies where there is a shrinking configuration of social opportunities, widening inequalities, poor distribution of capital, and inequitable state policies. Our data show that hope for the future is central to resilience, but that access to school has raised aspirations to the point of certain disillusionment, as families anchor their children to school despite significant socioeconomic impediments, to achieve the promise of a school-leaving certificate, a good job, and socioeconomic advancement. Paying close attention to resource provision and social processes is important: social policies and intervention programs that build up hope and raise expectations must not promise more than they can deliver.

Conclusions

How does this research speak to the impact of violence on mental health and the cultural values that foster resilience? For general mental health, what matters most is family connectedness, as measured by the local concept of family unity. For resilience, what matters most is a sense of coherence pertaining to cultural and social trajectories, the expression of social hope. Resilience is best understood in terms of trajectory, a sense of meaning-making that orders the world and gives coherence to the past, present, and future. In conflict zones, we often conceptualize and measure resilience as merely the absence of mental health problems despite exposure to significant trauma. This is a significant shortcoming, focusing as it does on the past as it affects the immediate present—the perspective peculiar to western, trauma-focused psychiatry. By contrast, an emic view of resilience in Afghan societal and cultural contexts is best captured by the expression of "life feeds on hope." This places the focus of attention squarely on the future, rather than the past, as it impacts psychosocial well-being in the here and now.

Our longitudinal work shows that family environments outweigh war-related violence in predicting children's psychiatric and depressive burden, but not post-traumatic stress. And continued attendance at school, per se, was associated with improvements in mental health: expressions of hope attest to the resilience of Afghan families striving to overcome life adversity, and education is, par excellence, an engine of hope in promising the young generation the opportunity of socioeconomic advancement. Thus present-day family relationships and future-oriented hopes for socioeconomic improvements are central to developing resilience. What matters for Afghan well-being are cultural values that make sense of day-to-day suffering, underpin a sense of social order, and give a promise to life. These generate, however, problematic tensions regarding social aspirations and likely frustrated expectations, when cultural values themselves become a form of social entrapment. In brief, the "drip-drip-drip" of everyday socioeconomic stressors is one of the most critical determinants of mental health, even in conflict settings. Such stressors impose a major burden on family relationships, but they are counteracted by remarkable expressions of hope that provide the cornerstone of resilience in Afghanistan.

Notes

1. Nancy Hatch Dupree, "The Family during Crisis in Afghanistan," *Journal of Comparative Family Studies* 35 (2004): 311–331.

2. This chapter is adapted from: Catherine Panter-Brick and Mark Eggerman, "Understanding Culture, Resilience, and Mental Health: The Production of Hope," in M. Ungar, ed., *The Social Ecology of Resilience: A Handbook of Theory and Practice* (New York: Springer, 2012), 369–386.

3. Arthur Kleinman, *What Really Matters: Living a Moral Life amidst Uncertainty and Danger* (Oxford: Oxford University Press, 2006).

4. Catherine Panter-Brick et al., "Mental Health and Childhood Adversities: A Longitudinal Study in Kabul, Afghanistan," *Journal of the American Academy of Child & Adolescent Psychiatry* 50, no. 4 (2011): 349–363.

5. Catherine Panter-Brick and Mark Eggerman, "Suffering, Hope, and Entrapment: Resilience and Cultural Values in Afghanistan," *Social Science & Medicine* 71 (2010): 71–83.

6. Catherine Panter-Brick, Marie-Pascale Grimon, and Mark Eggerman, "Caregiver-Child Mental Health: A Prospective Study in Conflict and Refugee Settings," *Journal of Child Psychology and Psychiatry* (2013), online proof: doi.10.1111/jcpp.12167.

PART 5

EDUCATION: NURTURING THE FUTURE

This student at the Afghan Institute of Learning school in Kabul is proud to show off his alphabet knowledge. Photo by Ginna Fleming, 2008.

CHAPTER 15

Education in Transition:
A Key Concern for Young Afghan Returnees

MAMIKO SAITO

After decades of protracted conflict, according to 2007 United Nations High Commission for Refugees (UNHCR) statistics, half of registered Afghan populations in Pakistan and Iran were born in exile,[1] in a second or even a third generation of displacement. Refugees who returned to Afghanistan were usually considered economically less vulnerable than those who had stayed during the years of conflict, because of the education and skills they had acquired, as well as the savings some had accrued.[2] However, from the point of view of many of the respondents I encountered, returning to one's "homeland" did not necessarily mean "returning." Repatriation was often accompanied by a complex mix of stresses and emotional struggles.

Fieldwork for this qualitative study, including the intensive interviews with 199 purposively selected respondents, was conducted in three countries over different periods across twelve months, starting in April 2006. The main criteria for selecting Afghan refugee and returnee respondents (both male and female) were as follows:

- Candidates were 15–30 years old[3] and had spent more than half of their lives in Pakistan or Iran;
- (For returnees only) they had returned to Afghanistan after the Afghan Interim Authority was established in late 2001, and had lived in Afghanistan for at least six months.

Growing Up as Afghan Refugees

Young refugees often possess contradictory, multiple, and conflicting identities.[4] Relating or associating oneself to a particular group or groups becomes crucial for a sense of belonging in the presence of "others" who are markedly different. This is particularly relevant in the context of forced displacement and the effect of having a legal status different from that of the citizens of the host country: the "other" is not only a member of one's own family, kin, or other linguistic or ethnic group, but also a "national other."

Conrad Schetter argues that Afghan national consciousness, shared by the majority of populations in Afghanistan, first emerged in response to the fragmentation of the country due to war and the intervention of a foreign power.[5] Before the Soviet invasion, nationalism in Afghanistan was primarily Pashtun-biased, led by a Pashtun royal family and Kabul central government, utilizing Pashtun nomads for acquisition of land. After the Soviet invasion, the majority of the non-Pashtun population started identifying themselves with Afghanistan as a country—although such Afghan identity hardly shared any common experiences or values. In particular, Afghans in exile started to perceive the territorial border nostalgically, albeit hardly rooted in common traditions or experiences. Bernt Glatzer points out that the notion of *watan* (homeland) relates primarily to a limited geographical area in which individuals are well known to each other.[6] In the diaspora context, however, it takes on a wider meaning: anybody from Afghanistan is regarded as belonging to the same *watan*. Indeed, the national awareness of themselves as Afghans took on a process of transformation in the face of invasion by "others" as well as through refugees' experiences in exile among non-Afghan "others."[7] For young refugees who were born or grew up in exile, the sense of being Afghans was often reinforced in the face of Pakistanis or Iranians, rather than by the sentiments for bygone days that their parents felt.

The emergence of identity in relation to sub-groups among Afghans (among them Pashtuns, Tajiks, and Hazaras) in exile followed a path similar to that of their identity as refugees, through exposure to differing values over time. Young Afghans would have certain inherited memories of these divisions from their parents, and some experienced conflict over ethnicity or politics that related to their place of origin in Afghanistan during their time in Pakistan or Iran. However, this was more likely to be an issue for first-generation Afghan refugees, or was more frequently referred to as an issue within Afghanistan. Therefore, for Afghans born or brought up in Pakistan and Iran, the more dominant feeling of difference was—as refugees—the sense of being residents with a status inferior to that of native citizens of the country.

Returning to one's homeland involves significant amounts of psychological stress and does not necessarily represent a return in the conventional sense, as many also have a profound attachment to the host country in which they grew up.[8] For groups of young refugees, intentions to return are less motivated by recovering an idealized past, kept alive through stories from relatives and other refugees, than by the ideas of rights, access to property, and citizenship—which they have not been necessarily able to fully acquire while growing up in refuge.[9] It is important to note that many young Afghan refugees embraced these expectations of their country as part of their return. If these high expectations were not met, disappointment for some was sharp and led to thoughts of onward movement—re-migrating to the host country or moving elsewhere.

Education in Pakistan and Iran

The government of Iran provided free education to all Afghan children until the mid-1990s. This was later reduced to only those with valid legal status, and the government's accelerated repatriation attempts eventually resulted in the introduction of schooling fees. The vast majority of literate respondents attended Iranian state schools, while others went to informal self-run Afghan schools—particularly children who were undocumented.

In Pakistan, many literate respondents attended a wide range of Afghan schools, located primarily in refugee camps[10] and areas with a high concentration of Afghans. In addition to some schools established as a result of refugees' efforts, various donors also supported Afghan schools in Pakistan, although a decline in funding prompted increased dropout rates after 1995. In sending children to Pakistani schools, two major factors affected the decisions of households: either the perceived benefits of (mostly private) Pakistani schools or a lack of Afghan schools in the neighborhood.

The high quality of education in Pakistan and Iran was referred to positively by the majority of respondents compared to that in Afghanistan. The perceived advantages included facilities (e.g., buildings, furniture, libraries), resources (e.g., up-to-date textbooks, labs, and learning materials), teaching approaches (e.g., trained teachers, practical work to complement theory), and organized systems (e.g., discipline and standardization, opportunities for event participation, and prizes for talented students).

Overall, Iranian state schools and Pakistani private schools were highly evaluated in all respects, although enrollment at the latter was limited to households that could afford the high fees. In Pakistan, private schools were often more attractive because English was the language of instruction, compared to government schools, where Urdu was primarily used. Acquiring English at a younger age was regarded as another benefit in Pakistan, and this included attendance at readily available language courses. The quality of Afghan schools in both countries appeared to depend on availability of support. Negative views were primarily related to physical resource constraints caused by limited funding. Nevertheless, Afghan schools in exile were much more positively rated than those in Afghanistan.

Values and Religious Learning

Not all young Afghans benefited equally from access to the education available in Pakistan and Iran and its quality. Around a quarter of returnees interviewed in Afghanistan did not receive formal education in exile, and the ratio was higher among those from Pakistan than among those from Iran. Reported causes for remaining uneducated or dropping out of schools at an early age were contextual: distance or unavailability of schools, lack of fixed residence, difficulties with registration, reductions in foreign funding, unfamiliarity with locations as refugees, and lack of interest/poor performance among children. However, two major factors frequently appeared: insufficient household funding to cover the direct costs and opportunity costs involved, and social norms preventing enrollment—particularly for girls. In Afghanistan, domestic influences are common; school enrollment for girls can be detrimental to family honor, as it is often viewed negatively by others.[11]

In addition to fear-related gender concerns, the widespread perception of formal schooling was powerful. Some families had no tradition of schooling, not only for daughters but also for sons. By way of example, a twenty-nine-year-old male who returned to Kabul had acquired a profound knowledge of Islamic matters during his sixteen years of learning in various *madrassas* (religious schools) in Pakistan.[12] As a teacher at a madrassa in Kabul, he recalled why secular schools were disliked by some Afghans:

> There were schools supported by UNHCR, and no fees were payable. But most Afghans didn't send their children to school due to negative images from Afghanistan. There was a feeling that if children went to school, they would be taught to become communists. It's thought that children going to madrassas will become rounded human beings.

Some females whose families regarded it as shameful for girls to attend external schooling were allowed to undergo religious education. This was usually limited to the early years before puberty. Learning the Qur'an and having lessons in Islamic matters was generally perceived as a duty and a spiritual reward (*sawab*) for both male and female Muslims, whereas not knowing about Islam was considered a sin (*guna*). In Pakistan, such education was provided by madrassas, mosques, knowledgeable neighbors, and children's own parents. In particular, some well-equipped madrassas were reported to be systematic, including basic school subjects along with dormitory facilities and overseas scholarships for qualified students.

According to some male respondents with extensive experience of Islamic learning in Pakistan, some madrassas were supported by the Pakistani government and Arab countries at the time of their learning. It was also reported that there was support from America during the Cold War.[13] On the other hand, the situation of religious training in some urban areas of Iran appeared further structured under the authority of *ayatollahs* (high-ranking Shi'a clerics) in Qom. Seminaries called *hawza ilmiyya* were usually accessible to boys and girls regardless of nationality. There were many highly educated young Afghan females from religious families in Iran whose male relatives supported girls' education regardless of secular and religious institutions.

Opportunities

Whether or not respondents had attended schools in Pakistan or Iran, many reported acquiring new technical skills, a better understanding of health and hygiene, and the ability to communicate with different people appropriately. "Boys who grow up in Pakistan are like domestic animals, while those who grow up in Afghanistan are like wild animals," a twenty-four-year-old Afghan male who was a university student in Peshawar said. This was due to different environments through which many respondents were exposed to a variety of information—simply seeing towns and cities, different ways of living and people, and learning from modern technology in the form of TV[14] or the Internet. These would not have been available if they had remained in isolated villages in Afghanistan. Being away from war and physical danger also gave them time to think with less tension. Similarly, prevailing social attitudes among Pakistanis and Iranians also had a great impact on respondents' households. Parents in some exile households decided on education for girls without telling extended family members in Afghanistan, regardless of the negative remarks that it might have brought. A nineteen-year-old female returnee in Herat said, "My parents became open-minded. If they hadn't gone to Iran, they wouldn't have been what they are now, and neither would I."

In particular, education in Iran was strongly supported by religious scholars, and this was perceived by Afghans as the ideal situation for Muslim men and women, and also as their responsibility. The positive aspects of Iran—a country perceived as cultured, respectful of women's rights, Islamic, and less patriarchal—were praised by most respondents who grew up there. The increased literacy rate appeared to symbolize a transformation of the values of individuals, families, and Afghan social norms in exile, and this eventually linked to the various behaviors and opportunities pursued.

Generational transformation in education was observed among returnees from Pakistan and Iran. Parents with higher levels of education often sent their children to schools in exile, albeit with gender and contextual differences. Meanwhile, uneducated parents showed more contrasting trends: some changed their attitudes toward educating their children, while others remained the same. It should also be noted that some highly educated male young Afghans (such as a non-governmental organization [NGO] officer working on a girls' education project) had entirely non-literate female family members due to tradition.

For children and youths, educational opportunities are primarily decided by family context, residential location, and the wider social and political situations of the country of refuge. Indeed, prevailing values are important but never fixed—particularly among young Afghans raised in Pakistani or Iranian social spheres. This is relevant when considering the future of these youths and the situation of the next generation. Overall, many respondents in this study benefited from various learning opportunities compared to their parents and members of their own generation who remained in Afghanistan during the war.

Fear of Return and Challenges of Reintegration

About a quarter of the returnee respondents indicated that they had not been happy with their household's decision to go back to Afghanistan. Among those who disagreed with the decision to return, most were females—many educated, although a few less educated also felt this way. Around half of this group reported that they had argued against the decision and tried to persuade the power-holders in the household to change their minds. For the other half, despite being unhappy with the decision, it was not possible to voice their disagreement because of their position in the family. Meanwhile, in some cases, disagreement surrounding the decision to return caused households that used to share the same income to split—leaving part of the family in exile and severing financial ties. There were cases of both male- and female-educated respondents doing this, with one individual going back to Afghanistan alone to pursue opportunities in higher education or work.

Major factors leading to strong negative return perceptions among respondents were the fear of losing the opportunity of quality education, along with apprehension toward unknown Afghanistan. For some respondents, return meant disruption to, or discontinuation of, their education, and denial of further educational opportunities that might have been available to them in the place of asylum. Besides this, the degree of attachment to the place where they grew up compared to their "homeland" was another key factor influencing their return attitudes. Returning to Afghanistan brought pain and sadness in leaving the one place they knew best and the opportunities for education or religious learning available there—perhaps sentiments similar to those their parents had felt on leaving Afghanistan years earlier.

Language and Accreditation

Native-language constraints were a major obstacle for some respondents in Pakistan. For instance, a twenty-three-year-old woman who went to an Afghan school in Peshawar was interested in returning to Kabul in the hope of finding work based on her status as a young English-speaking female. However, her two brothers, who had studied in the Pakistani educational system, were opposed to returning.

> Only my brothers are not happy about going back. They say that they've been studying in Pakistani schools and now in a Pakistani university. If we go to Afghanistan, they'll have to study from 12th grade in an Afghan school, which is difficult for them. There's no value in Afghanistan for education received in Pakistan. My brothers can't read and write Dari—they didn't go to any private Dari course (which is our mother tongue).

Differences between returnees by country included knowledge of languages, although the mother tongues of refugee populations and selected research sites varied. Some respondents who grew up in Pakistan had difficulties with the Dari language, and such issues were often related to living in and/or being educated in an all-Pakistani (Urdu-speaking) environment or in entirely Pashtun surroundings. This was not necessarily the case for many returnees from Iran, who were easily identified by their Persian-accented Dari. Rather, the majority of them could not speak Pashto, while many from Pakistan could.

Linguistic challenges experienced during the process of reintegration varied with individual backgrounds and return destinations in Afghanistan.

People expect greater returns from larger investments of time and money into formal education. Accordingly, recognition of degrees obtained and work potential are fundamental priorities among educated Afghan youths. However, not all qualifications approved in Pakistan and Iran were transferable upon return. Returnee students generally had to enter lower grades to continue studying in Afghanistan, especially when they had linguistic problems or when the required documentation was lacking.

First, non-registration of schools by the government of Afghanistan was a hindrance to obtaining certification. One student whose Afghan school was supported by a Pakistani political party was not allowed to take a university entrance exam in Afghanistan; another who studied at a non-registered Afghan school could secure neither approval nor employment as a formal teacher in Afghanistan. Accreditation was particularly necessary for government jobs.

Second, bureaucratic differences between the countries resulted in problems. One returnee who had studied at the newly established Nursing Department at the University of Tehran did not know how to get her degrees approved. When a student enters university in Iran, the pre-university certificate (twelfth grade) is kept by the Iranian government, but is required for degree approval in Afghanistan. Upon discovering that her nursing degree would not be useful in finding work, this returnee wished to study again at Kabul University, but could not take the entrance exam without the certificate.

Finally, administrative errors and poor treatment during processing created challenges. Upon return, some certificates were found to be lacking authorization stamps from Pakistan and Iran. It was difficult for young returnees to go back again without facilitation, especially for females who had returned to provincial areas. The difficulty of obtaining passports and visas to do this, particularly for re-entering Iran, was another practical issue. There appeared to be a lack of standardized, accessible information on procedures for approval and acceptance of certificates from schools and universities in Pakistan and Iran. Some reports also detailed procedures being affected by bribery.

Access

Not all literate respondents could continue their schooling upon repatriation, as they had feared. Gender norms, economic conditions, and lack of access to post-primary education, particularly in remote areas, were major hindrances. The mobility of young female returnees generally decreased in Afghanistan, not only because of more restrictive social norms but also due to security concerns (e.g., harassment and kidnapping) and limited infrastructure and facilities (e.g., inadequate roads and a lack of secure public transportation).

Although the selected research sites in Afghanistan were not characterized by a high risk of physical danger (e.g., attacks on female students, teachers, and schools), it was often considered inappropriate for females to go outside. Elders also considered post-war Afghanistan less safe due to their inerasable memories of war and their feelings of fear: "Something bad might happen to women and girls," said the mother of a teenage returnee in Baghlan. "It would bring great shame on our family, relatives, and the village."

Access to secondary schools and above for both male and female returnees in rural areas was particularly challenging simply due to the distances involved. Three male respondents living in urban areas had been able to leave their villages to pursue further education thanks to their financial resources and/or the fact that they had relatives to live with in towns. Access to education was one of the primary reasons given by rural respondents (both educated and uneducated) for preferring to settle in cities.

Discipline for Quality

Many educated respondents understood before repatriation that the quality of schooling in Afghanistan would not be the same. What disappointed them the most was not the obvious material deficiency of the schools, but people's attitudes. The laziness of less trained teachers combined with inappropriate teaching methods and a lack of student ability/motivation were sometimes voiced, particularly outside urban centers. Most of all, unequal treatment and various forms of discrimination in education severely discouraged some returnees.

Social rejection of returnees by other Afghans who had remained throughout the conflict was sometimes reported in the early stages of reintegration— most often among young, educated females. This happened when there were obvious differences in appearance and social interaction, which caused clashes with local cultural expectations and social codes. One student who was not fluent in Dari was told by her teacher, "Shame on you. You forgot that you are an Afghan!"

Corruption in school and university entrance exams, as well as a lack of access to scholarships after return, caused some to feel betrayal in their own homeland. Along with other concerns, this caused a loss of interest in studying or led to thoughts of leaving Afghanistan again. It was believed that only those with power and money could access the best opportunities in Afghanistan, and the rights of talented students were ignored. One twenty-one-year-old female who returned to Baghlan from Iran was labeled "*Iranigak*" (little Iran) at school:

> I got the highest mark in my theology exam, but it was announced that I came third. I didn't complain or approach the teacher to object. When I had a chance, I asked her about it. She frankly told me that one of my classmates had recently gotten married, so she had given her first position out of sympathy. Second place went to her daughter. If a teacher of theology, who should be faithful, honest, and know the right thing to do, perpetrates such injustice, what should I expect from other teachers? . . . If teachers received adequate pay from the government, they wouldn't ask students to pay bribes.

Profound Meaning of Education

The basic principles of Afghan education are often referred to in relation to the concepts of *talim wa tarbia* (knowledge and discipline). The more educated a person is, the more he or she should be punctual, dutiful, and acquiescent.[15] Respondents shared similar views, and the concepts of tarbia were particularly emphasized as fundamental attitudes required by Afghans to rebuild Afghanistan.

There was no doubt that an immediate result of being educated would be the ability to find a good job. As a household investment strategy, such jobs were expected to provide high salaries via white-collar work rather than the low income of hard physical labor. Besides, respected professions like medicine and engineering were seen as a way to help people in need through knowledge in places where such human resources were still limited.

Concerns were raised regarding the trend toward employment with exaggerated emphasis on timely skills in Afghanistan, even though the desire to acquire such skills was also pervasive among young Afghans. A twenty-year-old jobless male in Herat who graduated from an Afghan high school in Pakistan said, "People who don't know English and computers are uneducated." One twenty-nine-year-old female NGO worker in Peshawar noted the growing gap between rich and poor:

> NGOs have wrecked Afghanistan. All the people there want to work in an NGO because of the high salary. There's no one who wants to work for the government because of the low salary. The UN and NGOs don't pay atten-

tion to Afghan education. The youth have become crazy for dollars, and don't pay attention to education any more.

The ability to read and perform basic calculations was viewed as an important way of avoiding risk, especially among less educated males. It was essential for income earners not to make losses in self-employment or when dealing with money transfers—an area in which some respondents could help their fathers. For some females, the ability to read signs or count change provided some level of autonomy, however small. Literacy also allowed people to read books and learn about true Islam. In contrast, being uneducated was often linked to vulnerability to exploitation, marginalization, or a lack of belief in one's abilities. Feelings of fear and inability appeared to influence mobility and cause people to remain at home.

Beyond the meaning of schooling (i.e., gaining basic knowledge, work-related skills, and qualifications), the notion of tarbia was understood as the ideal moral behavior of human beings and the highest development of interpersonal skills. Educated people, whether religious or not, were perceived to have favorable characteristics. This was connected to the ideas of being a good human being and a good Muslim, rather than necessarily involving qualifications. For instance, some male teenagers expressed a preference to marry educated women because they would be able to respect elders, take care of family members, and do housework properly. Tarbia also encompasses the culture of society as a whole, which was addressed as the fundamental position for rebuilding Afghanistan. A seventeen-year-old married returnee student in Herat said:

> Afghans look for others' support like beggars, but Iranians are not like this. They want to stand on their own two feet and think about improvement. In this respect, the tarbia of Iranians is advanced. . . . Correct tarbia for children is very important because they are the next generation. If children develop good minds now, they can change the future of Afghanistan.

It was stressed that Afghans must utilize their wisdom for good deeds, work hard, and earnestly help their compatriots while overcoming old sectarian ideas and building national solidarity. The majority of respondents voiced strong disapproval of the current situation in Afghanistan, including power abuses, corruption, and ethnic/political and sectarian divisions. Such selfishness, prejudice, and ignorance were identified as root causes of Afghanistan's destruction. An eighteen-year-old male student who had returned to Kabul from Pakistan said, "Afghans should behave like human beings, not like animals." A few married women with brutal life stories also commented that injustice against women was due to "uneducated Afghans."

Many young Afghans interviewed in this study unanimously voiced the desire for education for themselves and the next generation. Equal opportunities for quality education and future employment were one of the critical concerns influencing their settlement places. Reflecting the growing needs of young returnees, the fear of losing these opportunities must be addressed by continuing to improve access to quality education in Afghanistan, particularly in remote areas. Access to higher education not readily available to Afghans in Pakistan and Iran is a strong pull and one of the factors that can encourage educated refugees back to Afghanistan.

Migration has impacted Afghan refugees as a whole, but more so for younger generations who grew up in the place of refuge. The values of the two host countries linking to broader political and sociocultural environments had a significant impact on individuals, particularly those who had interacted to a greater degree in the public sphere. Nearly all respondents—regardless of their education, gender, or emotional contentment—saw themselves as more open-minded in relation to their attitudes and worldview than those who had remained in Afghanistan. Based on values constructed in Pakistan or Iran, returnees often critically evaluated the situation in Afghanistan as if from an outsider's perspective. Coupled with more general challenges related to adolescence, young returnees developed new understandings of "home" and their futures within it as they spent more time there.

Evidence from the field reveals lack of certainty about future intentions among young returnees. Over a quarter of the returnee respondents interviewed in Kabul, Herat, and Baghlan provinces still had hopes or expectations of leaving Afghanistan again in either the short or the long term. Despite the profound complexities and challenges involved, the large-scale repatriation of young Afghan refugees from neighboring countries should be seen as a crucial asset for Afghanistan. Returnees bringing back various skills and ideas can have a long-term constructive influence on the recovery of Afghan society, where the wounds of conflict and distrust still remain. Many respondents spoke of their feelings of dislocation and a degree of social exclusion in their homeland. For them, all residents of Afghanistan—regardless of class, gender, ethnicity, or sectarian differences—are compatriots. Education is not simply about school attendance; it also involves understanding the ways of humanity and Islam, while controlling one's own greed and bias. Such a gradual transformation can be achieved through patient, mutual efforts to communicate with and understand people characterized by dissimilar ideas and behaviors.

Notes

1. United Nations High Commission for Refugees, *UNHCR Global Appeal 2008–2009* (Geneva: UNHCR, 2007).

2. Altai Consulting, *Integration of Returnees in the Afghan Labor Market* (Kabul: ILO and UNHCR, 2006).

3. Perceptions of childhood, adolescence, and young adulthood varied among respondents along with their conventional reported ages. For example, respondents in the study covered a range of diversity spanning from a 15-year-old housewife to a 24-year-old single female university student.

4. Dawn Chatty, "Researching Refugee Youth in the Middle East: Reflections on the Importance of Comparative Research," *Journal of Refugee Studies* 20, no. 2 (2007): 265–280.

5. Conrad Schetter, "Ethnoscapes, National Territorialization, and the Afghan War," *Geopolitics* 10 (2005): 50–75.

6. Bernt Glatzer, "War and Boundaries in Afghanistan: Significance and Relativity of Local and Social Boundaries," *Weld des Islams* 41, no. 3 (2001): 379–399.

7. Pierre Centlivres and Micheline Centlivres-Demont, "State, National Awareness and Levels of Identity in Afghanistan from Monarchy to Islamic State" *Central Asian Survey* 19, nos. 3/4 (2000): 419–428; Nancy Hatch Dupree, "Cultural Heritage and National Identity in Afghanistan," *Third World Quarterly* 23, no. 5 (2002): 977–989.

8. Tania Ghanem, "When Forced Migrants Return 'Home': The Psychosocial Difficulties Returnees Encounter in the Reintegration Process," RSC Working Paper No. 16 (Oxford: University of Oxford, 2003).

9. Roger Zetter, "Reconceptualizing the Myth of Return: Continuity and Transition amongst the Greek-Cypriot Refugees of 1974," *Journal of Refugee Studies* 12, no. 1 (1999): 1–22; Nancy Farwell, "'Onward through Strength': Coping and Psychological Support among Refugee Youth Returning to Eritrea from Sudan," *Journal of Refugee Studies* 14, no. 1 (2001): 43–69.

10. In 2007, 45 percent of Afghans in Pakistan lived in camps, while in Iran the figure was less than 2.5 percent as of 2004. United Nations High Committee on Refugees, *Afghanistan: Challenges to Return* (Geneva: UNHCR, 2004); Government of Pakistan and UNHCR, *Registration of Afghans in Pakistan 2007* (Islamabad: Government of Pakistan and UNHCR, 2007).

11. Pamela Hunte, *Looking Beyond the School Walls: Household Decision-Making and School Enrolment in Afghanistan* (Kabul: AREU, 2006).

12. The madrassa system traditionally includes any type of educational institution, whether Islamic schools, other religious schools, or secular institutions. They have existed for centuries. In recent years, they have been associated with radical Islam.

13. Ameena Ghaffar-Kucher, "The Effects of Repatriation on Education in Afghan Refugee Camps in Pakistan," in *Education in Emergencies and Post-Conflict Situations: Problems, Responses and Possibilities*, ed. Dana Burde, vol. 2 (New York: Columbia University Press), 2005.

14. Not all the respondents who grew up in urban areas had access to television;

this varied not only by economic status but also according to household context and gender.

15. Chaman Ali Hikmat, "The Effects of English Teaching Methods Course of the English Department of Kabul Education University on Secondary School English Teachers," master's thesis, University of Massachusetts, Center for International Education, 2009.

CHAPTER 16

Primary and Secondary Education: Exponential Growth and Prospects for the Future

OMAR QARGHA

The stability of Afghanistan, and the region, is directly connected to how well Afghan youth are prepared for dealing with the many challenges they face now and in the decades to come. This is one of the most important, yet most difficult, development goals for the country. Afghan children today are the heirs to now more than four decades of conflict. They have grown up in the midst of war, and have never experienced security, prosperity, or peace in their homeland. Their environments are shaped by trauma, foreign interventions, and dependency. The legacy includes the following:

- An estimated 1.8 million Afghans killed between 1979 and 1992;
- In the same period, millions lost their fathers through targeted killings and imprisonment of the male population;
- Afghans continue to be the largest refugee population in the world;
- The disabled population is estimated at upwards of two million individuals;
- The internal fighting between 1992 and 1996 resulted in the worst ethnically motivated atrocities in the region;
- Between 1996 and 2001, women were banned from public life, a perverted version of Sharia (Islamic law)[1] was put in place with draconian measures, and Afghanistan became the world's most isolated country and a haven for extremism;
- For more than a decade, more than 130,000 soldiers from fifty-two nations, plus a fragile Afghan government, have been trying to bring security and stability to the country.[2]

Despite an estimated $242.9 billion USD spent on international military operations, $26.7 billion USD in international aid, and $16.1 billion USD spent on security resources, the situation in Afghanistan is anything but stable. Violence, suicide bombings, and military operations are the daily norm. On average, sixty people per month fall victim to the ten million landmines scattered across the country. Afghanistan has the world's worst maternal mortality rate and is ranked second-worst in infant mortality and third-worst in adult literacy. Economically, its GDP per capita is in the bottom ten percentile. It is estimated that 97 percent of the official GDP is related to foreign military and aid expenditure, and the country remains the world's largest producer of opium.[3] This state of overall insecurity has manifested in physical, psychological, and emotional trauma for the entire nation, and particularly its children. Despite the importance of Afghanistan for the region's civil, economic, and military stability, Western scholarship is mostly silent regarding the condition of Afghan youth. With some reports estimating that 42 percent of Afghanistan's population is below the age of fourteen, the need for studying this population is not only essential for the development of Afghanistan, it is also crucial for global long-term stability.

The complex problems facing Afghan children range from the immediate need for survival to the challenge of becoming contributing members of the global community. However, for the nation's long-term stability and sustainability, there is no sector as important as a robust and healthy educational system. Education is directly related to better health, economic growth, and a unified civil society. Education is the mechanism through which a nation prepares for its future and transfers its values. But most of all, quality education is a right that every child worldwide deserves in order to reach his or her full potential. Education is not the silver bullet that will solve all of Afghanistan's problems, but it is certain that access to quality education will need to be an essential part of any strategy that intends to move the country toward social and economic stability.

The provision of quality education is a monumental task even in secure societies. In nations experiencing conflict, this challenge is exponentially more complex. Yet there are few other clear avenues that can break the cycle of violence, poverty, and despair. Therefore, it is crucial to examine Afghanistan's educational system and to consider ways to overcome the challenges it faces.

A Brief History of Education in Afghanistan

Historical accounts that describe the shape and form of education in ancient Afghanistan are limited. It is likely that organized education started with religious schools focused on preparing priests for various religious traditions.[4] The Zoroastrian Sassanid Dynasty (224–621 C.E.) was the last pre-Islamic empire in the region and is credited with establishing an elaborate system of education called the *dabiristan*. The primary purpose of these institutions was to prepare civil servants. The curriculum seems to have included a wide range of subjects from religious texts, history, literature, philosophy, and drafting administrative documents, to horse riding, javelin throwing, cooking, music, and archery. At its height, there might have been over 30,000 students enrolled in these schools in the area that is now Iran and Afghanistan. The dabiristan schools seem to have survived until the twelfth century, well into the Islamic era.[5] Although there are no studies that focus on the connection between the dabiristan and institutions of higher learning called *madrassas*, it is likely that the madrassa system incorporated many elements of the dabiristan.

When Afghanistan became part of the greater Islamic world in the seventh century, there was a surge in the number and type of educational institutions. A variety of Islamic institutions of learning either were introduced to or originated from Afghanistan. The most prominent of these institutions were the mosque schools, or *maktab*s, learning circles, or *halaqa*s, and the madrassas.

The maktab was housed within the mosque, whose *imam* (prayer leader) taught children the recitation and memorization of the Qur'an, reading, writing, arithmetic, and basic religious duties. The teacher either performed this task voluntarily as a religious duty or was paid by the parents of the children. It is not clear how many of these mosque schools existed across Afghanistan, but it is safe to assume that some sort of teaching took place in every mosque across the country.

The halaqas were also housed in the mosques, open to the public, and led by scholars who specialized in various subjects ranging from exegesis of the Qur'an to readings of poetry and discussions of literature. These circles might be very small or comprising hundreds of people, depending on the scholar's reputation and topic.

The most organized form of Islamic education started around the tenth century in the form of the madrassa. The madrassa, unlike the maktab and halaqa, was a physical structure specifically constructed for the purpose of education. These structures, and their operation, were funded through private endowments, known as *awqaf*, which provided faculty and students with lodging, food, and a stipend. It is important to note that a large portion of awqaf throughout the Muslim world were established and supported by women.[6] The curriculum of the madrassa was more advanced and the teaching more structured than those of the halaqa and the maktab. There is disagreement among historians of Islamic education about the geographical origin of the madrassa, though there is strong support through written records and architectural remains that its birthplace was Khurasan and/or Bukhara in modern-day Afghanistan and Uzbekistan. Records indicate that there were more than thirty madrassas in the East, even before the first major one built in Baghdad in 459/1066, which is considered the cradle of the madrassa system.

The exact number of madrassas that existed in Afghanistan is not well known. However, historical records mention that seventy were built in Khurasan by the Seljuks (1037–1194 C.E.), four hundred existed in Balkh prior to the Mongol invasion in 1221 C.E. (most likely an exaggeration), many existed in Ghazna, and, according to the travel accounts of the Chinese Ambassador Zhen Zheng, there were thirty madrassas in Herat in the year 1414. Madrassas in Herat and Samarkand were the first to offer specialization outside the explicit religious sciences in such areas as mathematics, astronomy, literature, philosophy, music, and medicine. By the end of the fifteenth century, Herat had five hospital-madrassas dedicated to teaching medicine.

Access to these institutions was open to individuals from all social and economic classes, and the madrassas offered a means of social mobility. Most of the literature suggests that female access was limited, although a recent study by Dr. Mohammad Nadwi at Oxford University documents more than 8,000 female scholars across the Muslim world who taught both males and females in different institutions, including the madrassas.[7]

From 642 to 1868 (more than 1,200 years), Islamic educational institutions were the only systems of education in Afghanistan, but, although they did not entirely disappear, their vigor began to dwindle during the eighteenth century. By the first Anglo-Afghan war in 1832, the madrassa system had mostly retreated into defensive mode. In the vibrant days, however, the Greek sciences were either incorporated into the Islamic paradigm or rejected based on critical analysis because, to a great extent, Muslims felt secure about their dominant global position intellectually, economically, and militarily. With the decline of Muslim economic and military power, due in part to colonization of Muslim lands, came a decline in intellectual power. As a result, madrassas in Afghanistan, and across the Muslim world, began closing themselves off, adopting puritanical perspectives, and shunning the inclusion, or even discussion, of modern intellectual debates.

Madrassas traditionally operated independently and without a central structure. In 2007, Afghanistan's Ministry of Education (MoE) brought them under the central control of the government. The MoE argued that since the Constitution requires all types of education to be consistent with the tenets of Islam, there is no need to have the madrassas operating independently. Furthermore, the MoE argued that centralizing these institutions would reduce foreign influence and curtail extremism. By the end of 2010, 518

Islamic Education Schools (their term for the madrassas), with 136,935 students (10 percent female), were registered with the MoE.[8]

Modern Schooling

The first recorded attempt at establishing modern schooling in Afghanistan dates back to 1868, with Amir Shir Ali Khan's opening of the military (*harbi*) school and the royal civil (*molki*) school. Access to either was limited to male members of the royal family and sons of other notables. The education was free and modeled after schools in British India and the Ottoman Empire, but this initial attempt was cut short by the second Anglo-Afghan war (1878–1880). In 1903/1904, Amir Habibullah Khan established the Habibia School first as a madrassa, but it quickly adopted the curriculum of British India and imported an Indian Muslim principal.[9] Soon after, a second school after the Turkish model was opened for the royal family (*maktabi malikzadaha*). It eventually became the Royal Military College (*madrassai harbi sarajia*), headed by a Turkish officer, with a curriculum that combined Islamic subjects, military sciences, and physical education. In 1907, the Office of Textbooks (*Darul Ta'lif*) was established and in 1914, the first teacher's college (*Darul Malimeen*) was founded.

In 1919, Amanullah Khan took the throne and that same year declared Afghanistan independent, initiating the third Anglo-Afghan war, which ended with an agreement to remove the restriction that Afghanistan could only enter into treaties with Great Britain. These changes started a nationwide expansion of modern schooling with support from several countries. The most notable accomplishments were the establishment of the Ministry of Education; a girls' secondary school called Masturat; and three high schools, Istiqlal, Nijat, and Ghazi, in addition to Habibia. In 1927, King Amanullah held a national grand assembly, or *Loya Jirga*, in which he proposed, among other policy changes, the expansion of education, especially for women, as well as a ban on men wearing beards and traditional attire in Kabul, and discouraged the *chadari* (veil, a.k.a. *burqa*). These reforms were in part influenced by Mustafa Kemal Atatürk's modernization efforts in Turkey. There was widespread backlash to these reforms, especially from the religious leaders and the population outside Kabul, which resulted in Habibullah Kalakani taking the throne in 1929. Kalakani reversed Amanullah Khan's edicts, and during the nine months of his reign, all modern schools were closed, mainly because of internal fighting. In September 1930, Nadir Shah took the reign from Kalakani in a coup d'état that resulted in Kalakani's execution. Nadir Shah reopened and expanded schools, including girls' schools, but established a committee of religious leaders to oversee them and ensure that they were in line with Islamic values.[10]

It was during the reigns of King Zahir Shah (1933–1973) and President Daoud Khan (1973–1978)[11] that modern schooling became firmly established throughout Afghanistan. With financial and technical support from France, Germany, the United States, the Soviet Union, and the United Nations, modern schooling expanded to rural areas and became more accessible to a greater portion of Afghan society. During this phase, primary education became compulsory, a national centralized bureaucracy was established, and several development plans were enacted. Educational expansion efforts increased primary and secondary enrollment from approximately 122,000 students in 1956 to an estimated 872,000 students in 1970. Nevertheless, access was not equal. By 1975, girls made up only 15 percent of the primary and 11 percent of the secondary student population. Furthermore, urban areas received most of the funding and the best teachers at the expense of rural areas.

With the Soviet invasion in 1979, a cycle of conflict began that continues today. The gains made in expanding modern schooling were set back. Student enrollment fell by 27 percent, from nearly 1,240,000 in 1980 to 910,000 in 1990; the teacher population was reduced by nearly half, from 41,634 in 1980 to 23,856 in 1990; and the number of schools was reduced from an estimated 3,800 in 1980 to less than 1,200 in 1990. Because fighting was concentrated outside the major cities, rural areas suffered most. During this same time period, the Afghan Mujahedin groups, with the help of international non-governmental organizations (NGOs), established many refugee schools in rural areas of Afghanistan, as well as in the neighboring countries of Pakistan and Iran. The exact number of these schools and the students attending them is not known.

In 1992, the Communist-backed government of Mohammad Najibullah Ahmadzai (known simply as Najibullah) fell and a period of internal fighting ensued, resulting in extended school closures for boys and girls. From 1996 to 2001, with the Taliban takeover, girls' education suffered a tremendous setback and all official girls' schools were closed. However, public schooling and attendance became comparatively more regular for boys compared to the previous period, although the quality remained very low. Despite the Taliban's official ban on girls' education, local communities and NGOs managed to provide school access for girls using creative strategies such as informal educational structures and home-based schools. It is estimated that nearly 500,000 students were enrolled in these alternative schools during the Taliban regime and that upwards of 60,000 girls attended home-based schools in

Kabul alone.[12] In 2001, just before the fall of the Taliban, nearly one million students were enrolled in the official primary and secondary schools, with girls making up only 2 percent of the official student population.

Since the fall of the Taliban, Afghanistan has seen an exponential, sevenfold increase in primary and secondary enrollment, unprecedented in Afghan history, rising to almost 7.5 million in 2010. The number of teachers has increased, from nearly 26,500 in 2001 to an estimated 170,000 in 2010. The number of schools has increased from just over 3,000 in 2001 to somewhere between 9,000 and 12,000 in 2010. Additionally, there are now more than 400 private schools.[13]

At least in terms of numbers, Afghan children gained more access[14] to schooling in the decade after the fall of the Taliban than in the entire previous one hundred and forty years of modern schooling put together. This is a commendable feat on the part of the Afghan Ministry of Education and the national and international NGOs that have provided critical support. Yet, simply increasing enrollment alone is not enough to reap the benefits of education. Improved access to schools must result in real learning, with all children having equitable access to quality education.

Moving from Simple Access to Increasing Quality of Learning

Quality of education is hotly debated, and defining and measuring it is extremely difficult. Even some things that are agreed upon, such as teacher quality, do not lend themselves easily to measurement. This is because a teacher's impact on individual students is based on factors that include, among others, how inspiring they are, how much they relate to the student, and how well they can relate the content to their particular students' experiences. In the case of Afghanistan, the difficulty of this task is multiplied, because of limited and questionable data. Except for the CONCOR university entrance exam,[15] there are no systematic mechanisms for measuring student performance. Because of Afghanistan's security concerns, rapid school expansion, and reporting irregularities, even the number of students and teachers is questionable. One study found that upwards of 20 percent of reported students were classified as "ghost students": reported as attending school but likely not enrolled. The reason for this discrepancy could range from schools wanting to report higher numbers for potential economical benefits to not updating records of dropouts or students that move from one school to another.[16] Any claim of determining the quality of Afghanistan's educational system has to be taken with caution and with an understanding of these limitations.

There is strong evidence from international data that student-teacher ratios, as well as the amount of time students spend directly on learning activities, are two indicators that can roughly gauge the quality of education students are receiving.[17] These can serve as relatively good proxies for looking at the quality of education Afghan youth are currently receiving compared to the education provided to them in the 1970s, prior to the start of major conflict, as against the quality of education provided to children in Organization for Economic Co-operation and Development (OECD) member countries.[18] In the interest of brevity and because of a lack of available data, the following comparison is limited to the core subjects of language instruction and mathematics. Again, this comparison provides a general gauge rather than a definitive analysis.

In 2010, Afghan students in grades four to six were intended to spend 255 hours on language and mathematics instruction. In 1975, the intended amount of time for the same subjects was 354 hours.[19] By comparison, nine- to eleven-year-olds in OECD countries spent, on average, 320 hours on mathematics and language instruction in 2008. In 2010, there were forty-four students for every primary teacher in Afghanistan. In 1975, the Afghan average student-teacher ratio was estimated at thirty-nine students per teacher. The average student-teacher ratio for OECD countries at the primary level in 2008 was sixteen students per teacher.

Today's Afghan students receive about one hundred hours less instruction time annually in language and mathematics than in 1975, and sixty-five hours less than in OECD countries. This difference may be an underestimate since it is based on intended curriculum time. The actual amount of time spent in school for primary school ranges from two to three hours. With the time needed for managing these large classrooms, how much actual time is left for instruction is unclear and worrisome. Although this analysis is based on two indicators with general country-level data, it does provide enough evidence to cause concern. It is clear that the quality of education Afghan children currently receive is drastically lower than that of children in OECD countries. With substantially more instruction time and noticeably smaller class sizes, it is not hard to imagine that the quality of education children received in the 1970s in Afghanistan was much better than what they are receiving now.

Determining whether all children receive equitable access is also not easy to deduce for similar reasons. However, the larger trends in access do provide a clear picture of the potential problem areas. Afghanistan has made huge strides in increasing general access to schools for girls, who made up only 15 percent of the official student population in 1975, a meager 2 percent in

2001, and now make up 39 percent of the total student population. However, there continues to be wide geographical disparity in the access girls have to schools. This disparity ranges from girls making up 9.3 percent of the student body in Uruzgan province in central Afghanistan, to 42 percent in northern Badakhshan province, with six other provinces having enrollment rates for girls below 20 percent.[20]

There are huge cultural and economic variations between provinces and rural and urban villages, as well as between individual schools. Class sizes alone tell the story. Although the average class size is around forty-four students, the variation between different localities is alarmingly high. Some areas have classes as small as thirteen students per teacher, while other areas have classes as large as 104 students per teacher.[21] The problem is exacerbated by the fact that more qualified teachers, as well as 80 percent of the private schools, are concentrated in the urban centers of Kabul (50 percent), Herat (18 percent), Balkh (8 percent), and Nangarhar (5 percent). These private schools have smaller classes, longer daily instruction times, and better teachers. With the emergence of private schools, access to quality education based on economic status is entering center stage. Wealthier families in urban centers are increasingly choosing to enroll their children in private schools, leaving the lesser quality public schools to lower-income families and rural populations. Finally, there are virtually no services in public or private schools for students with disabilities. Although considerable advancement has been made regarding general access to schooling, the quality of education that children receive seems to be based on their location, their families' economic status, and whether they struggle with disabilities. More research is needed to determine the underlying and specific contributing factors leading to these differences, but it is clear that not all Afghan children are receiving the same kind of education.

Discussion

Education is one of the fundamental rights of children. Afghanistan has signed numerous international declarations and covenants, such as the Universal Declaration of Human Rights, which universally acknowledges the importance of this right and places the obligation on the state to provide and protect education. The importance of education is religiously and culturally ingrained in the Afghan worldview, as evidenced in its long history of education and the numerous traditional literary works that praise education. This is perhaps best exemplified by a Prophetic saying that most Afghans have memorized: "Seeking knowledge is an obligation on every Muslim (male and female)."[22]

Despite this, for the last 150 years, the Afghan population has struggled to provide uninterrupted educational access for its children and to establish a uniform national system that meets high standards. Periods of growth have been followed by abrupt changes in form, function, purpose, and access. The current educational system is the latest manifestation of the growth cycle and has been the most ambitious effort to date at universalizing modern schooling. In order to maintain the gains, improve educational quality, and establish greater equitable access, creative solutions anchored in the lessons of the last 150 years must be devised.

There are many reasons for the cycles of educational expansion and educational contraction in Afghanistan; among them, as we have seen, are internal conflicts and foreign interventions.

Two general types of internal conflict have had disastrous consequences in the provision of education. The first is ideological and revolves around the types of values and attitudes education should nurture in Afghan youth. Examples of this include the revolts against modernization efforts of King Amanullah Khan, communization efforts of Soviet-supported regimes, and the Islamization efforts of the Taliban by large sectors of the society, who felt that the educational system was either being used to undermine children's Islamic values or was instilling a puritanical understanding of Islam in children without preparing them to be productive members of the global society. This conflict of ideology has been compounded by the fact that modern schooling and the madrassa system have operated independently, preparing Afghan children with different worldviews that are at best non-aligned.

The second type of conflict involves the effects of war on education and the use of educational systems for political means. Examples of this include national school closures during the time of Kalakani, the Afghan civil war of 1992–1996, and the Soviet and Mujahedin's politicization of the school curriculum. In all these cases, schooling was used as a means to an end. In the case of Kalakani and the Afghan civil war of 1992–1996, the school closures were much more a function of the overall unrest within the country and in the Soviet and Mujahedin's politicization efforts; curriculum was used to promote and enlist supporters for the war.

Foreign intervention has been a staple of the Afghan educational system since the introduction of modern schooling. This has manifested in both financial and ideological dependence. The financial dependence has been clear from the early days of modern schooling. Whether it has been the expansion of modern schooling or that of the madrassa system, Afghanistan has always depended on foreign aid for funding the major part of its educational system. Foreign aid by its nature has ideological dependence, such as the communization of the school curriculum by the Soviets or the radicalization of the madrassa curriculum by the Arab donors. Indirect dependence has come by adopting systems and mechanisms of educational delivery that meet the requirements of "best practices" by the donor agencies. The current educational system is a good example of this. Reforms that have taken place in areas such as curriculum development or teacher training are based much more on policies of multinational donors such as the World Bank and the United States Agency for International Development (USAID) than on the specific needs of Afghanistan. In either case, foreign intervention has resulted in tension between national and foreign interests and the creation of educational systems that are at best not entirely nationally driven.

What does this mean for the future of Afghanistan's educational provision, and how can these lessons inform the development of a sustainable, robust, and quality-based educational system for Afghan youth driven by their specific needs? The answer is complex and requires much more in-depth study. However, several key points are crucially important in moving forward. First, in order to reduce the potential for future conflict based on ideological perspectives, it is essential that serious effort be made to develop a system that synthesizes both modern and Islamic perspectives of education. Bringing both systems under one central administrative authority is not enough and not necessarily helpful. A more robust national intellectual debate, one that is participatory and democratic, should take place regarding the values and outcomes that Afghans desire from an educational system. The central approach for developing policy based on discussions between the leadership of the MoE and donor agencies is not conducive for long-term stability.

Second, divorcing education from politics is by nature neither possible nor desirable. However, *over*-politicization of education can be reduced by making sure that larger societal infrastructures are more just, equitable, and truly participatory in decision-making. There is essential need for Afghan youth to have clear avenues to higher education and obtaining good jobs. There has not been much progress made in either of these areas. Because large multinational donors shun funding for higher education, the growth of this sector has been much slower than that of primary and secondary education.[23] Additionally, because the quality of primary and secondary education has been wanting, there has not been a clear translation of education leading to good jobs. More access to higher education and economic opportunities has to be accompanied by equitable access for all Afghan youth, regardless of gender, locality, economic status, or disability. Experience has shown that neglecting or ignoring these factors can lead to over-politicization of education.

Finally, in order for Afghanistan to develop a truly national and sustainable education system, it must wean itself from dependence on foreign funding and rely more on national public and private funding. This is not going to be an easy task without a healthy national economy. Nevertheless, the debate about how to reduce dependence on foreign funding of education has to take central stage. Given the long history of Afghan perseverance, independence, and ingenuity, there is hope that these difficult challenges can be overcome.

Notes

1. The literal meaning of Sharia in Arabic is "a clear well-trodden path to water." It regulates all human actions and puts them into five categories: obligatory, recommended, permitted, disliked, and forbidden. Certain rulings in Sharia, such as the need to pray five times a day, are fixed, while a great deal of public dealing is situational and can vary based on time, place, and culture, as long as the central principles are maintained.

2. Shaista Wahab and Barry Youngerman, *A Brief History of Afghanistan* (New York: Checkmark Books, 2010), 244–246; "Death Tolls for the Major Wars," http://necrometrics.com/20c1m.htm; UNHCR Statistical Online Population Database 2010, http://www.unhcr.org/pages/4a013eb06.html; Unknown News, "Casualties for Afghanistan," http://www.unknownnews.org/casualties.html; Shabnam Mallick, "Case Study: Persons with Disabilities in Afghanistan" (Bangkok, Thailand: United Nations Development Program, 2007), http://regionalcentrebangkok.undp.or.th/practices/governance/a2j/docs/CaseStudy-01-Afghanistan.pdf.

3. Lydia Poole, "Afghanistan: Tracking Major Resource Flows 2002–2010" (Global Humanitarian Assistance Briefing Paper, 2011); International Campaign to Ban Land Mines, "Afghanistan: Landmine Factsheet," http://www.afghan-network.net/Landmines; Mark Memmott, "Billions in Afghan Aid May Not Do Long-term Good, Senate Report Warns," National Public Radio, 2011, http://www.npr.org/blogs/thetwo-way/2011/06/08/137055308/billions-in-afghan-aid-may-not-do-long-term-good-senate-report-warns.

4. Franklin T. Burroughs, "Cultural Factors in the Education of Ancient Iran," *Journal of Educational Sociology* 36, no. 5 (1963): 237–240.

5. For detailed analysis of Islamic education in Afghanistan and the rest of the Muslim world please refer to: Abdullodzhon Mirbabaev, "The Development of Education: Maktab, Madrasa, Science and Pedagogy," in *History of Civilizations of Central Asia*, ed. Clifford Edmund Bosworth and Muhammad Seyfeydinovich Asimov (Delhi: UNESCO, 2003), 31–43; Wadad Kadi, "Education in Islam: Myths and Truths," *Comparative Education Review* 50, no. 3 (2006): 311–324; George Makdisi, *The Rise of*

Colleges: Institutions of Learning in Islam and the West (Edinburgh: Edinburgh University Press, 1981); and Ahmad Shalabi, *History of Muslim Education* (Dar al-Kashshaf, 1954).

6. Mary Ann Fay, "Women and Waqf: Property, Power, and the Domain of Gender in Eighteenth-Century Egypt," in *Women in the Ottoman Empire: Middle Eastern Women in the Early Modern Era*, ed. Madeline Zilfi (Lieden, Netherlands: Brill, 1997), 28–47.

7. Mohammad Akran Nadwi, *Al-Muhaddithat: The Women Scholars in Islam* (London and Oxford: Interface Publications, 2007).

8. Islamic Republic of Afghanistan Ministry of Education, "2008–2009 Education Summary Report," July 2009, http://moe.gov.af/Content/files/078_MOE%20EMIS%20Summary%20Report%201387.pdf.

9. Habibia High School continues to operate in Kabul today as one of the best public high schools.

10. Wahab and Youngerman, *A Brief History of Afghanistan*; Saif Rahman Samady, *Education and Afghan Society in the Twentieth Century* (Paris: UNESCO, 2001).

11. Nadir Shah was assassinated in 1933 by a student and his son Zahir Shah took the throne. In 1973, after several years of civil unrest headed by student organizations in Kabul, Daoud Khan staged a bloodless coup, abolished the monarchy, and declared himself both president and prime minister.

12. Hassan Mohammed and American Institute for Research, *Education and the Role of NGOs in Emergencies: Afghanistan 1978–2002* (USAID, 2006).

13. Maiwand Safi and Mina Habib, "Afghan Private Schools under Scrutiny," Institute for War and Peace Reporting, ARR Issue 414, October 31, 2011, http://iwpr.net/report-news/afghan-private-schools-under-scrutiny.

14. The issue of school access was center-stage in the World Conference on Education for All in March 1990. The conference organizers—UNESCO, UNICEF, UNDG, and the World Bank—joined representatives from 150 countries, thirty-three intergovernmental bodies, and 125 non-governmental organizations to declare the goal of "universalizing primary education and massively reducing illiteracy by the end of the decade." This movement toward universal access was a result of research that showed correlations between educational access and increased economic and health indicators. It was argued that investment in education produced high economic returns and impressive health benefits especially for the world's poorest countries.

15. The CONCOR is administered to all students wanting to enter the public university system. This exam, which is derived from the French system, was originally (1978) designed to identify potentially successful university students in the general graduating student population. The grade on the CONCOR not only determines if a student is admitted to public higher education, but also which subject of study the student is admitted into. Medicine requires the highest grades, while teaching requires one of the lowest grades (http://aefnow.org/aef/projects/educational).

16. Craig Naumann, "October/November 2006 Reporting Data on Schools, Students and Teachers," Islamic Republic of Afghanistan Ministry of Education, Planning Department (USAID-BESST: Kabul, Afghanistan, 2006).

17. David Stephens, "Quality of Basic Education," paper prepared for the United Nations Educational, Scientific and Cultural Organization (UNESCO) EFA Moni-

toring Report Team (Paris: UNESCO, 2003), unesdoc.unesco.org/images/0014/00 1469/146968e.pdf.

18. OECD is an international economic organization, made up of thirty-four developed countries, with the aim of stimulating economic progress and world trade.

19. Calculation based on World Bank and United Nations data. Data is based on World Bank and United Nations databases as well as Samady, *Education and Afghan Society in the Twentieth Century*.

20. "Summary Report of Education Situation (2009–2010)," Islamic Republic of Afghanistan, Ministry of Education, EMIS Department, General Directorate of Planning and Evaluation.

21. Afghanistan Education System found in StateUniversity.com, http://educa tion.stateuniversity.com/pages/3/Afghanistan-EDUCATIONAL-SYSTEM-OV ERVIEW.html.

22. Reported in the collection of Prophetic sayings compiled by Imam Muhammad Bib Yazid ibn Majah al Qazwini, translated by Nassirudin al Khattab in *English Translation of Sunan ibn Majah with Commentary* (London, United Kingdom: Darussalam International Publications, 2007), Part 1, 224.

23. For a more in-depth analysis of this point see Steven Klees and Omar Qargha, "The Economics of Aid: Implications for Education and Development," in *Education, Economics, and Development*, ed. Macleans Geo-JaJa and Suzanne Majhanovich (Rotterdam: Sense, forthcoming).

CHAPTER 17

Music and Literacy:
A New Approach to Education

LOUISE M. PASCALE

My first introduction to the educational system in Afghanistan was in 1966. I had just graduated from the University of California, Berkeley, with a BA in music, and I held an elementary education teaching certificate. Two years after graduation I joined the United States Peace Corps and was assigned to Afghanistan to teach English to middle-school boys (aged twelve to fifteen), most of whom came from the outlying provinces. I would live and teach in Kabul. Before I left the States, the Peace Corps provided me with extensive training in teaching English as a second language (ESL).

I arrived the first day of class not quite knowing what to expect. I walked into a stark, rather dimly lit classroom to find thirty-plus seventh- and eighth-grade boys waiting eagerly for their new teacher—a foreigner and a woman, no less! There was excitement in the air. The classroom had one poorly maintained blackboard and old wooden desks with benches, with at least three boys to a bench. The cold building was made of concrete. Nothing hung on the walls.

The headmaster introduced me and, in a stern, authoritarian voice, made it clear to the students that they should listen and behave. Then he marched out and I was left to find my way in this completely new and unfamiliar teaching environment.

The students were used to only male instructors, so we all found ourselves in uncharted territory. I had no choice but to begin. I recited English words, as I had been taught, and the boys echoed them back to me. Occasionally, I wrote a word on the board. Most, but not all, of the students had paper and pencil.

This system of teaching continued for several weeks. Could the students construct sentences in English by themselves? I wondered. Were they able to put words together in sentences beyond what they were reciting back to me? Would they be able to converse with an English-speaking person on their own? I was beginning to doubt the teaching methods. I had learned that Afghan students are taught completely by rote and I observed that they were very comfortable being taught in that manner.

Rote learning primarily involves repetition. Throughout the Middle East, Central Asia, and much of the rest of the world, educational systems tend to emphasize memorization over critical thinking, even at the most specialized levels.[1] It was also the most common pedagogical strategy in the United States in the early 1900s, when more than two-thirds of the schools were rural, teachers had little to no formal education themselves, and educational resources were limited. Memorization, drill, and recitation were standard.[2] This is similar to the situation Afghanistan still faces in the twenty-first century.

An education system like Afghanistan's, which has long relied on rote memorization and dictation teaching methods, inevitably results in "decreases in the ability for students to learn decision-making, problem solving and critical thinking. This is further exacerbated by the lack of teacher-student interaction. If a teacher only promotes rote learning, students often become disinterested in attending school."[3]

Progressive reforms, such as outcome-based education, have put an emphasis on eliminating rote learning in favor of deep understanding. New curriculum standards in the U.S. call for more active learning, problem solving, critical thinking, and communication over merely recalling facts. The U.S. Department of Education found that students whose teachers emphasized "meaning and understanding" flourished. Teaching that was active and interactive, rather than passive and completely teacher-directed, motivated students and improved their critical thinking skills. Researchers have concluded that schooling that emphasized basic skills and tight control of instruction by the teacher was unhelpful and resulted in inadequate education and high literacy rates.[4] (Afghanistan's literacy rate, as of April 2012, is at 28 percent total—43.1 percent of males and 12.6 percent of females. Students on average have only nine years of school.[5] In a 2009 survey, Literacy Rates of the World, compiled by the CIA World Factbook, Afghanistan ranked 211 out of 213.[6]) Teacher-training institutions in Afghanistan are keenly aware of the need to overhaul the educational system and to create teacher-training opportunities that introduce new strategies and pedagogical approaches.

I reported daily for work at the middle school and the headmaster seemed to feel everything was going very well. Nevertheless, I began to question whether my students were learning anything at all, and anything that would be useful in their futures.

One day, I ventured beyond our rote lessons and tried engaging the students in a discussion. I found that this was much more difficult for them and that they had no practice in active participation. They seemed uncomfortable with the "freedom."

In the second year of my Peace Corps service, I was given the opportunity to teach music to young children. I had been curious about Afghan children's music and was delighted to be given the chance to learn more about it. Music was commonly heard in the bazaar and was always part of Afghan cultural festivities, but I discovered—and not surprisingly, given what I had experienced in the classroom—that music was not commonly part of a young child's education. Nor did there appear to be any music books available. Collecting children's songs seemed like a viable project and something I was interested in exploring further. I presented my idea to the Peace Corps and the Afghan government and everyone approved the project, a necessary step if I were to continue on this path. I was introduced to some Afghan musicians and poets, and together we assembled a small music book of sixteen traditional children's songs. With a harmonium (a small, accordion-like instrument) in hand, I tromped from one school to another, sharing the songs to the delight of the children and their teachers. Other than during my visits, even these young children were being taught by a rote method. As an extra bonus, I shared my small supply of crayons and had the children help illustrate the songbook with their delightful drawings. The children responded very positively to music time. They were allowed to move about, sing, and make art, all of which I noted had not only the children but the teachers engaged and interested in learning. I left Afghanistan in 1968 with a small published book which was to be distributed to elementary schools in Kabul.[7]

During the forty years since my Peace Corps experience, I've closely followed the news about Afghanistan and tried to imagine what was happening to the country I came to know and love. I wondered what had become of the children I taught, their families, and the friends I'd made before the devastation. Had they survived? I wondered, too, about the music.

Preserving the Music, Revitalizing Afghanistan's Musical Culture

In 2002, quite by chance, I came across my old copy of the songbook created while I was in the Peace Corps. I leafed through the torn and faded pages, sadly realizing that I no longer could read the Dari and although I knew the melodies, I couldn't remember the lyrics and had no easy way of translating them. As I stood in my living room, holding in my hands not only the songbook itself but all the memories that went with it, I came to the frightful realization—given the rigid decrees against music set by the Taliban[8]—that perhaps these songs were in danger of being lost to Afghan culture forever. At that moment, I vowed to return them to the children, somehow, someway. My immediate thought process was simple: the songs were at risk of being lost. They needed to be preserved. I had to return them. It was at that moment that the Afghan Children's Songbook Project was born.

In the documentary *Breaking the Silence: Music in Afghanistan*, the narrator stands amidst the devastation, on the top of a hill in a section of Kabul known as Kharabat Lane, a place considered to be "the cradle of Afghan music. . . . It was not about the rubble, the destruction of the buildings, or the loss of homes. It is not about that loss. When they took our music, they took our soul. It was the loss of our soul, our spirit. When they took the music, they took the soul of this country."[9]

The years I lived in Afghanistan, 1966–1968, are remembered by many Afghans as a "golden era," when music was prevalent, when children were singing, when trees were green, and the country was at peace. By the mid 1970s, that peaceful Afghanistan no longer existed.

Initially, I thought I'd just copy my old songbook and send it back, but it soon became apparent that that idea was not feasible. My copy, not the original, was in terrible shape and I had written the notation to each song solely by ear. I was sure there were errors. I was also concerned that the songs did not represent the total Afghan population and that people of varying ethnicities, often living in isolated circumstances, rural or urban, might not recognize or relate to them. I had worked primarily with one or two musicians and one poet. At the time, with my own limited knowledge of Afghan music, I had not thought to ask them to make sure the collection of songs was an inclusive representation of Afghanistan's various ethnic groups.

After much searching, I found an Afghan musician, Vaheed Kaacemy, living in Toronto. I told him about my project and he agreed to look over the old songbook. As a well-respected musician, composer, and former kindergarten teacher, Vaheed had the perfect combination of skills and background for this project. His reaction to my proposed project was profound. He burst into tears at seeing music that had long gone from his memory. He jumped headfirst into the project, hunting down the original sources for each melody and poem and finding Afghan children in the Toronto area to work on a recording. He felt strongly that a new songbook should be created and should include an accompanying CD. Verifying my concern that certain ethnic groups and languages were not represented, beyond Dari and Pashto, Vaheed searched out songs in Uzbeki and Hazaragi, thus broadening the scope of the songbook. When he sent me the first few recorded songs, the project truly came to life.

I then headed off to Washington, DC, to meet with the Afghan Ambassador's wife, Shamim Jawad, who I hoped would agree to support the project through her organization, Ayenda. I told her my story and my vision. She sat still, listening through headphones to the CD Vaheed had created of the first few songs, then gasped and actually seemed to stop breathing. "I haven't heard those songs since I was a child," she said, with tears in her eyes. "I never thought about the power music can have. I thought we needed to send computers to the schools. This is what the children need. They need their music back."[10]

Vaheed worked diligently to record sixteen songs. He insisted, emphatically, that Afghan children should have their own alphabet song, so he composed one using a familiar traditional melody from Herat. His alphabet song is now sung by thousands of children across Afghanistan.[11]

A moment that stands out among many and helps shed light on the vital power of music to strengthen cultural identity occurred at the release party held in March 2007 at the Afghan Embassy to celebrate the first printing of 3,500 songbooks, titled *Qu Qu Qu Barg-e-Chinaar: Children's Songs from Afghanistan*.[12] Two hundred Afghan Americans attended the event. I spoke, telling the story of the project, and then showed a short video of Afghan children singing one of the traditional songs, "Momardene Afghane." It is similar to the American song "This Land Is Your Land," by Woody Guthrie,[13] and speaks of the beauty of the country and the strength of Afghans, who are united as one people in one land.

As the video played, one woman in the crowd shouted, "We all know this song. We should all be singing." With that, two hundred Afghans raised their voices in unison. The room was melodiously filled with sound and I realized that there was not a dry eye in the room. It was an emotional, breathtaking moment.

The Songbook Project moved forward, and by 2009, 30,000 songbook packages, which each included not only a copy of the songbook, but a CD and cassette tape, had been distributed to schools and orphanages across Afghanistan. We were committed from the onset of the project to making certain that a songbook package was given to every child, not just one per class.

In that way, I hoped that children would begin not only to sing, but to notice the words on the page. All printing and distribution efforts were accomplished through TriVision,[14] an Afghan family-owned business located in Kabul, which, from the onset, was committed to making the project a success.

The songbook distribution plan, thanks to TriVision, is organized and efficient. Once a new printing is completed (TriVision prints in lots of five thousand), we send out an email to all our contacts—educational organizations, teacher-training institutes, individuals, etc., who have indicated interest in obtaining songbooks. We ask them to tell us exactly how many songbook packages they need and where they are specifically going to be distributed. We do not charge for the songbooks, but we do ask that they send us documentation and a brief report once they've completed the distribution process. Everyone needs to be able to pick up the songbook packages at the TriVision office in Kabul. Within twenty-four hours of an announcement that another 5,000 songbook packages are ready for distribution, they are all spoken for. It is clear that the need is great.

Through the generous assistance of many educational organizations, such as Youth Educational Services, Save the Children, Creating Hope International, Afghan Institute of Learning, PARSA, Aschiana, School of Leadership Afghanistan (SOLA), Canadian Women for Women-Afghanistan (CW4WAfghan), and many individuals interested in the project, the songbook packages have been distributed to elementary schools, orphanages, and women's centers, as well as traveling libraries, in thirteen provinces.

During these first few years of the project, due to my professional work in the field of arts and education, I kept hoping for a stronger connection between the Songbook Project and teaching basic literacy skills. I knew this was a natural fit but had not yet figured out how to make the link with Afghan teachers. Having spoken to many Afghans, I was aware that teachers were still using the same rote teaching methodology that I experienced while in the Peace Corps in the late 1960s. Not much had changed. I did, however, receive a photo and account from a school in Sheberghan, in the northwest corner of Afghanistan, where it was clear that not only were the children singing Vaheed's alphabet song, but the teacher was also using it as a teaching tool by writing on the blackboard as the children sang. I was encouraged to see this happening and wondered how to motivate other teachers to do more of the same.

The teacher began the lesson by having the children sing the alphabet song. The students were therefore immediately actively engaged in learning the alphabet. He then wrote the letters on the board and the children came up and identified the letters while singing. At times he asked a child to write out the letters themselves on the blackboard. As mentioned previously, teaching methodology is not typical in Afghanistan. Children are usually expected to remain in their seats throughout a lesson and are not encouraged to respond beyond responding by repetition. Many positive things occurred in this learning environment. The children were not only actively learning, but, through music, they were *experiencing* learning and in this case, learning language in a pleasurable way. Learning was personal and more relevant. Connections between sound and symbol were more apparent when the children were actively engaged in the process.

"Young children are naturally wired for sound and rhythm," Laura Woodhall and Brenda Ziembroski write in "Promoting Literacy through Music." "Besides providing enjoyment, music can play an important role in language and literacy development. Establishing a sense of rhythm can be used to increase a student's awareness of rhyming patterns, memorization and aural discrimination."[15]

The Literacy Connection

In 2009, I returned to Afghanistan to assess the project. As I visited schools and orphanages, I was reassured to see that the books were being put to good use. Children in every school I visited had learned all the songs. Whenever I delivered songbooks to a new site, the teachers were extremely grateful. None of the schools or orphanages I visited had any educational resources. The songbook was the children's only book. Surprising to me and also thrilling was witnessing children not only singing the songs, but intently following the words on the page. I had no idea this was happening, and it opened a new door for the songbook project.

I also observed that the teachers were not, for many reasons, able to take advantage of this phenomenon. They had clearly used the songbook to have children sing together but—and completely understandably, given their lack of resources and training, and their customary teaching methods—they had not imagined ways that the songbook could be used as a learning tool to enhance basic literacy skills.

Watching children earnestly trying to read the song lyrics finally provided me with the data I needed to expand the songbook's effectiveness by not only using it to help revitalize a part of Afghanistan's vibrant music culture, but also as a much-needed reading resource. I decided to add a training component to the project that would provide teachers with ideas for using the song-book as a text for improving basic reading and writing skills and to offer them alternative teaching strategies beyond rote learning. Aware of many research studies that demonstrate that participating in music activities improves early language development as well as builds creative thinking, imagination, and critical thinking skills, I was eager to create a new resource for Afghan teachers. This afforded me the opportunity I'd been hoping for.

I created a separate Teacher's Guide to accompany the songbook that took into consideration the lack of classroom educational supplies and resources and other physical limitations or cultural norms around teaching in Afghanistan. The guide, created with a team of Afghans, consists of five to six lesson ideas for every song. Each lesson suggests ways the songs can link to developing such literacy skills as letter recognition, letter sounds, vocabulary, listening skills, writing and print awareness, and reading comprehension. Just as we insist that every student in a school or orphanage receive her/his own song-book package, we also insist that every teacher receive her/his own copy of the Teacher's Guide. I discovered that there was often more than one teacher per grade level.

The Teacher's Guide has become a sought-after resource. We now include a small notebook and two pencils with each songbook package, allowing children to practice writing and enhance their creative thinking and problem-solving skills. Teachers remark that they are grateful to have access to innovative educational strategies. Teacher-training institutes in and around Kabul and organizations such as the Afghan Institute of Learning (AIL) are using the guide as one of their primary resources. Wahid Omar, senior graduate education manager at the Higher Education Project in Kabul and a board member of Afghans4Tomorrow, Inc., which has opened and maintains numerous schools in Afghanistan, gave guides to all one hundred of his student teachers. "The teachers really like them," he wrote in an email, "because it is a different way of teaching and it takes students away from the routine methods."[16] A teacher from the TOLO kindergarten in Kunduz sent an email after receiving the Teacher's Guide. "This Teacher's Guide is very helpful, because before we received this we did not know how to teach our students in a professional way. It is a big help to us."[17] AIL has organized several teacher-training programs across Afghanistan and works hard to change the way people think about education. They are particularly interested in expanding critical-thinking skills.[18]

"Ali Baaba" has been part of the Afghan children's song repertoire for hundreds of years and is among the most beloved of songs. The children's favorite part is to make the sounds of the animals.[19] Much like the farmer in the traditional American song "Old MacDonald," Ali Baaba has a garden and in his garden he has many animals—a goat, a dog, a duck, a cat, and even a rabbit.

English translation of an excerpt of "Ali Baaba":

Ali Baaba goes to his garden. In his garden, he has a goat.
Bah Bah Bah says the goat. Tell me now what else does he have?

Dari transliteration:

Ali Baaba baagh mayrowa. Dareen baagh yak bara daara.
Bah Bah Bah makona. Bogo daga chi daara.[20]

Beyond the simple joy of singing it, the song also provides an ideal opportunity to reinforce sounds and letter recognition, as well as a chance for children to offer their ideas, enhancing creative-thinking skills, imagination, and group collaboration. When the teacher asks the students to come up with a new animal for the garden, they are going beyond a conditioned answer. When they create their own story about an animal, they must use problem-solving skills. They are also reinforcing basic reading skills, thinking about sequencing and reading comprehension. Below are examples of suggested follow-up lessons provided in the Teacher's Guide.

"Ali Baaba"
Think of new animals that live in Ali Baaba's garden. Write their names on the board. What sounds do the animals make? What letters start with that sound?
Make up new verses to the song with new animals.
Make the animal sound and everyone guesses what animal it is.
Tell a story about an animal.
Write a few sentences on your paper:
   Name of the animal
   Sound of the animal
   Color of the animal
   Where you find the animal
   Draw the animal

"Grandmother Swings Me"
The Pashto song "Grandmother Swings Me" describes the happy memories

of a grandmother swinging a young child and the warmth and comfort a child finds in the arms of her/his mother or grandmother.

English translation of an excerpt:

> Grandmother, grandmother push my swing
> Push my swing high in the air
> If I get cold on the swing
> I know the warmth of my mother's arms will keep me warm.

Dari transliteration:

> *Boody boody taal raaka*
> *Taal day pame saal raaka*
> *Taal day pame saal raaka*
> *Taal kee bazen geezuma Demoor ghaze two day zuma.* (2X)

Below are suggested questions from the guide that specifically reinforce listening skills, comprehension, creative thinking, self-expression, and vocabulary:

- How do you feel when you go up in a swing? Write out the words on the board and on your paper. For example: happy, free, and silly. Say them together.
- What does a swing do? (Goes up and down, back and forth.) Write out and learn those words.
- What do you like about your grandmother? Write out the words. For example: nice, sweet, kind.
- Tell a story about your grandmother to another person (you can choose another older person).
- Tell someone about something special you like to do with your grandmother, grandfather, or older adult.
- What do you learn from them? Tell a story about that.

The Impact of Music on Language and Early Literacy

Current research provides evidence showing the power music has to engage children in learning early literacy skills, such as reading comprehension and verbal memory, listening skills, vocabulary development, phonemic awareness, and writing and print awareness. The implication for teachers is twofold. Music, while valuable for releasing the musical potential of every child, can significantly enhance children's language as well.[21] Now that the songbook has an accompanying Teacher's Guide, there is an opportunity to open doors to new ways of thinking about educating children. The lessons suggested in the

Teacher's Guide go beyond repeating words and deepen learning experiences by enabling personal connections, engaging the students in active learning, and allowing for creativity and reflection.

The Future Plans for the Afghan Children's Songbook Project

By the spring of 2013, a second songbook, with accompanying Teacher's Guide, will have been produced and five thousand copies will have been printed and distributed across Afghanistan. The new edition includes more Pashto, as well as songs in Tajik, Uzbeki, and Dari.[22]

It is evident that changing the educational system in Afghanistan is a slow process. Fortunately, there are many groups and organizations with teams of dedicated people, all putting a significant effort into bringing that change about.[23]

The Afghan Institute of Learning reported in an article on teacher training that "most of the curriculum was destroyed because of the years of war and civil strife. And the old curriculum did not incorporate interactive, student-centered lessons."[24] Afghanistan urgently needs updates to the existing curriculum. Many leaders in Afghan education realize this challenge. The Songbook Project is dedicated to being part of a concerted effort to improve the lives of children through the improvement of the educational process.

The future of Afghanistan lies with its children, who deserve to be taught the skills that will enable them to think critically and creatively, thus preparing them with the flexible skills they will need to face an uncertain future. Afghanistan needs people who are adaptable, innovative, can solve problems, and communicate well with others. Developing the capacity to be creative can enrich their lives and help them contribute to a better society.[25]

The Songbook Project uses music, specifically traditional Afghan children's music, as a conduit not only to revitalize Afghanistan's musical heritage, but to connect Afghan children to an important aspect of their cultural identity. Music is a vital force for building personal and cultural identity and strengthening community. When children sing songs from various ethnic groups, their view of the world is broadened and enlarged. Perceptions and assumptions are challenged. "The arts provide new perspectives on the lived world."[26]

When music is connected to teaching, it becomes a powerful curriculum tool. There are rhythms in learning, and feeling a pulse internally is essential to learning to read. There are rhythms in reading, in math, in language. Children who can sustain a pulse can also sustain attention.[27] Brain research shows that music aids memory and provides creative outlets.

"We cannot know through language what we cannot imagine. Those who cannot imagine cannot read."[28] There is no doubt that Afghan children face many obstacles. Those obstacles, however, can be overcome through the capacity to "look at things as if they were otherwise and to be able to break with what is supposedly fixed and finished. Imagination allows us to carve out new orders of experience."[29]

The Afghan Children's Songbook Project is committed to nurturing Afghan children and their teachers, as well, in developing an educational environment that is not just about learning facts but about shaping students who can think clearly and creatively, implement their own plans, communicate their ideas, and thus make a positive impact on the future of Afghanistan.[30]

Notes

1. Jon B. Alterman, "Investing in a More Robust Public Policy Environment in the Middle East," analysis paper, Center for Strategic & International Studies (CSIS) Middle East Program, June 2011, 5.

2. "The 1900s: Education: Overview," http://www.encyclopedia.com/doc/1G2 -3468300064.html.

3. Sam Eldakak, "The Modern Effects of Teacher Education on the Arab World," June 23, 2010, http://www.eric.ed.gov/PDFS/ED510606.pdf.

4. Alfie Kohn, "Poor Teaching for Poor Children . . . In the Name of School Reform," *Education Week*, April 27, 2011, vol. 30, issue 29, 32–24; Eldakak, "The Modern Effects of Teacher Education."

5. The online CIA World Factbook is updated weekly. CIA World Factbook, https://www.cia.gov/library/publications/the-world-factbook/geos/xx.html, April 2012.

6. Literacy Rates of the World provides statistics by map and charts of 213 countries (http://world.bymap.org/LiteracyRates.html).

7. The original songbook, *Children's Songs*, was published in 1968 by Kabul Press. The illustrations for the book were drawings created by children in the Kabul schools where I taught.

8. The Taliban, in power from 1996–2001, among other human rights violations, banned all music. But at least ten years prior to the Taliban's rule, music censorship had already reared its ugly head. With the Taliban, stereo systems, video cassette players, and TV sets were destroyed in public. Musicians tried to bury their instruments in order to hide them. One Afghan musician tells of hiding his precious *sarinda* (stringed instrument similar to a lute or fiddle) in his woodpile. Cassette innards were ripped out and hung in effigy. Musical instruments were burned in the public stadium. The only "music" allowed were religious chants. Another musician, fearing he might lose his mind without hearing or making music, bought doves, which he let loose in his house. He was then surrounded by the cooing of doves. The Taliban's list of forbid-

den things grew to include dance, theatre, film and television, cameras, photography, sculptures, magazines, newspapers, most books, festivities, children's toys, applause, and even . . . squeaky shoes. John Bailey, "Can You Stop the Birds Singing? The Censorship of Music in Afghanistan," in *The World Forum on Music and Censorship* (Denmark: Freemuse, 2001). "A woman could be arrested for humming to her child" (Andrew Solomon, "An Awakening from the Nightmare of the Taliban," *New York Times*, March 10, 2002).

9. Simon Broughton, director, *Breaking the Silence: Music in Afghanistan*, BBC, London, 2010.

10. Personal conversation with Shamim Jawad, Afghan Embassy, Washington, DC, September 2006.

11. Children at the Small Heaven Orphanage, Kabul, singing alphabet song, November 2009, http://www.afghansongbook.org/videos.html.

12. Louise Pascale, ed., *Qu Qu Qu Barg-e-Chinaar: Children's Songs of Afghanistan*, musical director Vaheed Kaacemy. Funders and sponsors include: Ayenda Foundation; National Geographic Society Mission Program; Roshan; Flora Foundation; Aga Khan Foundation; Bayat Foundation; Eastman Fund; CW4WAfghan; U.S. State Department Public Affairs Section, U.S. Embassy, Kabul, Afghanistan; Flora Foundation; Richard Pascale; Jason Soules; TriVision TV, publisher, 2006, www.afghansongbook .org.

13. Woody Guthrie wrote "This Land Is Your Land," one of the United States' most famous folk songs, in 1940. It was recorded in 1944 and published in 1944. He used a familiar Carter family melody. "The song is truly a great song about America, its natural wealth and beauty that kids in classrooms ought to know and learn to sing. The original version of the song had a pointed political message, but the published version omitted the last two verses, making 'This Land' a celebration of America." From the *Los Angeles Times* Pop & Hiss blog, "When Woody Guthrie's 'This Land Is Your Land' Went to School," http://latimesblogs.latimes.com/music_blog/2012/05 /woody-guthrie-centennial-this-land-is-your-land-school-folk-music.html, *Los Angeles Times*, May 10, 2012.

14. TriVision TV is a marketing and media production company owned and operated by the Lutfi family that has locations in Kabul and Chantilly, VA.

15. Laura Woodhall and Brenda Ziembroski, "Promoting Literacy through Music," *Songs for Teaching: Using Music to Promote Literacy*, http://www.songsforteaching .com/1b/literacymusic.htm.

16. Email correspondence from Wahid Omar, June 12, 2011.

17. Email correspondence from Zarghuna, kindergarten teacher, Kunduz, June 20, 2011.

18. "Training Increases the Reach of Education and Healthcare," *Afghan Institute of Learning*, http://www.afghaninstituteoflearning.org/teacher-training.html.

19. Children from the TOLO Kindergarten in Kunduz singing "Ali Baaba," November, 2009, http://www.afghansongbook.org/videos.html.

20. Pascale, *Qu Qu Qu Barg-e-Chinaar*, 9, 25.

21. "The Impact of Music on Language & Early Literacy: A Research Summary in Support of Kindermusik's ABC Music & ME," http://kindermusikkids.files.word press.com/2010/02/abc-research-paper.pdf.

22. This latest iteration of the Songbook Project involves reprinting and creating a second songbook and is funded by the Eastman Fund, CW4WAfghan, and the U.S. Department of State Public Affairs Section, U.S. Embassy, Kabul, Afghanistan.

23. Such as AIL, Afghans4Tomorrow, CW4WAfghan, and PARSA.

24. Afghan Institute of Learning, "Teacher Training," http://www.afghaninstitute oflearning.org/teachertraining.html.

25. Robert Fisher, "Expanding Minds: Developing Creative Thinking in Young Learners," *CATS: The IATEFEL Young Learners SIG Journal* (Spring 2006): 5–9.

26. Maxine Greene, *Releasing the Imagination* (San Francisco: Jossey-Bass Publishers, 1995).

27. Nick Page, *Music as a Way of Knowing*, The Galef Institute (Los Angeles: Stenhouse Publishers, 1995).

28. Harry S. Broudy, *The Role of Imagery in Learning*, occasional paper no. 1, Getty Council for Education in the Arts, Los Angeles, 1987.

29. Greene, *Releasing the Imagination*, 19.

30. For information about the Songbook Project, to order a songbook, or to view videos and photographs of children singing in Afghanistan, go to www.afghansong book.org.

PART 6

COMMUNICATING EMPOWERMENT

Young men use computers in an Internet café, Cafe Sori, in Karti Char district, Kabul. Photo by Beth Wald, 2009.

CHAPTER 18

"Thanks God for the Twitter and the Facebook! Thanks God for That!"

LAURYN OATES

I was slumped in the backseat of a cab darting down Granville Street in Vancouver. It was late at night and I was yearning for bed after thirty-six hours on five different flights through three continents, making my way home from Kabul to the small island where I live on Canada's west coast. It was July 2011, and my Kurdish cab driver was bowled over with the still unfolding revolutions in the Middle East, and how Twitter and Facebook were being used to such effect in mobilizing the masses. An immigrant from Turkey, he was abuzz as he argued that governments could no longer hide, even in those places where regime change still looked to be far at bay, like in Iran or Uzbekistan. His hands banged on the steering wheel as he spoke excitedly and breathlessly about how ordinary people were using social media to report what was happening inside their countries, to tell the outside world what their governments were really doing. The governments' power might still have been well entrenched, but the charade had become much harder to maintain when any individual could broadcast the truth.

The cab made its way across the Lion's Gate Bridge, suspended over the dark, sparkling Pacific Ocean, and up the gently sloping hill of Taylor Way to the highway. We chatted about the change sweeping over the masses in Bahrain, the courage of the protestors risking—and sometimes losing—their lives in the bloodied streets of Syria, and the unfolding war in Libya. It was indeed an exciting thing to watch, a potential new wave of democracies being born from the ground up. Despite my exhaustion his enthusiasm infected me too, and by the time we reached the quiet darkness of Horseshoe Bay, where the boats and ferries come and go to nearby islands, he was warmly shaking my hand with both of his, exclaiming, "I wish you all the best of luck over there!" He drove off, and I picked up my luggage from the road. A cloud of Kabul's brown dust puffed off of the bags into the night air.

Over *there*, too, people were watching the Middle East . . . very carefully.

Corruption, Repression, and Corrosion

Officially, Afghanistan is a democracy. But in the last few years, Afghans, who've waited more than three decades for peace and political change, have been watching the latest government compromises increasingly with each passing month, the country's nascent democratic institutions eroding as President Hamid Karzai seems ever more embracing of tribalism over transparency, of patronage over parliament. The initial euphoria with which Afghans had met the introduction (or re-introduction) of institutions like a progressive constitution, legislative assembly, the rule of law, and free and fair elections is rapidly receding as the post-Taliban government comes into its thirteenth year.[1]

The maiming of these new institutions of democracy is happening despite a massive international presence inside Afghanistan. The world's eyes are firmly fixed on this small country in the heart of Central Asia: there is consistent international media coverage; cash pouring in from Western governments; and an army of humanitarians, think-tankers, analysts, advisors, and researchers siphoning in and out of Kabul International Airport like a revolving door. Yet the scrutiny of all of these actors has still failed to hold the Afghan government to account. It's a sad irony that a country on the receiving end of a massive infusion of foreign assistance from countries all over the world, in one of the most ambitious and complex multinational interventions in history, is tied with Burma (Myanmar) as the second-most corrupt country on earth, after Somalia, according to Transparency International's 2010 corruption index.[2]

It's not for a lack of resources that the Afghan government is failing in its ability to exercise accountable and effective leadership and provide basic services for its people. It is a failure to recognize the essential role of good governance in bringing peace and prosperity to a ravaged nation, and the failure of those holding the purse strings to enforce this recognition in any serious way. Whenever the role of good governance is paid lip service by the international donors financing Afghanistan's rebuilding, it's rarely followed up with any robust insistence that the reforms promised by the Afghan government actually be realized.

Time and time again, Karzai's regime has demonstrated its lack of will to seriously combat corruption, to appoint ministers with progressive agendas who will get things done, and to improve the quality and reliability of the services that should by now be accessible to most Afghans, like clean water, good schools, and the rule of law.

The international donor community in Afghanistan may be willing to tolerate poor governance, but Afghans are no longer willing to contend with the broken promises and the lethargic pace of democratic reform and social development. A rumbling has started, particularly among the youth, as they observe citizen protest movements making serious gains in the Middle East, and this rumbling is swelling rapidly.

And in Afghanistan, youth matter. They constitute the overwhelming majority of the population.

Friending for Reform

Estimates for 2010 by the United Nations' Population Division[3] put 65 percent of Afghans under the age of twenty-four—about 45 percent of the population are under the age of fifteen, while about 20 percent fall into the fifteen to twenty-four category, with the median age in the country at only sixteen years old. These metrics mean that the vast majority of those alive in the country today were born into war. Some are survivors of the civil war, many have experienced what it is to be a refugee, and most have been eyewitnesses to the brutality of the Taliban. Yet, though they have never known peacetime and have little direct experience with good governance, these young people are fed up with the status quo. And the role of social media in uniting those who share a growing disillusionment and a desire for alternatives has not been lost upon the increasingly tech-savvy youth of Afghanistan.

Facebook groups calling for reforms, an end to corruption, or for President Karzai to step down are springing up constantly, with names like "Reformists" or "Karzai Must Go!" At the same time, Afghans are making it clear that in their opposition to the behavior of the current government, they also reject Taliban ideology. In fact, much of the youths' anger directed toward Karzai stems from the Afghan government's unpopular effort to initiate peace talks with the Taliban without having consulted the population on what kind of peace is acceptable—to the country's women, to its youth, to its minorities. The president's repeated references to the Taliban as "our Afghan brothers" have left a deep wound for many Afghans, offended by the official wooing of the very men who continue to murder Afghan civilians in the streets, in schools, banks, and grocery stores.

One of the Facebook groups started in Afghanistan is called the Anti-Taliban Movement. When it launched in March 2011, it reached more than 7,500 members within days, riding a wave of popular anger in response to the president's launch of the High Peace Council, a body established to reach out to the Taliban to initiate negotiations. However, in the same month, the group was hacked by someone posing as a group administrator, who proceeded to delete all the members. Many suspect the hacker was from the Afghan government, noting the resources that would have been necessary to detect and penetrate the site so quickly. Nevertheless, the group quickly relaunched under a slightly different name, with more than 6,000 members rejoining within twenty-four hours. By July 2011, membership had reached over 12,300. The group's administrators monitor it closely and update it daily.

One of those administrators is Omar Ahmadparwani, a twenty-eight-year-old sociology student at Kabul University. He and the others who started the Facebook group never anticipated the kind of response they would receive: "People were adding their friends, posting about it. Yesterday I saw about 10,400 posts are on there, from a span of four months. There are 1,600 pictures that have been posted to the page."[4]

When the group was hacked, Omar and his friends worked for days on end, staying up all night, to rebuild it and track down the original members. Previously, Omar says he might have checked his Facebook account maybe once every three months or so. Suddenly he was online constantly, struggling to keep up with the hourly requests from people wanting to join the group and the need to moderate the posting of content and remove potential infiltrators.

From his desk in an office in one of Kabul's sprawling neighborhoods, Omar, originally from Parwan province, explains that it's generally too dangerous to organize demonstrations in the streets. "We moved our political movement to this medium," he explains. People can stay off the radar of the government and the Taliban. Plus, by using Facebook, youth from across Afghanistan can connect virtually.

"Mostly we want to share our ideas, of the young generation," he says. "It's become more than what we expect. People post their ideas, the news of the day, analysis of the news. . . . If we find something that the media is not reporting, we share things happening behind the scenes."

As a result, media outlets have come to rely on the Facebook group's wall as a source. It is also widely visited by members of parliament, civil society activists, and even government officials. "We were inspired by the events in Egypt," notes Omar. "It gave us the idea how to oppose government, using the only thing accessible to us: making a group, gathering our friends, sharing the ideas."

Taking it to the streets can be risky. "They don't want the civil society to be active in Afghanistan. They want to force us to be quiet." Online too, the youth have to be vigilant. Many people use pseudonyms and avoid posting photos. Omar and his colleagues are aware that they are being monitored by the government. But they're undeterred. One consequence of having lived through the Taliban era and come of age during a period of intense violence is resilience and a fierce determination not to be subdued any longer.

"In this country we have daily crises. We don't fear these things," says Omar. "We have to be careful, but we are in war."

The attention of the government is one sign that Facebook organizing is having an impact. The old political elite, who often harbor radical Islamist leanings, is also taking notice. Burhanuddin Rabbani—leader of the old Mujahedin party, Jamiat-e Islami Afghanistan (Islamic Society of Afghanistan), assassinated by a suicide bomber in September 2011—expressed his anxiety about the potential power of the "Facebook and Internet kids" if "religious leaders fail to play a leadership role in the society."[5]

As Afghanistan's fairly open media covered events in Libya, Bahrain, Egypt, Iran, Tunisia, and elsewhere, the power of social media as a catalyst for protest movements was demonstrated.[6] Politicians are right to be nervous that they will be subject to a transparency not previously possible in Afghanistan's political environment. In the rapidity of its spread among youth,[7] Facebook in Afghanistan has largely slipped out of the control of government. So, too, has the Afghan blogosphere.

"I Think, Therefore I Blog"

Masuma Ibrahimi estimates that there are 30,000 Afghan bloggers. She's the general director of Afghan Cultural House (ACH), a unique center in Kabul's Karte Se neighborhood, where from morning to night there's a steady stream of traffic made up of mainly university students in their twenties. The stately old building tucked away behind an unassuming purple gate is a hub of activity, hosting an art gallery, an Internet café, a library, weekly film nights, and a busy schedule of lectures and conferences. Concerts are sometimes held in the courtyard, and young men and women freely mingle here, debating everything from art to politics to philosophy, as they sip tea and sit around the plastic tables dotting the lawn.

ACH offers blogging workshops and tries to bring together bloggers every month to network with each other face to face. A poster for a blogging workshop shows an image of Rodin's sculpture, *The Thinker*, with the headline "I think, therefore I blog." The poster introduces the concept of citizen journalism, describing it as "members of the public playing an active role in the process of collecting, reporting, analyzing and disseminating news and information," and promises to help registrants learn "how audiences are shaping the future of news and information. The intent of this participation is to provide independent, reliable, accurate, wide-ranging and relevant information that a democracy requires." It's one of several workshops that ACH offers "for young people in Afghanistan to express themselves," as Masuma, who just turned thirty, explains it.[8]

She got the idea three years ago from a blogger named Nasim Fikhrat who runs kabuli.org and presented his own course to help others learn how to blog in 2008. Masuma and ACH took the idea and held similar workshops in Bamiyan, Herat, Mazar-i-Sharif, and even in the turbulent Helmand province. On August 31, 2010, they held a celebration for World Blogging Day,[9] and have plans to establish blogging awards in Afghanistan. They have partnered with the Afghan Association of Blog Writers and recently hosted a visiting delegation from Google.

ACH also wants to make more Afghan blogs accessible to the English-speaking world. Yonus Entezar is ACH's deputy director. He thinks it's a shame that the international community in Afghanistan isn't privy to the rich information and analysis being generated by bloggers writing from diverse regions of the country:

"We discuss very critical issues. For example, in Bamiyan, one of the remote provinces, you can get firsthand information from bloggers. Or from bloggers in Badakhshan. This is a good tool for remote areas. People have access to the Internet from their mobiles and that kind of thing."[10]

ACH's first priority, however, is to help bloggers break free of censorship. Most Afghan bloggers are using Iran-based blogging platforms that facilitate writing in the Perso-Arabic script, like Persian Blog, BlogFa, or Blog Sky. However, these weblog services are filtered by the Iranian regime for content they deem "inappropriate." Masuma, who launched her Girl from Waras[11] blog in 2003, when she was twenty-two, used Persian Blog until her access was twice blocked, the second time after the BBC profiled her. Referring to Iran's hardline Islamist government, Masuma says, "The Iranians won't allow political subjects or good news from Afghanistan, or good things about international people. If anyone wrote that things are getting better in Afghanistan, they would block that." She explains, "When I write to the service provider, they don't reply or give any explanation. They shut it down for a while. Then you understand."

Censorship from within Afghanistan is less severe, but it still exists. The Ministry of Information and Culture has often been a thorn in the side of free expression rather than an incubator for progressive communications and arts. Many bloggers suspect that the ministry is also filtering some blogs and keeping an eye on popular bloggers. "It's hard to track what is being censored and blocked," Yonus explains. "The government says people can have websites, but the policy isn't clear about blogging. The Access to Information Law is not developed yet. Blogging is very new. The government is not sure how to deal with this issue."

He thinks the ministry is merely keeping an eye on the blogosphere. Yet already a popular blog run by an Afghan poet living in Norway has been blocked. And Yonus, who also has his own blog, has received death threats on his mobile phone. "I'm blogging on political issues. I am a Hazara[12] and I was writing about ethnicity. Those circles who don't want open discussion, they have been warning me," he says. Still, the Afghan government may be more malleable than the Iranian government. "The government needs to learn this is good for building democracy and governance, that it's not a waste of time or harmful. It can be used for education," says Yonus. "They are afraid of the technology and of blogging, so we need to change their minds."

ACH is working on developing its own Afghan-owned blog service provider free of Iranian censorship, where people can write posts in Dari, English, and Pashto. In the meantime, Masuma abandoned her Persian Blog and started a new one[13] under her nickname, Suma. She writes on a variety of topics, but often about life in Afghanistan as a woman and life in Kabul. She's rebuilding her following since closing down Girl from Waras. Controversy helps generates traffic to her new site. After she linked to an interview she had given to the BBC where she was shown without a head covering, a lively discussion erupted in the comments section. She was flabbergasted that readers were fixated only on the veiling issue, hardly paying attention to the subject of the article, but she says the incident still demonstrates the value of the medium since it engaged readers in an open discussion where diverse views were freely shared.

Media Renaissance on Twitter

Other young Afghans have found voices on Twitter. In particular, young journalists are using Twitter to report the news as they see it unfold. For instance, when Kabul's Intercontinental Hotel was attacked by insurgents on the night of June 28, 2011, several Afghans were live-tweeting the attack. Lotfullah Najafizada, a manager at Tolo News, was one of them. That night, he first tweeted hearing gunfire in his neighborhood. Within thirty minutes, he reported via Twitter that the Intercon, as it's known in Kabul, was under attack. Throughout the night he tweeted updates to his followers as the situation developed, from details about the security response, number of attackers, and casualties, to his personal observations about what it was like to be so close to the violence: "Gunfire near my ears not letting me sleep," he tweeted in the early hours of June 29.

A few days after the Intercon attack, I was with Lotfullah and his colleague Ehsan Amiri, a producer and senior researcher, at Tolo News headquarters in Kabul's upscale Wazir Akbar Khan neighborhood. Tolo News is one of the media outlets owned by the Moby Group, which also owns Tolo TV, the country's most popular television station and one of the first independent commercial stations to open after the fall of the Taliban. Tolo TV is popular not only for its range and quality of content, but for pushing the boundaries in what it broadcasts. The station has earned the wrath of religious conservatives in government for airing Bollywood soap operas where women are shown unveiled and with bare arms, even featuring the occasional kiss. The station's singing talent show *Afghan Star*, in the spirit of *American Idol*, can draw more than ten million viewers an episode, but has put at least two female contestants in hiding for appearing on the show. A political satire show, *Kankash*, openly criticizes members of the government in its commentary and skits.

As I look around the heads bent over keyboards and people carting around camera equipment, everyone in the station seems incredibly young. Lotfullah, himself only twenty-four, confirms this: "There are rarely people above the age of thirty working here, which means there is a vast motivation and enthusiasm for doing things for the country. That's not limited to our company. You'll find it throughout all the channels."[14] He points out that while youth don't have a strong presence or voice in the government, they are the force behind the country's media renaissance. "The machine functioning this country is run by youth," he says. "People in public affairs, the information technology sector, and many other sectors are run by a very young individual, which is a sign of progress. Youth play a significant role in the country. From being a journalist, I see that we are important and we make decisions for a big number of people."

Social media is taken seriously at Tolo, with staff among the company's 900 employees dedicated solely to updating the Facebook and Twitter feeds. What Lotfullah calls "citizen journalism" is used to drive decisions at Tolo, as the company solicits the views of their audience using social media: "People should be involved in their society and what's happening around them. We want to make sure people get their voices heard through us."

For Lotfullah and Ehsan, Twitter is also a way to document the experience of life amidst war. As Lotfullah was returning from a weekend trip to the picturesque Panjshir Valley, just north of Kabul province, he remarked on the changing security environment: "You know, there is just one tiny gate to enter Panjshir and nowadays you are very thoroughly checked by security forces to make sure no insurgent enters the province. It wasn't the case a year ago. I found it interesting and tweeted it. It was like entering a different country, just to go to Panjshir."

Bilal Sarwary, in his late twenties, is an Afghan journalist with the BBC in Kabul. His career in journalism inadvertently started after 9/11, when he was working at the Intercontinental Hotel in Peshawar, which was suddenly flooded with foreign media as the world's attention turned to that corner of the world. He found himself thrust into the role of fixer (translator and guide) for Abu Dhabi TV, and before he knew it was accompanying reporters to Tora Bora as the Taliban fled Kabul and Osama bin Laden made his escape over the mountains. Since then, he's worked in TV, radio, documentary film production, and online news. A prolific tweeter, he never sets down his Blackberry as we sit talking in the garden of the BBC's compound in Kabul, a fountain serenely gurgling into a small pool nearby. He pauses occasionally to check his Twitter feed and acknowledges being an addict: "If I am in a province or far away, I feel as if my fingers are itching."[15]

Sent to cover a military operation in a remote area in the north, he encountered a villager in the mountains and asked him whether he had seen any Taliban in the area. "And he said they are like clouds. They appear and they disappear. I tweeted what he had said, and it was picked up by five or six different countries, it was re-tweeted everywhere."

It was when Bilal won a full scholarship in 2006 to study for a degree at Middlebury College in Vermont that he discovered Facebook. By the time he returned to Kabul in 2010, he noticed that journalists everywhere were using Twitter. "I just started by tweeting about life in Afghanistan," he recalls, "then I started with newsy items, not hard news, but soft news about, say, farmers' complaints, for example. I got four hundred followers in about a week. I got all sorts of messages from people in Africa and other parts of the world."

His followers soon grew to nearly 2,000. He tweets in Dari, Pashto, Urdu, and English. He also uses Twitter to keep in contact with other Afghan journalists: "We're connected by Twitter, we rely heavily on it. It decreases the phone bill!" he laughs. He's helped others open Twitter accounts, including Kabul's police chief, General Mohammad Ayub Salangi, who is now tweeting regularly. "It's good. Politicians should do this," says Bilal, who thinks that the more politicians communicate with their constituents, the better it is for democracy. Bilal also uses Twitter to consume information from others. He follows news sites, organizations, and even Oprah. Sometimes, he tweets verses from poems he likes or from poetry he's written himself. He can't seem to stop typing.

Afghanistan is a country that yields story after story, from the uplifting to the wrenchingly painful. And as Bilal roams from province to province, it's become automatic for him to report what he sees as he sees it, and to express what he thinks and feels about the complicated world in which he lives. It's one way to cope with the perpetual violence and loss, and with the risk inherent in being a journalist in Afghanistan. "I've made my decision to do this work. There are days when I leave for a trip or for work and I think I might not come back," he tells me. "Sometimes I can't contain my emotions on Facebook or Twitter, when I have lost friends, like people who work for the government who are killed."

Bilal's contention that Twitter is a powerful means of disseminating information has been validated numerous times as he's unearthed new information by live-tweeting from the scene of a story. When hundreds of Taliban made a daring escape from the Kandahar city jail in April 2011, he interviewed a shopkeeper near the prison who was disgruntled over money owed to him by Taliban commanders who had been getting soft drinks from the shop as they came and went from the area in the weeks leading up to the attack. It was evidence that Taliban commanders had been present for a while and had been planning the attack for some time.

Fighting with Words, Not Bullets

Despite the prevailing weak governance, the Karzai administration's apparent keenness to bend toward the Taliban, and the general uncertainty of the future, for young Afghans like Masuma, Yonus, Bilal, Ehsan, and Lotfullah there is no going back. The country has fundamentally and profoundly changed in their view, and they insist that the change is irreversible. "In Afghanistan we were like birds in a cage, totally cut off from the outside world, but now we understand the world is a global village. It's a cliché, but it's true," says Bilal. "The whole world is in Afghanistan now, so maybe it's not surprising. Political rivalries are being fought on social media. It's better for people to fight with words, not bullets. It can heal the wounds from bullets. It's better to fight with words."

Indeed, it may be the "Internet kids," as the old warlord Rabbani called them, who precipitate the shift to a peace that *is* tolerable — that includes justice and human rights. As their government implodes in its own inefficiency and fails to invest in democratic process, it's these "kids" who are actually embodying the idea of citizenship and taking up the right to demand the accountability that was promised to them. They are refusing to self-censor, despite the risks. "We don't believe in censorship," Lotfullah says. "We can't work under that kind of pressure. We have a commitment to the country. Yes, some powerful people try to warn us sometimes, but it doesn't mean we follow those instructions."

And they see clearly the relationship between the media, an open society, and democracy. Lotfullah explains, "We consider our mistakes and what happened to this country in the past, so we think we have a greater responsibility now to strengthen democracy and help people have their right to be informed. This is the motivation. It's responsible journalism, looking at how we can impact the society. Nothing like this has occurred in the history of Afghanistan. We are the luckiest journalists in the history of Afghanistan. We have a great amount of freedom, which we never had before."

Bilal, too, is savoring the right to report the truth as he sees it, and to have a voice. "If you look back at the history of this country, during the communist time, you could get put in jail and tortured if you listened to the BBC or Radio Free Europe," he says. "It's powerful today that you can speak like this." He is ardent that social media serves as a check on the government, and the more people who have access to this form of communication the more forceful will be the change.

Omar, of the Anti-Taliban Movement, emphasizes that he and his collaborators created their Facebook group to demonstrate young people's discontent with the government's efforts to negotiate with the Taliban and to counter the idea that Afghans "don't deserve democratic government.

"We oppose being sacrificed for Karzai's irrational decisions. We oppose having tribal political systems. We oppose being killed politically for big powers' wishes. We oppose the U.S. not keeping their promises made to Afghanistan's people. We oppose being once again left to neighboring countries' hands. We don't want the world to make a decision so carelessly to leave us alone. We oppose losing all we have achieved in the last ten years. We want to fight for our future."[16]

In Afghanistan, good citizenship has evolved before good statehood, and it may be these young citizens who end up becoming the first true architects of democracy in their country.

Notes

1. Afghanistan's first constitution was adopted in 1923, as a result of an urban-based political movement for constitutional monarchy that started during the reign of Amir Habibullah Khan in the late nineteenth century. It was replaced in 1931 after the deposition of King Amanullah. Afghanistan's 1964 constitution was considered especially progressive and held up as a model in the Muslim world. It was replaced in

1976 after the fall of the monarchy. A new constitution was adopted by the communist government in 1987, and replaced again in 1990. Parliamentary democracy was also introduced in Afghanistan in 1964, but was cut short with the 1979 Soviet invasion and not reintroduced until after the fall of the Taliban in 2001. Despite the difficulty in sustaining democratic institutions in Afghanistan, the country nevertheless has a long and rich history of activism for democracy, from protests to the formation of democratic political parties.

2. From the 2010 Corruption Perceptions Index of Transparency International, wherein Afghanistan and Myanmar (Burma) tied for the rank of 176 out of 178 countries (http://www.transparency.org/).

3. A division of the UN's Department of Economic and Social Affairs of the United Nations Secretariat.

4. Omar Ahmadparwani, interview, June 30, 2011, Kabul.

5. Recorded March 3, 2011, during the General Meeting of Ulama in Afghanistan, Kabul.

6. Media freedom is enshrined in the 2004 constitution, and the media sector has seen exponential growth since 2002. There is a high number of independent television and radio stations, as well as newspapers and magazines. However, self-censorship is often practiced as many issues remain taboo, as was demonstrated when twenty-three-year-old Pervez Kambakhsh was sentenced to death in a hasty 2008 trial for reproducing critical material on Islam and women in an article for a local newspaper. The threat of being accused of blasphemy remains a very real concern for journalists, as the clergy and Islamist political leaders exercise undue influence. Further, female journalists, singers, and newscasters have been threatened and even killed. Thus, while media freedom has significantly improved since the fall of the Taliban, there remain important freedom of expression and human rights concerns in the sector.

7. In 2011, Facebook had nearly 200,000 users in Afghanistan, according to an estimate from an activist with Afghan Culture House.

8. Interview, July 4, 2011, Kabul.

9. Officially known simply as BlogDay, August 31 was declared World Blogging Day in 2005 by Nir Ofir, an Israeli blogger and web entrepreneur. The official website is http://www.blogday.org/.

10. Interview, July 4, 2011, Kabul.

11. Named for the district she comes from in Bamiyan province.

12. Hazaras are one of Afghanistan's many ethnic groups, representing an estimated 9 percent of the Afghan population, in addition to large populations living in Iran and Pakistan as refugees or migrants. The origins of the Hazara people lie in the migrations of male Mongols into Central Asia, including the raids of Genghis Khan and his army into central Afghanistan and elsewhere. Hazaras generally belong to the Shi'a sect of Islam, while approximately 75 to 80 percent of Afghanistan's population practices Sunni Islam. This has sometimes led to sectarian persecution and violence toward Hazaras. However, Hazaras have also experienced discrimination because of their distinctive physical features that easily distinguish them from other ethnic groups like Pashtuns and Tajiks. This discrimination has included forced migration (such as when Hazaras were expelled from Helmand province), subjugation of Hazara areas (such as by the nineteenth-century Afghan king Abdur Rahman Khan), and massacres of Hazaras by Pashtuns, culminating most recently in massacres perpetrated by

the Taliban in Bamiyan and Mazar-i-Sharif (8,000 civilians killed in 1998, as documented by Human Rights Watch).

13. See http://masumaibrahimi.blogspot.com/.
14. Interview, July 3, 2011, Kabul.
15. Bilal Sarwary, interview, July 2, 2011, Kabul.
16. Personal correspondence, March 19, 2011.

CHAPTER 19

The New Storytellers of Afghanistan

JOANNA SHERMAN

We are driving on the dusty road to Shamoli, surrounded by the rocky hills that grow into craggy mountains in the distance. We are actors from Bond Street Theatre,[1] and we are going to meet a storyteller—one of the last of Afghanistan's old traditions, and the roots of its theatre.

We walk through the village, dirt paths well worn under our feet. A passel of kids runs alongside us and up ahead. We attract attention as foreigners—foreigners haven't been seen here since the Soviet invaders came and left. The kids are mostly boys. We passed girls busy washing clothes in the stream, little ones just four or five years old, with older sisters maybe seven or eight. The girls work; the boys play. This is the way it is in Afghanistan. I am here to make theatre happen and am determined to include the girls.

The storyteller is an old guy with a long, scraggly white beard and a goofy smile revealing a few brave teeth still hanging in there. He settles down with the other grownups on the cushions that line the room, Afghan-style, and the kids fill in the gaps, crawling over each other to get closer to the action. They surround the house and peer in the glassless windows. We all patiently have tea. Nothing happens without first having tea.

This fellow is a true storyteller, through and through. He acts out every part, his voice changing with each character, arms and legs waggling in gesture, his face a myriad of expressions. He is telling us about the funny war times—those laugh-a-minute years when the Soviets blew up homes, forced young men to join their militia, pillaged, raped, slaughtered. Not funny at all, but the old guy is telling us how he was stuck in a hole with a few other fellows and they're all drinking tea (of course). There's just one little air hole in their lair. Pretty soon nature calls and our narrator is desperate. His friends exclaim, "Hey! You can't do that in here!" But what to do? There's no leaving the hiding place with Soviets outside shooting anything that moves. His friends say, "Stick it out the little hole." "No!" he cries, "they'll shoot it off!" By now, the room is howling with laughter at the image—the crowded hiding hole, the tea, the urgency. The kids are squealing with delight and poking each other.

All his stories are a little raunchy and often scatological. There was the one about how the Soviets finally find him and force him to fight on their side. But he is such a clumsy, inept soldier that during his first task to fix the out-house, he falls backward into the muck. The boys are howling, the men—who have no doubt heard these stories a million times and watched them grow over the years to outlandish proportions—are laughing out loud nonetheless. We foreigners get the joke a minute later (after translation), but we can't help laughing along. The guy is a gem. And all the grownups become kids in his presence.

Another story starts bubbling up, but we tear ourselves away. As we leave the village, we pass the girls, now busy gathering wood or fetching water to bring to waiting mothers, busy and efficient as little girls can be. All of them are dolled up in sparkly little dresses. Little girls love their sparkles, no matter where in the world. I tell myself that surely they've heard the storyteller before. Surely they get their chance to play.

We stop by the side of the road near a deserted Soviet tank and watch as a group of kids push the giant, protruding gun barrel with all the energy their little hands can muster until it's totally turned around and facing in the oppo-site direction. Quick as they can, they jump aboard and catch a ride while the giant gun swings a wide arc around to the other side. It stops with a bump, dropping the laughing kids on the ground. Then they're up and pushing it again for another ride. It's a Soviet-tank amusement park! The best toy ever. Who needs a slide or a jungle gym? And the girls were taking rides right along with the boys. See? Girls have some fun.

If the Soviets Had Won the War

Sometimes I think it would have been better if the Soviets had won the war. They believed girls should be educated as engineers or doctors, should have choices in their lives. They brought modernity. Women drove cars, went to movies, ate at restaurants in the open, not hidden behind "women only" cur-tained areas. There were science books, literature, theatre, and the arts. Hard to imagine these days. It's like time flew backward.

I know about these wild times thanks to Anisa Wahab,[2] the Shirley Temple of Afghanistan. Her story is singular. Her father was an art-loving man who encouraged his children to cut their own paths. Anisa was a precocious and natural actress. Few parents would have seen and nurtured her potential at age seven. It was 1963 and there was an audition notice for a child to play a little boy in a TV show. Anisa's father encouraged her to audition despite being clearly a girl. She beat out all the boys and got the part! Her first role put her in public view and she won their hearts. Audiences just loved her. She was cute, infectious, and could play any part. Years later, when I worked with her, she was still nimble and versatile, playing a little boy, an old woman, a musician, and a young mother with grace and ease in our historical play about Afghanistan, *Beyond the Mirror*.[3]

Anisa's childhood was a dream: travel, fame, the love of her whole country. She was an icon of little girlness at its best—energetic, talented, and funny, her films immensely popular. Her star power continued as she grew. It helped that she never really grew "up." She was tiny, maybe four foot ten inches, and I doubt if she weighed more than eighty pounds.

Then the Soviets left and chaos reigned. Many fled Afghanistan and Anisa, no longer able to appear in public, spent years in Pakistan waiting for a chance to return to the country that loved her. That's where I met her, frail but spirited, a refugee in Peshawar, creating theatre in the limited environment of refugee life as a member of a group of exiled actors who called themselves Exile Theatre, a group that became our long-time collaborators.

When the time was right to return, in 2002, Anisa was no longer a child, but she was still a star. As Afghanistan emerged from ruin, she reemerged on television, and everyone remembered her. As she walked down the streets of Kabul, the children would whisper, "Anisa! There's Anisa Wahab." She returned to a TV career without a second thought, although now she was playing the funny aunt or gossipy neighbor. She was still cute, though the years of hardship had taken its toll on her. Her smile was still often and infectious, but I wonder how her life would have been . . . if the Soviets had won the war.

Performing in the Refugee Camps

I came to the country in 2002, just after September 11 reminded us that Afghanistan was on the map. Actually, I went to Pakistan first, with members of my theatre group, Bond Street Theatre, to work in the refugee camps. This was a likely destination for us, having spent years using theatre to tackle thorny issues in countries in crisis. We had worked in refugee camps in Kosovo, Bosnia, and Palestine; entertained street children in Colombia and Brazil; and presented political theatre in East Berlin while the wall was still standing. When we're asked, "Why do theatre for refugees? Don't they need food, shelter, medicine?" we quote the physician from Doctors Without Borders, who told us, "We are providing refugees the necessities for human survival—food, medicine, shelter—but you are providing them with food for the soul. You are restoring their humanity."

The Afghan camps were architecturally diverse depending on which stage of which war you left to settle here. Some were composed of scrappy tents raised in a hurry that hardly gave shelter; some were tidy, well-organized tents provided by the United Nations; and some were villages with high mud walls surrounding attractive, although rudimentary, mud homes. Many children had been born in these camps and had colorful maps and pictures of Afghanistan on their walls, a promise they would return home someday to these green hills and wide boulevards. Imagine their surprise upon returning to see hardly stone upon stone, let alone green gardens and boulevards.

We went to work in the refugee schools, giving workshops to boys and girls in theatre games to help open their minds and hearts, and circus skills to challenge them. We also performed. In some camps where the families had recently arrived, the children were pale, with the kind of relentless fear that makes even the face of a child seem old. Some were children of Taliban who had fled NATO warplanes that routed them out of their villages. Ironic that those fleeing the Taliban's harsh rules were suddenly mixed together with the Taliban themselves.

This thought gave us pause when performing in the quickly assembled camp schools. Who was our audience this time? Were they aghast that a woman was performing, sharing the stage with a man? At one show, our hosts asked us exactly what we would be doing. We explained it was just a funny show to make the kids laugh. After all, they had not laughed in a long time.

"So you aren't on stage together then, are you?"

"Oh yes, we perform together."

"You don't touch, do you?"

"Yes, because we are doing some acrobatic routines and we must touch each other."

"Well there's no music, is there?"

"Yes, for the dancing."

"Dancing! You're dancing?"

"Well, yes, but just on stilts."

"What?"

We decided to show them a video. We flipped open the camera and they watched our show on a 2- by 3-inch screen. After just a few moments they agreed. Apparently, we were dressed and behaving in such an unusual manner that we wouldn't really be seen as being male or female or even human.

Perhaps cartoon characters. And we made the children laugh a lot. After every show, the kids told us their faces hurt from laughing, "because we never laugh."

The children were most intrigued with the stilts. Long pants hide the wooden poles strapped to our legs, making us appear as giants, impossibly tall, yet comical and non-threatening. Knowing children's awe at such magic, we brought kid-size stilts with us for the children to try. If our post-performance workshops taught nothing else, the art of stilt-walking was the most uplifting, physically and emotionally. Children, suddenly taller than their parents and teachers, strode about, wobbly, but beaming with pride. Girls, rarely allowed to be so physically adventurous, were thrilled. To achieve something easily that looks impossible is empowering in every sense. We have taught stilts to rural women in India, barefoot in their saris; hefty cleaning staff at the Pentagon; eighty-year-old grandmothers; and four-star generals—all of them skeptical, then hooked.

Afghanistan Recovering

In 2003, we went into Afghanistan with the goal of finding the children and setting things right again through the exhilarating experience of theatre. We performed in villages broken down by years of war. Everyone turned out to see these shows outdoors in the dusty schoolyards. No swing sets or basketball courts here. Just dirt. The kids sat in front, but the ring of adults behind them got bigger and bigger with each village we visited. Word had traveled ahead of us that something amazing was coming to town, and everyone, not just the children, was hungry for diversion. These villagers had never seen a performance, ever, and we wondered if they would laugh at the same things that made us laugh—the funny business and slapstick.

If there's one thing I've learned in my travels, it's that what makes kids laugh anywhere in the world is the same. If you fall down, kids laugh; if you squirt water from your mouth, kids laugh; if you accidentally on purpose smack someone, kids laugh. It seems to be the universal kid heaven—adults making fools of themselves. I often think it's because they have learned not to fall and know how to eat, and seeing a grownup that doesn't have these basics together is hilarious. They aren't laughing with us, they're laughing at us. And we don't mind a bit.

Except at one school. Word had gotten out that something wicked was coming. One teacher was clearly fresh with Talib teachings and had instructed his class of older boys that the foreign "guests" were not to be welcomed. We set up stage in a patch of dirt and the boys all eagerly gathered around, little ones sitting in the front, a bit older squatting behind, and standing behind them all the older boys. We couldn't help but notice their grim faces.

We began our show—a pratfall or two—the little ones falling over each other in delight, until, SMACK! The older ones hit the kids on the back of the head. Another comic bit, the kids giggle happily. SMACK. Another hit on the back of their heads. How could they help but laugh? This is the first comedy they'd ever seen—cartoon characters come to life. Every time the kids laughed, they received a smack until the audience was stone silent. We were surrounded by a ring of sullen, uncomfortable, confused, gray faces.

Now we were up to the acrobatic routine. I felt the first stone hit my face— a tiny one and it stung. Then another and my performing partner whispers between clenched teeth, "Let's get out of here, and fast." We finish our show, bow to the ring of sullen faces, grab our gear, and head for the office, tiny stones still pelting the back of our necks. We were crushed, not for ourselves, but for the little ones who weren't allowed to laugh. I can only hope our antics remained in their minds to enjoy in their private musings. Later, we heard that the teacher had been dismissed.

This was Afghanistan in 2003—so much hope for the future amid a backdrop of rubble. Homeless children wandered the streets in little family clusters: big brothers with small parades of siblings now left to their own devices. The orphanages quickly filled with boys. Girls, considered more vulnerable, were more often taken in by relatives.

Besides offering these children a little laughter, we gave them social skills. Little kids who live on the streets make their own laws, generally centering around who is biggest—survival of the fittest. Our workshops using simple theatre games were a revelation. "Let's make a circle." No one ever asked them to do this before. "I'm going to give out these pencils one at a time." One at a time! A brand-new concept to kids who could kill each other over a pencil. And the biggest surprise of all were the games—the idea that you could follow rules and actually have more fun in the process. Duck duck goose, cat and mouse, *kaka ama* (uncle aunt). If this sounds a lot like kindergarten, it is. Because that is what they had missed, that setting where one learns to cooperate with others, share, win and lose, and see oneself as an active player in a game not of your own construction.

But how do you gather street-working children scattered throughout the cities? Food. Children's centers put out the word they are offering a hot lunch. News travels fast. Once the children are there, the center squeezes in an hour of schooling before the children must go back to work the streets. We gave our shows and workshops during that hour of peace before they returned to the streets. But, even in that hour, their eyes are opened, their minds stimulated, and they take the games with them.

Afghanistan Regressing

More than a decade has passed. The hopefulness of 2003 has slowly eroded. The lingering war, the growing influence of Pakistan, the corrupt officials, the suitcases of money in the hands of a few, have made people skeptical, yet more self-reliant. Afghanistan is reeling backward to not-so-distant memories of chaos and war. Women and girls have problems now that they thought were over. Our work in Afghanistan has changed with the times. The children we first met are teenagers now, and laughter is not enough. They have more to say.

I first saw Behnaz[4] on the stage in 2005, when she was thirteen. A small group of girls from the northern province of Kunduz had created a theatre group, completely on their own with no apparent outside influence or training. They were presenting a play at one of the first post-war Kabul Theatre Festivals[5] held in the newly patched theatre at Kabul University, a building that the Taliban had failed to thoroughly demolish in their attempt to eliminate everything they deemed un-Islamic. After so many lost years, most of the acting was clumsy and amateurish but with a passionate determination to talk about the war.

Then Behnaz took the stage, dressed as a little man with a fake moustache and turban, a servant to two bearded scholars. As they pored over their tomes, she dusted around them, peered over their shoulders, and carried on a monologue concerning how little about life they knew from their books. She was witty and wise, with the comic timing of a pro, and kept the audience in stitches. Unflappable, she improvised around the two straight men and stole the show.

Behnaz obviously had the genes of a storyteller, a comedienne, perhaps the next Anisa Wahab. Afterward, I asked how this small group of girls got it into their heads to form a theatre group, practice intently with no training, and head hundreds of miles from Kunduz to Kabul to perform for scores of strangers. The Taliban had strictly forbidden all arts—no music, dancing, singing, painting, performing. What was the girls' influence, their model? They shrugged. This idea to perform, to tell a story onstage with funny characters, a comic plot, and a heady message was pulled out of some corner of their imagination, some intrinsic need to comment on life.

Two years later, in 2007, a small prop plane flew us up north to Kunduz to offer the group some actual theatre training. Behnaz, at age fifteen, was now the director, commanding a troupe of twelve girls and four boys, ages twelve to seventeen. She trained them as well as she could, instilling the discipline to work hard at their craft, and they all were poised and confident onstage. We worked with the group every day for two weeks, giving them a crash course in physical theatre—from the essentials of body language to physicalizing text, plus mask-making, mime, puppetry, *commedia*, martial arts, vocal techniques, and, of course, stilts. They loved it all!

Over the weeks, we got to know the girls' aspirations. They wanted to become astronauts, teachers, and politicians. The theatre training is a good preparation for their eventual careers, and they learn to speak out with self-assurance. Yet each day they slip beneath the veil as they step out the door. "In a few years things will be different," says Behnaz. "We don't mind it, but too bad it covers the whole face," says another.

At the end, the group demonstrated the techniques they had learned to the local community. Behnaz stood in front of rows and rows of men much older than she and told them how performing on the stage was not forbidden in Islam, and should be encouraged as a way for young people to speak about important topics. They all looked at her in amazement, her courage completely disarming. I hope they were listening.

However, as the audience began filing into the courtyard, the other girls' faith began to falter. When confronted with an audience of men, maybe a future husband, they begged me, please, could they wear their masks for the entire show. But finally, the girls did perform, unmasked, and the audience response was superlative. It remains remarkable that these young women decided to create theatre against all odds.

By 2011, Kunduz was off-limits. The Taliban had taken control of much of the province and Behnaz's group had to disband. Most left the area for safer cities. Behnaz went to Kabul to study law, planning to use her prodigious performance skills and sense of humor to win legal debates on the rights of women. She has found the perfect stage for her talents in a country where women and girls have little access to justice.

A Tentative Future

I am working in a Pashtun area now—Nangarhar and Kandahar, home of the Taliban, whoever they are. It's not like a club you join. It's a convenient label for insurgents who often are just impoverished young men looking to "join the army and see the world," or incited by an unjust death in the family, or answering the need for a paycheck, or swayed by a teacher like the one we encountered in the refugee school back in 2002, eager to throw a stone at foreigners.

We still bring theatre to children as a means to uplift and heal, but now theatre has a new imperative as a way to bring information to isolated communities. The messages in our plays—about women's rights, children's rights, domestic violence, rule of law, corruption—are becoming more and more urgent. The target audiences are children who must be able to imagine a peaceful, productive future, but also the men and women who influence them.

These days I am focused on creating all-girls theatre troupes that perform for all-female audiences, the only acceptable way women dare appear onstage. However, this path is fraught with challenges: women rarely leave their homes or villages, most cannot read or write, few have electricity or access to media, and misinformation and harmful traditional practices rule their lives. The process of bringing together women or girls interested in joining a performance project who can also gain permission from their families is near impossible. Theatre is not widely known and is easily confused with Bollywood or television dramas and films from outside Afghanistan that don't conform to the traditional view of dress and behavior, particularly for women. Television is forbidden to girls in many homes, and even radio is often considered a male domain.

Nonetheless, we have created four all-female theatre groups in four provinces so far, and are working to unite them for mutual support and security. Our best method is to work in tandem with all-male groups (as most groups are), where men dress as women to play female parts. In our women's groups, the girls dress as men. I have often suspected that the men enjoy mincing about as women, with floppy wigs and ill-fitting dresses, but I assure you that the women love playing men. They have no trouble taking on the role of an abusive husband or dismissive policeman.

However, theatre has become a dangerous occupation again, even for the men. We can no longer travel blithely into the villages where we once were gladly greeted. Even the local theatre groups are hesitant to visit some areas. Our work has turned more to training than performing.

Women, especially, live on a fragile precipice. They are like Behnaz and Anisa, full of talent and hope, yet they keep themselves hidden. Dare to step out of bounds by working with a foreigner, having a job, walking alone, going to school, showing your face, or ankle, or foot—all can bring the wrath of some righteous man upon you. Or woman. Virtually all the young women we have trained are plagued by death threats. Text messages say, "I know where you live and this is a warning, next time a bullet," and "Hear these screams?

They will be yours." How can these messages be ignored? Go to the police? Maybe they are involved. Even in your burqa they recognize your feet, your gait, your hands. This is what keeps bright young women behind the high walls of their homes, and keeps women from taking the stage. Yet, undaunted, they still come to our workshops and make plays out of their stories.

Women are allowed to perform for other women. But, to avoid misunderstandings, we always invite the mullahs to see what we are doing. We tell them about the workshops: we are teaching the girls how to solve problems in the family. The training focuses on themes of conflict and solutions, using the girls' experiences and perceptions to explore the issues and then creating plays that the girls devise themselves.

The workshops also highlight self-expression and communication skills, and all means to build self-confidence. A most compelling exercise is one in which the girls stand in a line and, one by one, each girl yells her name loudly as though calling over a mountain. The group then echoes her name back to her. If, for your entire life, you have been taught to be neither seen nor heard, it's difficult to yell your name. In the next step, each girl goes forward and faces the line of girls as though they are the mountain. Then she calls out her name, and the mountain again echoes back loudly. Even for a professional, it is a bit shocking to hear your name thrown back at you so dynamically. But as one girl told us, "This is the first time I have felt like a real person. Yes, I am Marzia!"

The girls, all in their mid-teens, were eager to show their play to the mullahs, although a bit shy in front of these important guests. Two clerics came to the private showing—one old and smiley, the other young and sullen. The girls bravely enacted their drama.

The play is about a new young bride now living with the husband's family. The mother-in-law is a grim, angry woman who rails against the young girl at every chance, complains to the husband about how lazy she is, and lies that she saw the girl in the marketplace with her face exposed. "You must beat your wife," she tells her son. "Aren't you man enough?" The mother-in-law is played by a girl of thirteen, but clearly she knows women like this and plays every nuance perfectly. We discover that the mother-in-law, as a young bride, had been treated the same by her mother-in-law, and probably hers before that in a long line of woman-on-woman abuse. The powerless seek out those with even less.

A friend comes to visit the old woman and sees her beating the young bride. "Why do you beat her," she rails, "what has she done? Don't you recognize yourself? Look at me, I abused my son's bride and she burned herself. Now the girl is dead, my son has left me, and I am alone. I wait to hear someone knock at my door. Is this what you want?" The old woman replies, "But it is too late for me, I cannot change."

In the end, she reconciles with the young girl and the son is glad. And so is the sullen young mullah. The older one wipes away a tear. "I didn't know what theatre was," he says. "This is a good message. You can continue your work." And then, "I want you to do this play at the mosque."

It is beyond unusual to request a performance by women at a mosque. Perhaps more important, each troupe of girls has also presented their performance at the women's prison in their province. In Herat, an inmate told the young actors that she wished her own mother-in-law had seen their show, because she was in prison for killing the mother-in-law after years of abuse. Often, women cry and embrace the girls afterwards, so appreciative are they of the girls' talent and message. I am sure this is what keeps the girls going. No matter how it's presented, live theatre, right in front of people's eyes, is a wondrous new experience, and audiences are entranced, hanging on the actors' every word.

Samira's Story

Samira is not the daughter of a mullah, but she may soon be a mullah's wife. At seventeen, she is only in the ninth grade, having missed years of schooling, and she is determined to hold off this wedding forever . . . or at least until she finishes high school. Government law says she has the right to consent or refuse any proposed marriage, but custom says her nearest male relative has final say.

Samira was born in Laghman, a poor farming region with tidy mud-walled houses, well-swept dirt floors, and the unfortunate reputation of being home to "stupid backward folk." Laghman jokes abound in Afghanistan like "redneck" jokes do in the United States. Her mother died while giving Samira life, leaving her, her father, and older brother, Nabil. When the father found a new wife, she refused to marry him unless he divested himself of his children. Nabil and Samira were packed off to live with her mother's mother in an even more remote district where schooling was not an option. The two children clung to each other and, when the grandmother passed on, were shuffled to a relative in Pakistan, where at least they could begin school. Samira has not seen her father since he gave her away.

When I met Samira she was living with her uncle, a mullah, in a household of six girls and four brothers. Nabil had married and lived apart. The mullah was an open-minded man who permitted his girls to go to school, strictly enforcing their study time and demanding perfect grades. Four of these girls and Samira attended our theatre program, a tribute to this mullah.

We paid each girl a small stipend to attend the workshops, a typical incentive although it attracts a few attendees just interested in the fee. I don't mind; the theatre training will help those girls too. They will learn to speak out loud without giggling, hold their heads high without hiding their faces, and stand up straight and speak to the world with confidence.

The mullah's daughters were the best actors in the group, smart and courageous, and Samira was the best of them all. Her face, always tight-lipped and pinched, relaxed and gave way to a new countenance as she slipped into her roles. She became formidable and fearsome playing the abusive father, animated and clever as the narrator, determined yet gentle as the young mother. When she finished her part, her face sank back into its usual look of patient despair, the gaze of someone much older.

It wasn't long before the mullah changed his mind about Samira's future: wasn't it about time she married? Her betrothed, another mullah, was now thirty and getting impatient. And the sisters decided having this freeloading cousin wasn't so much fun anymore. It was okay when she was her usual downcast self, but she was stealing their glow when she lit up the stage. She moved in with her brother, who has remained her sole true friend. But, like a bad fairytale, his wife turns on her whenever the brother turns his back.

I visit Samira when I can. She is still a pale beauty with the same tense gaze, still going to high school with her cousins, still trying to keep the girls' performing group alive, and still quietly warding off the imminent threat of marriage. In the end, her brother will make that call.

The New Storytellers

I would love to drive to Shamoli to see the storyteller again, but it's a much more dangerous journey now. Does he know that Anisa Wahab has died? The old storytellers are the last link to one of the country's most essential traditions.

Theatre opens the doors to young minds and hearts, giving kids a way to tell their own tales. It allows them to imagine a future where the abusive husband learns his lesson, where the mother-in-law realizes her mistake, where the girl marries the man of her choice. If you can't imagine a better future, you can't go there. Hopefully, creating and telling these stories gives the children of Afghanistan the courage and strength to demand happy endings in their own life stories.

When the old storytellers pass on, who will act out stories for the children of Afghanistan? Who will make comedy out of tragedy, make tears of joy from tears of sorrow? Why, the children themselves, of course!

Notes

1. Bond Street Theatre was founded in 1976 by a group of physically skilled actors dedicated to innovative theatre and motivated by a passion to be useful in this world. The company creates theatre works that address social and environmental issues and uses the performing arts as humanitarian outreach in areas of conflict, poverty, and post-war crises. The ensemble collaborates with local artists to enjoy the benefits of artistic exchange and promotes the arts as a means to advance human rights and shape a peaceful world. Current focus areas: Afghanistan, Haiti, Guatemala, and Myanmar. Bond Street Theatre is an NGO in association with the United Nations and receives support from the United States government, the United States Institute for Peace, private foundations, and individual donors. The company has performed in major festivals and theatres around the world and reached critical communities on five continents.

2. Anisa Wahab was born in 1957 in Kabul, worked over forty-six years in theatre and cinema in Afghanistan, and died in 2010. To see Anisa in action, visit http://www.youtube.com/watch?v=o8JqLGtPF_c; to see her in *Beyond the Mirror* with Exile Theatre and Bond Street Theatre, visit http://www.bondst.org/activities/12/us-premier-of-beyond-the-mirror.

3. *Beyond the Mirror*, collaboratively created by Bond Street Theatre of New York and Exile Theatre of Kabul, was presented in Afghanistan, Japan, and the U.S. in 2005, and again in the U.S. in 2009. The production received acclaim from the *New York Times*, *Washington Post*, *Baltimore Sun*, *San Francisco Chronicle*, CNN, NPR, and other news media as the first-ever U.S.-Afghan theatre collaboration, and the first Afghan theatre group to perform in the United States. The play was directed by Joanna Sherman and Mahmood Shah Salimi.

4. For the girls' safety, all names, except for Anisa Wahab, have been changed.

5. The first postwar Afghan National Theatre Forum took place in Kabul in 2004, with 49 performances presented by theatre makers from across Afghanistan. Minister of Higher Education Dr. Sharif Fayez announced, "My wish is that our great sons and daughters once again delight in their artistic abilities." The first version of *Beyond the Mirror* was presented at this Festival in 2004, and the fully developed version at the Festival in 2005. The play introduced a new "stylistic method that is physical, visual and non-verbal . . . rather than a narrative dialogue-based play" (ISAF News, March 2005). The seventh Afghan National Theatre Festival took place in Kabul in 2012.

CHAPTER 20

Six Epiphanies: Testament to Change from Inside an Afghan Orphanage

IAN POUNDS

The following are select narratives from my time as an American volunteer in Afghanistan in 2009. After an initial summer living and teaching inside a girls' orphanage, I was invited to stay. I moved my life to Kabul as a permanent volunteer for four years. Toward the end of 2012 I was compelled to leave after a fatwa *was issued, situating me as a direct target, endangering the people around me.*

The Afghan Child Education and Care Organization (AFCECO) was founded and is directed by Andeisha Farid, a young and fearless Afghan woman who as a small child was displaced by war after the Soviets destroyed her village. AFCECO's principle is simple: transform a tragedy—the endless stream of orphaned Afghan children—into a source of positive change from within. These narratives by definition are not necessarily about joyful moments in the orphanage. Joy for all of us there was a daily occurrence. Here I wish to relate those moments that illustrate the unique combination of innocence and wisdom these brave and willing children exhibited, and how I learned more about myself as an American than I ever could have gleaned back home. While Afghanistan in many ways reeled, AFCECO thrived. It expanded to twelve orphanages serving more than 2,000 children over time, and it implemented a full athletic program for boys and girls, a learning center, music and art, as well as a foreign cultural exchange. (During the winter of 2011–2012, I toured the United States with six of the children in a 33-foot RV for three months, covering 10,000 miles.) All these programs were meant to enhance the inadequate public education, to adhere to notions that a true democracy stems from a liberal arts education. Unfortunately, today AFCECO is under tremendous pressure from extreme elements in the Afghan government. Additionally, money is drying up as the military economy withdraws. Regardless, AFCECO will continue to serve children, because now a generation of children, having grown up in the orphanages, will keep the mission alive.

There is no better example of this outlook than a most memorable moment when three older girls from my leadership workshop visited a West Point middle school. These students' military fathers and mothers were serving in Afghanistan. At the end of the girls' presentation, wherein they shared their life stories, all 450 students in a unified, unprecedented action gave the girls a one-minute standing ovation. The principal shook his head; he'd never seen anything like it. How could such a tough audience of ten- to fourteen-year-olds be so moved? Perhaps the answer is related to how the girls consistently responded to the oft-posed question, "Wouldn't you like to live in America?" The girls turned to me as if to ask, Is this a trick question?

They then turned to their audience and answered, "I live in Afghanistan. My people need me. It is my home."

I

The most important thing about this night is that we had watermelon with our meal. It was also my first night living at Mehan, an orphanage in western Kabul. I'd moved in with sixty-five girls between the ages of seven and sixteen from every tribe: Uzbek and Nuristani, Pashtun and Tajik and Hazara. I'd come to volunteer as their English teacher and had already learned my first lesson. Only an hour before, at five minutes to seven, the sun down and cool April air seeping through the sashes and jambs, fourteen-year-old Mahbooba, one of the few who knew some English, looked up at me with the most incredulous brown eyes and let me know under no uncertain terms just what education means to the children. I was tired. I'd taught all day with a half hour for *naan* (bread) and *chai sabz* (green tea) at noon. First had been the Sitara I orphanage, eighty boys and girls between five and nine years of age in one room, sitting on the floor, notepads in their laps, pencils poised. I had no idea where to begin. I rubbed my tummy. "Hungry," I moaned. They put their pencils down, rubbed their tummies too, giggling. *Hungry* . . . Then it had been Sitara II, all the older boys, rolling a soccer ball around playing elimination with questions and answers in conversational English, and then mid-afternoon, back to Mehan for classes with the eight-to-twelves. Now was my last session, ten of the older girls, and I decided to let them out early. "Bas," I said, *enough.*

"Ian jan,"[1] Mahbooba asked. "What time is it?"

I looked at my watch. "Five minutes to seven."

Mahbooba launched into a discussion with her classmates in Dari, then back to me. "Ian jan," she said, matter of fact, "we want our five minutes."

Dinner was in the basement of the three-story building. Sixty Afghan girls and one adult American male sitting on the floor around a plastic red mat that had been rolled out for the occasion. *Shola* was served, a steamed lentil and rice dish with a chalky sauce poured on top. I watched for a sign that the girls were altering their behavior due to my presence, but I couldn't detect anything drastic. Those whose turn it was tended to serving the shola and then collecting the plates; the rest of the girls chatted and every now and then glanced at me and smiled.

After shola, Mahbooba descended the stairway with a large ripe watermelon in her arms. She proceeded to cut it up with a very small knife and other, smaller girls handed the bright pink wedges out to their appreciative sisters. A girl named Frishta, ten years old and three feet tall, handed me a ridiculously large piece. I nodded thanks and noticed just about all the girls in the room watching me as I took my first bite. It was as if they were looking to see what effect one of their prized luxuries would have on this strangest of visitors. I gazed at them, and involuntarily my mouth maneuvered the pulp from the seed. The first satellite traveled in a graceful arc the entire length of our dinner mat, landing with a "plink" in Fatima's metal saucer. Sixty pairs of eyes stared in amazement not only for what I had done, but that *I* had done it. After an initial three seconds of complete silence, an eruption of laughter. Battle lines were drawn and lips were puckered. A generation of Afghan girls learning to spit watermelon seeds. I raised my fist into the air, spit another seed, and—more to myself—said out loud beneath the excited voices in the echoing basement of the orphanage, "Take that, Taliban!"

II

At Sitara II the boys, ages ten to seventeen, are more carefree. Every day, besides going to school, they play soccer. The code of ethics in these orphanages includes tolerance and equality. But Sharia laws linger in Afghan society as one set of extreme fundamentalists, the Taliban, was replaced by another, the "Northern Alliance." Outside, the boys have a leg up no matter what. Still, they do not come cleanly into the world. Though they gallivant around, spar with one another, emote a sense of confidence that verges on cavalier, they carry with them a sense of immediacy, heaviness of spirit, even foreboding that I do not sense in the girls. Perhaps that is why they easily wrap arms around each other's shoulders, hold hands as they walk down the street. The separation of genders emboldens the need for intimacy, nurtures a rather heartwarming appreciation for all things beautiful and fragile, roses, for example, and kites. Take Dariush. He is thirteen, Pashtun, strikingly south Asian in his looks, almost fierce with his pronounced jaw, his mustache and sideburns so black as to be painted. Yet he is by far the gentlest of the older group. This is not to be confused with passivity. He is first to volunteer, as active a participant in our lessons and discourse as his more aggressive peers. He wishes to be a journalist. He may succeed. He has the knack to be present without being detected. He wrote down a dream he had one night, which he shared with photography class. In the throes of an obvious mix of stage fright and untapped emotion, he clasped a single piece of paper between both thumbs and index fingers. The page trembled as he read out loud his description of the dream:

> One day I went to hospital and saw two persons near to me, and facing me they said come. I went near to them. They said this box, give the box and put another name. I said no, no, I am not working for you. Suddenly I saw the other man bring a rifle out. They tell me go. I went to another place, a home with the box. I saw one police near to me. What is this? I said I don't know. He said give me. I gived he. He opened the box and he saw in box. He said what is this! I saw a bomb. He said how got this box. I said they gave it to me. They escape. After, police tell me let's go. I said where? To jail. I said why? He said let's go. I went into jail. I was two days in jail. Suddenly, I saw one tormentor near to me. He tells me, who give box to me? I said they gave to me. He said no, you lie me, and he bring out knife he said tell me. I said I don't know. He to thrash me with knife. Suddenly I to awaken. I saw to dream.

In photography class I teach the children to see with new eyes, to ignore the obvious and exaggerate the particular. It is not by accident I brought six boys together with seven girls in this one class. Early on I shared an assortment of pictures off the Internet, all taken in Afghanistan over the past ten years. There are photos of soldiers fighting, unending panoramas of the Hindu Kush, pictures of markets flooded with color and humanity, classic shots of babies beside warriors and close-ups of white-bearded Sufis with wisdom oozing from their eyes, but the children unanimously chose as their favorite a photo of the destroyed Darul Aman Palace framed by a foreboding cloud-filled sunset and three homeless children stoically traversing the rubble.

I handed out cameras like little portholes into freedom. The boys sauntered back to Sitara II fully armed, snapping pictures along the way, harmless portraits of Ulfat doing a handstand, Omid among the roses, but also some not so innocent, burned-out buses stacked upon one another, a glass-cloaked wedding hall surrounded by shanties, a dog tied up to a stake in a pile of trash. It was the buses Dariush tried to capture. I'd taught him to make the ordinary strange, the strange ordinary. A security agent came up behind Dariush and pulled the camera from his hands. "What is this? Where did you get this? Who gave it to you? You want to go to jail? Come with me." Dariush pleaded with the guard, and in the end escaped for the price of a roll of film. He ran back to Mehan; the dear child wanted to apologize to *me*. He was ashamed; he bowed his head and opened his camera, exposing the empty chamber.

"It was his dream," one of the girls in photography class later said in a hushed voice. "The one about the package with a bomb. He saw to dream."

III

My most intensive class is with Maria, Sitiza, Pashtana, and my hopeful young star Yasamin. Two Kabulis, a Pashtun and Nuristani, all around fifteen. They are not the brightest students I have, and there are others who speak English better, but they have a work ethic and a combined determination of heart. I push them. Yesterday I gave them Shakespeare. After reading the speech about the seven stages in a man's life, they looked at me in horror. Yellow highlighters in hand, they proceeded to mark almost every word. What is a pard, and what is a capon lined? Explain, please, a bubble reputation, mewling and puking, and what on earth is a shrunk shank? Then there is pronunciation. I almost lost them. They were distracted and tired. I assigned specific lines to the speech. Three of the four girls are in drama, so they took to this strategy easily, but Yasamin struggled to understand. The others teased her, and she turned away to wipe silent tears from her eyes. I consoled her as best I could. I know now how fragile these girls are, but also how extraordinarily strong, adaptive, and determined. Having acknowledged the tears and frustration, as Yasamin herself modeled, we eased back into the lesson, undaunted. I put my pen down and looked at the white board. There I'd written Shakespeare's seven ages, ending with the dying man who fades into oblivion, sans everything. "This is a man's life, yes?" I queried. "What about a woman's?"

"In Afghanistan?" Pashtana asked.

"Yes, does an Afghan woman follow these stages?"

It was as if the door across the room had been suddenly slammed shut by the wind. Maria did not hesitate to answer. "Two stages: infant straight to dying old woman."

I raised my eyebrows. "Really?" I asked the other three. They all nodded.

"Look," Maria adjusted in her chair, the teacher now. "Look at these stages—after infant is schoolboy." She looked at me. "How many girls go to school?" I could not argue. "Then lover." Pause. We all shook our heads. "Soldier, justice, retired man. What woman in Afghanistan goes through these stages?"

Sitiza added that many women don't go from infant to old lady. They just die. So often these children arrest me with their frankness. They say things to me I do not know if they ever have said to an adult. As I negotiated the impact of Maria's lesson, I looked each of the girls in the eyes, amazed. They did not flinch. "This is something you are here to change," I said. "You are here in this class, in this orphanage, in this city, in this country to add stages to your lives, maybe even the lives of all Afghan women." I will not forget the confident smiles that came upon the faces of those young ladies in that moment. Before letting them go I asked the girls to please put down their markers, close their eyes and listen. I took a deep breath, sighed, and began.

All the world's a stage, and all the men and women merely players . . .

IV

We hold these truths to be self-evident, that all men are created equal, that they are endowed by their Creator with certain unalienable Rights, that among these are Life, Liberty and the pursuit of Happiness.

These are the words that greeted the fifteen older girls in my leadership workshop (grades ten through twelve). I'd written them on the board beforehand, alone in the room. Just writing them sent some electricity through my body. It wasn't only their weightiness, but the anticipation of sharing them with a group of adolescents who had never seen or heard the words before. How to begin for the first time in a year to talk to my students about my own country, its history, its people, and ultimately its role in their lives and the lives of every Afghan?

We walked through Thomas Jefferson's declaration word for word. *Unalienable* was difficult to explain. *God-given, natural, unalterable? Rights* is another word not easy to explain. Then came *pursuit of happiness.* Just try and figure out what he meant by happiness. We read the sentence out loud together. "There is one thing odd," I said, "one thing that seems it may be wrong, out of place in these words; what is it?" The girls jumped at the challenge, but were on the wrong tangent. They assumed I'd meant some sort of grammatical error. I shook my head. They kept trying to stab at word order or usage. I was about to give up when Pashtana said one little word from the very end of the table, a word I almost missed beneath the din.

"Men."

"Hold on, everyone. *Nako!*"[2] I waited until it was quiet. "What was that, Pashtana?" The other girls looked at her as if she had won a prize.

"Men," she repeated a little more confidently. "All *men* are created equal?" Pashtana is Pashtun; she lived in AFCECO's Pakistan orphanage in Peshawar for many years and then moved to Kabul. I'd recently asked the class to memorize a poem that had been taught to me by a Japanese Zen master in Kyoto. It was Pashtana who recited it without hesitation, without a single error in pronunciation. *Each day in life is training, training for myself. Though failure is possible, living each moment equal to anyone, ready for everything, I am alive, I am this moment, my future is here and now.*

"Men!" I repeated Pashtana's revelation. The girls smiled and nodded. They offered some replacement words such as *people*, *humans*, and even *animals*. Then Sitiza wanted to discuss the meaning of humanity. She has been showing real desire these past weeks, to reach beyond what her very restrictive family dreams for her. I think her good friend Maria is rubbing off on her. So we went down the road of humanity, and if I wanted we could have spent the two hours on this one word. Thus we began our journey to America.

V

There is a saying in Afghanistan that a window only breaks once. When trust is given it is given for life. If it is broken, it is also broken for life. One week the Mehan house parents, Nasifa and Yasin, threw a birthday party for their two-year-old daughter, Marwa. The girls blew up balloons and decorated the foyer at the entrance to the orphanage, set up chairs and a tape player, and then changed into their best and most colorful clothes for the occasion. At teatime several guests arrived, some with children. Afghan pop music blared through the house. One of the younger guests, dressed in jeans, took center stage and pulled one and another of the girls from their seats. Most Afghan women and men love to dance, and they are quite good at it. The oddity is, their style of dancing (albeit less flowery and more folk-rooted) is remarkably reminiscent of the individualized, improvised, floating dance of hippies at a Grateful Dead concert.

Every class has a clown, just as every ancient ceremony has its fool. Three years in residence at Mehan, Sadaf maintains sole ownership of that role. She is thirteen, from Farah Province, one of those Afghans whose looks herald from the Middle East. Her hair is black, black as pure tar but without the shine. It is the kind of black from which no amount of light is repelled, one of the two most coveted marks of beauty here in the heart of the continent (the other being light skin). Once, I played Beethoven over the stereo in the library. I inquired as to whether Sadaf liked the music. She smiled innocently but betrayed herself with her glinting brown eyes. "When does the *music* start?" she asked.

Sadaf makes people laugh, but as with all class clowns something sad underlies her nonchalance towards the future, her own well-being, sad because it is not a self-destructiveness that fuels her, nor is it a crazy brevity of spirit; the world for whatever reason has married her to the moment. There is no foresight, but then again there is a crystal-clear vision of what is happening as it happens. Unlike with other children, I do not want to know what happened to her. Not for lack of caring, more for a sense of caring more.

The sun had set and the moon waxed full and Sadaf was first of the orphans to dance alone. She wasn't very good. Stiff, a little one-dimensional, she nonetheless sashayed about the floor as happily, it seemed, as if she were a princess parading for an adoring court. In less time than it takes to survey a room she pulled on my arm. Fools have a knack for bringing out the fool in everyone. (The girls have worn out their collection of Charlie Chaplin's movies.) The pulsing *dhol*, the somehow stylish, rapid-fired string of the *rebab*,[3] the lung-filling drone of the harmonium filled my senses. I imagine I danced something akin to Celtic prancing infused with land-locked water ballet. The birthday party wound up its gears a few notches and I was not permitted to leave the floor. It was then Sadaf motioned for me to teach her how to swing dance. It is possible, dare I say, to swing to anything, even to measures of music timed in seventeenths. Sadaf followed well. For added flair I twirled her around and around, then twirled myself, then both together. Tunes tend to be rather long here, seven to ten minutes. We lasted, barely, and were rewarded with applause. I sat at a corner table, pleased with myself. Chai and hard lemon-drop candy were brought over as my reward.

The evening should have ended there. It was going on 8:30. I could have left the party without appearing rude. I was tired. I wanted to type a few words and read a little poetry and quietly go to bed. Sadaf stood beside me and pointed at something across the room. "Stand up," she said. It is not often she speaks English, even though she understands quite a bit of it. I stood up. There was nothing there. I sat down. There was no chair; Sadaf had pulled it out from behind me. My ass landed full-force on the floor.

No mitigating factors entered my head in that moment, not in front of everyone, all the children, the staff, the only American. I stood up, pointed my finger at Sadaf, who was laughing, and said in a low but forceful tone, "How can I ever trust you again?"

The evening wore on, blurred. Sadaf was absent. I asked around, but nobody seemed inclined to answer. Finally Nafisa, one of the older girls, could not withhold her knowledge any longer. "Ian! Sadaf—she cries!" Nafisa pointed upstairs. I went immediately. I'd realized my folly almost as soon as I'd committed it. Sadaf was alone at the top of the third-floor stairs, sobbing uncontrollably. I shooed the curious followers away and sat beside her. I took her shaking fist, unclenched it, and held her hand in my own. Whether her action or mine or both, a window had been broken. It was not going to be put back together through force, negotiation, or apology. I am here but a brief wistful spring and summer. For Sadaf there is no such thing as pulling stakes and laying claim to another piece of ground.

VI

The girls of Mehan walk a tightrope between the world outside and their blossomed freedom inside. When they go to school they wear black uniforms. On their heads they wrap white scarves. They do not have "recess." After school they return directly to the orphanage. This is due to security as much as the strength of conservative mores—kidnapping of girls is lucrative business. Once back inside the gates of Mehan, off come the conservative uniforms, whereupon the girls dress freely and imaginatively, even though their choices are few. Modesty is expected here; for both genders the exposure of skin hardly goes beyond face, hands, and feet. This, combined with a multicultural population, makes for a society where the expression through clothing is dizzying, a pure extension of ancestry, distinctive from all others. The girls amalgamate these distinctions, making every day a costume party, or at the very least reminiscent of "dress up," as if they have discovered a never-opened trunk up in the attic of grandmother's house. Add to these traditional articles the contributions from sponsors in the West, and what would have been a bow to lineage is now self-expression. Orange skirts over jeans; crimson saris with T-shirts; brown boys' overshirts worn with yellow sarongs; track suits with scarves of every color worn across the chest, the waist, or lavishly around the neck and head.

Regardless, the girls can ill afford to be obsessive about their clothes, or their hair for that matter. Their priority is to be useful and valued among their peers, while applying themselves to their studies. To them what is important is what is developing *inside*. Farzana is a case in point. She is Hazara, a thirteen-

year-old from Bamiyan province where, when she was five, all the men including her father were massacred by Taliban. She often hung around my room,
mostly silent, as if simply being there would glean something. She has a face
shaped like a teardrop, black eyes and oversized cheekbones, with raven-black
hair, unkempt just past her ears—a tomboy. One day she inquired about a
book I was reading, a collection of poems by Rumi, the twelfth-century Sufi
poet who was born in northern Afghanistan before fleeing Genghis Khan. I
handed the book to her.

"Take it. It's yours."

She refused. "I will borrow it."

Months later I asked her about Rumi. She had not even hinted of its existence after that initial exchange. "Oh yes," she said, as if she'd been merely
waiting for me to ask. She went to her room and returned with the book. She
had made a cover for it out of rose paper. She handed it to me and I flipped
through it, taking note of dog-eared corners and stained pages.

"Do you have a favorite?" I asked.

Farzana stuck her finger out and leafed through the pages while I held the
book. "This one."

I handed the book back to her. "Would you please read it for me?"

Begrudgingly, she acceded. Softly, timidly for a tough girl like her, she
read, until she got to the fourth line, when she suddenly lifted her voice and
question into the air. "The way of love is not a subtle argument. The door there
is devastation. Birds make great sky circles of their freedom. How do they
learn it? They fall, and falling they are given wings."

Once, as dusk fell upon Kabul on a sultry evening, I gathered with five of the
girls around the outdoor burner used to heat water. It was the closest thing
to sitting around a campfire they'd ever experienced. A full moon had risen.
Red roses had begun to bloom in the small courtyard; we could just make out
their faint, sweet perfume. In a hushed voice I related what it had been like
for me as a kid to be afraid in the dark, and how I came to brave it. Farzana
was there, helping to translate. In a while the deepening night and brightened
fire must have emboldened her. She launched into a kind of confession. The
other girls listened intently, but they didn't have enough of a grasp of English
to know what Farzana was saying. Her confession was directed toward me.
"When I was five," she said, "for a while I didn't think my father was dead. I
mean, I knew he was dead, I saw him get taken away. But one night he came
to me in a dream. He asked me to make tea for him. I made him tea. He was
so real, I believed he was alive."

What is an orphan but an opening line cut off from the rest of its story? In these children are a pinch of Russian poetic, a sprinkle of Chinese aesthetic, a dollop of Persian propriety, and a dash of Indian ecstatic. This is Afghanistan. Who's to say there is anything that cannot be imagined?

Notes

1. Jan (Dari): Suffix denoting endearment.
2. Nako (Dari): "Stop" or "Don't do it."
3. A dhol is a drum thought to have originated in North India. A rebab is a two-stringed fiddle, considered one of the national instruments of Afghanistan.

The car being too full to fit them, children ride in the trunk of a taxicab in Kabul, Afghanistan. As the photographer watched the boy on the far right struggle to keep the trunk lid from banging down on his and the others' heads, she noted that in the United States this might be treated as child abuse. "My Afghan companions expressed surprise at this," she writes, "stating that this was far from abuse— after all, the children weren't being made to run after the car." Photo by Anne E. Brodsky, 2002.

Epilogue: Imagining the Future

ASHRAF ZAHEDI

If we act now with realism and foresight, if we show courage, if we think globally and allocate our resources accordingly, we can give our children and youth a more peaceful and equitable world. One where suffering will be reduced. Where opportunities and hope are within every young person's reach. This is not a dream. It is our responsibility.
JAMES WOLFENSOHN, WORLD BANK PRESIDENT 1995–2005,
"CHILDREN AND YOUTH: A FRAMEWORK FOR ACTION"

The future and sociopolitical strength of a country lies in its investment in its children. Failure to envision and implement a child-centered national policy can have serious consequences for the future of any nation and can negatively impact the physical, mental, emotional, and social development of its children and in turn lead to the loss of human capital. Afghanistan exemplifies this case.

Afghanistan has chronically suffered from uneven socioeconomic developments. Even during Mohammed Zahir Shah's rule (1933–1973), a period that some Afghans refer to as a "golden era," poverty was rampant, as it is today, particularly in the rural areas. In addition, more than three decades of war and destruction, beginning with the 1979 Soviet invasion, exacerbated the problem and destroyed the country's infrastructure and social institutions. Crucially important, it has also deprived Afghan society of whole and healthy children, who are vital to rebuilding Afghanistan and securing the path to peace.

The regime change in Afghanistan in 2001, when the United States and its allies invaded the country and routed the Taliban, heralded a new beginning for the Afghan people. The Afghan government, along with international donors and United Nations agencies, promised access to education, health care, and employment, and depicted a bright future. Billions of dollars have been allocated to support these promises.[1]

But what has been achieved for Afghan children and youth? While there has not been sufficient time to make a historical analysis evaluating Afghanistan's investment in its children, the years since the fall of the Taliban should be sufficient for gauging political commitment of the Afghan government and their international donors.

In the years since 2001, investments, mostly in urban areas, have provided great opportunities for many Afghan upper- and middle-class families, particularly returnees from the diaspora in the West. Their children, who have come of age since the country has again opened to the world, stand to largely benefit from sociopolitical and economic developments in Afghanistan. Unlike the poor, these children's social aspirations continue to be fulfilled and they are, for the most part, enjoying the promises of prosperity. They stand to lose everything if the civil war intensifies and, in turn, poor children lose hope for prosperity.

Children and young Afghans constitute 68 percent of the Afghan population.[2] Young Afghans are a distinct social group, claiming the public sphere as "youth." They are learning to be youth, a privilege not afforded to past generations of Afghans who, during decades of political conflicts, had to bypass "youth"—the period between childhood and adulthood. Youth is, indeed, a historical and social construction shaped by culture and social structures. One learns to become a youth. It is a socialization process during which young people need emotional, intellectual, and cognitive spaces to develop. Youth, however, is not a homogeneous group. It is divided by social class, gender, ethnicity, religion, and region.

These differences notwithstanding, Afghan youth are claiming the public spaces. They are attending Afghanistan's fifty-four public and private universities in record numbers.[3] They are working for international nonprofit and civil society organizations, forming clubs and youth organizations, and taking part in politics. They are playing a significant role in Afghanistan's thriving mass media. A brief examination of their role in Afghan society sheds light on social changes taking place in Afghanistan.

Openings in the political system have provided them with opportunities to venture into politics and seek political offices. Many Afghan youth, male or female—who have drawn on family name recognition or gained popularity through their involvement in politics, mass media, entertainment, and sports—sought public office in the 2005 and 2010 elections. A few 2005 examples: Malalai Joya, who, at age twenty-seven, was elected to Parliament and became world-famous for voicing her dissention to corruption and misogyny. Sabrina Sagheb, at twenty-four, was the youngest woman that year to stand and win a seat in the Parliament. At twenty-seven, Farida Tarana, a popular singer from the Tolo TV show *Afghan Star* (similar to *American Idol*), ran for the twenty-nine-seat Kabul Provincial Council (akin to the U.S. state legislature) and was elected.

In 2010, Robina Jalali, a popular figure and former Olympic runner, ran for office at age twenty-five but did not receive sufficient votes. Controversy surrounding her election notwithstanding, at twenty-nine, Farkhunda Zahra Naderi, an attorney, was elected to Parliament. Baktash Siawash, a popular blogger and television personality, became the youngest member of Parliament that year at twenty-five. Fawzia Koofi, who was elected in 2005 at age thirty, was reelected in 2010. She ran for the Afghan presidency in 2014 on a platform of equal rights for women, promoting universal education and the opposition to political corruption.[4]

Affluent Afghan youth are experiencing a variety of activities and enjoying leisure time. They frequent newly opened luxury malls in Kabul and indulge themselves in consumer products. Along with older Afghans, they watch Western, as well as Bollywood, movies, glimpsing other societies. Decades ago Afghans watched movies in Kabul's many cinemas, but these were shut down during the civil war and Taliban rule. Half a dozen cinemas again operate in Kabul, yet due to security concerns they are not well attended. People prefer to watch films in the safety of their homes.

They enjoy listening to music, banned under the Taliban. In fact, music has a special place in Afghanistan for people of all ages. No wonder *Afghan Star* is such a huge hit.[5] The music industry is thriving and many youth bands, playing traditional as well as modern songs, are gaining recognition. In 2009, the first rock band emerged, called Kabul Dreams.[6] Its ethnically diverse members have lived in the diaspora and performed in the West. In addition to entertainment, Afghan television and radio programs highlight youth perspectives and social concerns.

Girls and boys take part in various sports. Some gather at Ghazni Stadium, the site of Taliban public executions, to skateboard in a section called Skateistan. There is even a bowling alley in Kabul, popular with boys and girls who can afford it (at $35USD an hour). Girls now have their own soccer and cricket clubs in Kabul and have been playing competitive soccer with opportunities to compete in tournaments outside Afghanistan. Boys compete in many sports, but cricket and soccer are seen to be the most popular.

Afghan youth are enjoying arts, culture, and intellectual exchanges in organizational settings, such as Afghan Cultural House in Kabul, which offers young Afghans unique opportunities to socialize and exchange ideas. The center has a café, Internet service, library, training center, and art gallery. Armanshahr (Open Asia), a French non-governmental organization (NGO), is another venue that attracts youth. It promotes human rights and progressive ideas among young people by sponsoring meetings and cultural events and publishing analytical articles in English and Dari.

Afghan Youth Voices Festival is a forum where creative young people can meet, produce stories, collaborate, and have fun. It sponsors a women's blogging project, an Afghan memorial project, and a national poetry competition.

Young Women for Change aims to raise public awareness about gender inequality. Its highly publicized Walk against Street Harassment campaign in Kabul on July 14, 2011, received much international attention. It sponsors many cultural and political events. Some events are mixed, boys and girls; others are exclusively for girls.

Some youth activities have political undertones and aim for engagement in the political process. Afghanistan Young Leaders Initiative, established in 2011 in cooperation with Asia Society Twenty-First Century, is one such organization. It attempts to educate and mobilize Afghan youth at the grassroots level to rebuild Afghanistan and enhance the quality of life for all Afghans.

Some youth activities are in fact organized by the Afghan government and the United Nations Development Programme (UNDP). In 2007, the UNDP initiated a two-year National Joint Youth Programme to increase Afghan government capacity to support and provide services to youth; improve their quality of life and access to livelihood opportunities; and encourage their participation in governance, sociopolitical process, and peace building.[7] In line with this program, the Youth Parliament of Afghanistan was held in Kabul in June 2007 in order to familiarize high-school students with the workings of Parliament and the process of decision making.[8]

The Afghan government has also established a National Youth Council with branches in many Afghan cities such as Kabul, Herat, and Balkh. It has created a sub-ministerial position for dealing with youth issues, namely the Deputy Minister of Youth Affairs. This deputy position works within the Ministry of Culture and Information.[9]

Additionally, the Afghan government, in cooperation with the United Nations Children's Fund (UNICEF), has established Youth Information and Contact Centres in fourteen of Afghanistan's thirty-four provinces.[10] These centers are tasked to provide information, guidance, and counseling for youth. It is not clear how effective these centers have been in terms of impact and outreach.

Afghan youth who can afford them have been using mobile phones, and these phones are viewed as an "affordable luxury." Through the use of mobile phones and the Internet, Afghan youth have become well connected to each other and the outside world. But where social networking has served as a medium for political mobilization in other countries, young Afghans, concerned about security, were not taking to the streets. Instead, those who are not trying to bring about change by working through existing political channels have tried to register their discontent with and disapproval of the government through social media such as Facebook.

Although President Hamid Karzai discouraged youth involvement in politics—recalling student involvement in the Afghan upheavals of the 1960s and 1970s that eventually led to the 1978 Saur Revolution and the Soviet invasion—he nonetheless opened the June 2012 National Youth Peace Jirga, where some 1,700 youth gathered to debate the reconciliation process and the development of an "alternative" peace strategy, the future of the U.S. military presence in Afghanistan, anti-corruption and the role of Afghan youth in it, unemployment and its effects on youth in an insecure environment, and educational problems.[11]

Emerging Pictures

Afghan youth are gradually leaving their marks on the society. But this is only part of the story, the story of middle- and upper-class urban youth. Most young Afghans have yet to benefit from the social changes of the past decade. Eighty-five percent of Afghans live in rural areas, facing socioeconomic hardships, so it is unlikely that these youngsters have the opportunities to participate in arts, culture, and civic activities. They do not have the luxury of being youth and engaging in non-income-generating activities.

How would urban and relatively affluent youth and economically pressed rural youth envision their futures, respectively? Both groups envision an Afghanistan that offers social opportunities and political stability. Both aspire to better lives for themselves and their families. But the structures of socioeconomic opportunities are not there to fulfill the social aspirations of rural and low-income urban youth. How do these alienated and disenfranchised youth deal with the growing socioeconomic disparities in Afghanistan? How will they channel their dissatisfaction? Will they glorify the past and gravitate toward insurgent groups? These are sobering questions, and the best way to prevent such scenarios from unfolding is to invest in Afghan children and youth and provide them with chances of social upward mobility. It is here that a child-centered national policy and fully dedicated ministry to implement it become essential. Political will and allocation of resources are central to the future of Afghan children.

Afghanistan is a signatory to and has ratified the United Nations Convention on the Rights of the Child. The Afghan government, with the help of UN agencies including the UNDP, UNICEF, and the United Nations Educational, Scientific and Cultural Organization (UNESCO), as well as international donors, has developed many strategic plans for the country. The Afghanistan National Development Strategy, the National Education Strategic Plan, and the National Heath Strategy have significant bearings on the lives of Afghan children. Additionally, the Afghan government, with the help of UNICEF and in partnership with international and local NGOs and donors, developed the National Plan of Action for At-Risk Children in 2004.[12] In May 2006, the government adopted it as the National Strategy for Children at Risk (NSFCAR).[13]

NSFCAR identifies specific groups of children particularly at risk and in need of protection:

- Children with disabilities (mental and physical);
- Street children (working and street-working children);
- Children in conflict with the law;
- Kidnapped children;
- Trafficked children;
- Child soldiers and other war-affected children;
- Children deprived of parental care;
- Girls forced into marriage or early marriage;
- Internally displaced and returnee children;
- Children from ethnic minority groups;
- Children using drugs and/or selling drugs;
- Children experiencing abuse (sexual, physical, emotional, neglect).[14]

Most issues identified by NSFCAR have been fully examined by contributors to this volume.

This plan of action is central to the government's strategy for protecting children and is under the leadership of the Ministry of Labor, Social Affairs, Martyrs, and Disabled (MoLSAMD), together with the Child Protection section of the Ministry of Interior.[15] The plan, however, lacks sufficient funding and professionally trained staff and is limited in outreach and impact.

Another child-protection program—in line with the National Plan of Action for At-Risk Children—is Child Protection Action Networks (CPANs), which have been in operation since 2003. UNICEF, in cooperation with the Afghan government, NGOs, and community leaders, has been funding and operating CPANs, which are currently active in twenty-eight provinces.[16] CPANs have been facing challenges in certain rural areas, due to insecurity and thus inaccessibility, and a lack of trained professionals in law and social welfare. Sadly, despite CPANs and the Afghan government's efforts, NSFCAR reports that "the majority of 'at risk' or vulnerable children and their families receive no support."[17]

While development of the NSFCAR and CPANs is a positive step, these plans suffer from lack of leadership, oversight, and political will. Addressing children's needs seems to be of low priority, and the implementation of the plan by the Ministry of Labor, Social Affairs, Martyrs, and Disabled, which is tasked with a hodgepodge of different activities, signifies weak commitment to children. Professor Wasil Noor Muhmad, deputy minister of MoLSAMD, has acknowledged that "there are also various gaps in capacity, knowledge, and commitment of MoLSAMD management."[18] The text of the 2004 National Plan of Action for At-Risk Children recommends implementation of a comprehensive child protection plan and requires "establishment of a child protection Secretariat with the Ministry of Labor and Social Affairs."[19] As of this writing, no such position has been established. Many countries—such as India, Canada, Malaysia, and Nepal—have created government ministries especially for the protection of children.[20]

Addressing Perennial Poverty

Poverty is a major challenge to the work of CPANs and NSFCAR in Afghanistan. Poverty is also a serious development issue that severely impacts Afghan families and their abilities to support and protect their children. To address poverty, the Afghan government adopted the Afghanistan National Development Strategy (ANDS) in 2008. This strategic plan was based on the World Bank and International Monetary Fund vision of poverty reduction captured in their "Poverty Reduction Strategy Papers."[21] It aims to reduce poverty and sustain socioeconomic developments through the private sector in a market-led economy. This approach may serve certain advanced post-industrial countries with well-established safety nets, but it is not a good policy approach for Afghanistan. Market-led economies promote top-down economic growth and expect trickle-down benefits, which often does not happen. As it recovers from the decades of war, loss of human capital, and capital flight, Afghanistan is now in the process of rebuilding its infrastructure and social institutions. There are still not sufficient social safety nets and social protections programs in place to offset the potential negative effects of a market-led economy.

The market-led policy approach views poverty in terms of income and the lack thereof. Low income is the result of poverty, not the cause of it. Addressing poverty requires recognizing its multiple causes. Poverty has a whole host of causes, including social class, gender, ethnicity, age, disability, access to resources (land and credit), lack of marketable skills, and access to markets. In Afghanistan, poverty is also caused by poor health, internal and external displacement, the loss of assets due to war and conflict, and living in remote and resource-poor regions—thus denying full access to education and the labor market. What is more, the experience of other countries indicates that a "market approach to reconstruction and development may inevitably" impact negatively on the poor.[22]

Investing in Poverty Reduction

Cash transfers as a means of reducing poverty have been implemented worldwide. Two popular programs are unconditional cash transfers and conditional cash transfers.[23] While unconditional cash transfers programs are often used in humanitarian emergencies and/or in post-conflict situations, the conditional cash transfers (CCT) programs have become a preferred tool for immediate poverty reduction. The preference is based on its potential for human capital development.

CCT programs initiated in Mexico in 1997 and have been widely used across the globe ever since.[24] The World Bank is a major player in CCT and provides funding and technical support to local governments. The program objective is to combine long-term human capital development with short-term poverty alleviation. It aims to reduce poverty while setting certain criteria for the recipients, who must belong to poor households and agree to the terms and conditions of cash transfer, which demand that recipients enroll their children in public schools, take children to heath clinics (for vaccinations and checkups), and use the cash to improve children's nutrition. The payment can vary from country to country and range from $3USD to $9USD a month per child. It also varies in the number of children covered in a family and their age limits.[25] Though the money is for the family, the cash recipient is the mother or female guardian. The program effectively improves the status of women in the family. The CCT programs provide the family with steady income that can be used in times of catastrophe and illness and are regarded as an investment in human capital development.

While CCT programs are not a panacea and do not deal with structures of socioeconomic inequalities and power disparities, they can address some aspects of poverty. They are a form of intervention that would disrupt the cycle of poverty and protect children from its many problems. The CCT programs have been widely monitored by academics and practitioners, and their effectiveness rigorously evaluated. Their success in Latin America, particularly the model Bolsa Familia program in Brazil and the Oportunidades program in Mexico, has demonstrated how they can not only address education, health, and nutrition, but effectively narrow the gap between social classes.[26] Similar successes have been documented in Africa and Asia. According to a UNICEF report, the positive impacts of CCT programs can be measured in three ways: direct expenditure on children health and education; expenditure on food, fuel, and shelter for the household as a whole; and indirectly through investment in livelihood.[27]

The World Bank CCT programs cover many countries with similar socioeconomic conditions as Afghanistan, such as Pakistan, Bangladesh, and Yemen. But as of 2013, the World Bank had not offered CCT programs to Afghanistan (except for the families of martyrs and the disabled). My request in 2013 to speak with World Bank officials and inquire about the reasons for not implementing CCT in Afghanistan went unanswered. While the World Bank has financed many reconstruction projects in Afghanistan for the purpose of building its infrastructure—and in the long run positively impacting Afghan society—it has shied away from a program that can bear fruit in a short time and improve the quality of life for millions of Afghans, particularly children. Corruption and administrative issues are often concerns for CCT implementations. But research shows that in other countries, concerns regarding insecurity, misuse, and corruption related to cash programs are, according to UNICEF's Susanne Jaspor and Paul Harvey, generally "not borne out in practice and these risks can be minimized through good program design."[28]

CCT programs in Afghanistan can impact many issues that poor children face and could effectively impact Afghanistan's future. If implemented, the immediate impact would be on the Afghan family. The family is the most enduring social institution in Afghanistan. Afghans—young and old, rich and poor, male and female—draw strength from their families and the family continues to be the source of resilience and affection. Yet decades of war, conflict, and internal and external displacement have shaken and disrupted Afghan family-support networks and effectively eroded their collective resources and capability to provide for children.

CCT programs can be one way to restore Afghan families' financial capabilities. Such programs can impact families by helping to improve children's education in low-income families. Afghans indeed have a strong desire for education, regardless of social class, and cash transfer can fulfill this desire.

Poor diet and limited access to nourishing food caused by poverty contribute to the health problems of Afghan children. As one of the three criteria for cash transfer, recipients in other countries are expected to give nutritious food to their children to improve their health. CCTs can therefore also lead to food security and nutrition for the rest of the family.[29] A CCT program in Afghanistan can complement the current Ministry of Health's Basic Health Package program, particularly in urban areas.

CCTs can effectively impact all poverty-related issues such as disabilities, street children, children in conflict with the law, trafficked children, child soldiering, orphans, child labor, early marriage, and child sexual abuse.

It must be reiterated that CCT programs are not long-term poverty reduction solutions and cannot address all causes of poverty. They are supplements to larger poverty reduction efforts to reduce socioeconomic and political disparities. CCTs in Afghanistan must be designed around the existing supply-side challenges—lack of sufficient health clinics and schools—and be flexible in dictating terms of conditionality.

The Future of Afghan Children and Youth

Afghan children are resilient and have high social aspirations. The challenge facing the Afghan government and international donors is how to channel children's resiliency into improving their own lives and rebuilding Afghanistan, and in turn fulfilling their social aspirations. While rebuilding Afghan infrastructures and social institutions and developing poverty-reduction programs are crucial for the country's path to peace and prosperity, changing cultural attitudes and customs is also highly important for the betterment of Afghan society and the protection of children.

There is an urgent need for a national campaign to raise awareness about children and their social, physical, mental, and emotional needs. Cultural practices harmful to children should be exposed and their impacts on the family and society highlighted through the media, particularly radio programs. Youth Radio and Voice of America–Karwan are just two examples of radio programs raising public awareness. High-profile Afghans—politicians, singers, athletes, talk show hosts, business figures, tribal and religious leaders—should take an active role in raising awareness and supporting the campaign.

Members of the Afghan parliament can play an important role in child and youth advocacy. Parliamentarians are in the best position to champion child protection and youth development. They can pass legislation and allocate resources in favor of children and youth and mainstream their issues into national policies. Likewise, they can support a ministry or secretarial position dedicated to child and youth affairs.

A minister or secretariat in charge of child protection and youth development programs should have a proven record of commitment to children, demonstrate leadership in improving the status of Afghan children and youth, and address their real needs, setting the foundation for fulfillment of their social aspirations. Currently, those tasked with children's well-being and youth affairs in Afghanistan are political appointees, not experts in the field, and lack vision, expertise, and political determination.

Many developing countries with large youth populations have long recognized the importance of a dedicated, well-financed ministry exclusively for children and youth.[30] Such a ministry is often tasked with designing a comprehensive national policy including access to education, employment, and engagement in social affairs and governance. The national policy is often implemented in partnership with the business sector and civil society organizations, as well as with the support of multi-sector ministries.

Contributors to this volume have provided a comprehensive analysis of issues facing Afghan children and have recommended ways to address them. It is up to the Afghan government and international donors to draw on these and other recommendations from agencies experienced in child protection and youth affairs and to develop a comprehensive plan to improve quality of life for Afghan children and youth and secure their future.

It is imperative for international donors to sustain their funding and technical support for Afghan children and child protection programs. Failing to do so will increase the socioeconomic gaps between middle- and upper-class children and poor urban and rural children. Socioeconomic disparities may aggravate political division between the beneficiaries of Afghanistan's achievements and those who have been left out. What course of action will these disenfranchised youth take, and to which political alternatives will they turn? Will they meet political challenges peacefully or resort to violence? The future remains to be seen, but it is highly dependent on the political will of the Afghan government and the financial commitment and sustained support of international donors and aid agencies.

The departure of international forces and decline in foreign aid will certainly impact the Afghan economy and in turn Afghans' confidence in their government. The uncertain financial climate may lead to capital flight of Afghans and non-Afghans, thus impacting the job market. The World Bank, drawing on the experiences of other countries, has cautioned against an abrupt drop in foreign aid and its impact on job market and political stability.[31] A decline in foreign aid is bound to increase the rate of poverty and will affect children's well-being.

If the international community is serious about political stability and peace in Afghanistan, it must go beyond mere political peace. It must make commitments to demand-driven, socioeconomic developments in Afghanistan and address social and economic aspects of peace. Investing in children and youth is central to building human capital, fostering development, and securing a lasting peace. This is not just a sound policy choice but a moral obligation.

Notes

1. According to Afghanistan's Ministry of Finance, Aid Statistics, "Since the establishment of the interim Government, a total of USD 90 billion in aid has been pledged for Afghanistan (for the period of 2002–2013) by the international community . . . Pure commitment for reconstruction and development purposes for the period (2002–2010) stands at USD 37.6 billion out of which USD 28.1 billion has been disbursed so far" (http://www.budgetmof.gov.af/index.php?option=com_content&view=article&id=78&Itemid=64&lang=en).

It needs to be noted that not all these billions of dollars are actually benefiting the Afghan people. According to a World Bank report, "despite the large volume of aid, most international spending 'on' Afghanistan is not spent 'in' Afghanistan, as it leaves the economy through imports, expatriated profits of contractors, and outward remittances."

"Afghanistan in Transition: Looking Beyond 2014, Volume 1: Overview" (Washington, DC: World Bank, 2012), 2.

2. United Nations Development Programme, "National Joint Youth Programme," Annual Report 2008, http://www.undp.org.af/whoweare/undpinafghanistan/Projects/dcse/prj_youth.htm.

3. According to the Afghanistan Central Statistics Organization, there are twenty-four public and thirty private universities in Afghanistan. Eighty-four thousand one hundred eighty-four students attended these universities—69,084 male and 15,100 female—in 2010–2011 (http://cso.gov.af/en/page/4846).

4. While Fawzia Koofi's website (http://www.fawziakoofi.org/), as of November 2013, declared her candidacy for the presidency of Afghanistan, the official election registration does not reflect her candidacy. She may be too young—according to Afghan law, candidates must be forty years old. Like most Afghans, however, Koofi does not have a birth certificate, so her age cannot be verified.

5. The *Afghan Star* documentary, made in 2009, follows four contestants in the Afghan music competition (http://www.imdb.com/title/tt1334510/).

6. Videos of Kabul Dreams can be seen on YouTube. Here is one example: http://www.youtube.com/watch?v=i4kAvjgqh-U.

7. United Nations Development Programme, "National Joint Youth Programme," Annual Report 2008, http://www.undp.org.af/whoweare/undpinafghanistan/Projects/dcse/prj_youth.htm.

8. One hundred and one high schools boys and girls who were in the top of their class participated in a five-day meeting in Kabul in June 2007. The five-part video of this event can be viewed on YouTube at http://www.youtube.com/watch?v=syOS_yH9Lhg.

9. In many countries, there are both a minister and a dedicated ministry to address youth issues.

10. Wasil Noor Muhmad, "Child Protection System, Prevention And Response to Child Protection in Afghanistan," High Level Meeting on Cooperation of Child Rights in Asia Pacific Region, Beijing, November 2010, 3, http://www.unicef.org/eapro/DM_shanghi_CPAN_meeting.pdf.

11. Kazemi Reza, "Split Unity: Afghanistan's Controversial Youth Peace," Afghanistan Analysts Network, July 7, 2012, http://www.aan-afghanistan.org/index.asp?id=2864.

12. "Afghanistan National Strategy for Children At-Risk," Islamic Republic of Afghanistan 2004, http://lib.ohchr.org/HRBodies/UPR/Documents/Session5/AF/AFG_Afghanistan_National_Strategy_for_Children_at-risk.pdf.

13. Muhmad, "Child Protection System," 2.

14. Afghanistan National Strategy for Children At-Risk, 6.

15. Afghanistan National Strategy for Children At-Risk, 6.

16. Muhmad, "Child Protection System," 4.

17. Afghanistan National Strategy for Children At-Risk, 18.

18. Muhmad, "Child Protection System," 4.

19. Afghanistan National Strategy for Children At-Risk, 19.

20. Just a few examples are: India, Ministry of Women and Child Development; Canada, Ministry of Children and Family Development; Malaysia, Ministry of Women, Family, and Community Development; and Nepal, Ministry of Women, Children and Social Welfare.

21. Low-income countries seeking aid and/or debt relief are required to develop a poverty-reduction strategy based on the Poverty Reduction Strategy Papers of the International Monetary Fund (IMF) and World Bank and follow their terms and conditions of debt relief.

22. Daud Saba and Omar Zakhilwal, "Afghanistan National Development Report 2004: Security with a Human Face" (Islamabad: United Nations Development Programme, 2004), 54. For more information on poverty reduction in Afghanistan please refer to Paula Kantor and Adam Pain, "Rethinking Rural Poverty Reduction in Afghanistan" (Kabul: Afghanistan Research and Evaluation Unit, 2011), and Paula Kantor and Adam Pain, "Poverty in Afghan Policy: Enhancing Solutions Through Better Defining the Problem" (Kabul: Afghanistan Research and Evaluation Unit, 2010).

23. For more information on unconditional cash transfer, please refer to Joseph Hanlon, Armando Barrientos, and David Hulme, *Just Give Money to the Poor: The Development Revolution from the Global South* (Sterling, VA: Kumarian Press, 2010); Espen Villanger, "Cash Transfers Contributing to Social Protection: A Synthesis of Evaluation Findings" (Oslo: Norwegian Agency for Development Cooperation, 2008); and Bernd Schubert and Rachel Slater, "Social Cash Transfers in Low-Income African Countries: Conditional or Unconditional," *Development Policy Review* 24, no. 5 (2006): 571–578.

For an in-depth discussion of conditional cash transfer programs please refer to Ariel Fiszbein and Norbert Schady, "Conditional Cash Transfers: Reducing Present and Future Poverty" (Washington, DC: The World Bank, 2009); Laura Rawlings and Gloria Rubio, "Evaluating the Impact of Conditional Cash Transfer Programs," *The World Bank Research Observer* 20, no. I (Spring 2005); Sudhanshu Handa and Benjamin Davis, "The Experience of Conditional Cash Transfers in Latin America and the Caribbean," *Development Policy Review* 24, no. 5 (2006).

24. Fiszbein and Schady, "Conditional Cash Transfers," 21.

25. In some countries there is a ceiling on the number of children supported, perhaps as a form of family planning (Rawlings and Rubio, "Evaluating the Impact of Conditional Cash Transfer Programs," 31–32).

26. Kathy Lindert, Anja Linder, Jason Hobbs, and Benedicte de la Briere, "The Nuts and Bolts of Brazil's Bolsa Familia Program: Implementing Conditional Cash Transfers in a Decentralized Context" (Washington DC: The World Bank, 2007); Jere Behman, Susan Parker, and Petra Todd, "Do Conditional Cash Transfers for Schooling Generate Lasting Benefits? A Five-Year Follow Up of Progresa/Oportonidada," *The Journal of Human Resources* 46, no. I (January 2011).

27. Susanne Jaspars and Paul Harvey et al., "A Review of UNICEF's Role in Cash Transfers to Emergency Affected Population," New York, UNICEF, 2007, 6.

28. Jaspars and Harvey et al., "A Review of UNICEF's Role in Cash Transfers," 6.

29. Lucy Basset, "Can Conditional Cash Transfer Programs Play a Greater Role in Reducing Child Under Nutrition?" Washington DC: The World Bank, 2008.

30. There are some regional examples of a dedicated ministry addressing youth issues: India, Ministry of Youth Affairs and Sports; Iran, Ministry of Youth Affairs and Sports; Pakistan, Ministry of Youth Affairs; and Sri-Lanka, Ministry of Youth Affairs and Skills Development. For more information on national youth policies and youth ministries, please refer to World Atlas of Youth Policies. Available at http://www.planwithyouth.org/resources/youth-policies/.

31. "Afghanistan in Transition: Looking Beyond 2014, Volume I: Overview" (Washington DC: World Bank, 2012), 8.

Selected Bibliography and Filmography

Abdullah, Morag Murray. *My Khyber Marriage: Experiences of a Scotswoman as the Wife of a Pathan Chieftain's Son*. London: The Octagon Press, 1990.

ABLE Books (Afghan Centre at Kabul University Boxed Library Extension). Louis and Nancy Dupree Foundation. Kabul: Samsoor Printing, 2004, http://www.dupreefoundation.org/able.htm.

Afghanistan Research and Evaluation Unit. *The A to Z Guide to Afghanistan Assistance 2012*. Kabul: AREU, 2012.

Ahmad, Aisha, and Roger Boase. *Pashtun Tales from the Pakistan-Afghanistan Frontier*. London: Saqi Books, 2003.

Ahmed, Laila. *Women and Gender in Islam: Historical Roots of a Modern Debate*. New Haven: Yale University Press, 1992.

Ayub, Awista. *Kabul Girls Soccer Club: A Dream, Eight Girls, and a Journey Home*. New York: Hyperion Books, 2010.

Badkhen, Anna. *Afghanistan by Donkey: One Year in a War Zone*. Washington, DC: FP Group, 2012.

Bauman, Richard. *Verbal Art as Performance*. Long Grove, IL: Waveland Press, Inc., 1984.

Beah, Ishmael. *A Long Way Gone: Memoirs of a Boy Soldier*. New York: Farrar, Straus and Giroux, 2007.

Brett, Rachel, and Margaret McCallin. *Children: The Invisible Soldiers*. Stockholm: Rädda Barnen, Swedish Save the Children, 1996.

Brett, Rachel, and Irma Specht. *Young Soldiers—Why They Choose to Fight*. London: Lynne Rienner Publishers for International Labour Organisation, 2004.

Brodsky, Anne E. *With All Our Strength: The Revolutionary Association of the Women of Afghanistan*. New York: Routledge, 2003.

Bronfenbrenner, Urie. *The Ecology of Human Development: Experiments by Nature and Design*. Cambridge, MA: Harvard University Press, 1979.

Buck, Alfred A. *Health and Disease in Rural Afghanistan*. Johns Hopkins Monographs in International Health. Baltimore, MD: York Press, 1972.

Coburn, Noah. *Bazaar Politics: Power & Pottery in an Afghan Market Town*. Stanford, CA: Stanford University Press, 2011.

Coles, Robert. *The Political Life of Children*. Boston: Atlantic Monthly Press, 1986.

Dalrymple, William. *Return of a King: The Battle for Afghanistan, 1839–42*. New York: Knopf, 2013.

Denker, Debra. *Sisters on the Bridge of Fire: One Woman's Journey in Afghanistan, India, and Pakistan*. Tucson, AZ: Schaffner Press, 2001.

———. *War in the Land of Cain*. Columbia, TN: SynergEbooks, 2011.

Donini, Antonio, Norah Niland, and Karin Wermester, eds. *Nation-Building Unraveled? Aid, Peace and Justice in Afghanistan*. West Hartford, CT: Kumarian Press, 2004.

Donovan, L., and L. Pascale. *Integrating the Arts Across the Content Areas*. Huntington Beach, CA: Shell Publishing, 2012.

Dufour, Charlotte. *Amitiés Afghanes—dix ans de vies partagées*. France: Editions Fayard, 2011.

Dupree, Louis. *Afghanistan*. Oxford: Oxford University Press, 1997.

Elliot, Jason. *An Unexpected Light: Travels in Afghanistan*. New York: Picador St. Martin's Press, 1999.

Emadi, Hafizullah. *Culture and Customs of Afghanistan*. Santa Barbara, CA: Greenwood Press, 2005.

———. *Repression, Resistance, and Women in Afghanistan*. Westport, CT: Praeger, 2002.

Erikson, Erik H. *Childhood and Society*. New York: W. W. Norton and Co., 1963.

Esposito, John L. *The Oxford Dictionary of Islam*. Oxford: Oxford University Press, 2003.

Ewans, Martin. *Afghanistan: A New History*. Richmond, Surrey, England: Curzon Press, 2001.

Fitzgerald, Paul, and Elizabeth Gould, with Sima Wali. *Invisible History: Afghanistan's Untold Story*. San Francisco: City Lights, 2009.

Freire, Paulo. *Pedagogy of the Oppressed*. London: The Continuum International Publishing Group Inc., 2010.

Gankovsky, Yuri V., et al. *A History of Afghanistan*. Translated by Vitaly Baskakov. Moscow, Russia: Progress Publishers, 1985.

Goodson, Larry P. *Afghanistan's Endless War: State Failure, Regional Politics, and the Rise of the Taliban*. Seattle: University of Washington Press, 2001.

Greene, Maxine. *Releasing the Imagination: Essays on Education, the Arts, and Social Change*. San Francisco: Jossey-Bass Publishers, 1995.

Grima, Benedicte. *The Performance of Emotion among Paxtun Women: "The Misfortunes Which Have Befallen Me."* Austin: University of Texas Press, 1992.

Grossman, Dave. *On Killing: The Psychological Cost of Learning to Kill in War and Society*. New York: Back Bay Books, 2009.

Hall, Stuart, ed. *Representation: Cultural Representations and Signifying Practices*. Thousand Oaks, CA: Sage Publications, 2002.

Hanlon, Joseph, Armando Barriento, and David Hulm. *Just Give Money to the Poor: The Development Revolution from the Global South*. Sterling, VA: Kumarian Press, 2010.

Heath, Jennifer. *A House White with Sorrow: Ballad for Afghanistan*. Boulder, CO: Roden Press, 1996.

Heath, Jennifer, and Ashraf Zahedi, eds. *Land of the Unconquerable: The Lives of Contemporary Afghan Women*. Berkeley: University of California Press, 2011.

Hosseini, Khaled. *The Kite Runner*. New York: Riverhead Books, 2003.

Hunte, Pamela. *Looking Beyond the School Walls: Household Decision-Making and School Enrolment in Afghanistan*. Kabul: Afghanistan Research and Evaluation Unit, 2005.

Jalil, F. *Mini Survey Report on Corporal Punishing*. Kabul: Save the Children Sweden, 2003.

Kamali, Mohammad Hashim. *Law in Afghanistan: A Study of the Constitutions, Matrimonial Law and the Judiciary*. Leiden, The Netherlands: E. J. Brill, 1985.

Katib, Lina. *Filming the Modern Middle East: Politics in the Cinemas of Hollywood and the Arab World*. London: I. B. Tauris, 2008.

Katrak, Sorab K. *Through Amanullah's Afghanistan: A Book of Travel*, second edition. Karachi: Din Muhammad Press, 1953.

Kleinman, Arthur. *What Really Matters: Living a Moral Life Amidst Uncertainty and Danger*. Oxford: Oxford University Press, 2006.

Louv, Richard. *Last Child in the Woods: Saving Our Children from Nature-Deficit Disorder*. New York: Algonquin Books, 2005.

Marten, James. *Children and War: A Historical Anthology*. New York: New York University Press, 2002.

Mills, Margaret. *Rhetorics and Politics in Afghan Traditional Storytelling*. Philadelphia: University of Pennsylvania Press, 1991.

Moghadam, Valentine M. *Modernizing Women, Gender and Social Change in the Middle East*. Boulder, CO: Lynne Rienner Publishers, 2003.

Moghissi, Haideh. *Feminism and Islamic Fundamentalism: The Limits of Postmodern Analysis*. London: Zed Books, 1999.

Nawid, Senzil. *Religious Response to Social Change in Afghanistan, 1919–29: King Aman-Allah and the Afghan Ulama*. Costa Mesa, CA: Mazda Publishers, 2000.

Nojumi, Neamatollah, Dyan Mazurana, and Elizabeth Stites. *After the Taliban: Life and Security in Rural Afghanistan*. Lanham, MD: Rowman & Littlefield, 2009.

O'Connor, Ronald W., ed. *Health Care in Muslim Asia: Development and Disorder in Wartime Afghanistan*. Lanham, MD: University Press of America, 1994.

———. *Managing Health Systems in Developing Areas: Experiences from Afghanistan*. Lexington, MA: Lexington Books, 1980.

Omar, Wahid. *Afghanistan: A Nation in Performance, A Comparative Study Between Medieval France and Contemporary Afghanistan*. Saarbrücken, Germany: VDM Publishing, Verlag Dr. Müller, 2010.

Omidian, Patricia. *Aging and Family in an Afghan Refugee Community*. New York: Garland Publishing, Inc., 1996.

Ong, Walter J. *Orality and Literacy*. New York: Routledge, 1982.

Page, Nick. *Music as a Way of Knowing*. The Galef Institute. Los Angeles: Stenhouse Publishers, 1995.

Panter-Brick, Catherine, and Malcolm T. Smiths, eds. *Abandoned Children*. Cambridge, UK: Cambridge University Press, 2000.

Pascale, Louise, ed.; Vaheed Kaacemy, music. *Qu Qu Qu Barg-e-Chinaar: Children's Songs of Afghanistan*. Washington, DC: National Geographic Society, 2008. www .afghansongbook.org.

Raonaq, Mohammad Ali. *A Manual for Spoken Dari in Afghanistan*. Translated by Wahid Omar. Kabul: Danish Press, 2008.

Rashid, Ahmed. *Descent into Chaos: How the War against Islamic Extremism Is Being Lost in Pakistan, Afghanistan and Central Asia*. Noida, India: Penguin, 2008.

———. *Taliban: Militant Islam, Oil, and Fundamentalism in Central Asia*. New Haven: Yale University Press, 2000.

Saed, Zohra and Sahar Muradi, eds. *One Story, Thirty Stories: An Anthology of Contemporary Afghan American Literature*. Fayetteville, AR: University of Arkansas Press, 2010.

Save the Children Sweden and Norway. *Disciplining Children: An Exploration of the Impact of Physical and Humiliating Punishment of Children in Afghanistan*. Kabul: Save the Children Sweden and Norway, 2006.

Sharif, Sharifa. *On the Edge of Being: An Afghan Woman's Journey*. Toronto: Sumach Press, 2011.

Shepler, Susan. *Conflicted Childhoods: Fighting Over Child Soldiers in Sierra Leone*. Berkeley: University of California, 2005.

Slugget, Cath, and John Frederick, eds. *Mapping of Psychosocial Support for Child Sexual Abuse in Four Countries in South and Central Asia: Afghanistan, Bangladesh, Nepal and Pakistan*. Save the Children Sweden-Denmark, 2003.

Smith, Deborah J. *Challenging Myths and Finding Spaces for Change: Family Dynamics and Family Violence in Afghanistan*. Kabul: Afghanistan Research and Evaluation Unit, 2009.

———. *Decisions, Desires and Diversity: Marriage Practices in Afghanistan*. Kabul: Afghanistan Research and Evaluation Unit, 2009.

———. *Love, Fear and Discipline: Everyday Violence toward Children in Afghan Families*. Kabul: Afghanistan Research and Evaluation Unit, 2008.

Solinger, Rickie, Madeline Fox, and Kayhan Irani, eds. *Telling Stories to Change the World: Global Voices on the Power to Build Community and Make Social Justice Claims*. New York: Routledge, 2008.

Stone, Emma, ed. *Disability and Development: Learning from Action and Research on Disability in the Majority World*. Leeds: The Disability Press, 1999.

Tapper, Nancy. *Bartered Brides: Politics, Gender and Marriage in an Afghan Tribal Society*. Cambridge, UK: Cambridge University Press, 1991.

Turner, Graeme. *Film as Social Practice IV*. New York: Routledge, 1988.

Ungar, Michael, ed. *The Social Ecology of Resilience: A Handbook of Theory and Practice*. New York: Springer, 2012.

UNHCR. *The State of the World's Refugees 2000: Fifty Years of Humanitarian Action*. Oxford: Oxford University Press, 2000.

Wahab, Shaista, and Barry Youngerman. *A Brief History of Afghanistan*. New York: Checkmark Books, 2010.

Wessells, Michael. *Child Soldiers, From Violence to Protection*. Cambridge, MA: Harvard University Press, 2006.

Selected Children's and Young Adult Books

Abouraya, Karen Leggett. *Hands Around the Library: Protecting Egypt's Treasured Books.* Illustrated by Susan Roth. New York: Dial Books, 2012.

Ahmedi, Farah, with Tamim Ansary. *The Story of My Life: An Afghan Girl on the Other Side of the Sky.* New York: Simon Spotlight Entertainment, 2005.

Banting, Erin. *Afghanistan: The People, Land and Culture.* New York: Crabtree Publishing Company, 2003.

de Eulate, Ana A. *The Sky of Afghanistan.* Madrid: Cuento de Luz, 2012.

Ellis, Deborah. *The Breadwinner Trilogy.* Toronto: Groundwood Books, 2009.

———. *Kids of Kabul: Living Bravely through a Never-Ending War.* Toronto: Groundwood Books, 2012.

Haskins, James, and Kathleen Benson. *Count Your Way Through Afghanistan.* Illustrated by Megan Moore. Minneapolis: Millbrook Press, 2006.

King, Dedie. *I See the Sun in Afghanistan.* Illustrated by Judith Inglese; translated by Mohd Vahidi. Hardwick, MA: Satya House Publications, 2011.

Knox, Barbara. *Afghanistan: Many Cultures, One World.* Mankato, MN: Blue Earth Books, 2003.

MacKay, Sharon. *Thunder Over Kandahar.* Photography by Rafal Gerszak. Toronto: Annick Press, 2010.

Reedy, Trent. *Words in the Dust.* New York: Arthur A. Levine Books, 2011.

Senzai, N. H. *Shooting Kabul.* New York: Paula Wiseman Books, 2011.

Shah, Idries. *Neem the Half-Boy.* Illustrated by Midori Mori and Robert Revels. Los Altos, CA: Hoopoe Books, English edition, 1998; Dari-Pashto bilingual edition published in 2011. www.hoopoekids.com; www.booksforafghanistan.org.

———. *The Silly Chicken.* Illustrated by Jeff Jackson. Los Altos, CA: Hoopoe Books, English edition, 2000; Dari-Pashto bilingual edition, 2010. www.hoopoekids.com; www.booksforafghanistan.org.

Sullivan, Michael P., and Tony O'Brien. *Afghan Dreams: Young Voices of Afghanistan.* New York: Bloomsbury USA Children's, 2008.

Weber, Valerie J. *I Come from Afghanistan: This Is My Story.* Milwaukee: Weekly Reader Early Learning Library, 2006.

Williams, Karen Lynn. *Kindergarten Stepping Stones.* Dubuque, IA: Kendall Hunt Publishing, 2007.

Winter, Jeanette. *Nasreen's Secret School: A True Story from Afghanistan.* New York: Beach Lane Books, 2009.

Selected Filmography

Afghan Working Children: Enforcing Laws, Ensuring Their Rights. Aria TV with War Child Holland, 2013. http://www.youtube.com/watch?v=9F7JJwUzaRM.

Barmak, Siddiq, director. *Osama.* Afghanistan: Barmak Film, LeBrocquy, Fraser Productions, 2003.

Foster, Marc, director. *The Kite Runner.* United States: Dreamworks, Sidney Kimmel Entertainment, Participant Productions, et al., 2007.

French, Sam, director. *Buzkashi Boys.* United States: Department of State, 2012.

Greenwald, Robert, director. *Rethink Afghanistan*. Culver City, CA: Brave New Foundation, 2009. http://rethinkafghanistan.com/then-and-now.php.

Khan, Kabir, director. *Kabul Express*. India Yash Raj Films, 2006.

Majidi, Majiid, director. *Baran*. Iran: Fouad Nahas, 2001.

Makhmalbaf, Mohsen, director. *Alefbay-e afghan* (Afghan Alphabet). Iran: 2002.

Marking, Havana, director. *Afghan Star Documentary*. United Kingdom, United States, Afghanistan: Kaboora Production and Roast Beef Productions, 2008.

No Strings International. *Landmine Awareness*. http://www.nostrings.org.uk/ and http://www.youtube.com/watch?v=VCHS2MTNWe8&list=UULa4PxiL0g2Nq cvlv_dwjgA.

Quraishi, Najibullah, producer. *The Dancing Boys of Afghanistan*. United States: Frontline, 2010.

Samizay, Gazelle, director. *Nosh-e Jan* (Bon Appétit), 2008; *9,409 miles*, 2009; *Upon My Daughter*, 2010; gazellesamizay.com.

Vickers, Jill, and Jody Bergedick, directors. *Once in Afghanistan*. United States: Dirt Road Productions, 2008.

Winterbottom, Michael, director. *In This World*. United Kingdom: Film Consortium, British Broadcasting Corporation, 2002.

About the Contributors

Hangama Anwari has worked for human rights in Afghanistan since she was fifteen years old, when her father helped her type articles. After civil war forced her family from Kabul to northern Afghanistan, she graduated from university in Balkh province with a degree in law and political science, lectured there, and worked at a community-based organization, Community for Development Organization. The Taliban conquest of the north, coupled with the loss of her father, forced her, at twenty-two, to move to Islamabad, Pakistan, where she could work and care for her young siblings. On staff at United Nations Habitat, she traveled to Afghanistan to assist underground home-based organizations working on education, income generation, and other key services. She returned after the fall of the Taliban to create a non-governmental organization, the Women and Children Legal Research Foundation, designed to illuminate the impact of harmful traditional practices enforced by Afghanistan's informal justice system and to render a clear picture of their negative influence "not only on women, but on children, society, and the process for development and democracy."

Fitsum Assefa is a public nutrition specialist working with UNICEF. She has twenty years' experience in Africa and Asia working with non-governmental organizations and the United Nations, in assessment, design, implementation, and management of nutrition and food security programs both in humanitarian and development contexts. Her work experience in Afghanistan dates back to 1995. She is one of the lead professionals who supported national public nutrition assessments, programs, and policy in Afghanistan during the period of 2002 to 2005. She currently resides and works in Niger, where she is the chief of UNICEF's nutrition section.

Annalies Borrel has twenty years of program and policy experience in humanitarian, transition, and development contexts with United Nations organizations, non-governmental organizations, Tufts University, and governments in Africa, the Balkans, and Afghanistan. Her work has been predominantly in the area of food and nutrition security, but she is also experienced in poverty reduction, disaster risk management, social protection, livelihoods, public health, and national capacity development. Throughout her career, she has supported a multi-sectoral approach to food and nutrition security, recognizing the complex and diverse social, political, and economic factors that impact on food and nutrition, and their implications for analysis, policy, research, and programs. She currently resides and works in Ethiopia.

Delphine Boutin works on issues of labor and development economics at EDHEC Business School (France), with a specialization in children. She is also a consultant for the International Labor Organization and the Understanding Children's Work project. She has written two articles published in French by the Université Montesquieu-Bordeaux IV, referring respectively to the repercussions of child soldiering and the market for child soldiers in the African Great Lake region.

Anne E. Brodsky received her PhD in clinical/community psychology from the University of Maryland, College Park. She completed her clinical internship at Massachusetts Mental Health Center, Harvard Medical School, and a postdoctoral fellowship at the Johns Hopkins Bloomberg School of Public Health. She is currently a professor of psychology and associate dean in the College of Arts, Humanities, and Social Sciences at the University of Maryland, Baltimore County. Her teaching, research, and practice focus on resilience, psychological sense of community, and the role of communities in creating and resisting societal risks and oppressions, including violence, poverty, racism, and sexism. Between 2001 and 2007 she made regular research trips to Pakistan and Afghanistan, interviewing more than two hundred Afghan women, children, and men about Afghan women's risk and resilience. She is the author of more than thirty articles and chapters, as well as the book *With All Our Strength: The Revolutionary Association of the Women of Afghanistan (RAWA)* (Routledge, 2003).

Sam Chen served as physician to U.S. Peace Corps Volunteers in Afghanistan from 1966 to 1968.

Teresa Cutler-Broyles has a master's degree in cultural studies and comparative literature, is a PhD candidate in American studies with a focus on American Orientalism and film theory, and teaches film classes at the University of New Mexico. She is the author of *A Dream That Keeps Returning* (2007), a series of travel essays about Italy, and *One Eyed Jack* (2012), a young adult novel. A chapter in *Belly Dance Around the World: New Communities, Performance and Identity*, edited by Caitlin E. McDonald and Barbara Sellers-Young (McFarland, 2013), looks at the globalization of dance. She also owns a small business, InkWell International LLC, through which she runs writing workshops in Italy and Turkey and provides a variety of writing and editing services.

Charlotte Dufour has been working on food security, nutrition, and livelihoods since 2000, predominantly in Afghanistan. After obtaining a masters in public health nutrition, she worked with Action Contre la Faim in Afghanistan, Paris, and Ethiopia. She returned to Afghanistan regularly between 2002 and 2005, while working with Groupe URD on project evaluations and training. She moved to Kabul in 2005 and worked with the United Nations Food and Agriculture Organization in the Ministry of Agriculture as nutrition officer until the end of 2008. She continued regular consulting in the health and agriculture sectors until early 2010. She lives in Rome and works with the FAO on nutrition in sub-Saharan Africa. In 2011, *Amitiés Afghanes—dix ans de vies partagées* was published by Editions Fayard.

Mark Eggerman (MPhil) is a research scientist at the Macmillan Center for International and Area Studies at Yale University and an independent fieldwork management consultant specializing in the Middle East and Islamic societies. His work in Afghanistan has included studies of public opinion, media use, education, politics, and mental health for clients such as the BBC World Service Trust, Intermedia Survey Research Institute, Durham University, and Afghanistan Research and Evaluation Unit. He has provided expert witness reports for legal aid caseworkers representing Afghan child and adolescent asylum-seekers in the United Kingdom.

Ginna Fleming is a freelance photographer living in Mill Valley, California. She has photographed people and cultures around the world. Her fine art photos have been shown in juried shows and publications. She was one of eight women photographers exhibited at UNESCO headquarters in Paris to mark International Women's Day in March of 2011. Her work in photo-journalism includes documenting the work of four non-profit groups in Afghanistan in 2008, and publication of a book titled *Another Afghanistan* (www.ginnafleming.com).

Jennifer Heath is an independent scholar, award-winning activist and cultural journalist, critic, and curator, the author or editor of numerous books of fiction and nonfiction, including *On the Edge of Dream: The Women of Celtic Myth and Legend* and *The Echoing Green: The Garden in Myth and Memory* (both from Penguin/Plume, 1998, 2000); *A House White with Sorrow: A Ballad for Afghanistan* (Roden Press, 1996); *The Scimitar and the Veil: Extraordinary Women of Islam* (Paulist Press, 2004); *The Veil: Women Writers on Its History, Lore, and Politics* (University of California Press, 2008); and *Land of the Unconquerable: The Lives of Contemporary Afghan Women* (University of California Press, 2011), coedited with Ashraf Zahedi. She came of age in Afghanistan, founded Seeds for Afghanistan in 2001 and the Afghanistan Relief Organization Midwife Training and Infant Care Program, later known as International Midwife Assistance. Her many touring art exhibitions include *Water, Water Everywhere: Paean to a Vanishing Resource*; *The Veil: Visible & Invisible Spaces*; *Black Velvet: The Art We Love to Hate*; and *The Map Is Not the Territory: Parallel Paths — Palestinians, Native Americans, Irish.*

Esther Hyneman is a professor emeritus of English at Long Island University. She received her BA from Goucher College and her MA and PhD from Columbia University. She sits on the board of directors of Women for Afghan Women and often spends about six months a year in Afghanistan.

Amina Kator-Mubarez graduated from the University of California, Berkeley, with a BA in political science and a minor in global poverty and practice and is currently pursuing an MA in national security affairs from the Naval Postgraduate School in Monterey, California. Her love and passion for Afghanistan has led her to travel there on several occasions and conduct extensive research about the region. She was a fund recipient of the Afaf Kanafani Scholarship for the best paper on the topic of women in South Asia and received a travel grant through the Blum Center at UC-Berkeley to conduct research and interview youth in Afghanistan regarding their hopes and aspirations for the future. In addition, she's actively been involved in events such as the Rebuild Afghanistan Summit and has provided project-level technical leadership on gender and other social issues related to design, implementation, monitoring, and evaluation of international development projects in Afghanistan.

Lael Adams Mohib specializes in rural development in Afghanistan and has an MA in international relations from Boston University. She has worked for the Afghan Ministry of Rural Rehabilitation and Development and FLAG International, Afghanistan. She is also project manager for the Enabled Children Initiative, a fundraising project hosted by the Afghan Professionals network to support disabled orphans in Afghanistan. Her writings have appeared on Foreign Policy's AfPak Channel, the *New York Times* At War blog, the *Islamic Monthly* magazine, and the *Boston Globe* online. She recently produced a documentary film, *Voice of a Nation: My Journey through Afghanistan.*

Lauryn Oates is a human rights activist focused on education in conflict zones. She works in close partnership with a variety of Afghan women's organizations and international charities and is currently programs director of Canadian Women for Women in Afghanistan, providing leadership for projects such as the Fanoos ("Lantern") Teacher Training program, from which more than 5,000 teachers have graduated, and a network of village library and literacy centers called Afghanistan Lowalee!/Afghanistan Reads! Oates is the recipient of several awards and distinctions, including a Queen's Diamond Jubilee Medal for community service in 2012. She holds a PhD in literacy education from the University of British Columbia and divides her time between the West Coast of Canada and Kabul.

Wahid Omar was born in Kabul and left Afghanistan shortly before the Soviet invasion in 1979. He lived in France as a political refugee until 1987 and received his PhD from the University of Colorado in 2010. He has worked in Afghanistan since 2001 in project development, implementation, and feasibility studies, and as an educational advisor for the United Nations Development Program, training university professors and building capacity at the University of Kabul. Under his leadership, forty-five projects have been implemented, ranging from school and community centers, teacher training, water improvement projects, and microlending to humanitarian aid and relief efforts. He has won many awards for his teaching and writing, and his work in collecting and preserving Afghan folklore has garnered the attention of the Smithsonian Institution. He is the author of *Afghanistan: A Nation in Performance—A Comparative Study between Medieval France and Contemporary Afghanistan.*

Catherine Panter-Brick (DPhil) is professor of anthropology, health, and global affairs at Yale University. Her focus on youth in global adversity has included research with street children, refugees, famine-stricken families, and war-affected communities in areas of conflict and humanitarian emergencies. She has directed more than forty international projects, including the first large-scale survey of child and caregiver mental health in Afghanistan. She is the senior editor (Medical Anthropology section) for the international and interdisciplinary journal *Social Science & Medicine*. She received the 2011 Lucy Mair Medal for Applied Anthropology, an award that honors excellence in the application of anthropology to the relief of poverty and distress, and to the active recognition of human dignity.

Louise M. Pascale has been an associate professor for Lesley University in the ITA Creative Arts in Learning program for more than fifteen years. In 2003 she launched the Children's Afghan Songbook Project, a project that strives to preserve traditional Afghan children's songs and return them to the children of Afghanistan. These songs almost completely disappeared from Afghan culture due to the devastation that has afflicted Afghanistan over the past thirty years. The project is rooted in her years as a Peace Corps volunteer during the late 1960s. More than 30,000 copies of the songbook *Qu Qu Qu Barg-e-Chinaar: Children's Songs from Afghanistan* have been distributed to and are in use in schools and orphanages across Afghanistan. In 2009, an accompanying Teacher's Guide was published to provide teachers with ways to use the songbook to enhance basic literacy skills. In 2013 a second songbook, *Awansana See Saana*, and an accompanying Teacher's Guide were published. As of 2013, 45,000 songbooks and 4,000 Teacher's Guides have been distributed. Pascale edited an English translated version of the songbook *Qu Qu Qu Barg-e-Chinaar* in 2008; it was published by National Geographic. It is distributed primarily in the United States and Canada.

Ian Pounds began his education traveling 10,000 miles on the angle of a genetically transmitted hitchhiker's thumb. He sailed around the world with Semester at Sea, a shipboard campus devoted to global studies. He acquired his BA in creative writing from the Evergreen State College, and later studied Elizabethan literature at Oxford University. For three years he practiced Vipassana meditation, and for three years he homesteaded an otherwise deserted island in Southeast Alaska. His plays have been showcased at Seattle's New City Theatre and Olympia's Black Box. He's been a stonemason, a performance poet, a counselor of runaway teens, and led workshops with the Association for Experiential Education and the Vermont Stage Company. He was a scholar at the Bread Loaf Writers' Conference, where he served for more than ten years on the admissions committee and coordinated the Bakeless Literary Prizes. He recently completed a draft of a memoir, *Undestroyed*, about his four years as a volunteer living with and teaching orphans in Kabul, Afghanistan. He is now on the faculty at the Asian University for Women in Chittagong, Bangladesh.

Omar Qargha (BS, MEd, MA) is a partner at Afghanistan Holding Group and leads Afghanistan Research Services. He has served as an academic advisor for USAID's Higher Education Project (HEP), where he developed the National Standards for Teacher Education Programs, developed and implemented a two-year science and math training program for more than 350 professors, and established the National Association of Science and Mathematics Educators of Afghanistan (NASMEA). As a research associate for USAID's Building Education Support Systems for Teachers (BESST) project, he developed the National Teacher Competency Framework and advised the Afghan Ministry of Education on teacher development and credentialing in policy. He was assistant director at Help the Afghan Children, where he developed training curriculum and monitoring and evaluation systems, managed school construction, and oversaw the implementation of all programs. He received a master's degree in international comparative education from Stanford University's Graduate School of Education, as well as a master's degree in curriculum and instruction from George Mason University. He is currently completing his doctoral degree in international education policy at the University of Maryland.

Mamiko Saito started working in Afghanistan and Pakistan in 2003, at the Afghanistan Research and Evalution Unit (AREU), with a particular focus on youth and young adults. She currently serves as a coordinator for Japan International Cooperation Agency's project in Kabul. She holds a master's degree in education and development studies from the University of East Anglia.

Sheryl Shapiro is a freelance photographer and travel writer based in Boulder, Colorado. Her passion is photographing indigenous people living traditional lifestyles. She has traveled extensively in the developing world, including Afghanistan, Iran, Myanmar, Yemen, Tibet, and Pakistan. Sheryl's work has been published both nationally and internationally in *Practical Horseman*, *FHM Magazine*, the *Melbourne Herald Sun*, and the *Brisbane Sunday Mail*, to name a few. She has taught courses on independent third-world travel and presents educational slide shows of her travels for public and private audiences. Her photos can be viewed at www .sherylbshapiro.com and www.picasaweb.google.com/sherylbshapiro.

Sharifa Sharif is an Afghan-Canadian independent consultant/expert on Afghanistan culture and society, mainly in the fields of women, culture, and development. She has worked in adult education, women and development, community development, journalism, and politics in Afghanistan, Canada, India, and the Czech Republic. She obtained her PhD in education policy at the University of Illinois. Her published works include a memoir, *On the Edge of Being: An Afghan Woman's Journey*, and two collections of short stories, *The Guilty Judges of Stoning* (in Dari) and *Window* (in Pashto).

Joanna Sherman cofounded Bond Street Theatre in 1976 and has served as artistic director since 1986. Under her directorship, the company received a MacArthur Award for its innovative intercultural programming. As director, choreographer, and actor for Bond Street Theatre, she directed productions that toured to major theatres and festivals worldwide and initiated company projects in East Asia, South America, Eastern and Western Europe, the Middle East, Pakistan, India, Afghanistan, and Myanmar. Sherman has been a speaker on the role of the arts in areas of conflict at the United Nations, the National Council on Women, the UN Conference on Women in China in 1995, the UN Youth Assembly, the Association of Performing Arts Presenters, Theatre Without Borders, arts councils, and arts-in-education forums, and has been featured on CNN, BBC, and National Public Radio, among many others. She has directed, lectured, and taught internationally at universities worldwide; her writing has been published in numerous periodicals and she has received various grants and awards. Recent projects include collaboration with Afghanistan's Exile Theatre to depict true stories of life during wartime. The piece was presented in Afghanistan, Japan, and the United States, and is the first U.S.-Afghan theatre collaboration in history. She is currently conducting a theatre-based conflict resolution project in Afghanistan with support from the U.S. Embassy and U.S. Institute of Peace. She plays tenor saxophone with Bond Street Theatre's Shinbone Alley Stilt Band.

Amanda Sim is the research and evaluation specialist for the child protection and women's protection and empowerment sectors at the International Rescue Committee. She currently oversees evaluations of family strengthening and child mental health programs in Thailand, Ethiopia, and Liberia.

Prior to her current role, she managed the child and youth protection and development programs for the IRC in Afghanistan and Liberia. Amanda was with the Afghanistan Research and Evaluation Unit (AREU), based in Kabul, from 2007–2008, where she led a research project on child labor. Her research interests include children affected by conflict, child psychosocial well-being, and cross-cultural research in conflict and displacement settings. Amanda holds an MA from the Fletcher School of Law and Diplomacy at Tufts University, where she specialized in humanitarian studies.

Deborah J. Smith has worked in Afghanistan for the past six years, primarily in the fields of gender, community-based dispute resolution, and justice. Prior to this she researched public health issues in Malawi and Zambia. Deborah holds a PhD from the London School of Economics and Political Science for which she conducted fieldwork in India. She currently works as an independent consultant.

Steven Solter has worked in international public health since 1971, mostly on long-term projects in Asia. He has spent nearly six years in Afghanistan (including three years prior to the Soviet invasion of 1979). He has also worked for twelve years in Southeast Asia (Indonesia, Philippines, and Cambodia), as well as two years in Iran. He has mostly advised Ministries of Health at central or provincial levels in an effort to reduce maternal and child mortality, especially through the use of community health workers based at the village level and through using data for decision-making. He recently retired from Management Sciences for Health, a nonprofit group based in Cambridge, Massachusetts, where he had been employed since 1976. He was based in Kabul from 2008 to 2010 as technical director of a large USAID-funded project aimed at enhancing the capacity of the Afghan Ministry of Public Health. He now lives in Northern California and does occasional short-term assignments. He received his MPH from Johns Hopkins University and his MD from Stanford University.

Ashraf Zahedi, PhD, is a sociologist who has conducted research at Center for Middle East Studies, University of California, Santa Barbara; the Beatrice Bain Research Group at the University of California, Berkeley; the Institute for Research on Women and Gender, Stanford University; and the Center for Middle Eastern Studies, University of California, Berkeley. Her research interests include political ideology, social movements, transnational feminism, gender and development, and social policy. Her research is focused on the United States, Iran, and Afghanistan. She has published many articles in academic journals including *Iranian Studies, Journal of Middle East Women's Studies, International Feminist Journal of Politics*, and *Women's Studies International Forum*. She is, with Jennifer Heath, the coeditor of *Land of the Unconquerable: The Lives of Contemporary Afghan Women* (University of California Press, 2011).

Index

Convention on Worst Forms of Child Labor; legal protection; National Strategy for Children at Risk; orphans; prostitution: and sex work; street children; *and specific kinds of labor*

child marriage, 8, 9, 99, 112–123, 170, 176, 177. *See also* child bridegrooms; child brides; legal marriage age; legal protection; marriage laws; marriage practices

child mortality. *See* infant mortality

Child Protection Action Network (CPAN), 137, 140, 142n12, 173, 221, 328, 329, 335n10

Children in Crisis (CIC), 214, 224n6

children in film, 6, 69–77

children in prison, 8, 26n33, 54, 63, 96–111; and *Osama*, 75; and Putney School, 103; and school, 99, 100, 102–104. *See also* Children's Support Center; legal protection; Women for Afghan Women

Children's Support Center (CSC), 96–107, 108n1, 110nn16,21,22,24,26. *See also* children in prison

Child Rights International Network, 26n33

Child Sexual Abuse (CSA), 95n4, 142n9, 175–177, 332. See also *bacha bazi*; *bacha bereesh*; child trafficking; dancing boys; legal protection

child soldiering, 153–168; and coerced enrollment, 156; and demobilization, 154, 160, 161, 168nn48,50,55, 169nn61,63, 170; and education, 157, 166nn32,34,35,37,44; and 2007 Paris Child Soldiering Conference, 160. See also *bacha bazi*; *bacha bereesh*; child labor; drug use and drug trade; HIV/AIDS

child trafficking, 11, 109n11, 113, 164n15, 176–180, 182nn25,26,27, 183n28. *See also* Convention on Preventing and Combating Trafficking in Women and Children for Prostitution; legal protection; sexual abuse; United

Nations Convention Against Transnational Organized Crime

China, 51, 142n12

Chinese investors, 195

CIA World Factbook, 31n76, 270, 280n5

civilian casualties, 24n23, 25n23

civil war, 1, 4, 22, 39, 50n10, 52, 54, 55, 57, 59, 64, 67n22, 115, 120, 195, 220, 264, 287, 324, 325

Cold War, 5, 245

Colombia, 157, 167n40, 300

colostrum, 190, 210n28; and breast milk, 196n3, 202, 205; "breast milk deficiency," 202. *See also* breastfeeding; health care; nutrition

Communist/communism, 23n5, 38, 39, 45, 59, 64, 67, 114, 115, 154, 229, 260, 294, 295, 296n1. *See also* Saur Revolution; Soviets

community-based health care, 191, 194, 196. *See also* health care; immunization; midwifery; Ministry of Public Health

Community-Based Rehabilitation (CBR), 218

community development, 138, 335n20

community health workers, 13, 92, 188, 190, 192, 193, 196n8

CONCOR (university entrance exam), 261, 267n15

conditional cash transfers (CCT), 331, 332, 336nn23,26; and unconditional cash transfers, 330. *See also* World Bank

congenital diseases/disorders, 29n61, 218–220; and birth defects, 7, 199, 209n12, 216, 217; and cerebral palsy, 214, 216, 222; and club foot (talipes equinovarus), 216, 217, 219; and hip dysplasia, 216. *See also* birth; disabilities; interfamilial marriage

Consortium for Street Children, 11, 28n52

Constitution of the Islamic Republic of Afghanistan, 12, 121nn3,8, 152n14, 173, 258; and 1923, 1964, 1987, 1990 constitutions, 296n1

and Consortium for Street Children, 11. *See also* child labor; Parakeet Boys; prostitution

suicide, 66, 229, 232; and suicide bombings, 227, 231, 256, 289; and suicide missions, 154, 158, 163n7. *See also* child soldiering; mental health

Sullivan, Mike, 1

Sunni Islam, 5, 50n7, 296n12. *See also* Taliban

Supreme Court of Afghanistan, 109n14

Swedish Committee for Afghanistan (SCA), 218, 219

Tajik people, 2, 23n6, 37, 39, 41, 42, 45, 52, 103, 122n17, 155, 164n18, 242, 296n12, 312. *See also* Ismail Khan

Takhar province, 101

takleef asabi (affliction of the nerves), 232

Taliban, 24nn19,20,22,23, 32n90, 40, 44, 51, 52, 54, 55, 57, 58, 64, 65, 66n1, 70, 74, 75, 94, 97, 99, 116, 119, 143, 158, 220, 286, 287, 289, 292, 293, 294, 296n1, 297n12, 301, 304, 305, 313, 320, 323, 324, 325; and Afghan civil war, 39, 64; and Anti-Taliban Movement Afghanistan, 287, 295; and child soldiering, 154, 155, 157, 163n12, 166n35; and cultural crimes, 14, 77, 110n26, 272, 280n8, 304, 325; and education, 16, 18, 30n74, 55, 57, 58, 68n27, 166n35, 220, 236, 260, 261, 264; and employment, 11, 120; and ethnicity, 164; and health care access, 189, 191, 192; and Karzai, Hamid, 287; and marriage practices, 115; and media, 288, 296n6; and mental health, 229, 235; "new," 5, 24n22; and nutrition, 30n67, 203; and prison, 108; and Sharia, 313; and Sunni Islam, 5, 50n7, 115

talim wa tarbia (knowledge and discipline), 250

Tapaye Zanabad (the hill that women built), 9. *See also* widows

Tarana, Farida, 325

Tarzi, Mahmud Beg, 3

Teacher's Guide. *See* Afghan Children's Songbook Project

Teenage Writer's Workshop, 17

television, 20, 71, 253n14, 281, 292, 296n6, 300, 306, 325; and Afghan National Television, 152n24

Terre des Hommes (TDH), 172–175, 181n7

textbooks, 18, 31nn82,83,84, 243, 259; and child soldiering, 157, 166n33; and CIA textbook scandal, 31n81, 166n33. *See also* Afghan Children's Songbook Project

theatre, 20, 21, 32n93, 281, 298–310. *See also* storytellers *and specific theatres*

Theatre Circus Afsana, 21, 32n93

Tiefenbrun, Susan, 155, 164n15

Tolo News, 291, 292; and Tolo TV, 292, 325. *See also* media; social media

Tora Bora, 293

toys, 5, 14, 222, 223, 281, 299. *See also* cultural practices; play

traditional birth attendants. See *dais*

Transitional Houses, 106, 107

TriVision TV, 274, 281nn12,14

tuberculosis, 190; and BCG vaccinations, 197n11

Turcoman people, 23n6

Turkey, 3, 259, 285

Twitter, 19, 285, 291–294. *See also* blogging; Facebook; journalism; media; social media

undernutrition. *See* malnutrition

unexploded ordnance (UXO), 15. *See also* disabilities; landmines

United Kingdom, 222

United Nations (UN). *See specific UN institutions*

United Nations Afghanistan Disability Support Program, 214

United Nations Assistance Mission to Afghanistan (UNAMA), 24n23, 122n18, 160

United Nations Children's Fund